Ploughing The South Sea

A History of Merchant Shipping on the West Coast of South America

[signature]

E. JOHN McGARRY

Bloomington, IN   Milton Keynes, UK

AuthorHouse™
1663 Liberty Drive, Suite 200
Bloomington, IN 47403
www.authorhouse.com
Phone: 1-800-839-8640

AuthorHouse™ UK Ltd.
500 Avebury Boulevard
Central Milton Keynes, MK9 2BE
www.authorhouse.co.uk
Phone: 08001974150

© 2006 E. JOHN McGARRY. All rights reserved.

No part of this book may be reproduced, stored in a retrieval system, or transmitted by any means without the written permission of the author.

First published by AuthorHouse 2/13/2006

ISBN: 1-4208-2985-8 (sc)

Printed in the United States of America
Bloomington, Indiana

This book is printed on acid-free paper.

Front Cover depicts painting of Pacific Steam Navigation Company's paddle steamer Santiago II launched 1865. Rear Cover shows painting of the same company's first steamship ss Chile of 1840, entering the Peruvian port of Callao.

Covers designed by Elena McGarry.

About The Author

E. John McGarry was former Crew Purser on Pacific Steam Navigation Company's flagship *ss Reina del Mar*. He left that company in 1964 after marrying Elena whom he met on that liner. Employed for thirty years by various Local Government Authorities in North Wales, the New Forest and ultimately in Yorkshire, he retired from Local Government in 1996 after 23 years service as a Town Clerk to a small Yorkshire Local Authority. He then entered the service of Ofsted as a School's Lay Inspector before finally retiring in 2002 to finish researching and writing "*Ploughing The South Sea*". Fluent in Spanish, which he studied at Liverpool College of Commerce, he also holds a BA degree in Mathematics and Technology

Dedicated to my ever-patient wife Elena.

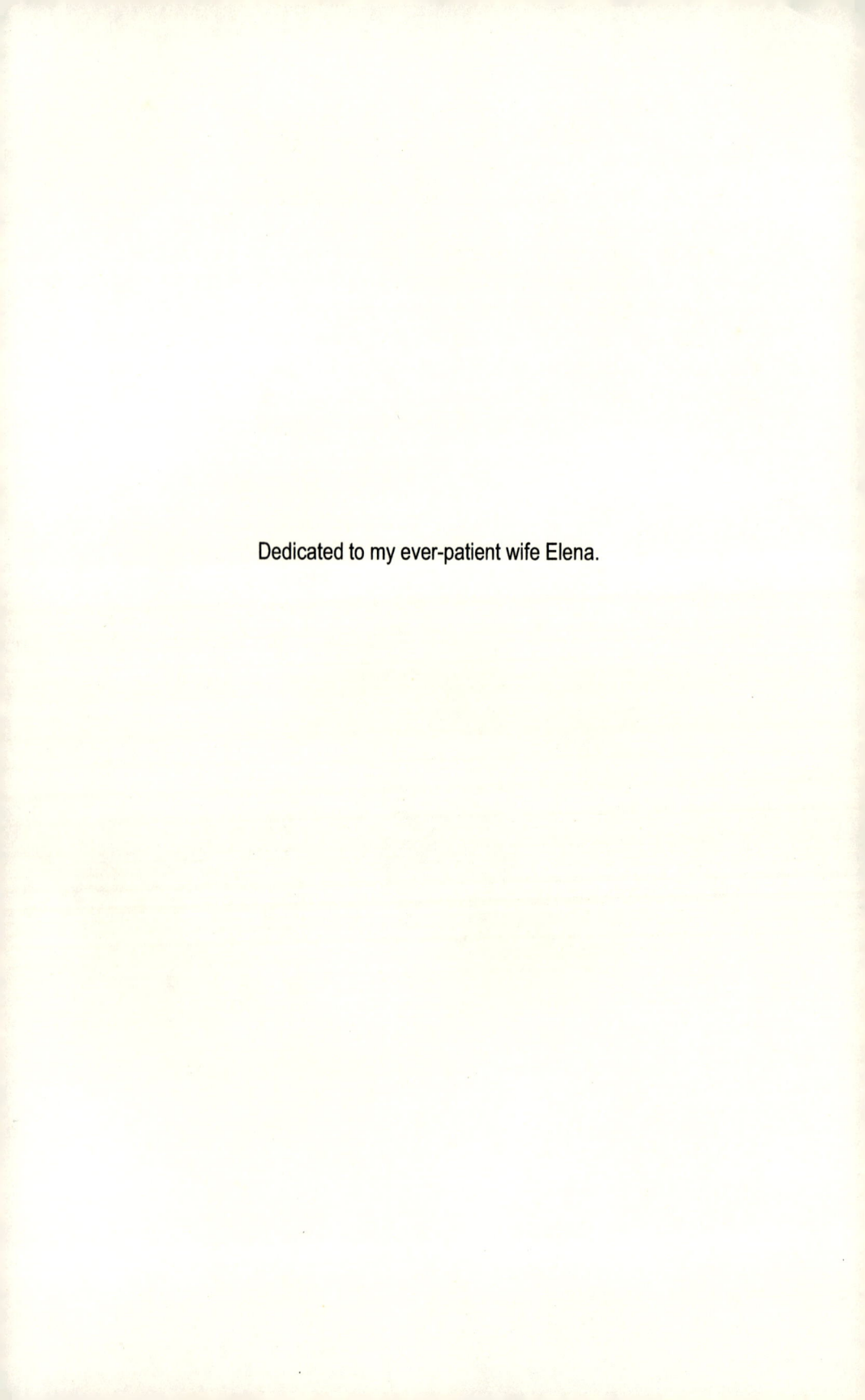

Table of Contents

Introduction 1
1. Setting The Scene.   1503–1835 8
2. Visions of Steamships and Political Conflicts   1824-1839 28
3. A Problematic Venture   1835-1840 54
4. First Steamship Line.   1839-1845 74
5. Growing Pains   1845- 1849 83
6. Political Developments   1845-1848 110
7. Panama and The Railroad   1849-1860 121
8. War With Spain.   Panama Railroad Dispute   1860-1871 146
9. West Coast Competition   1869-1878 177
10. Preludes To Protectionism.   1873-1889 198
11. War Of The Pacific. Causes and Affects.   1879-1898 222
12. Sailing Towards Protectionism.   1890-1915 245
13. Affects of Protectionism.   Return to a Free Market.   1915-1994 261
14. Grancolombiana Line, Peruvian Line, Ecuadorian Transnave and Flopec Lines.   1946-1973 289
15. Modernise Or Wither.   1946-2000 306
16. Conclusions 322
Bibliography 342
Endnotes 347

Map of South America: courtesy of Texas University Library

Introduction

Little has been written in the United Kingdom of the development of merchant steam shipping on the West Coast of South America (WCSA). Consequently, details of the interactions of shipping companies operating in that region such as the once powerful Pacific Steam Navigation Company (PSNC) of Liverpool, England, the American Grace Line of New York, and the Chilean Compañia Sudamericana de Vapores (CSAV), remain largely unknown here. Even less is recorded of the younger South American shipping firms such as the Ecuadorian Transnave, the Compañia Chilena Naviera Oceánica (CCNI), and La Grancolombiana. The development of steam navigation and its affects on the WCSA, apart from Claudio Véliz's detailed history of the Chilean merchant marine up to 1922, and valuable contributions from René De La Pedraja's general view of Latin American shipping[1], has been sadly neglected.

Ploughing the South Sea is an attempt to fill that gap. It is not a specific or conclusive history of PSNC, although the "*English Company*", as it was called in Latin America, did play a dominant role, and is used in this study as the vehicle to bring all known and related historical data together. To produce such an undertaking with only passing references to PSNC would be like baking an apple pie without the filling. This book's objective is to provide a revealing insight into the political, social and economic backgrounds and their influences on merchant shipping, principally in a 19th Century age when codes of behaviour, business ethics and proper treatment of the poorer classes were more notably absent than they are today.

This publication may, therefore, disappoint those seeking a neat chronological and nostalgic history extolling the glories of PSNC; such publications do exist, for example, John E. Lingwood's, "*The Steam Conquistadors-A History of the Pacific Steam Navigation Company*"[2] in which he acknowledged that his work relied heavily on Arthur Wardle's 1940 book commemorating the company's centenary and entitled "*Steam Conquers the Pacific*".[3] For this company's post-1940 history John E. Lingwood, PSNC's Archivist, naturally resorted to its records. Both books are currently out of print and copies are quite rare.

In his commemorative work, Wardle, in acknowledging his reliance on PSNC's archives, revealed that some company records from its early years were, unfortunately, lost. It is clear from his text that he was obliged to borrow heavily from Argentinean historian Juan Bautista Albérdi's biography of North American William Wheelwright, published in 1876, as "*La Vida y Los Trabajos Industriales de William Wheelwright en La America del Sud*" (Life and Industrial Works of William Wheelwright in South America). Wheelwright, regarded from the onset as "*the father of PSNC*", has been bestowed, certainly in Albérdi's text, with heroic attributes for his role in its formation and for other public projects completed in Chile and Argentina.

Apart from works by Véliz and De La Pedraja, those titles already cited are mostly commemorative publications. Anyone pursuing an interest in the development of PSNC and its contribution to Liverpool and WCSA, might gain the impression from the afore mentioned bibliography, that William Wheelwright truly was a heroic figure setting PSNC on a straightforward growth path by his initial foresight, care and attention.

PSNC was, undeniably, a very powerful force on the WCSA, but in order to appreciate the reasons for the development of merchant shipping in that region, investigations of the interplay and relationships between the *"English Company"* and its other competitors are essential. The impact of these firms must be assessed both individually and collectively, and not only on each other, but also on the West Coast nations themselves.

Basic questions need to be addressed; why, for example, haven't some once famous shipping enterprises, particularly PSNC and Grace Line, survived and why have others, often lesser known establishments in the 19th Century, become more powerful? Why did PSNC commence operations on the WCSA and not initially involve British ports? Was it really a pioneering adventure on which Wheelwright embarked, or was there a ready-made gap in an existing market that remained to be filled, which others could have undertaken? Did Wheelwright merit the praise and fame heaped upon him? Many other questions arise which cannot readily be answered without further research. Detailed investigations were, therefore, required, especially as all known existing histories of PSNC, whilst accurate in terms of the limited data available to their authors, painted a one-sided, mostly benevolent, and too sympathetic a picture.

Albérdi's biography of William Wheelwright, for example, was the result of 19th Century fashion for South American historians to eulogize at least one national hero. At the time of its compilation, Juan Bautista Albérdi, an Argentinean ex-politician and historian, was living in exile in Chile when cultural conflict characterized contemporary South America. The Creoles,[4] or élite ruling classes in South America after early 19th Century independence, were fixated with the progress and modernization of industrial Europe and the United States. In seeking to Europeanise their own countries, they sought to import and impose, rather than apply, these much-extolled foreign techniques and philosophies on their young nations, as well as imitating European culture and French society especially.

These ruling élites firmly believed that the European super powers and the United States, would not only provide solutions to problems then painfully afflicting South American societies, but that their values and philosophies would also embrace and underpin their own life styles. In other words, they were keen to adopt anything that would enhance and preserve their privileged positions. In the first half of the 19th Century, such was the élites' desire for "*progress*", that is the ambition to recreate their nations as closely as possible to European and North American models, that they actively encouraged the importation of super powers' technologies, their thought, literature, investment finance and the attraction of entrepreneurs such as William Wheelwright.

Given Albérdi's choice for his biographical work, it would have been a breach of established etiquette for him to voice negative aspects of Wheelwright and his contributions to PSNC's launch. While his biography is a useful study of contemporary events, care must be taken in considering whether Albérdi's assessment of his subject's life and environment might have omitted any unflattering detail or even exaggerated Wheelwright's successes.

Fashionable thought on the need to Europeanise South America subsequently changed. More intense nationalistic sentiments emerged, leading to the replacement of Anglo Saxon and European philosophies by more introspective considerations of likely home-grown heroes rather than foreign personalities such as Wheelwright, despite him being previously considered a subject worthy of recording for posterity. Albérdi attempted to circumvent this literary difficulty by declaring that the former United States citizen "*had died only to be reborn as a South American*" to live and breathe most of his life there, and as a result of this miraculous transformation, was able to achieve meaningful benefits for South America. Clearly, claimed Albérdi, Wheelwright, by these actions, had demonstrated that, if not a natural South American, he was one at heart and, therefore, a proper and acceptable figure to be reserved a place in history.

Accordingly, Albérdi's work cannot provide a true perspective of events surrounding Wheelwright and PSNC's creation. It must be considered flawed because, according to contemporary fashion, it was interpreted as an historical eulogy written by a member of the élite about an élite and targeted at an élitist readership. It, therefore, carries the danger of bias and the likelihood of discriminating against any actions or thought detrimental to or critical of, not only his subject, but also his peers.

Wardle's book is, I submit, similarly one-dimensional. Due to the loss of PSNC's archives for its early years and the need to rely heavily on Albérdi's biography of Wheelwright, it must, consequently, inherit some of the afore-mentioned defects. Moreover, Wardle's work is a commemorative publication commissioned by PSNC to celebrate its centenary in 1940. While he may have had unrestricted access to this company's records, the latter could have been at odds with actual events, particularly where incidents arose in bitter conflicts with other steamship firms, or where significant issues could even have been disregarded.

Such omissions may not have been deliberate, since it must be accepted that a commemorative work might afford only limited capacity for publication of historical detail and, therefore, the author may have had to be both selective and restrictive in content to highlight glorious achievements. Some avoided facts and incidents may not have been entirely favourable to PSNC, and it is likely that this company's Directorate would have retained editorial control to ensure that this was done. In any case, authors of commissioned works would surely not want to bite the hand that fed them. Accordingly, alternative sources must be found to either substantiate or repudiate claims made by Albérdi and Wardle.

Both authors, in specifically focusing on Wheelwright's role in PSNC, mostly neglected to portray the true state of contemporary economic and political affairs on the WCSA. PSNC did indeed play a major role in 19th Century development of this region, and because of its successes, many ex- employees and others associated with that firm, often speak proudly and nostalgically of events, details of which have been passed down by predecessors and by the company itself. Undoubtedly, other British companies originating in Liverpool and elsewhere are still held in high esteem for similar benefits they allegedly brought to those areas in which they operated, and to the port of Liverpool and its hinterland. Were these benefits widespread and who were the beneficiaries? Who gained, who lost?

With the passage of time, knowledge of actual events passed down by a succession of historians and researchers inevitably becomes blurred, and those authors commissioned by shipping companies to publish respective commemorative histories, may have been influenced, perhaps sub-consciously, to have glossed-over events where the reality was entirely different. They may have tended to depict heroic images of their founding entrepreneurs in the early years of such shipping lines; they would probably neglect to inform of the warts and inappropriate behaviour of the companies concerned, especially their affects on the societies of those nations with which they had commercial intercourse. These actions today might be considered socially and politically unacceptable.

PSNC Archivist John E.Lingwood introduced his PSNC history with the following passage:

"It was once quoted that the record of The Pacific Steam Navigation Company is one of dogged endurance in the face of adversity. Yet the company, in spite of continuing odds, still moves forward, ever adapting to changing circumstances, maintaining its identity undiminished as it moves forward to the year 1978..."

Whilst there were instances of such adversity, probably also experienced by other contemporary shipping companies, the true reasons for PSNC's success are those deriving from a considerable chunk of good fortune accompanied by beneficial political circumstances beyond the company's control.

The main theatre for PSNC's operations was the WCSA, from Panama to the Strait of Magellan at the tip of Chile. There was little competition in the early years, from 1840 up to 1870, but political, economic and social developments eventually attracted interest from other foreign and British shipping firms, especially from those countries with whom PSNC traded. This, according to Chilean historian Claudio Véliz in his "*Historia De La Marina Mercante De Chile*", bred a collection of myths; one in particular being that Chile, during the 19th Century, enjoyed a strong and extensive merchant fleet until it was destroyed by PSNC's attempts to build a monopoly on the Pacific coast. This book, therefore, explores any such occurrences and circumstances contributing to this myth, if myth it was; the real situation needs to be recorded.

William Wheelwright, in all of the above-mentioned PSNC histories, as well as in the early South American press, has been portrayed as a hero. Certainly, he was successful, much admired and, undoubtedly, a very moral businessman according to 19th standards. One suspects, however, that this success might have been acquired mostly through influential contacts combined with specific political requisites of the nations concerned. Could his accomplishments have been achieved by being in the right place at the right time? Could they have been attributable to considerable influences and pressures exerted within the Governments of the West Coast nations, the Chilean Government in particular, the aristocracy of the then ruling élite class, and the South American business community, a large part of which comprised British, North Americans and Europeans?

Is it possible that Wheelwright was simply being used by West Coast Governments for the development of their own national economies? He was at one stage, the United States Consul in Guayaquil and, accordingly, might have been identified by these nations as a potential link in establishing most favoured trading links with the United States. It is true that Wheelwright had to surmount difficult obstacles to attract investment to fund his proposed enterprise, but research undertaken for this book explores a far wider scenario in order to place PSNC's operations in perspective. Peruvian and Chilean Navies adopted steamships shortly after independence; it was inevitable that their commercial sectors would eventually adopt this type of transportation.

It is, therefore, appropriate to study the development of merchant sailing-ship trade in this region from the Spanish Imperial era to 1840, and to ascertain whether and/or when any earlier attempts were made to employ and operate steam-powered vessels. It is also necessary to identify causes for the initial lack of investment interest in commercially operated steamships on the WCSA, and indeed, in the world at large. Wheelwright did eventually launch his steamship enterprise, and an examination of the factors contributing to its emergence must be made to gauge the extent of his claimed heroic feats.

After Wheelwright's departure from PSNC in 1855, this company continued to enjoy success, but was this necessarily due to good management, or was it because the company had sailed into advantageous political waters in which it could not expect to founder? Importantly, did PSNC's West Coast operations provide benefits to the South American public generally, or were its achievements at the expense of the West Coast nations themselves?

"*Ploughing the South Sea*" is, accordingly, a study of economic, social and political factors contributing to the development of merchant shipping along the WCSA, from the Spanish Imperial Era to the end of the 20th Century. The "*South Sea*" was the name given by Balboa in 1513 to that stretch of the Pacific Ocean south of the Bay of Panama and extending to the Strait of Magellan. The phrase "*Ploughing the Sea*" is borrowed from the text of a letter sent by Simón Bolívar to one of his lieutenants, complaining that governing his country with its never-ending problems was like *ploughing the sea*; no sooner had the difficulties been pushed aside, they would, inevitably, after a short period flow back again to their original chaotic state.

The development of shipping and trade generally on the WCSA during the 19th century was, undoubtedly, aided by the relatively few occurrences of war when compared with the Atlantic and Caribbean. The conflict with Spain from October 1865 to March 1866, resulting in the blockading of some of the principal ports on the West Coast, would logically have affected PSNC's operations as well as the merchant ships of the nations concerned. Similarly, the 1879-1883 War of the Pacific between Chile, Bolivia and Peru, three countries constituting the principal arena of PSNC's West Coast operations, must not only have severely impacted on maritime trade, but have also tested the loyalties of its employees in these three republics and the company's oft-declared policy of neutrality. The causes, affects and the aftermath of these conflicts need to be assessed in relation to PSNC's contemporary operations.

Other considerations such as the political disappearance of the Bolivian coastline would also have influenced PSNC's services, given that Wheelwright, in 1840, had obtained a decree from that country granting PSNC the right of coastal trading within Bolivian waters. Any meaningful investigation would also need to address the reasons and circumstances for the rapid introduction of steamship services between Europe and the WCSA.

An examination of the issues and events leading to the construction of the Panama Railroad in 1855 and the Panama Canal in 1914, still widely regarded as being opened for the benefit of all nations, are included in this work. Both facilities imposed changes not only on PSNC and on competing North American shipping lines, but also promoted an upsurge of national feeling within the West Coast nations; their impact on the WCSA needed to be measured.

Two World Wars had a distressing affect on Europe; to what extent did the South American nations benefit from her troubles, and how did PSNC and other shipping lines cope with these and other crises? It is clear that after these nationally debilitating wars, the British Merchant Navy suffered a rapid decline. There are many who believe that had the British Government made financial efforts to subsidize its mercantile fleet in the same way as Chile and Peru, then PSNC and other British shipping companies would have been better placed to survive; might this have been the case?

As this study commences with an investigation of the commercial conditions and maritime situation prevailing on the WCSA before PSNC's operations, it would be appropriate to close it with a review of the conditions and the situation in this region after PSNC ceased operating. It would also be fitting to ascertain whether its demise, like many other British and foreign shipping companies operating in the Americas, was inevitable.

Finally, some of the English press advertisements and other documents set out in the text have been back-translated from the Spanish text of Arthur Wardle's "*El Vapor Conquista el Pacífico*"; they are, therefore, unlikely to agree word for word with the English originals The value of the peso has been taken at 48d (i.e. old pence -240d to the pound). This level was remarkably stable until the latter stages of the 19th Century. Dollar equivalents of sterling values have been made using the rate of $US1.80 to the pound. At the time of writing the dollar was falling in value.

1. Setting The Scene.   1503-1835

The mention of trade between Spain and her Latin American possessions in the first half of the 16th Century usually conjures up visions of a one-way traffic to the mother country in vast quantities of gold and silver. The tendency is to forget that the daily needs of her colonists were also provided by merchandise transported on outward voyages of Spanish galleons. In the process, many new plants and products were introduced to the West Coast of South America (WCSA), principally items such as seeds, animals, grain, oil and wine. Apart from gold and silver, other exports from that region included cacao, cotton, potatoes, corn and a wide variety of drugs like coca and quinine. These contributed to the development of Spain's WCSA Empire, but the latter's agricultural progress rated only second in importance to her preferred gold and silver imports.

Enormous quantities of this precious metal extracted from her New World colonies, and shipped home to the official port of Seville, eventually found their way into mainstream Europe where they helped finance industrialization outside Spain. The mother country had squandered these precious resources to finance lingering wars in support of the Catholic Church's struggles against the Protestant rebels of the Netherlands, Elizabethan England, France and the Turks. In return, the Church bestowed her approval and recognition of Spain's sovereignty over her sector of the Americas. In meeting such military commitments, Spain's imported wealth was generally used unproductively. By 1598, the country was bankrupt, overwhelmed by continued imposition of taxes and the twin plagues of inflation and economic depression, leading eventually to widespread famine. Desperate for new revenue, the Spanish Crown focused its attention on the gold and silver producing territories along the WCSA.

The Casa de Contratación[5], a supreme Spanish regulatory body founded in 1503, was made responsible for overseeing the nation's import and exports. It enjoyed total control over licensing ships, organizing transatlantic fleets, inspecting and registering cargoes, collecting taxes, duties and above all, ensuring the safe passage of Spain's share of wealth derived from the *"Quinto Real"*, a tax imposed on a one fifth portion of any gold and silver mined in the Spanish colonies. This Royal Authority ensured the continuation of the Spanish Crown's monopoly of its trans-Atlantic trade by channelling all related commercial activity through a small number of Spanish ports, principally Seville, and later Cadiz in the 18th Century. Trade in both exports and imports was actually conducted by a group of merchants in Seville known as the *"consulado"* to whom the Spanish Crown had granted exclusive trading rights with the Indies.

Although Spanish colonists introduced domesticated animals and crops alien to the American sub-continent, careful stock rearing converted once unproductive

Setting The Scene. 1503–1835

land into large profitable grazing areas, and the plough's introduction enabled the exploitation of previously unmanageable terrain. Indeed the Spanish Crown actively promoted agriculture by exporting new seeds, plants, livestock, farming implements, and most importantly, technical advice. This led to the establishment of a successful agrarian trade on the WCSA. The port of Guayaquil, linked to Spain's principal trades routes by the 18th Century, had begun to export bananas and cocoa to other West Coast colonies. As the latter progressed economically, so too did demand for goods such as twine, saffron, and paper needed to satisfy local demand from the ever growing bureaucracies of the Catholic Church and the many administrative institutions associated with the Spanish Crown.

Latin American locations of Spanish maritime commerce were strictly controlled. Three ports, designated as official control centres, monitored the access and egress points for the authorized fleets; Cartagena de Indias handled maritime traffic to and from New Granada;[6] Vera Cruz served Mexico and Central America; Nombre de Dios (later Portobello), on the Caribbean coast of Panama, handled cargo transhipments across the Isthmus onwards to Peru and Chile. Principal trade routes between Cadiz, Spain and Panama extended over 11,500 kilometres. A voyage to Peru's main port of Callao via Cape Horn, by contrast, entailed a trip of 17,000 kilometres.

The Seville consulado's merchants were also allowed to operate branches of their business houses in the capitals of the Audencias, the principal administrative areas in 16th Century Spanish America. As trade between these colonies expanded, the control centres began to operate independently of their headquarters in the mother country, and were eventually awarded their own separate status, the consulado of Lima being granted in 1613. A monopoly was thus created at both ends of the trade routes, allowing merchandise supplies to be manipulated to obtain the highest prices; in many cases generating profit levels of up to 100% on exports to the Spanish colonies. The Casa de Contratación also effected price rises in the Americas by imposing punitive levels of duty and tax, its officials working in close collaboration with the consulados' merchants.[7]

Spain, failing to satisfy demand from the Indies for manufactured goods from within her national resources, resorted to importing these from the more industrialized European nations, and then re-exporting them to the appointed consulados, in the process, becoming nothing more than a clearinghouse. In acquiring these goods from the more advanced countries, Spain was obliged to release into general European circulation, considerable amounts of imported gold and silver, further depleting her wealth. Such European manufactures commanded excessively high prices, augmented by the restrictive practices of the Casa de Contratación and associate consulados. This led to widespread circumvention of its highly and centrally regulated system. Moreover, this ever-increasing contraband was imported by European enterprises at prices substantially lower than those set by the monopolistic Spanish authorities.

Sailing voyages to the three official ports of Cartagena de Indias, Nombre de Dios and Vera Cruz, basically followed the routes formerly mapped by Columbus; vessels leaving Seville would head for the Canaries to replenish supplies, and then sail for about a month towards the south Caribbean before proceeding to Cartagena de Indias. There fresh supplies would be loaded prior to heading for Nombre de Dios on the Caribbean coast of Panama, where cargoes were discharged for transhipment across the Isthmus to Panama's Pacific port to be re-loaded onto sailing ships bound for the Peruvian port of Callao.

Panama, at that time, could hardly be described as a permanent port. When ships were due to call, temporary stalls would suddenly appear on the shore along with increased human activity; no permanent port facilities in the usual sense existed. Cargo conveyed northwards across the Isthmus from Panama to Porto Bello would be collected and taken to Havana for onward shipment to Spain. Similar activity took place at Porto Bello. Jorge Juan and Antonio de Ulloa, having visited the latter port in the mid 18th Century, provided the following record of the typical hustle and bustle generated by the arrival of sailing ships:

"The ships are no sooner moored in the harbour than the first work is to erect a tent made of ship's sails in the Square for receiving its cargo, at which the proprietors of the goods are present in order to find their bales by the marks, which distinguish them. These bales are drawn on sledges to their proper places by the crew of every ship and the money given to them is proportionally divided.

While the seamen and European traders are thus employed, the shore is covered with droves of mules from Panama, each drove comprising more than one hundred and loaded with chests of gold and silver from the merchants of Peru. Some unload them at the exchange, others in the middle of the Square, yet amid the hurry and confusion of such crowds, no theft, loss or disturbance is ever known. He who has seen this place during the *tiempo muerto*, or dead time, solitary, poor and a perpetual silence reigning everywhere, the harbour quite empty, and in every place wearing a melancholy aspect, must be filled with astonishment at the sudden change, to see the bustling multitudes, every house crowded, the Square and streets encumbered with bales and chests of gold and silver of all kinds, the harbour full of ships and vessels, some bringing by way of Rio de Chape [Chagres] the goods of Peru, such as cacao, quinquina or Jesuits' bark, vicuña wool, and bezoar stones [for medicinal purposes]; others coming from Carthagena loaded with provisions. Thus a place, at all other times detested for its deleterious qualitites, becomes the warehouse and the market of the riches of the Old and New Words and scene of one of the most considerable branches of commerce in the whole world.

After the ships have been unloaded and the merchants of Peru together with the President of Panama have arrived, the fair is ready to begin. Representatives of the various merchants and traders then go on board one of the principal galleons in the harbour and there in the presence of the commodore of the galleons and the President of Panama, the former

Setting The Scene. 1503–1835

as the patron of the Europeans and the latter, of the Peruvians, the prices of the various goods and merchandise are settled. After three or four meetings, agreements are made, signed, and made public. In accordance with them, each sets about to make his sales and purchases. In that way, all fraud is avoided. The purchases and sales, as likewise the exchange of money, are transacted by brokers, both from Spain and Peru. After this, everyone begins to dispose of his goods; the Spanish brokers embarking their chests of money and those of Peru sending away the goods they have purchased."[8]

By 1560, exports of silver from Spain's colonies had increased to such an extent, that the Spanish monarchy was obliged to organize armed escort fleets to deter piracy. Ships sailing to or from the Indies were thus required to join one of two units or "*flotas*". Operating as separate groups, the "*flota*" destined for New Spain[9] would leave the mother country each spring for Vera Cruz, accompanied by vessels heading for the silver producing Honduras. The second fleet, leaving Seville in August, would sail for Nombre de Dios, laden with cargoes for South America. This latter grouping, assembled specifically to collect stocks of silver produced in the Potosí region[10] of the Vice-Royalty of Peru, was escorted by at least six Spanish galleons. These were the typical ocean-going warships operated by the continental European naval powers in the 15th and 16th Century. They were large, cumbersome three-masted vessels, square rigged and with two decks accommodating their main cannon batteries in broadsides; the Spanish authorities considered them suitable for conveying treasure and other cargo from the Americas to the Indies, and from the WCSA to the Panama Isthmus.

Their naval weakness, however, was clearly demonstrated in the defeat of the Spanish Armada in 1588, when the lighter and swifter English sailing ships, designed and constructed by John Hawkins, easily outmanoeuvred these unwieldy vessels. They were also no match for those smaller and more responsive ships in the calmer, light breezed environment of the Pacific coast of South and Central America. Over the winter period, both galleon fleets would remain together in Havana, returning to Spain the following spring.

By the close of the 16th Century, the strain of maintaining a far-flung empire had begun to weigh on Spain's economy. Despite having received substantial resources from the silver-producing tax, the "*Royal Fifth*", her wealth was rapidly depleted, not only by the financing of continual war in Europe, but also by the increasing costs of administering and defending her colonies. Dutch fleets had begun to penetrate into areas hitherto regarded as the preserve of Spain. In 1628, Dutchman Piet Heyn captured an entire Spanish treasure fleet in the Bay of Matanza off Cuba. The Dutch had also acquired valuable territory in 1634 when seizing Curaçao and other islands. The French and English, following the Dutch example, took and occupied a large assortment of islands in the Caribbean. A measure of the value of a typical galleon's cargo can perhaps be assessed by a report of May 7, 2002, from Reuters News Agency in Panama, announcing that a sunken galleon dating from the Spanish Conquest, and carrying a cargo valued at US $50 million (£28,000,000 approximately), had been found by scientists off Panama's Pacific coast. The ship *San Jose* had sunk on June 17, 1631, in the archipelago of the Pearl Islands approximately 60 miles south of Panama Bay.

The threat of further losses to her empire was such that Spain was eventually forced to retain large amounts of silver within the Indies to finance the provision and re-enforcement of coastal defences, particularly along the western seaboard of South America. Business confidence in trade between Spain and her New World possessions consequently collapsed. Moreover, silver production, heavily dependent on the mother country for supplies of mercury, fell steadily because of her financial inability to supply this commodity. The outcome was that, by 1640, no silver was reaching Spain from the Indies or the Americas. Due to lack of revenue, Spain was, therefore, unable to supply her colonies with the European manufactured goods they craved.

The mother country retained regulatory control over her commerce and the entire colonial administrative system was still subservient to the Spanish Crown. Restrictions applying to Spanish territory on the West Coast South America before and up to this period were unquestionably severe; such was Spain's fear of penetration of her colonies by other nations, Britain especially. Any person found guilty of trading with a foreign nation other than those authorized by the regulatory *"consulados"* was sentenced to death. Spanish nationals (peninsulares), that is, those from the Iberian Peninsula, were not even allowed entry into her colonies without special permission. No foreigner had been permitted to visit any of the Spanish South American colonies; any communication between colonial provinces was controlled in case revolutionary sentiments were fostered by inter regional discourse. Nobody was allowed to reside in the colonies unless born in Spain. No South American was permitted to own a ship or receive a cargo. No financial capital other than Spanish could be introduced into the colonies. Any foreign ship in distress venturing into a South American port was liable to be seized and her crew imprisoned.

The logical solution to Spain's financial crisis would have required her to make peace with her enemies and wind-down her military commitments, thus allowing her to concentrate on the development of her own economy in tandem with those of her colonies. The Spanish Crown, however, continued to rely on the Catholic Church's recognition of its legitimacy both in Europe and in the Americas; in turn, the Church continued to demand Spanish military commitment to opposing the former's enemies.

As Spain's economic and military might began to collapse, her grasp on the colonies loosened, allowing them to develop according to their resources and at their own pace. This led to an increase in the numbers of Hispanic elements resident in the colonies compared with the indigenous majority population; powerful local oligarchies soon formed from amongst the minority land and property owning Creoles[11] who eventually emerged as the ruling élite class of South America. Coastal trading along the WCSA was undertaken and controlled by Lima ship-owners until the monopoly was removed by the Spanish appointed Administration and transferred to the emerging Lima élites, and subsequently, to foreign business houses and merchants; a sure recipe for conflict.

Edward Williamson in his *"History of Latin America"* suggests that the fall in recorded shipments imported through Seville, indicated that the greater amount of silver, having being retained in the Indies, was used not just to pay for defence and administration, but was also applied as investment in local enterprises. He remarked:

"This was after all, the great age of public construction and architectural embellishment in Spanish America- ports, fortifications, roads, churches, palaces and mansions were built in the main centres of Spanish settlement."

At the end of the 17th Century, there already existed an active inter regional trade, especially between Peru and Chile. This coastal based commerce increased considerably over the following century as authorized maritime routes were established and developed between Callao and Valparaiso, a distance of 2400 kilometres. Both ports, at the time, were within the Vice-Royalty of Peru; Valparaíso being viewed by the latter as the poor relation. The amount of cargo carried between these two centres was recorded as having quadrupled in the period from the end of the 17th Century to the end of the 18th, and the value of such goods as having increased by a factor of eight.[12]

Peruvian trade was extremely important to Chile, because the majority of her agricultural produce, such as wheat and tallow for making candles, was exported to Callao. As far as Peru was concerned, commercial links with Spain still took precedence, but Chile was the main recipient of exports from Peruvian coastal regions such as textiles, sugar and tobacco, the latter two requiring a tropical climate that Chile lacked. As well as agricultural products, Chile exported precious metals and copper to Peru. In the 17th Century, trade in cereals between the two countries had been practically non-existent, such absence being attributed to the high cost of prevailing freight charges. However, a disastrous earthquake in Lima in 1687, having adversely affected Peruvian agriculture, enabled considerable Chilean grain supplies to be directed towards feeding Lima's inhabitants and its suburbs. As a result of Chile providing shortfalls, a trade in the supply of wheat to Lima was created, an activity that continued throughout the 19th Century.[13]

An important Peruvian export, probably contributing mostly to the strengthening of commercial ties between the two ports, was the supply of home-produced low cost textiles, along with the re-export of the more expensive European manufactured fabrics. Various records maintained by religious institutions such as convents and hospitals reveal that "*tocuyo*", a coarse cotton cloth exported from Peru, was an important element in Chilean imports. The most heavily traded commodity exported to Chile was sugar, where consumption was widespread both for cooking and medicinal purposes. This commodity was produced by huge coastal area plantations owned and managed by powerful and influential élites. Due to increases in Peruvian sugar and wheat from Chile's central regions, the Peruvian merchant fleet in 1789, based in Callao, amounted to 29 sailing ships compared with just two vessels registered in Valparaíso and Guayaquil.[14]

European textiles constituted an important part of imports by the Vice-Royalties of South America. Those Creoles and Spanish immigrants, who had managed to purchase high office or, had manoeuvred themselves by other means into influential positions, were more financially able to acquire these European manufactured fabrics re-exported to the Vice-Royalty by Spain. Included in this imported merchandise was fine linen from Flanders used in the embroidery of sheets, altar cloths, and shirts. It was not rated as highly as other European textiles and despite its general availability in local shops, it was often used as medium of exchange for work undertaken. One other product that assumed great importance was paper from France and Geneva, re-exported via Spain and used particularly by the Colonial bureaucracy, religious institutions and their associated organizations. Other imports included spices, cinnamon, pepper and of lesser importance, the more expensive Spanish saffron, used mainly for medicinal purposes.

Increased commercial maritime activity, together with reduced competition from Spanish shipyards, led to the emergence of a Pacific shipbuilding industry located principally at Guayaquil, which provided ships for the Callao-Panama link. The industry declined in the 18th Century, having been overtaken by technical advances in European vessels that had become actively involved in Spanish America's international commerce.[15] From 1700, galleons that had sailed to the Atlantic via Cape Horn gradually disappeared as trade with Peru was conducted via an overland crossing of the Isthmus of Panama, fed by maritime movements between the latter and Callao.

The Vice-Royalty of Nueva Granada, created in 1739, incorporating Panama and Guayaquil, loosened previously strong links with the whaling and fishing industry in Paita and the port of Callao, which remained in the Vice-Royalty of Peru.[16] Moreover, Spain and her Vice-Royalties granted licences to smaller individual vessels capable of using the Cape Horn route. In 1776, new problems appeared for Lima and Callao following the creation of the Vice-Royalty of La Plata, whose élite landowners and merchants, having been granted concessions similar to those held by their Lima counterparts, emerged as competitors in the lucrative trade with Bolivia. Free Trade policies introduced by the Spanish Administration created more problems for the monopolistic élites, bringing in their wake additional shipping companies from Spain, which once firmly established in Lima, posed serious threats to existing enterprises.

Due to trade liberalization, navigation became more flexible, faster and more regular. Additionally, Cadiz, having replaced Seville as Spain's most important port, ceased enjoying the monopoly rights to handle exports; in 1778, a similar fate befell Callao. Other ports along the WCSA were soon opened-up and allowed to trade freely with each other. In this same period, the system of recovering taxes and duty became more simplified, leading in some cases to meaningful reductions. One external factor that contributed to this was the steady influx of goods from contraband activity, which was responsible for considerable declines in tax and duty revenue. In the 18th Century, in the Pacific as well as in the Spanish Caribbean and Spanish Atlantic colonies, smuggling and associated illegal trading were endemic.

Undertaken by the French originally, the South American authorities had tolerated this practice because France was then allied with Spain during the Spanish War of Succession (1739-1748). The English, subsequently, infiltrated this lucrative contraband trade, assisted by a concession granted to them by the terms of the 1713 Treaty of Utrecht, including the right to trade in slaves and use of the port of Buenos Aires as a regional trading base. Towards the end of the 17th and up to the latter quarter of the 18th Centuries, England enjoyed facilities available at the Portuguese port of Colonia do Sacramento, on the opposite shore to Buenos Aires on the River Plate estuary. From this port regular contraband trading was conducted with the Spanish colonies. In 1790, a Spanish treaty, signed with the United States and Great Britain, allowed both countries to operate their merchant fleets in the Pacific, provided they were outside the 10 miles shore limit. They were only allowed to enter West Coast ports in an emergency, but their presence in the Pacific marked an increase in contraband, not only of much demanded merchandise but also of books, magazines and ideas that inclined towards more liberal trade policies and intellectual thought detrimental to the Spanish colonial system.[17]

Between 1788 and 1796, 26 ships from Boston had been recorded in Chilean ports, but for the same period in Peru, 226 vessels had been observed. It was unsurprising that the number of actual emergencies had been very few, but it led to the Spanish Authorities trying to control their shores with Coast Guards. It was clear that during the period 1810 to 1820, North American business merchants had become firmly established in the Peruvian whaling ports, but for reasons other than whaling. Between 1808 and 1821, the contrast was even greater; 81 frigates and 77 brigantines entered Callao compared with 44 sailing ships in Valparaíso.[18] Throughout this era, further improvements in navigation and increases in ship sizes led to reduced freight charges and larger shipping volumes. Between 1717 and

1749, vessels of around 300 tons gross weight comprised about 67% of trading ships, but between 1750 and 1778, this figure reduced to 46%. In the latter case, the growth of cargo measured against a reduction in ship numbers was an obvious indicator of vessels becoming larger.[19]

In fact, trade between Peru and Chile from the end of the 17th to the end of the 18th Century increased by around 150%. This is attributed partly to the larger sailing ships constructed in Europe, which, after rounding Cape Horn, remained in the Pacific to operate on coastal and inter regional trade. Vessels on the West Coast continued to grow in size, again prompting lower shipping rates. Before 1730, maritime trade between Peru and Chile had mostly ceased to operate in winter due to poor sailing weather conditions, but thereafter, a notable increase in shipping movements was recorded following significant progress in navigational systems and sailing techniques, thereby lessening the risk of being shipwrecked.[20]

The biggest factor affecting commerce was war. The 18th Century witnessed bitter international conflicts such as the War of Jenkins Ear (1739-1748) between England and Spain, arising initially from the former country's illicit trade in Spanish America, and later, by the War of Austrian Succession (1740-1748), and the American War of Independence (1779-1783). Throughout these campaigns, Spain found herself in direct confrontation with England, the only naval power then capable of seriously obstructing trade with her colonies. The decline in Spanish shipping activity occurred not only because of considerable vessel losses, but because, given the conditions then operating in periods of war, unaffordable increases in insurance levels militated against effective commerce.

The War of Jenkins Ear and the Seven Years War, especially in the year 1762, when Spain entered the conflict and the English captured Havana, were especially destructive for Spanish trade, judging by the huge number of ships captured or destroyed. Even by the end of the 17th Century, the convoys plying the historic route from Spain to Panama had virtually disappeared, leading to a serious drop in commerce. This was only addressed around 1730, once the restrictions on monopoly trading between Spain and Peru had been lifted. By contrast, inter regional activity along the Pacific coast had increased during the remainder of the 18th Century, aided by the fact that the Pacific Ocean was then relatively free and unaffected by international conflict.

Towards the end of the 18th Century, increasing contraband supplies were still unable to meet the WCSA's insatiable demand for goods, particularly, the regions around Lima. This shortage effectively contributed to the growth of this still illicit activity; more merchandise was shipped via the Cape Horn route, even though it was substantially longer and more time consuming than shipment via the Panama Isthmus. The voyage round Cape Horn, however, had the advantage of not only creating lower costs compared with the expense of transporting merchandise from Panama, but also of avoiding the statutory intervention of Lima's élite middlemen.

One extra benefit introduced by contraband trading generated from vessels rounding Cape Horn, was the appreciable price reductions in Chile of imported textiles. In the 17th Century, Spanish and Creole business houses had been able to rake-in profits of between 100 and 300 per cent. By the 18th Century, due to growing European imports, these levels had fallen dramatically, resulting in some colonial enterprises being bankrupted but quickly replaced by a growing number of European establishments as the illicit trade mushroomed.

The removal of trade restrictions did not affect all products; sugar, for example, was not considered suitable for import from the Indies due to the long distances it had to be conveyed, although some was legally acquired from Brazil and Cuba towards the end of the 18th Century. Moreover, Peru's influential sugar producers had applied considerable pressure on the authorities to protect their interests. Wheat exported from Chile, on the other hand, figured in a growing market with Peru and returning ships brought back sugar and textiles on lower rates of freight.

Towards the end of the 18th Century, shipments from Valparaiso to Callao were 40% higher than those from the latter to the former port. One reason for this was the monopoly awarded to Lima's official grain-dealing business houses; they were allowed to purchase this commodity in Chile, convey it to Lima, and sell it there at far higher prices. Chilean firms, on the other hand, were prohibited from setting -up similar operations. Chile was still administered as part of the Vice-Royalty of Peru and the latter's business houses, unlike their Chilean counterparts, continued to exert considerable influence on the Spanish monarchy's appointed Executive in Lima, by making effective use of "*donations*" or "*loans*". Corruption was rife, mostly at the lower administrative levels to which officials usually appointed on poor salaries and short-term contracts, sought alternative sources to supplement their meagre finances. The powerful Creole élites, content to participate in such bribery, were thus more able to influence local tiers of government, especially during the period of that long-standing and strict policy of isolation, which Spain had long imposed on her colonies and, which had been assiduously enforced by the self-serving Creoles.

Furthermore, Spanish administrators had become increasingly incapable of physically supervising the thousands of miles of the West Coast. Foreign vessels, accordingly, in the late 18th Century, especially from the United States, began to take advantage of this weakness. Small, but relatively fast ships, from Baltimore especially, sailed warily round Cape Horn into the Pacific in search of valuable business, bringing with them the much sought-after manufactured goods from Europe, which the greater part of West Coast residents had never enjoyed. The United States, repressed as a British colony, had not then developed industries of her own, and her merchant ships imported cargoes of mainly British manufactured goods acquired in the West Indies. News of this lucrative activity soon leaked to other merchantmen in that area eventually leading to British dominance of this illegal trade. All along the West Coast, the entrepreneurial *contrabandistas* located suitable sheltered waters where vessels could secretly discharge their own treasure troves of merchandise to satisfy ever-increasing demands of the local population, safe in the knowledge that this fast growing stealth trade was facilitated and protected by the many layers of official corruption.

The Spanish Colonial Administration, eventually aware that local craving for imported goods had become overwhelming, issued a decree in 1810 consenting to the transportation of British goods across the Isthmus of Panama, and permitting their onward shipment to the Peruvian port of Callao. Such merchandise was, however, still subjected to an import duty of 37.5%, even before other local taxes were applied. Despite this seemingly crippling fiscal burden, British ships continued to make fortunes by trading on the Peruvian coast.

In September 18, 1818, following the emergence of Chile's first independent Government, Juan Martinez de Rojas, son-in-law of a shipping magnate in Concepción, aware that many foreign ships, the majority North American, were trading illegally along the Chilean coast, decided that opening all Chilean ports to foreign vessels would be nationally advantageous. Unfortunately for Chile, this far-sighted policy was not supported by any measures to protect sea routes; defence policies concentrated on protecting harbours and the provision of cavalry patrols which could be quickly mobilized against any invading landing parties. Given Chile's lengthy coastline, these limited protective measures left her vulnerable to potentially hostile maritime forces.

Spain, beset with internal strife, eventually lost control of her colonies and with it the capacity to supply them with their essential commodity requirements. She was obliged, therefore, to tolerate direct commercial intercourse with Britain as a substitute source for such goods. By 1818, British sailing ships were entering Callao to land their cargoes with little action being undertaken by the Authorities to expel them. In 1819, this port was declared officially open to trade with Great Britain for a period of two years, and the latter's merchants permitted to settle there.[21]

The British business community, as well as those foreign merchants already on South American soil, became increasingly entrenched as their numbers expanded. The amount of UK ships involved in trading with the WCSA became so great, that the British Government, bowing to the demands of its mainland ship owners and investors, instructed the Royal Navy to afford them her protection, especially from American privateers and from the forces of the Vice-Royalty of Peru. Visits by British Royal Navy ships to the Peruvian and Chilean coasts became more frequent, particularly as British traders having exchanged their goods for silver, began employing them to ship this specie to the UK. Although merchants were heftily charged for these services, the arrangement was considered much safer than conveying bullion by merchant vessels, and further benefited by the application of lower insurance rates. As the Spanish colonies finally gained their independence in the first quarter of the 19th Century, barriers to free commerce were removed, but would later lead to trade disputes and eventually war.

An important factor in the struggle for Chilean independence was the involvement of British banks in lending considerable sums to the Chilean Government to finance her own war of Independence, although the British Government had throughout the 1820s still not officially recognized Chile as a sovereign state.[22] Chile had, in fact, made considerable progress with positive economic and social reforms during the years 1818 to 1823, under the Government of Liberator Bernado O'Higgins. Given the length of her coastline, the physical constraints of mainland travel, her dependence on foreign trade and her European outlook, it is surprising that she did not then possess a strong and viable merchant fleet. Chilean historian, Claudio Veliz claimed in 1961, that there was still a firm but unfounded belief that Chile, at one time, possessed a very powerful merchant marine, which had disappeared due to infiltration by foreign concerns.[23] This may have been attributed to O'Higgins' grand vision for creating a merchant navy superior to that of the United States; his dream was of an alliance with Great Britain; she would control the Old World order while Chile would assume responsibility for the New World.

A large part of what could be classed as the Chilean merchant fleet during the period 1817-1821 was operating as corsairs. These vessels, privately funded and operated, were sanctioned by the country to which they belonged to plunder enemy ships . They were useful to the Government of Chile in that they positively disrupted Spain's sea trade in the Pacific and allowed Chilean crews to gain practical navigational experience, potentially useful in the service of her national navy. Considerable profits were to be made from these plundering adventures, but the increasing numbers of Chilean vessels occupied in such forays only reduced the number of ships available to serve in a genuine merchant fleet. Moreover, scarce investment capital was often applied to the purchase of vessels, whether old or new, to embark on these risky but remunerative privateering quests, rather than be committed to strict merchant marine operations.

Typical of these sorties was the occasion a group of British and North Americans, under the command of adventurer William Mackay, chartered a very old and decrepit schooner called *Death or Glory*. With astounding luck, her crew captured a Spanish 400 tons sailing ship, together with cargo valued at 300,000 pesos(about £60,000 or $US108,000). This prize capture was taken to Valparaiso where others, having heard of the rewards involved, were determined to follow the example of the fortunate adventurers.[24] Apart from privateering's counteracting influences, the main reasons for lack of investment in merchant shipping was the perception by businessmen then operating in Chile, that such enterprises were risky, returning little profit in comparison with their traditional industries.

In simple terms, these entrepreneurs could be divided into three distinct commercial groups; agricultural producers and exporters from the southern regions of Chile; mining interests of the arid northern parts and the bankers, business houses and importers of the middle regions where most of the nation's population dwelt. These three groups were more interested in ensuring that import duties and freight charges for their respective cargoes be kept as low as possible. They reasonably believed that sustaining a Chilean merchant marine would generate higher taxes and increases in freight charges.

Although there was no shortage of investment capital in Chile at the time, the afore-mentioned business interests preferred to re-invest in their own established industries and in the business sectors with which they were already well acquainted, rather than gamble on enterprises of which they were less knowledgeable. The Chilean Government had, therefore, been obliged to resort to other measures to encourage investment in a national merchant fleet and, throughout the O'Higgins years, had steadfastly refused to remove its policy of cabotage, officially restricting foreign vessels from trading along the Chilean coastline. This policy had been introduced in an attempt to encourage Chilean business houses to invest in and operate coastal shipping, and at the same time, to expand and accelerate the Chilean shipbuilding industry.

Despite advantageous reductions in duties and generous subsidies, there was no interest from the national business sector except for one small group of Chilean nationals who, seeing an excellent business opportunity because of their country's free trade policy, formed Eyzaguirre y Compañia in August 1819, for the purpose of operating a sailing ship service to India.[25] Between 1817 and 1825, at least 75% of all of Chile's copper exports had been transported to Asian ports, Calcutta especially. Imports of this metal had been arranged by Great Britain as part of a triangular operation.[26] Eyzaguirre y Cia envisaged a similar plan; its ships would sail for Asian ports with copper and return to Chilean ports with tea, spices and other exotic products naturally unavailable in Chile. This company's strategy, formed to take advantage of the generous financial awards by the Chilean Government to encourage this type of operation by national ship owners was, accordingly, exempted from all export taxes and benefited from considerable reductions in import duty.

In 1819, this company's frigate *Carmen* duly arrived in Calcutta with 3,200 quintals of copper (one quintal = 100 pounds). The ship reportedly arrived in such bad condition, that the shipping agent recorded that he had been obliged to charter the frigate *Stanmore* as a replacement which had sailed for Valparaiso with a cargo of tea, spices and other Asian merchandise. The Chilean company, once again, chartered this vessel for the return to Calcutta laden with copper. The Chilean Government was heartened that its efforts in launching economic incentives were seen to be having the desired affect. Unfortunately, the conduct of Eyzaguirre y Cia was fraudulent, involving actions, which, according to Claudio Véliz, were then quite common in merchant shipping.

The *Carmen* had not arrived in Calcutta in the decrepit state reported by her shipping agent, and the charter of the *Stanmore* was, therefore, unnecessary. Eyzaguirre y Cia, having benefited from exemptions of export taxes on her cargo of copper to Calcutta, had sought to acquire similar British duty reductions on this commodity imported into India. To obtain this, the company would have had to charter a British registered vessel. It met this requirement by chartering the British registered *Stanmore* and selling the *Carmen*. The cargo carried by the *Stanmore* out of Calcutta accordingly benefited from reduced British export duty. In order to attract reduced duty on cargo imported into Chile, the company passed-off the *Stanmore* as a Chilean vessel. This was technically allowed because the latter had been a direct replacement for the Chilean registered *Carmen*.

Flushed with the success of this operation, Eyzaguirre y Cia continued with its subterfuge by operating two Chilean-registered vessels on the basis that the company was founded and based in Chile, while declaring them to the British Authorities as British ships registered in the name of their British captains. The Chilean company came unstuck when the British Authorities, somewhat tardily, discovered from periodic lists of shipping movements submitted by their consuls at the subject ports, that the company was changing the nationality of its vessels on each voyage. In any case, the Chilean Government, drawing most of its revenue from import and export duties, had by then raised taxes on copper exports, increasing their cost by between 15 to 18% at a time when Great Britain, undergoing a financial crisis, was prompted to seek cheaper copper imports from alternative sources. The Chilean copper trade to India, accordingly, collapsed completely.[27]

In the period 1818-1823 under President Bernado O'Higgins, considerable progress was achieved with financial and social reforms, creating a favourable economic climate and attracting considerable immigration from Europe, especially from Britain. Once established in Chile, the British business community invigorated her economy and way of life, previously conducted on the considerably more rigid culture of the Spanish ancien regime. Mrs. María Graham, otherwise known as Lady Calcott, a noted Chilean resident and close friend of Chilean hero Admiral Cochrane, recorded in her "*Journal of a Resident in Chili*" in 1822:

"English shops are prevalent; small wares and woollen goods are the main items for sale. On every street, tailors shops, shoe shops, saddlers and English taverns can be seen. And it is surprising how many people here speak English."

After Chilean Independence, there were in Valparaíso alone, several dozen British import-export houses, needing continuous stocks of merchandise in order to maintain trade. The goods they sold were mainly shipped-in from Europe. British banks financed European business; international enterprises, mainly British, proliferated, thereby assisting the growth of regular merchant shipping activity on the WCSA. It is no wonder that many in Britain and her expatriates in South America came to regard this region as the unofficial part of the British Empire.

For the 12 years before 1818, there had been no shortage of merchant ships plying Chilean shores. However, most of these were foreign-owned and thus not available for Chilean Government requisition in times of crisis. During his period as Chilean President, Liberator Bernardo O'Higgins had seen fit to launch an expensive military and naval campaign to free Peru from Spanish control. Chile had assembled a formidable naval force, having already secured further large British loans and obtained official recognition by the United States. The unsuccessful Peruvian campaign caused Chilean public discontent, mainly because of its high cost.

O'Higgins' liberal reforms, and his authoritarianism in implementing them, had only served to inflame the élites' passions. They eventually forced him to flee into exile in Peru. Soon after, Chile fell into chaos; political control was assumed by the military whenever a sequence of short-lived Governments was dissolved. Grandiose public schemes and plans for improvement lay dormant; public works, which had already started, lay abandoned and Government employees remained unpaid; crime both in the capital and in countryside flourished. In the midst of these disorders, economic progress came to a complete standstill; the state of the nation was such that the Chilean Navy comprised just one vessel.

Once hostilities with Spain had ended, there were so few merchant ships available that Chile was unable to cope with the demands of both coastal and foreign trade. To overcome this problem, her Government allowed foreign flag vessels to conduct coastal operations. This encouraged the entry of English ships into Talcahuano and Valparaíso; they brought with them the fashionable and much-in-demand goods from England and Europe. Once their merchandise had been discharged, these vessels would then proceed about 220 miles north of Valparaíso to the port of La Serena to load precious cargoes of copper, gold and silver.

The war and internal strife, having diminished Chile's financial resources, caused her to default on her loan repayments to Great Britain who, accordingly, downgraded her to a very low position in the hierarchy of credit-worthy South American republics. By 1825, the British Government had already recognized the nations of Gran Columbia, Brazil and the United Provinces of La Plata as sovereign states; the latter included the territories now forming Argentina and Uruguay. Chile applied to Great Britain for official recognition as a sovereign nation, but the latter's Government considered her to be too disorganized, a view based on a report from her official representative in Valparaíso which claimed:

Setting The Scene. 1503–1835

"At present the State is so generally convulsed that it may be said there is no Government in the country"

The Chilean public had strongly criticised the expense of the country's military operations to liberate Peru from Spanish forces. The question of recovering most of the costs from her was an issue that would bitterly occupy both nations for years. During Chile's liberation campaign, 50% of her national expenditure had been concentrated on military spending while 65% of her revenue derived from Customs' taxes and duties on imports and exports. It would, therefore, have been difficult for the Chilean Government to have promoted the establishment of a merchant marine and a national shipbuilding industry while, as a country at war, she was committed to increasing revenue from shipping, of which the greater part was foreign.

As a Spanish colony, Chile had been dominated by a small ruling élite whose power and prestige were founded on wealth derived from their huge agricultural and other land ownerships, and to a lesser extent, on mining and commerce. The élite groups vociferously complained at the cost of the Peruvian campaign; there was no body or person to speak on behalf of the landless, uneducated, poor indigenous majority. Nevertheless, the ruling class began to successfully reorganize Chile. Given her extremely long coastline endowed with many small harbours, they eventually accepted that the sea was the conduit to contact with the outside world.

It is unsurprising that Chile, at this stage, still did not possess a merchant marine. Her cabotage policy had previously barred foreign vessels from her minor ports to the detriment of national revenue. Importantly, the lack of interest by the small numbers of Chilean national ship owners in calling at these lesser status ports, especially within the northern Chilean coastline, meant that mining interests in that area suffered a virtual communications' blackout. A similar situation occurred in the wealthy timber areas of the country's southern regions. Both areas relied on the import of goods and materials, which could only be supplied by the other, and could only be transported by sea.

The scarcity of ships created a vacuum filled, at the time, by foreign vessels calling at major ports. The Chilean Senate had previously refused requests to remove its cabotage policy and in 1819, had even declined to licence a French shipping enterprise to transport timber cargoes from the River Maule to mining concerns in the country's northern sector.[28] A similar application from British entrepreneurs to bring ore from the minor port of Huasco to Coquimbo had also been rejected. Mining interests and their associated trades in these two minor ports were substantial. Prices of goods in the two locations, because of the infrequency of visiting ships, rose considerably and mine owners were unable to ship out their mineral ores.

"*Mining Guild*" protestations led to a Chilean Senate review of cabotage restrictions, but the main reason why there was no expansion in the Chilean merchant fleet or increases in the numbers of Chilean ship owners, as envisaged in the nation's protectionist policy, was the general uncompetitiveness of their ships compared with foreign vessels Claudio Veliz drew attention to a report submitted to the Chilean Government three months before the review of its cabotage policy[29]:

" [Experience of sailing across oceans and into numerous ports] are advantages only enjoyed by foreign registered ships carrying away the fruits of the nation's labours to far flung destinations while our 40 Chilean registered vessels are unavailable for unacceptably long periods to transport cargo between our national ports.
The English discharge their imported cargoes in Talcahuano and from that port transport timber for use here in the province of Valparaiso. Once the latter cargoes are unloaded, their ships, rather than sail away in ballast, are loaded with stores and provisions for shipment to Coquimbo. Again, instead of taking-on stone for ballast, they charge for minimum quantities of whatever type of cargo may become available, thereby saving the cost and labour of providing ballast and enabling them to sail away to load-up with copper, having already contracted with shippers in the northern ports".

In 1822, a Chilean Senate's review of the cabotage policy led to a reclassification of the status of her ports. Valparaiso continued its role as the nation's principal maritime centre; Coquimbo, Talcahuano and San Carlos de Chiloé were classed as major ports, officially opening the way for foreign vessels to undertake coastal operations between these locations; other ports remained classed as "*minor*" and from which foreign flag vessels were prohibited from trading.

The Chilean Government, in view of national opinion, had then considered it politically prudent to maintain cabotage as State policy, but in order to meet the demands of the mining sector, the former "*minor*" ports of Huasco and Copiapó were excluded in the national interest from the prohibited classification and allowed to export their copper on foreign ships. However, some differentiation in port dues was retained; for example, foreign ships had to pay five pesos (approximately £1) per mast for rights of anchorage while Chilean ships paid half of this rate.[30]

The Chilean Executive realized, by this time, that national revenue principally obtained through the levy of export and import taxes had declined due to cabotage policy. It had, importantly, failed to encourage the construction of Chilean vessels on the scale intended; it also calculated the potential loss of further financial resources by excluding foreign vessels from coastal trading and the minor ports.[31] Despite political instability, Chile's economy continued to grow, leading to increases in both foreign and national shipping movements. This is evident from the following table:

TOTAL TONNAGES OF MERCHANT SHIPPING FROM CHILE, GREAT BRITAIN, UNITED STATES, FRANCE ARRIVING AT VALPARAISO. DURING THE PERIOD 1825-1833[32]

YEAR	CHILE	GREAT BRITAIN	USA	FRANCE
1825	4727	15931	17695	1686
1826	8197	14965	15406	5230
1827	6137	11388	15753	6955
1828	8152	13869	19085	8050
1829	11635	15976	13740	5648
1830	11176	11343	16975	10836
1831	8556	8281	14827	9257
1832	9837	7216	11959	5909
1833	11197	11040	13953	7160

Chile's principal port of Valparaíso, strategically situated on her long "*runner-bean*" coastline, was the first major port of call for sailing ships rounding Cape Horn. Consequently, it assumed great economic importance in Chile's strategy to re-launch the country as an influential trading nation. The start of this process occurred when Joaquín Prieto became leader of the élite class' Conservative party and overthrew the ruling Liberals following the battle of Lircay in April 1830. One of the affects of this triumph was the political emergence of Diego Portales, a non-élite in the traditional sense, but a successful and highly influential Valparaíso businessman with strong political views. His merchant trading concern had required him to conduct business in Peru to where he headed in 1823. From there, he expounded the view:

"A strong Government [should be] a centralizing [establishment] whose members being true models of virtue and patriotism, should set citizens on the road to order and virtue. When these [citizens] learn to be conscientious, the Government will become completely liberal, free and idealistic, and one in which all citizens will participate".

From 1828 onwards, having purchased a newspaper concern in Valparaíso, Portales was able to circulate his strong political opinions, and soon became a renowned local figure. He was appointed to the Chilean Government as Minister with four portfolios, one of which was responsibility for the War and Navy department. Although instrumental in the presidential success of Prieto and the efficacy of the Conservative Party, he preferred to remain the power behind the throne, exercising control as a virtual dictator. The period between the battle of Lircay and his death were so replete with his policies, that it became defined as the "*Portalian Era*". He had ended the Liberal's exotic and utopian policies, which had caused turmoil throughout Chile. It was he who had insisted that Chileans must subordinate class and individual interests to the nation's urgent need for orderly government.

Portales' bullying of Prieto and the Conservative party did, however, result in the establishment of law and order, a fact which made the implementation and effectiveness of his strict and repressive policies acceptable to the élite ruling class. Opposition within the ruling party was not tolerated, and those members voicing dissent were removed from influential positions and often exiled in the process. Press freedom was withdrawn and political meetings controlled. Although Portales' methods were brutal and dictatorial, they were seen to be effective in reducing corruption, inefficiency and administrative abuse. A new constitution conforming to his ideas was adopted in 1833, giving the President power to act independently of the bi-cameral arrangement of Senate and Chamber of Deputies. An important addition was the Presidential right to assume emergency or extraordinary powers in times of crisis, in order to oppose legitimate dissent without the need for judicial procedure.

To ensure that power remained within the ruling élite class, anyone then wishing to register as a voter, was required to prove ownership of substantial property and demonstrate high literacy qualifications. More stringent requirements were needed for those seeking election to public office. In practice, only about 500 families in Chile could satisfy these qualifying requirements.[33] For more than thirty years, these 500 had been linked by blood, marriage, friendship or financial interest; they supported those of its number whom they had enabled to secure public office; they were also in a position to advise, chastise and censure the latter if their actions were incompatible with the families' overall interests.

Despite the harshness and discrimination shown by the Portales constitution, it did provide Chile with a long period of stability during which trade and the nation prospered. As previously noted, Portales had been both a resident and businessman in the port of Valparaíso and naturally, had been interested in promoting industry, commerce and shipping. Having assumed control of Government policy, Portales set out to make Valparaíso the centre of trade for the entire Pacific coast of South America, applying pressure to bring about improvements, expansion and repair of Valparaíso docks. Warehouses, in which goods in transit could be stored cheaply without incurring duty, were approved by the Chilean legislature at his request.

The Chilean Government confidently believed that the security and tax advantages offered by use of the port's facilities, would make Valparaíso the emporium of the Pacific, attracting European and Asian goods to be exchanged for valuable imports from Mexico and Peru. Valparaíso's stevedores and boatmen, essential to the successful operation of the port, where ships had to anchor in the open bay and be served by lighters, were, by 1837 organized into official "*gremios*" or guilds strictly controlled by the Government. The port was improved, therefore, not only to attract foreign business but also to accommodate a national merchant marine, and an already planned coastal steam navigation system to provide the backbone of her national defence. Preferential tariffs were applied to merchandise conveyed by Chilean registered ships whether Chilean-built or subsequently purchased by Chilean nationals, which in times of crisis could be requisitioned by the Government as military transports or converted to naval warships. An 1834 law allowed Chilean-registered vessels a 10% reduction on imported foreign goods if the subject vessel had been built in a foreign country, but a 20% exemption if the ship had actually been constructed in Chile.

Foreign ship owners, however, were easily able to circumvent these restrictions by arranging for their Chilean resident business associates to register their vessels in the names of their Chilean wives or children, and thus become eligible for reduced Customs duties. A further law in 1837 required that Chilean ships' crews comprise at least one quarter of Chilean nationals up to the end of that year; be composed of one half for the years 1838 and 1839, and three quarters thereafter. Similar legislation in 1836 demanded that captains of Chilean ships be of Chilean nationality and a twelve years period of grace was allowed in which to achieve this. The following tables indicate the extent of the Chilean Merchant marine in 1835[34]:

Captain	No. Vessels	Average	Largest vessel
British	17	133 tons	269 tons
Chilean	8	112	323
Italian	6	155	250

AVERAGE SIZE OF VESSELS BUILT IN:
USA	164.5 tons
Chile	67.8
UK	187.0

The total number of vessels comprising the Chilean merchant fleet amounted to 61, producing a combined tonnage of 7273 and giving an average of 119.23 tons for each ship, substantially smaller than those built in the UK and USA. Those built in Chile were approximately a third of the size of British-built craft. This was the situation of merchant shipping on the West Coast of South America at the beginning of 19th Century, when mostly unforeseen events would have a major impact on its development.

2. Visions of Steamships and Political Conflicts 1824-1839

Restored Liberty ship ss *Jeremiah O'Brien*.
Courtesy National Liberty Ship Memorial. San Francisco

Between September 27, 1941 and September 2, 1945, 2710 emergency Liberty ships, similar to the restored vessel *ss Jeremiah O'Brien*, were built mainly to provide World War 2 North Atlantic relief convoys. They were being completed so quickly at one stage, that their builders ran out of suitable names, obliging the United States Maritime Commission to adopt a policy of calling them after eminent North Americans who had contributed significantly to their country's history or culture.

One such ship was Standard Liberty vessel No. 2464, christened *ss William Wheelwright*. It is debatable whether Wheelwright actually contributed directly to his country's history or culture, although, certainly, he was highly regarded by his compatriots; his impact was felt more in South America, Chile especially, and in the UK, Merseyside in particular. He was, according to his biographer Juan Bautista Albérdi, born in Newburyport, Massachusetts on March 18, 1798, the son of an American captain employed in the West Indian trade, and directly descended from the Reverend John Wheelwright (1592-1679) of Lincolnshire, an English Quaker fleeing religious persecution.

Albérdi described Wheelwright as an impatient and restless student, initially attending a local primary school followed by admission in 1812 to the Phillips Academy Andover, Massachusetts, a highly reputable school of theology. He studied there for two years where, it was said, he was often ridiculed for daydreaming. Among his many and highly imaginative projects was a proposal for a canal across the Isthmus of Panama.

Undoubtedly influenced by his being reared in a family maritime business, it was hardly surprising that Wheelwright chose to pursue a naval career. It is clear from Albérdi's initial description of Wheelwright and his early upbringing, that he was born into a wealthy merchant family; importantly, from Albérdi's perspective, into an élite and privileged class. At age seventeen, he was allowed to experience the far from élite side of the lower ranks, by being assigned as a cabin steward on one of the family vessels. A year later, a merchant ship headed for New Orleans on which he was sailing as an ordinary seaman, ran aground on one of the Caicos (Bahamas Group) islands. Crewmembers saved themselves by quickly converting a large wooden cradle, used for loading and measuring cargo, into a makeshift boat.

Despite this narrow escape, Wheelwright signed Ship's Articles for a voyage to the West Indies, but most of the time was confined to bed with fever. At age nineteen, he was given command of a ship headed for Río de Janeiro, almost dying on the return voyage from injuries sustained from the brutal assault of a mutinous seaman. Aged 23, he eventually captained the *Rising Empire*, owned by William Bartlett, a reputable Newburyport merchant. Unfortunately, on trying to enter the port of Ensenada in the Plate Estuary, 30 miles from Buenos Aires, the vessel founded on the infamous Ortiz Bank. All but one of the crew was saved; survivors rowed for twenty-four hours before gaining the Buenos Aires[35] shore.

Albérdi related that native Indians, in exchange for muskets rescued from his wrecked ship, guided Wheelwright towards Buenos Aires where he arrived "*penniless and on foot*". The *Rising Empire's* owner,[36] he remarked, had not blamed him for her loss and had been more than willing to assign another vessel to his command. In correspondence to his family, sent shortly after his unfortunate experience, Wheelwright wrote:

"After the loss of my ship, I became weary and worn out with misfortune. Distance and active business, I hoped, would in some measure obliterate painful memories."

Clearly, the young North American had other plans; a few months later, he gratefully accepted the offer of a Purser's position on a Valparaíso-bound vessel. Some maritime historians have Wheelwright sailing on this occasion as an "*able seaman*", a "*sailor*" or described him as "*working before the mast*". He signed Ship's Articles, according to Albérdi, as a "*Sobrecargo*", Spanish for "*Purser*"; his responsibilities would have focused more on cargo administration than passenger welfare. The word was mis-translated in later English versions of Wheelwright's biography, which formed the basis for the early chapters of Arthur C.Wardle's "*El Vapor Conquista El Pacífico*" (The Steamship Conquers the Pacific) and subsequent histories of the Pacific Steam Navigation Company.

This might seem to be a trifling criticism over one mistranslated word from Albérdi's work. However, perpetuating the error not only fails to appreciate Wheelwright's background and the élite circles both in which he moved and, in which he was to generate wealth and influence, it also ignores the paradox that has always characterized South America, the wealth and potential richness of the sub-continent as opposed to the then abject poverty of the majority of its indigenous people.

Following the fall of Portugal and Spain to Napoleon, ambitious British entrepreneurs and merchants moved into South America. In 1810, approximately 120 British merchants resided in Buenos Aires, increasing by 1824, to 3000. E.Bradford Burns in his "*Latin America: A Concise Interpretative History*"[37] commented:

"The British sold more to Latin America than anyone else and in some cases almost monopolized the imports into certain countries. British firms handled the lion's share of Latin America's foreign trade and British bottoms carried much of it to distant ports. The English Government maintained men of war in Latin American waters to protect British Commerce to safeguard the rights of Englishmen, and on occasion to transfer specie. London supplied most of the loans and investments to the new nations."

Given South American society's class structure at this time, it would have been highly surprising if Wheelwright, a Captain in his own right, a highly educated man from a wealthy background, who had probably frequented circles of the ruling class and business merchants in Buenos Aires, had taken a position as a deck rating. Had he done so, he would have subjected himself to the most inhospitable and dangerous conditions when rounding Cape Horn. Penniless then he might have been, but he was one of the elite's very own and recognized as such. He would surely have been labelled "*creditworthy*" given his shipping connections in the United States port of Newburyport and the nearby port of Ensenada; the Buenos Aires merchant class would undoubtedly have assisted him.

It was during his stay in Buenos Aires that Wheelwright assimilated the then progressive views of a group of intellectual élites whose objective was to convert Argentina into a great and wealthy power by "*making her a copy of Europe*". [38] Heavily influenced by European enlightenment, even to the extent of wanting to make Buenos Aires the Paris of South America, this group strongly advocated the importation of European culture, from France especially, its new technologies, and the encouragement of immigration from the developed European nations.[39] These views struck a harmonious chord with Wheelwright. His subsequent experiences gained on the trip around Cape Horn to Valparaíso, according to Albérdi, prompted his awareness of the poor trading conditions on the WCSA; there were no proper harbours or support facilities, regarded as essential for stimulating the development of a nation's trading position.

Wheelwright would have also been conscious of the political situation prevailing in South America during the early 19th Century. The non-Portuguese areas of the sub-continent had been largely under the severely restrictive control and deliberately suffocating influences of Spain, fearful of foreign infiltration of her colonies. This had resulted in a cramping of free trade with any nation other than the mother country; immigration had also been banned, along with the employment of foreign labour. The crucial elements needed for progress and economic development of the WCSA were foreign capital and entrepreneurs capable of applying it to European technology-based enterprises already located there, or to be later invited-in.

After the young republics had gained their independence, there was, simply, little in the way of a communications' infrastructure, apart from well-used roads between Lima and Callao, and from Santiago to Valparaíso[40]. Other major routes and bridges were notoriously lacking; the few existing harbours were both inadequate and dangerous. A postal service of sorts had operated, but it was slow, insecure and unreliable. Nevertheless, in 1827, Pedro Allessandri with his sailing ship *Paquete Volador* established "*the first regular passenger service between Callao and Valparaíso*".[41] It is not known how regular was this service, but because it relied on a sailing vessel, it would have been subject to the vagaries of winds impeding the operation.

Wheelwright arrived in Valparaíso in 1824 during the concluding period of Bolivar's revolution. Southern Chile was still controlled by the Spanish Royalist party and the Peruvian port of Callao continued to suffer Spanish occupation, even after Bolívar's success at the battle of Ayacucho. Despite trading links established by the Authorities of the Vice-Royalty of Peru between Callao and Valparaiso, the latter then had little to offer in the way of commerce in comparison with the former port serving the influential Lima business houses. Valparaíso's importance could be measured by the fact that the nearest Customs House was, at that time, located at inland Santiago, ninety miles away over the mountains. Juan Bautista Albérdi wrote:

"The port of Valparaíso [in 1824] was a simple landing place with no more that 15,000 inhabitants. It was far from being the Emporium of the Pacific, as it later was, for the simple reason that [international] maritime trade had not then commenced even in that region.

Ploughing The South Sea

The business houses to which Wheelwright would look for support to fund his steamship line did not yet exist."

Moreover, feelings of insularity had then emerged amongst Chilean élites:

"The run of the mill Chilean aristocrat of that era was untravelled, poorly educated, and completely wrapped-up in the interests of his own limited environment. His isolationism was closely related to Chile's physical isolation, for news from the outside world was hard to come by".[42]

**Valparaíso around 1800. Believed to be an engraving by George Vancouver.
Courtesy: Barry Lawrence Ruderman. Antique Maps La Jolla California**

All the great reforms were then taking place in Gran Colombia whose main port was Guayaquil with a population of 22,000. Wheelwright, consequently, headed northwards to that city, then the principal West Coast location, and a place where business opportunities appeared more encouraging. The Republic of Gran Colombia then comprised the provinces of Venezuela, Ecuador and New Granada, the Isthmus of Panama forming part of the latter. By 1826, Wheelwright had established his own prosperous trading concern, winning wide respect particularly from compatriots in Guayaquil. His reputation contributed to his appointment there as United States' Consul. Most of the new South American Governments had not then been recognized by the older established nations, and the office of Consul in these circumstances, according to Juan Bautista Albérdi, was held in equal esteem to that of an Ambassador. By the mid 1820s, of all the South American countries, Great Britain had only granted official recognition to Gran Colombia, Brazil and the United Provinces of La Plata.

The American Consulate had been the first legation received in Guayaquil and, therefore, took precedence over those of other countries who later established embassies. Because almost all matters referred to Consul Wheelwright dealt with commerce, his official residence during those turbulent times was also the common meeting place for generals and leaders. The many contacts and friends that he made during this period of office were to become useful to him in subsequent commercial ventures.

In 1828, Wheelwright returned to Newburyport to marry Martha Bartlett. Their honeymoon included the essential and notorious mule journey across the Isthmus of Panama. From there, the voyage back to Guayaquil was made by sailing ship. Unfortunately, he was confronted on his return with the news that during his absence, his business had been ruined with accumulated losses of $100,000 (pesos)[43]. This financial disaster appeared to be the direct result of the country's internal political struggles leading to the eventual disintegration of Gran Columbia in 1830, following the resignation of Bolívar as leader shortly before his death, the latter provoking declarations of independence by Venezuela and Ecuador. In 1828, Colombia had been at war with Peru, the former emerging victorious only to find herself in dire financial and political straits. It was this state of affairs that Wheelwright encountered on his return from North America.

Certainly, the shipbuilding port of Guayaquil had declined in influence and commercial activity. As American Consul, Wheelwright would have been in a prime position to have anticipated these political and economic crises and, accordingly, to have taken appropriate avoiding measures before his departure for Newburyport. Perhaps the thought of his intended marriage had blinded him to the true state of affairs and their likely impact on the port. Commensurate with Guayaquil's decline, Valparaíso assumed a more important role as Chile extended her power and influence. The other South American nations, preoccupied with internal social, political problems and boundary disputes with their neighbours, had been too busy to take note. Under Portales' guidance, Chile had taken a more active interest in foreign affairs, especially the promotion of commercial relations with the outside world, and in planning countermeasures to possible threats of interference by other South American nations.

Chile, living up to her national motto, "*By Reason or Force*", had been careful to weave these policies with a fine thread of neutrality, embroidered with declarations of non-intervention in other nation's affairs, but such involvement became unavoidable. France, for example, had actually sought territorial rights in Chile, and Great Britain had refused to recognize her as an independent state; both issues, therefore, impelled Chile to become focused on the executive affairs of those countries that did or could affect her. For example, claims against Chile submitted by resident nationals of those two Great Powers were supported, as a matter of course, by the subject elder States. Accordingly, Chile wisely chose, initially at least, to follow a policy of open accord with these powerful nations, intending to buy sufficient time to achieve her economic and domestic objectives. She had hoped that success in these areas would earn her the respect and recognition of the world's more powerful and influential nations.

Chile continued to adopt a cautious stance in case of military threats from other republics. The three new nations, New Granada, Venezuela and Ecuador, arising from the break-up of Gran Columbia, were perceived by Chile to pose no real danger to her security. Neither was Bolivia seen as a threat; the Atacama Desert was deemed to act as an adequate buffer between the two countries even though the regions' official boundaries had not been settled. Bolivia, in fact, regarded the Atacama as valueless and, in any case, was preoccupied with her own relations with Peru. It was the latter nation, which Chile, in the early 1830s, identified as the greatest potential threat. The citizens of these two republics had developed a deep-seated loathing of each other; conflicts had arisen over a number of issues. Mutual dislike and mistrust had been generated long before their respective independence. Vice-Regal splendour and living standards in Peru, for many years, had sharply contrasted with the simpler way of life in the Captaincy General of Chile when still subservient to that Vice-Royalty.

The Peruvians' higher living standards were bitterly resented by Chileans; anger was fuelled by Peruvian displays of contempt for their simpler and poorer lifestyles. Furthermore, the Chileans' deep frustration and resentment were heightened by past economic discrimination by Spain and the Vice Royalty, a practice that Lima's ruling élites had encouraged for their own benefit for two centuries at Chile's expense. The latter's crowning bitterness, however, derived from the fact that this young nation, having struggled to win her own independence from Spain, had mounted a military campaign at considerable expense and effort to help Peru seize hers.

Having achieved this, disputes arose between the two countries, the most bitter focusing on Peru's non-payment of the Chilean Navy's payroll, as had been promised when Chile agreed to contribute her naval forces to the Peruvian campaign. It is recorded that the word "*ingrate*" was increasingly used in Chilean society to denote a "*Peruvian*".[44] To make matters worse, Liberator San Martín's forced flight from Peru enabled the Spanish to resume attacks to recover their former colony. Chile returned to Peru with troops to again assist her in successfully repulsing them. The two independent republics finally agreed the terms of loan repayments to Chile of one million pesos (approximately £200,000 or $US 360,000) together with Peruvian compensation for the cost of sending Chilean arms, military ships and supplies to deter Spain from retaking Peru.

A long period of political upheaval followed, witnessing rapid turnovers of Peruvian Governments. None of these short-lived administrations ever attempted to honour agreed loan repayments and compensation when Chile was suffering her own severe economic and financial difficulties; continued default by Peru only exacerbated the Chileans' already inflamed and lowly opinion of Peruvians. Chile, nevertheless, stuck doggedly and realistically to diplomatic procedures to recover her debts. Peru was, after all, her largest foreign trading partner; her national treasury and ruling élite were heavily dependent on exports of grain and flour to Lima. These commodities, during the 1820s, represented about 50% of her total exports to Peru.

Chilean diplomatic initiatives, therefore, attempted to regularize trade with her northern neighbour by having her withdraw those high tariffs and duties imposed during the Spanish colonial period against Chilean exports. Because of these punitive and discriminating taxes, the United States was emerging as a competing and cheaper supplier of wheat to Peru. Chile, consequently, launched further diplomatic missions in 1830, in an attempt to rationalize commerce with the latter by securing a Peruvian trade agreement and an accord on the outstanding compensation and loan repayments.

Further conflicts arose between the two nations, and one, which principally focused on the port of Valparaíso. Chile, shortly after gaining independence, had formulated a policy of encouraging trade with the wider world, Europe especially. In pursuit of this ambition, she had declared that she would make Valparaíso the major port on the WCSA. The implication, not lost on Peru, was that it would be at the expense of Callao, her major port. Peru let it be known that she had the ability to seriously affect Chile's proposals by introducing favourable tariffs to persuade ships to make directly for Callao after rounding Cape Horn, bypassing Valparaíso.[45] Chilean diplomatic activity was, therefore, organized to prevent this. Another important issue that Chile had tried to include in her negotiations with Peru was the question of preventing Chilean political exiles, based within the latter's territory, from mounting revolutionary expeditions and crossing back into Chile. The period 1830-1836, being especially difficult to launch these diplomatic offensives, did not prevent Chile from concluding a Trade and Friendship treaty with the United States in 1834, which contained reciprocal measures for exempting each nation's ships from taxes, duties and port dues. Its importance and impact on the development of West Coast merchant shipping would not be fully appreciated until its agreed expiration in 1854.

Due to the considerable turnover of Peru's Governments and her fragile and complicated confederated relationship with Bolivia, the Peruvian Administration was left in turmoil, making it almost impossible for Chilean diplomats and other appointed representatives to identify and establish contact with their proper Peruvian counterparts. This then, was the state of political affairs in Chile greeting

Wheelwright when he decided that a complete relocation from Guayaquil to the beautiful port of Valparaíso would provide him with better trading prospects. Shortly after his arrival, he established a sailing packet line operating a service between Valparaíso and Cobija, then the principal port of Bolivia. He launched this operation with a 60 tons schooner called the *Fourth of July*. This one ship enterprise quickly blossomed into a line of vessels. Wheelwright taking command of an American built schooner, *La Veloz Manuela*, soon earned his company an excellent reputation for punctuality, speed, and treatment of passengers.

This renown was achieved despite contemporary views that sailing ship voyages, although the essential means of transport along the West Coast at that time, had long been considered tiresome and uncomfortable. Indeed, as in the Spanish colonial period, it was still considered too risky to travel along the coast by sailing ship in winter. Although favourable winds and currents tended to assist voyages northwards along the WCSA, sailing southwards presented vastly different problems. Sailing ships steering towards the equator, with their destination lying to leeward, were often taken beyond their intended port and had to double back southwards to try to reach it. Sailing ships were still experiencing these problems in the early 20th Century. Basil Lubbock in his "*Nitrate Clippers*" described how, in 1903, the *Lindisfarne*, bound for Antofagasta from Australia, was taken past her destination by the current and was compelled to sail south-west for 1300 miles passing south of Antofagasta and then coming-about to sail up the coast again to reach her intended destination. The time that had elapsed from the moment she was carried beyond the latter port to the date she gained it on her second attempt was exactly one month.[46]

Further examples highlight the difficulties for sailing ships on the West Coast. In 1908, the *Hougomont* left Coquimbo for Tocopilla. She also failed to make the anchorage and drifted past it; she continued northwards by 400 miles, whereupon her captain abandoned his contracted call, sailing off in disgust for Australia. The following year the *Buteshire* left Panama for Caleta Coloso, and after 80 days, struggling to make progress to the South, was obliged to return to Panama arriving after a fruitless passage of 91 days.[47]

These difficulties were common on the WCSA and Wheelwright's professional drive and foresight would, therefore, have attracted the Chilean business community's attention including, most notably, the powerful and influential Minister of War and Navy Departments, Diego Portales, who, as an importer of Peruvian tobacco, would probably have used Wheelwright's reputable shipping line. Certainly, the latter's ideas for regular and shorter voyages using steamships would have especially appealed to the politically powerful Portales. Indeed, Wheelwright's proposals for improving trade had stimulated such thinking in many other influential businessmen in both England and South America, although evidence exists of similar proposals having being aired elsewhere in the American sub-continent.

Albérdi reported that Wheelwright, during his stay in Valparaíso, had already launched major public and private initiatives there, and supervised their construction through to completion. Such works, he added, encouraged by the Chilean Government's modernization policy, included the erection of a badly-needed lighthouse, the installation of water distillation and gas distribution networks, and the completion of a brick-making factory. Wheelwright was also said to have become involved in a number of other improvements of Valparaíso streets, then badly paved, unclean and unhealthy.

Albérdi claimed that it was through Wheelwright's suggestion and personal initiative that these conditions were changed and soon copied in other cities throughout Chile.[48] Wheelwright was also reported as having successfully undertaken land surveys leading to the discovery and production of coal, borax, and saltpetre, otherwise know as sodium nitrate. His engineering and commercial activities were promoted as exemplifying the very entrepreneurial attitude, which the new Latin American nations, Chile especially, had been trying to encourage.

As advised in the introduction to this study, care must be taken with the accuracy of data provided by 19th Century South American historians who eulogized their subjects, as was the fashion, for their contributions to society and the nation. Albérdi, in having to surmount this requirement to record national heroes rather than foreign élites, would quite possibly have exaggerated Wheelwright's accomplishments in order to demonstrate that, although officially a US citizen, he was spiritually, if not to all other intents and purposes, a South American, worthy of a biography.

A clear example of this type of historical exaggeration has been uncovered in Dr.Samuel J. Martland's thesis *"Southern Progress: Constructing Urban Improvement in Valparaíso, 1840-1918"*[49], detailing events leading to the introduction of gas lighting and supply in Valparaíso between 1843 and 1863. It quite clearly demonstrates that Wheelwright's scheme, considered more favourable than others submitted to the port's Municipality, was never actually approved. Although some work did start, land required for the gas works' installation was never handed-over by the Local Authority; the latter abandoned the project in 1852, having failed to agree a basis with Wheelwright for calculating the price of supplying gas based on the market price for coal.[50]

According to that part of Maitland's thesis sub-titled *"Cuando el gas pasó de moda: la élite de Valparaíso y la tecnología Urbana,* (When gas went out of fashion; Valparaíso's élite and urban technology) *1843-1863"* the first recorded promoter of a gas utility was Joseph Waddington, an acquaintance of Wheelwright. In 1844, the latter had recommended that a gas works in the port would send a clear political signal of the type of progress to which the nation aspired. He was

Ploughing The South Sea

subsequently approached by certain Councillors asking him to obtain information from their London counterparts where an extensive scheme had long functioned successfully. It was not until 1848, that French Engineer Alejo Cornou submitted the first concrete proposals for a Valparaíso project. A contract was approved in November 1848, but never ratified and the proposal withered. Not until 1850 did Wheelwright submit his own proposals for generating and distributing coal gas. Despite not being the pioneer of this gas project, and not the first to propose the introduction of steam merchant shipping on WCSA, Albérdi attributed Wheelwright with pioneer status on both accounts.

Albérdi claimed that observations and experiences drawn from Wheelwright's many voyages along the West Coast, and his strong links with interested Chilean ministers such as Portales, had led him to conclude that there was a huge demand for a more rapid means of transport on both land and sea. It was generally acknowledged that the calm waters and very gentle southerly winds in the Pacific central coastal regions were not generally suitable for sailing ships; voyages by such vessels were mainly long and unreliable, not the best recipe for promoting trade and travel. Moreover, sailing ships were prone to remaining in port for days awaiting favourable winds, and passengers with reservations would have had to fund additional expenses for food and accommodation while awaiting the departure of their ship.

Furthermore, suitable overland transport and communications, extending for thousands of miles, were almost impossible to undertake due to the difficulties presented by the West Coast terrain. Based on his experiences of port requirements and navigation, Wheelwright compiled a realistic and feasible plan for improving maritime transportation. He had recounted to Albérdi his boyhood memories of Robert Fulton's first steamboat trials on the River Hudson, and his own subsequent research into this remarkable development in European and North American waters. One or two experiments with steamships had already taken place along the Chilean coast, and although not completely successful, had been sufficient to fire Wheelwright and others with enthusiasm for this mode of transport.

In December 1818, the paddle steamer *Rotherhyde*, her engines having been removed, had been laid-up at Deptford, London. Lord Cochrane and his brother commissioned her builders, Brent & Co., to completely refit her as a warship for the former's intended campaign to liberate Chile. Renamed *Rising Star*, the vessel had been constructed specifically for Arctic exploration, with the former name of *North Pole*. Little else is known of this ship, but she was thought to have been fitted with two 35-horsepower engines and two funnels positioned forward of amidships. Having crossed the Southern Atlantic, arriving at Valparaíso in April 1822, this vessel was described in the local press as being a fully fitted [sailing] ship with auxiliary [steam] engines.

The *Rising Star*.
From an engraving in the National Library, Santiago. Chile.

Lord Cochrane, and others, had let it be understood that she was the first steamship to have actually crossed the Atlantic entirely under steam to reach the Pacific. Maritime historians have subsequently confirmed that her crossing had taken as long as any other contemporary sailing ship, her engines having only been operational for a total of nineteen hours during the entire outward voyage. Moreover, this steamship, aiming to rely exclusively on steam power, suffered an ignominious breakdown on the voyage from Valparaiso to Quintero.

Lord Cochrane (1775-1860), otherwise 10th Earl of Dundonald, had been a British Naval Commander serving in the Napoleonic Wars. The British Admiralty had regarded him as a troublemaker and too radical in his behaviour. Discredited after being court-martialled for overtly criticizing his commander-in-chief, he was in 1814, also widely, but falsely, accused of implication in a stock market fraud. Dismissed from the Royal Navy, he was enticed in 1818 to Chile and appointed by the latter's first President, Bernardo O'Higgins, as Vice-Admiral of Chile and Commander-in-Chief of of the Republic's Naval Forces. Prominent in the liberation of Peru and Chile, he became a national hero. Returning to the UK in 1832, he was pardoned, rejoined the Royal Navy, eventually becoming an Admiral

Another unsuccessful steamship appeared in 1821; a small sailing barque, the *Telica*, owned and captained by one Mr. Mitrovich, had crossed the Atlantic from Europe under canvas, and after rounding Cape Horn, arrived at Guayaquil where she was fitted with steam engines. His objective appeared to be similar to Wheelwright's later proposals. Having loaded cargo and embarked passengers, she had sailed for Callao under the flag of Colombia. The *Telica*, struggling through heavy mist, was forced to reduce speed, causing her not only to fall behind schedule, but to also exhaust all her fuel in the process. Her passengers, angry at the unexpected delays, repeatedly subjected her captain to considerable threats and demands.

According to Wardle,[51] he became so unstable and unsettled at the passengers' provocative attitude, that whilst anchored in the Peruvian port of Huarmey, he is alleged to have deliberately fired his pistol into a barrel of gunpowder, the resulting explosion blowing up most of the ship. Mitrovich, his passengers, and crew all perished except for one sailor, appropriately named Thomas Jump, apparently responsible for providing this version of events. For many years after this incident, the wrecked hull of the steamship was seen beached on the coast just outside Huarmey. In his "*History of Steam Navigation*", US Rear-Admiral Preble advanced a more plausible explanation for the actions of the *Telica's* captain, submitting that the vessel was blown-up because she was either losing her owner/captain money or citing the possibility that a boiler explosion had been the cause of the accident.

In 1823, Simón Bolívar had authorized the granting of a twenty years' exclusive privilege to Juan Bernardo Elbers to provide a fleet of steam riverboats on the Colombian River Magadalena network. The latter flowed towards the port of Barranquilla and out into the Caribbean. Although these steamboats were never intended for the open sea, they confirm that steam navigation was already operating well before Wheelwright's scheme had materialized.

Jiménez de Quesada.
**Typical of early steamboats on the River Magdalena.
Reproduced from Antonio Montaña's. "A Todo Vapor".**

Steamships had already appeared in Brazilian waters in 1819 and by 1839, a steamship line connected Rio de Janeiro with the northern provinces of the then Brazilian Empire. By 1843, the steamship *Guapiassú* travelled the 900 miles from Belém to Manaus in nine days, but undertook the return trip in four and a half days. Prior to this event, sailing ships had normally taken two or three months to complete this same voyage. Wheelwright, as US Consul in Guayaquil, must not only have been aware of the steamships' progress in Brazil and developments on the Colombian River Magdalena, but also of the *Telica* tragedy; certainly he would have been acquainted with the *Rising Star's* history. These events, rather than causing him to lose interest in steamships, only appeared to have strengthened his belief in them.

Convinced of the wealth of natural resources to be found on the Pacific coast, Wheelwright strenuously strove to enthuse Valparaíso merchants with the feasibility of his pioneering project for operating regular passenger and cargo steamship services along the WCSA. Initial local support for this scheme not being forthcoming, he decided to strike out on his own. In the early 1830s, he was still planning, searching for coal resources and seeking financial capital for his proposed operation. Many financiers had already distanced themselves from him; others considered his proposals utter madness. It was extremely difficult for a foreigner to try to convince South American élites that had still not discarded the Old Spanish colonial outlook. His proposals were not then seen as visionary; even the President of Peru had believed that Wheelwright had taken leave of his senses, and it was, therefore, unsurprising that people should turn their backs on him.[52] Albérdi reported that youth on the streets of the Peruvian capital Lima had hooted at him derisively, ridiculing him for his wild ideas. One English diplomat had even ordered his servants not to allow "*that insane Wheelwright*" to enter his quarters.

One of the main criticisms directed against his proposals derived from a general and deep conviction that there was a complete lack of local coal resources on the WCSA for steamships. This belief held fast despite Wheelwright's claims to the contrary, and the fact that His British Majesty's Navy had previously used coal from Concepción in Chile. Indeed, Wheelwright had already demonstrated to various Chilean statesmen how their locally produced coal could be converted into coke. Moreover, Chilean national hero Lord Cochrane had already testified to the existence of plentiful coal deposits in Talcahuano, more than adequate to continually fuel a line of steamships. Cochrane himself had already made use of this resource during his period of command of the Chilean Pacific squadron. His confirmation of its use was supported by the eventual success of the steamship *Rising Star*, she had used local coal supplies following her arrival at Valparaiso in 1822.

Apart from a generally perceived lack of coal resources, Wheelwright's failure to generate sufficient interest in his steamship proposals was probably more attributable to the political situation in the period 1830 to 1836, and the uncertainty it created. This had arisen from Chile's relations with her northern neighbours Peru and Bolivia. The latter nation, known as Alto Peru throughout the Spanish colonial period, had been part of the Vice-Royalty of Peru until 1776 before being integrated into the newly created Vice-Royalty of La Plata. In 1810, Alto Peru reverted to the control of Lima until liberated by Bolívar's military forces. She had then rejected advances from the Governments of both Lima and Buenos Aires to merge with those nations, choosing independence instead and adopting the name of Bolivia.

This nation was weak and disadvantaged from the moment of her creation. Cobija, her main seaport, was too distant from her own population centres, and her traditional commercial routes to the outside world had to cross Peru's territory to access the latter's important port of Arica. To survive and develop, Bolivia needed alternative and more suitable maritime outlets; many Bolivians had even proposed the forceful annexation of Arica or political integration with Peru. Peruvian leaders wishing to thwart Bolivian independence, of course, favoured the latter option.

By 1830, the first year of Chile's new Conservative Government, both the Bolivian and Peruvian Presidents, although sworn enemies, were in favour of confederation. General Gamarra of Peru and General Santa Cruz of Bolivia had each wanted to remove the other from power to become sole ruler of a confederated state of Bolivia with Peru. Both had together successfully overthrown Bolívar's successor in the latter country, but Gamarra had then expelled Santa Cruz from Peru who, having successfully gained the Presidency of Bolivia, went on to render skilful and valuable service to that nation. Both presidents continued to scheme and plot against each other but there were, at that time, several other groups in Peru which, for their own individual reasons, planned to wrest control from Gamarra. Accordingly, a situation of constant turmoil and upheaval prevailed in Lima, further fuelled by looming threats of war with Bolivia.

One would have thought that a Bolivia-Peru confrontation would have appealed to Chile, given that the preoccupations of her divided northern neighbours would have reduced the risk of military threats to her from either. Unfortunately for Chile, this situation actually hampered diplomatic progress and severely hindered trade development. Factions within Bolivia and Peru contrived to manipulate the Chilean Government into supporting their respective causes, a scenario that it was determined to avoid at all costs. Chile, still clinging to the diplomatic path towards trade agreements, instructed her representative to seek a commercial pact with Peru to allow the import of each country's agricultural and manufactured goods and exempt them from all duty. There was a strong logic to this proposal since both countries would benefit; Chile would have gained a favoured position for her wheat and flour within her largest export market, while Peru would have been guaranteed a privileged position for the export of her tropical produce, sugar especially, of which Chile was the largest importer. Chile argued that other trade aspects would evolve from this treaty to mutually benefit the two nations.

To complicate matters, the Peruvian Government was aware of its own heavy reliance on revenue generated from customs duties on imported Chilean goods. Sections of the Chilean Government had expressed concern that if Chile was granted the monopoly for exporting grain and flour to Peru, the United States, being more competitive in supplying these commodities, might oppose the arrangement, prompting the Peruvians to blame Chile for any conflict with Washington, and also for any high rise in Peruvian bread prices. Chile, therefore, felt obliged to submit alternative proposals, even including one that would have substantially reduced the amount of the still outstanding Peruvian debt. Ultimately, the Peruvian Government insisted that any trade agreement be supported by a commitment that, if the territory of either country was ever invaded, the other would come to her aid.

It was then clear to Chile that war between Peru and Bolivia was inevitable. The Chilean Government, not wishing to be drawn into conflict between these two countries, refused to sanction the trade treaty. Matters were further complicated when Bolivia sought to drag Chile into her own dispute with Peru. Chile, therefore, decided that the only solution was to act as mediator between the two warring republics. In 1831, she managed to force the early signing of a treaty whereby Peru and Bolivia agreed to maintain their forces at purely defensive levels, *"to remain eternally at peace"* and never to intervene in each other's internal affairs. Both nations then asked Chile to guarantee the terms of the treaty but her conservative Government, having become even more committed to a policy of strict neutrality and non-intervention, tried to extricate the country from further involvement to concentrate on improving her own national development and economy. Thereafter, Chile announced her willingness to co-operate with any Spanish American countries to secure mutually advantageous commercial accords.

By 1832, Chile's diplomatic offensives for a Peruvian trade pact had stalled. The situation further deteriorated when the Peruvian Government declared Callao a *"port of deposit"*. This action, designed to provide that port with financial advantages over Valparaíso, adversely affected Chilean exports of flour and wheat. These commodities, on reaching Peru before their intended sale there, would usually have been stored at the unloading port, mostly Callao. In February 1832, the Peruvian authorities instructed that all such imports so discharged had to be weighed and removed from storage whether sold or not; failure to do so incurred penalties. The Chilean Government countered this strategy by demanding that Peru immediately repay her outstanding loan and by promptly imposing prohibitive rates of duty on imports of Peruvian sugar.

Diego Portales considered that such actions would inevitably lead to war and advised his Government to prepare for a military struggle. The Peruvian Government responded to Chile's counteractions by not only doubling duty on Chilean produce, but by also seeking to entice trade away from Valparaíso by imposing additional duties on goods not shipped directly to Callao as first port of call on the Pacific coast. Relations between the two countries, thereafter, deteriorated to the point where Chile decided to seek a loan from Bolivia to purchase a frigate for her national navy. Her approach was rebuffed because by granting it, Bolivia claimed she would be compromised in the Peruvian-Chilean conflict.

Chilean fears were partly dispelled when Peruvian President Gamarra was forcibly removed from the Presidential palace after refusing to quit on the expiry of his legal term; his counter-revolt was ineffective. Strong protests, meanwhile, from Peruvian enterprises hard hit by the imposition of the Chilean Government's high taxes on imported Peruvian sugar, obliged their Government to sign a commercial treaty in January 1835. This accord fulfilled many of Chile's objectives. It reduced, for example, the duty to one half of the former import taxes, provided the subject goods were conveyed only in either Chilean or Peruvian ships. The agreement helped to consolidate the trade in sugar and wheat which, enjoying legal protection, nurtured the growth and prosperity of the contemporary Chilean merchant marine. Furthermore, Valparaíso succeeded in fulfilling Governmental ambitions to ensure its role as the supreme port on the West Coast of South America.

A further short period of revolution followed in Peru, during which ratification of the treaty was placed in doubt. By July 1835, General Salaverry appeared to have taken control of most of that country and finally sanctioned the agreement, causing national rejoicing throughout Chile. The Chilean Congress was confirmed in its belief that stable and orderly government was the only foundation for national progress and economic development. Valparaíso continued to expand and prosper, managing between 1831 and 1835 to triple its customs' revenue and by the end of the latter period, the Chilean Government had managed to overcome internal debt problems.

Towards the end of 1835, Wheelwright realized that the health of his wife had deteriorated to such an extent due to the local climate, that she was obliged to return immediately to the United States. She and her two young daughters boarded a sailing ship that was to take them 65 days to travel via Cape Horn back to Newburyport in Massachusetts. After his family's departure, Wheelwright resumed his campaign in Valparaíso to introduce merchant steamship navigation on the West Coast. Earlier in June 1835, a meeting was convened at the Valparaíso residence of Joshua Waddington, an influential English businessman, to discuss Wheelwright's grand scheme. Among those present were Chilean Minister of the Interior, Diego Portales, and Captain Robert Fitzroy, Commander of *HMS Beagle*, (the ship in which Charles Darwin undertook his voyage around the world). It is

Visions of Steamships and Political Conflicts 1824-1839

obvious from contact with the politically powerful figure of Portales that Wheelwright moved in very élitist and influential circles.

Given Portales' experiences as a Valparaíso entrepreneur with his own set ideas on promoting strong international shipping connections for Chile, it is hardly surprising that he would lend him his support. It was probably due to his urging that Wheelwright petitioned for the appropriate licence to operate his steamship enterprise along Chile's coastline, safe in the knowledge that it would be granted without question. Having assured Portales that his own United States Government would support the project, Wheelwright lost little time in petitioning the Chilean Authorities for these exclusive rights. There is no basis to establish that the United States had actually been willing to participate in Wheelwright's scheme, and later events were to disprove his assertions. Nevertheless, it would certainly have been an assurance that Chile would have wanted to hear; links with that country were important to her Government's thinking. A permit to implement Wheelwright's proposals was essential at that time because regulations, inherited from previous Spanish administrations, required that all WCSA coastal trade be restricted to national vessels. This policy, known as "*cabotage*", was already widely practised by the United States, European nations and Britain especially, who had extended it to her colonies by promulgation of 17th Century Navigation Acts. Chile had thus continued with that practice during her "*Europeanization period*".

The attendance of Captain Fitzroy at the meeting at Waddington's residence was highly significant. At the end of the Napoleonic Wars, Great Britain was the only nation capable of policing the high seas to ensure safe trade for her own rapidly growing empire. South America was one of the regions in which Great Britain encouraged trade, so eager was she to secure new resources to feed the demands of her growing Industrial Revolution. At the beginning of the 19th century, much of the South American coastline had remained uncharted, and as trade relations with the new republics evolved, the task of compiling charts and coastal maps assumed real urgency.

The evident need for reliable navigational charts in 1795, led to the establishment of the British Admiralty's Hydrographic Office. Before its creation, owners and captains of British ships had been obliged to purchase the subject charts from specialist outlets in central London. Their quality and accuracy were often imperfect, but even Hydrographic Office productions, although much improved, still contained errors. A corps of Surveyors was eventually created to train naval personnel for this specialist work. Provided with six survey vessels, one of which was *HMS Beagle*, on which Robert Fitzroy sailed as a Lieutenant, its first mission in 1826 focused mainly on the east coast of South America, the Falkland Islands, the Strait of Magellan, Tierra Del Fuego and the southern coastline of Chile up to the Chiloé Islands.

Ploughing The South Sea

In 1831, Fitzroy was appointed commander of *HMS Beagle* to undertake the second expedition to map the remainder of the WCSA and, on this occasion, was accompanied by Charles Darwin. The information gleaned from Fitzroy's surveys, particularly those relating to the Strait of Magellan, were essential to Wheelwright's planning for the maiden voyages of the *Peru* and *Chile*. Fitzroy's discoveries would also have been of political and strategic importance to the Chilean Government prior to its occupation of the Strait.

Wheelwright clearly recognized at the onset, that there would be many setbacks to overcome if his proposed steamship operation along the extensive WCSA was ever to prove successful. Subsequent political events posed never-ending obstacles, but being a skilled diplomat and able negotiator; he most probably would have used the deep-seated enmity between Chile and the Confederation of Peru-Bolivia to advantage. The difficulties he faced must have been enormous, and similar to those experienced by Chilean representatives when trying to identify the incumbent Peruvian administrators or officials with whom to hold discussions.

The following descriptions of the long and convoluted political and military events are necessarily included to allow an appreciation of the difficulties not only facing Wheelwright and other commercial concerns, but also the Chilean Government. The 1835 Trade Treaty with Peru did not survive more than 18 months, and a situation developed inexorably drawing Chile into war. General Santa Cruz, as President of Bolivia, had been convinced of the need to establish a free trade policy to encourage and favour direct merchant shipping between the Confederation's ports and Europe. Accordingly, he declared that Arica, Cobija, Callao and Paita would be registered as "*Bond*" ports or ports of deposit; he improved the administration of the nation's Aduana (Customs) and introduced a fixed rate system of taxes on goods transported by ships visiting other West Coast ports before arriving in Peru.[53] Santa Cruz having rapidly and extensively improved her economy, brought an improved level of law and order to the country.

By 1836, the estimated value of total trade on the WCSA had risen to 12 million pesos (approximately £2,400,000 or US 4,320,000 dollars), of which 7 million pesos (£1,400,000 or US 2,520,000 dollars approximately) were generated by Peru.[54] Santa Cruz had, importantly, assembled a well-trained and disciplined army, and was thus prepared and determined to go into battle for the leadership of a Peruvian-Bolivian Confederation by removing General Salaverry, his opposite number in Peru. Although Salaverry did not then completely control all of Peru, Santa Cruz was concerned that when faced with an attack, his opponent would unite the entire nation against Bolivia. He, therefore, felt it prudent to ally himself with his old enemy, ex-Peruvian President Gamarra. They jointly seized power and created separate northern and southern Peruvian states, later to be united in a tripartite Peru-Bolivia Confederation, but only after Gamarra had defected from Santa Cruz forces to join with Salaverry.

Luís Orbegoso, at this time based in Arequipa in southern Peru, regarded himself as that country's true President, and sought Santa Cruz's assistance in overthrowing Salaverry. Santa Cruz, taking advantage of Orbegoso's invitation to enter Peru, then passed himself off as the country's saviour, contriving to manufacture excuses and situations to warrant his *"invited"* entry into Peru. He described the objective of his visit as a mission to *"rescue"* that nation and her neighbours *"from the monstrous disorders and cruelties perpetrated by General Salaverry"*. In defeating the latter, Santa Cruz's forces paved the way for Orbegoso to assume the position of *"Supreme Chief of Peru"*.

Having taken control of the Peruvian Executive, Orbegoso proceeded to renounce those approvals and agreements contracted by Salaverry, amongst them the accord ratifying the trade pact with Chile. This prompted the Chilean Administration to impose additional import duties on Peruvian goods, but with the proviso that the taxes be removed if Orbegoso confirmed and adhered to the previous trade accord. Orbegoso, however, in January 1836, had already pre-empted Chilean action by announcing that the subject treaty would expire at the end of four months *"to allow for the adjustment of Peruvian commercial interests"*.[55]

In February 1836, Santa Cruz having overrun Salaverry's army, had him executed. Having thus eliminated all Peruvian opposition, he then started to promote his long cherished dream of a Confederation of Bolivia with Peru. After arranging for Orbegoso to appoint him as Leader of the separate and independent state of South Peru, Santa Cruz confirmed Orbegoso as *"Supreme Leader"* of the similarly independent state of North Peru; the latter was, unsurprisingly, agreeable to Santa Cruz's proposals for confederation. The Chilean Government, perceiving that Bolivia and Peru were set for union under Santa Cruz's leadership, deliberately leaked details of its proposals for significantly expanding Chile's Navy. To this end, it approached some of the nation's wealthy citizens, inviting them to make secret loans to the State to enable the purchase of a number of warships. Although the Chilean Government's journal, El Araucano, emphasized that these proposals had no connection whatsoever with the Peruvian dispute, they did, as the Chileans had intended, cause considerable consternation in the Peruvian capital.

Chile proceeded to strengthen her military forces as Santa Cruz loyalists, having gradually gained control of the Orbegoso Government, appointed Juan Garcia Río, one of their own, as Finance Minister. He was specifically asked to review the ill-fated trade agreement with Chile. Having declared that its implementation would severely affect Peru's trade status in the Pacific, he advised the treaty's abrogation, reasoning that more advantageous and direct trade with Europe and the United States should be encouraged. Chile's annoyance at Peru's treaty renunciation turned to deep concern when Peru leased two naval ships to a group of Chilean exiles under the leadership of former President Freire, who

Ploughing The South Sea

had been actively plotting to overthrow the Chilean Government. Peru did not attempt to stop the vessels leaving Callao as they headed-out with a well-armed expeditionary force towards their revolutionary objective, the Chilean island of Chiloé. On July 28, 1836, the Chilean Government declared a state of martial law.

Fortunately for the Chileans, the crew of Freire's flagship, the *Monteagudo*, mutinied and sailed into Valparaíso Bay to hand-over the ship, together with valuable documentary evidence, to the Chilean Authorities. Incorporating the *Monteagudo* into her navy allowed Chile to re-deploy other vessels. In August, the Chilean sailing ship *Aquiles* was ordered to Callao to attack the Peruvian fleet as a reprisal for sanctioning the Freire expedition. She anchored in Callao Bay on August 21 and on that night, 80 men in five rowing boats entered the port. This assault force boarded all the Confederation's vessels so quietly and easily, that it was not until the following morning that the Peruvians realized the *Aquiles* had departed along with the three captured warships, seriously weakening her navy. This stealth action so enraged Santa Cruz that he imprisoned the Chilean Chargé d'Affaires, albeit for a few minutes only. Nevertheless, this was a considerable diplomatic insult threatening imminent war.

Great Britain tried to broker a peace agreement, but it was signed by Santa Cruz only. She, together with the United States, France and Germany had backed Santa Cruz's liberal policies, which once consolidated, would have allowed them access to a Peruvian market that would continue to be the most important on the WCSA, from the point of view of directness and competitive pricing. British support over the next few years was, at times, on the verge of being converted into direct intervention, but the Confederation's heavy defeat in 1839 precluded this.[56] Santa Cruz needed a state of peace to allow the establishment of his Peru-Bolivia Confederation. It was for this reason that Chile refused to sanction the brokered British accord, her prime objective being to stop the Peru-Bolivia union. Portales likened this to a campaign to achieve "*Chile's second Independence*", and on September 10, 1836, warned former naval hero Manuel Blanco Encalada, that he would have to lead a mission to secure it. Chilean President Prieto, on the other hand, still true to his belief in the diplomatic process, informed Santa Cruz that a Chilean negotiator, armed with full powers, would be dispatched to Lima. .

The Chilean Congress, however, had also authorized a declaration of war if its envoy did not receive reparations commensurate with the "*injuries*" inflicted on Chile during her campaign to assist Peru in her struggle for independence. The appointed representative, Mariano Egaña, was dispatched to Lima armed with the power to declare war if the following five demands were not met:

(i) That satisfaction be obtained for the jailing of the Chargé d'Affaires;
(ii) That Peru acknowledge her independence debt to Chile;

(iii) That a limit be imposed on Peru's Navy;
(iv) That all Chilean nationals in Peru be exempted from the obligation to make loans to Peru and from conscription into the Peruvian Army;
(v) That a reciprocal trade agreement be concluded with Chile and the independence of Bolivia be recognized.

The latter point was the most important Chilean objective. Chile informed Santa Cruz that she did not care whether he ruled Peru or Bolivia, as long as the two nations remained separate sovereign states.

Engaña reached Callao on October 30 1836, having travelled on one of five warships in convoy. The latter were refused entry pending the granting of Chilean guarantees about their intentions. Four of the Chilean warships then broke-away from the convoy, and headed for the port of Guayaquil to prevent the departure of three Peruvian vessels believed to be waiting there. Egaña, failing to secure the afore-mentioned demands from Santa Cruz, declared war on November 11, 1836. The main reason for Chile's war declaration did not arise in the stipulations attached to the negotiations. It originated out of fear of a Confederation of Bolivia and Peru; such an integration of these two republics would have led to a combined military and economic strength more powerful than her own, thus threatening the balance of power and hence her own security.

Probably the demands submitted by Egaña and the fears of military instability in the region were complementary, but commercial considerations did seem to have been at the forefront of Chile's initial concerns, while the question of her own defence was used to justify the war. It was an argument widely broadcast by Santa Cruz subsequent to the Chilean Congress' rejection of his peace initiative, and used to bolster his strategy of ordering representatives to Santiago to try to keep the Peru-Bolivia Confederation from being dragged into war. Chile rejected all of Santa Cruz's offers and, inevitably, discussions came to nothing. On December 24, 1836, the Chilean Congress confirmed Engaña's declaration of hostilities.

Chile, at this stage, was well aware of Argentina's concern at the Peru - Bolivia Confederation. Juan Manuel Rosas, had in 1834, assumed the powers of a dictator but was involved in bitter struggles with the Unitarios, opposed to his ambitions for Argentinean Federalism. The defeated Unitarios, expelled from their country, had been allowed by Santa Cruz to seek refuge in Bolivia where their active plotting to overthrow Rosas was deliberately ignored. Relations between Argentina and Bolivia, accordingly, became increasingly hostile. Rosas, mindful of the way in which Santa Cruz had successfully "*rescued*" Peru from the "*atrocities*" of Salaverry, feared that Santa Cruz would use the same ploy by supporting the exiled Unitarios in their seizure of part of Argentinean territory to merge it with Bolivia.

In February 1837, discussions between Chile and Argentina were launched to consider the prospects of an alliance for waging war on Santa Cruz. Chile found two issues unacceptable. Firstly, Argentina insisted that as part of the post war agreement, the Peruvian province of Tarija, which Argentina claimed as part of her State of Salta, be returned to her, and secondly, the Bolivian army be downsized. Chile refused to agree both these demands, emphasizing that she did not possess sufficient information about the province of Tarija to allow her to form a proper judgment. Tarija had been transferred by Spain in February 1807, from the archbishopric of Charcas to the then newly created bishopric of Salta, but it was uncertain whether this was done for spiritual or administrative purposes. At that time, the region of Atacama was part of the Intendency of Salta. In the face of disputes from the latter's Governor, Atacama and Tarija both elected to become part of Bolivia under her law of 1826.[57]

Chile's main objective in a post war period was to ensure that an un-Confederated Bolivia be sufficiently strong on her own account to resist military-backed overtures from Peru. To insist that Bolivia weaken her army would, in her view, defeat this strategy. Rosas, on the other hand, his country riven by internal feuding, saw war as the only realistic means of countering Bolivian threats and enforcing demands for the "*return*" of Tarija, an action that would successfully unite his deeply divided nation. On May 19, 1837, Rosas, without waiting for Chile, declared war on Santa Cruz accusing the latter, inter alia, of interfering in Argentinean affairs.

Chile, meanwhile, continued to prepare for war. Her navy had been equipped to engage hostile forces and ferry troops to Peru. Soldiers were conscripted, suitably armed and trained for battle. Unknown to her at the time, anti-Government elements, having already infiltrated the army whipping-up demands for isolationism and peaceful co-existence with Peru, caused a series of revolts within army barracks. Attributed to Santa Cruz and his agents, these seriously delayed the military expedition. Having applied harsh measures to eradicate any dissent or disloyalty, the Government, in June 1837, readied the task force to set out for Peru. War and Navy Minster Portales was to have accompanied the expedition, but a revolt by the Chilean Maipo Regiment resulted in his arrest while inspecting its troops. The uprising was successfully put down, but in the turmoil, a junior officer ordered the shooting of Portales. Chileans, stunned by the murder of its real leader, widely believed that Santa Cruz had planned the assassination. Indeed, many shared his view that Chile would not recover from the loss of Portales for a very long time, and would quickly sue for peace. The opposite occurred; Portales' legacy of leadership and strong government caused the country to fully support the Chilean Executive.

On September 15, 1837, a Chilean military expedition of "*Restoration*" led by Admiral Blanco Encalada, and comprising 3000 men and 400 Peruvian exiled volunteers, left Valparaíso under instructions "*to negotiate an honourable peace once victory had been declared*". Chile's required settlement terms were: satisfaction for Santa Cruz's imprisonment of Chile's Chargé d'Affaires, independence for Bolivia, and settlement of Peru's debt to Chile, a limitation of the size of Peruvian navy, and the production of a trade treaty granting Chile most favoured nation status. Encalada was also empowered to seek the removal of Santa Cruz from the Bolivian Presidency.

The Chilean offence force landed in Southern Peru without difficulty, but an expected Argentinean offensive never materialized, nor did an anticipated revolt in Bolivia. Contrary to Chilean intelligence reports, the Peruvians were generally apathetic to the idea of "*restoration*" and the contingent of Peruvian volunteers began quarrelling with the Chilean military. This enabled Santa Cruz to dig himself into an invincible position, such that the Chileans, on seeing that victory was improbable, accepted Santa Cruz's offer to negotiate and a peace treaty was signed at Paucarpata on November 17, 1837. This accord saved thousands of lives, but the benefits gained for Chile fell far short of her expectations. She did, however, obtain most favoured nation status, and an undertaking from Santa Cruz to be responsible for Peruvian debt to Chile plus interest. Chile, for her part, was obliged to agree to Peru's own special concessions, including an undertaking to broker peace between Santa Cruz and Argentina. Both Governments agreed to the principle of non-intervention, and to prevent their respective territories from being used as bases for revolutionary activities against the other.

Chile, in fact, would have made further and more valuable concessions had it not been for the Chilean Congress. Her representatives in Lima had agreed to return the three Peruvian ships captured by the *Aquiles*, in the process transferring naval superiority to the Peru-Bolivia Confederation. Most importantly, in signing such a treaty, Chile would have provided Santa Cruz with legitimate recognition of the Confederation rather than have it dissolved; her prime objective in waging war. Accordingly, in December 1837, the Chilean Government refused to ratify the treaty, and disassociated itself completely from the terms negotiated by its two representatives in Lima. The Chilean Congress resolved that war with Peru-Bolivia be pursued and that Santa Cruz be informed that a state of war continued to exist.

Chilean plans to form alliances with Ecuador and Argentina to invade Peru never materialized, but hoping that anti-Santa Cruz sentiment would assist her in dissolving the Confederation, Chile decided to mount the military campaign on her own. On this occasion, Peruvian volunteers supporting the Chilean initiative assembled as a Peruvian army commanded by Agustín Gamarra, Santa Cruz's archenemy and former President of Peru, but under the overall control of Chilean Manuel Bulnes. Chile had, by then, agreed with Gamarra that she would limit her military action to destroying the Peru-Bolivia Confederation, and undertook not to involve herself, thereafter, in Peru's internal affairs.

Chile's first expedition provoked considerable anger in Great Britain. The latter, seeing Peru as a progressive and well-administered nation, had expressed considerable sympathy for her Government. Great Britain's displeasure may have derived more from the fact that war between the two countries had caused both to default on repayments of British granted loans. An outbreak of peace, it was believed, would not only permit the two nations to resume their financial obligations, but would also allow British commercial interests in both countries to continue to prosper in an atmosphere of stability.

On July 10, 1838, the second Chilean expedition of "*Restoration*" set sail under the leadership of General Bulnes, but while en route, the State of North Peru, one of the three units of the Confederation, rose up against Santa Cruz and installed Orbegoso as her President. The latter, however, was still as opposed to Chile as the man he replaced. A battle ensued resulting in Bulnes occupying Lima and Agustín Gamarra being installed as provisional President of Peru. Bulnes and his forces proceeded to the country's interior to engage with Santa Cruz who had already decisively defeated the Argentinean military. On November 10, 1838, Santa Cruz retook Lima and, having forced Gamarra's withdrawal, entered the city triumphantly. The Chilean Government, having miscalculated anti-Santa Cruz feeling in Peru and, not having received expected military support from Argentina, decided to sue for peace with face-saving terms. Santa Cruz was again willing to negotiate a peace deal and offered safe conduct to the Chilean expeditionary force in exchange for Chile's recognition of the Confederation and acceptance of the latter's naval and military parity with Chilean forces. Chile's representative Mariano Egaña, counter-proposed that both Santa Cruz's and Chilean forces be withdrawn simultaneously to let the question of confederation of Peru with Bolivia be determined by a free vote of all Peruvians. This, unsurprisingly, was rejected by Santa Cruz and Chile's desired treaty remained elusive.

By January 20, 1839, Bulnes had prepared for the inevitable battle with Santa Cruz. He had wisely used the intervening period to assiduously train his forces to commit with superior numbers of Confederation troops. This contributed to a stunning and decisive victory at the battle of Yungay, forcing Santa Cruz to flee back to Bolivia where, faced with a revolt by his remaining troops, he sought exile in Ecuador. The outcome of Bulnes' victory was the emergence of several independent Governments in Peru and Bolivia who then proceeded to prepare for war with each other. In April 1839, Bulnes withdrew his forces from Peru following the desired collapse of the Peru-Bolivia Confederation.

Some historians have suggested that this lengthy period of instability delayed the introduction of merchant steamships on the West Coast. While it might appear that political unrest only contributed further to investor reluctance to participate in

Wheelwright's commercial maritime venture, he had during most of the convoluted military and political crises travelled to the United States and Great Britain to try to raise capital for his steamship enterprise. There is no evidence to suggest that the Chilean, Peruvian and Bolivian Decrees of 1835 and 1836 granted to his steamship enterprise were ever threatened with revocation by any of the respective three nations. Any such withdrawal of their individual licences to Wheelwright would have placed that nation at a commercial disadvantage to the others; Chile had more to lose from any such rescission. Apart from the initial paucity of investors in his scheme, the only difficulty then facing Wheelwright was his worrying search for coal.

3. A Problematic Venture 1835-1840

Relying on Portales' backing, Wheelwright submitted his petition for the necessary permits to operate in Chilean waters. It would, therefore, have come as no surprise to him to hear President Prieto proclaim on June 10, 1835:

"The introduction of these steamships will, undeniably, be of great use to our nation, particularly if one takes account of the benefits expected to be conferred on agriculture, mining, and industry. Actually, all that is being asked of us is to bestow a right that has already been granted to other inventors or pioneering engineers. These have previously been awarded on the basis that by doing so, processing speeds would not only be increased but costs reduced. Furthermore, because this navigation system has not yet emerged here, it will not be introduced unless the relevant permit is granted." [58]

The Senate issued its Decree, on August 25, 1835, awarding Wheelwright exclusive rights for ten years, to operate steamship services in Chilean waters and to establish whatever support facilities in ports and rivers then enjoyed by Chilean registered vessels. This licence was conditional on his steamship line being operational within two years. To fulfil the terms of this concession, Wheelwright was required to operate the franchise with at least two vessels of 300 tons each; It fell to the Chilean Government to identify those coastal locations where Wheelwright could establish workshops and stores necessary for the proper operation of his steamship enterprise.

Portales' support for Wheelwright's scheme could have been strengthened by the lack of interest from other commercial concerns, especially Chilean. Few national ship owners or other enterprises could then have financed such an operation. War and Navy Minister Portales would certainly have been aware that there were insufficient merchant vessels that could be readily requisitioned as a national fleet in times of conflict. The growth of the Chilean merchant marine had been curtailed by the war with Peru, formerly her main trading partner, but once ended, those remaining merchant ships were too few to meet Chile's needs for foreign-going activity as well as her coastwise trade.

Apart from the urgent requirement to overcome this shortage of commercial vessels, the Chilean Government had its own hidden agenda based on earlier liberalist policies of her first President Bernado O'Higgins. The latter, in the name of progress, that is the 19th century view of *"modernization"*, had sought the Europeanization[59] of Chile by attracting investment, new inventions, and entrepreneurs from the Great Powers. European and North American culture

A Problematic Venture 1835-1840

was already widespread given the considerable and increasing presence of their respective nationals and influences in that country.

After Independence, O'Higgins had carefully studied the territories bordering the Strait of Magellan and recognized the strategic trading position his country occupied on the sea-lanes between Europe, North Atlantic and the Pacific Basin. Unfavourable winds in this region and the narrowness of the Strait had never been conducive to sailing ship manoeuvres; such vessels had, for centuries, been obliged to take the longer and stormier voyage round Cape Horn. Various proposals had been floated in Chile, one of which was to employ steam-powered tugboats to tow sailing ships through the Strait.

The economics and benefits from state control of this ocean-connecting channel prompted the Chilean Government to plan for the occupation of this South American southern region, including the Strait of Magellan. In 1843, Chile's southern boundary had extended only up to the River Bío Bío near Concepción. On September 21 of that year, the Bulnes Government settled a permanent Chilean presence there to take advantage of the huge volume of steam ships that it envisaged would pass along this important route. The "*settlement*" occurred while Argentina was distracted by Civil War and she was, therefore, unable to mount a challenge to Chile's de facto sovereignty of that region.

O'Higgins had also envisaged that steamships negotiating the Strait would need plentiful supplies of coal and provisions; he had foreseen that Valparaíso's importance would increase as ships increasingly passed through the Strait to resume voyages northwards to Callao in Peru, or across the Pacific to Australia. In this respect, he had recommended the creation and expansion of shipyards, docks and Customs House in the Chilean port.[60] Portales subsequently implemented these plans when nurturing the reconstruction of Chile's Merchant marine. Naval schools were opened in Valparaíso and Ancud. Free cargo storage, not subjected to customs duty, was provided in new warehousing facilities constructed in the principal port. Importantly, financial support was made available for struggling ship owners.

1854 view of Valparaíso Bay with the Customs Buildings in the background. From a lithograph in National Historical Museum Library. Santiago. Chile.

It was fortunate that Wheelwright's steamship proposals dovetailed with Chile's own strategy for economic growth. Their implementation was certainly viewed as being essential to the development of both Chile's internal trade and, especially, her commerce with Europe. Without such foreign assistance, O'Higgins' deduced that his ambitions could never be achieved. Consequently, European shipping interests were encouraged to develop in Chile. Her Government had also realized that without such shipping firms, the extent of potential revenue losses would have been considerable. These arrangements with foreign shipping interests, however, were tacitly considered by the Chilean Government to serve only as short-term solutions until Chile was able to promote her own national development backed by her own resources; the seeds of nationalism had already been sown.

Chile had also been aware of United States' discussions on proposals for a canal across the Isthmus of Panama. It had been widely discussed for years, but the Chilean Government considered it an impractical proposition, never to be implemented. This view was still widespread in 1858. El Mercurio, Valparaiso's daily newspaper, suggested that the canal would never be built because of the Isthmus' unhealthy climate. Accordingly, Wheelwright's proposals for merchant steamships on the West Coast complemented Chile's own longer-term economic strategy centred on steamship routes through the Strait of Magellan. It was unlikely that Wheelwright, with so many contacts in the Chilean Government and other influential circles, would have been ignorant of this hidden agenda. Indeed, in years to come, Wheelwright would warn the Pacific Steam Navigation Company, the enterprise that he would eventually launch, that Chile would inevitably adopt a more nationally focused economy, relying more on her home registered enterprises, especially in shipping.

Since the beginning of the 19th Century, the concept of steam navigation had stimulated worldwide interest; there were many examples of individual successes. Before the *Great Western's* accomplishment in 1837, none had been sufficient to persuade investors to trust in Wheelwright's proposed operation. It is also reasonable to assume that his project might have emerged far earlier had it not been for trade and military conflicts between Peru and Chile. On the other hand, while some South American investor resistance did emerge because of uncertain political and economic outlooks, Wheelwright's project was more likely to have been delayed because the Chilean Government had intimated its preference for a European or United States establishment to finance and administer the proposed steamship enterprise.

Chile preferred to strengthen ties with the Great Powers rather than have Wheelwright's scheme supported by scarce Chilean finance. Had Chile's capital resources been readily available, her Government would most probably have applied these to improving and increasing her own merchant fleet and Navy; she had already been reduced to seeking secret loans from her wealthy nationals and

A Problematic Venture 1835-1840

Bolivia for this purpose. Even in the United States and Europe, investor leanings towards a South American shipping venture were, initially, very low due to the prevailing weak financial climate, the political uncertainty in South America, and the degree of risk embedded in the mechanics of the proposed operation. It took between three and a half to four months to sail from England to the WCSA; the route via Cape Horn was equivalent in distance to that well-established route to Calcutta and Singapore. The Cape Horn voyage also produced relatively high freight and insurance rates.[61]

Acute political instability in Peru also militated against investor confidence in South America, a perception only sharpened by remarks made by Peru's Foreign Minister in 1834, that his country "*had not enjoyed a tranquil moment since Independence*".[62] From 1826 to 1845, Peru's Government comprised military officers rather than elected members from the country at large; protectionism was allowed to flourish at the expense of liberal commercialism and foreigners in particular. Indeed, the British Ambassador expressed the view in 1834:

" ...That at least one half of the Deputies of the [Peruvian] Congress and Members of Government consider them [the foreigners] in the light of Public Robbers, as enemies to the community, and whose property is therefore lawful plunder".[63]

In the late 1830s, foreigners were prohibited from engaging in retail trade, and in some regions of Peru were even ordered to shut-down their business houses; some Congress members even demanded that all foreign enterprises be liquidated, and all consuls and agents obliged to leave the country. The only Peruvian President receiving the cachet of approval from the British Government for his adherence to the principles of economic liberalism was Andres de Santa Cruz, head of the short-lived Peru-Bolivian Confederation.

The Peruvian nation was always desperate for finance, a situation exacerbated by constant and costly warfare that had engaged her military-based Governments since Independence. Callao had lain mostly in ruins after the Spanish had been besieged in the port for over two years; foreign armies had ravaged many agricultural estates, both in the coastal and highland areas of the country.[64] Financing military requirements, rather than restructuring the nation's economy, had led to heavy borrowing, the procedures for which were usually arranged arbitrarily:

"...The only way to raise money in an emergency, real or contrived, was by forced loan or by coming to mutually convenient arrangements with individuals. The people with the largest amounts of cash were usually merchants and the most attractive of these were the European traders with their relatively easy access to metropolitan credit."[65]

Peru, therefore, was, considered a risky environment for foreign traders, especially when conducting business with her Government. There were occasions of contracts being annulled without compensation, particularly when Peruvian Governments considered them injurious to the nation.

After Independence, many Spaniards forming the backbone of the Peruvian bureaucracy fled; the immediate result was that Peru lacked the expertise to successfully manage her economy differently from the Spanish colonial system. For example, her Government was unable to arrange the most efficient method of disposing of her vast guano resources, and by 1849, her economy had been largely at the mercy of Anthony Gibbs & Son of London.[66] This firm had contracted with the Peruvian Government for exclusive rights to sell guano during that year to all Europe with the exception of France.[67] Gibbs and Co., like other business houses engaged in this trade, were usually required to advance or loan the Peruvian Government considerable amounts of finance to be repaid from future guano sales.

It is likely that the ease with which Wheelwright subsequently obtained the right to launch his proposed steamship line in Peruvian and Bolivian waters, is attributable to the fact that, as a foreign shipping concern, the Peruvian Government might have envisaged extracting much needed revenue from a foreign-owned enterprise. Peru would have also anticipated that steamship links, with an overland Panama Isthmus connection, would create stronger commercial ties between her and the Great Powers. Such a shipping enterprise, her Government believed, would assist Peru's emergence from the isolation into which she was sinking, and would also have calculated that by supporting Wheelwright's venture, the nation might be better placed to negotiate stronger credit positions with the United States or/and Great Britain, depending on where the majority of capital investment originated.

A history of bad debt, political instability and contract rescissions were significant factors in deterring potential investors from supporting Wheelwright's scheme. The successful and economic Atlantic voyages undertaken by the steamship *Great Western*, as well as attracting considerable publicity for the concept of ocean-going steamships, lent more credibility to the viability of Wheelwright's proposed project in the Pacific. Launched in July 1837 for the Great Western Railway Company, the *Great Western* had been designed specifically for the North Atlantic crossing almost three years after Wheelwright had published his own proposals for merchant steam shipping on the WCSA.

A Problematic Venture 1835-1840

Reproduced from a painting of the *Great Western*

    The competing British & American Steam Navigation Company (BASNC), anxious to be the first to cross the Atlantic entirely under steam, had already started construction of its own vessel, the *ss Royal Victoria*, but construction had been plagued by a series of delays. Knowing that the latter vessel would never be ready in time, BASNC chartered the *ss Sirius* for the proposed trip. She was a 700 tons coastal steamer normally plying the Cork-London route.

    On March 29, 1838, the *Sirius* left London, calling in at Queenstown in Ireland before the start of her Atlantic adventure. Not being built for ocean voyages, she had taken on board as much coal as it was possible to carry. Large amounts of it were heaped on deck and every available space below was filled to capacity with the precious fuel. The *Great Western* had still been tied-up in Bristol when the *Sirius* had departed, but set sail in hot pursuit 10 days later. The former had the more powerful engines, and the competing *Sirius* had to maintain a full head of steam to the very end.

    A storm in mid ocean slowed her down considerably; she was obliged to increase fuel consumption to such an extent, that the vessel eventually exhausted all her coal. The *Sirius'* crew scavenged the ship for auxiliary fuel; furniture, doors and even the emergency mast were requisitioned. Eventually arriving in New York harbour on April 22, 1838, she was thus recorded as the first vessel to have sailed the Atlantic Ocean entirely under her own steam. It was a hollow victory; the *Great Western* completed her crossing four hours later with 200 tons of fuel spare, having made the voyage in 14 days, 4 faster than the *Sirius*. The latter ship made two further transatlantic crossings for BASNC before reverting to coastal trade;

she met an undignified end after running aground in dense fog on the approaches to the Cork harbour with the loss of nineteen lives.

On September 13, 1836, Wheelwright received from the Peruvian Government a decree similar to that granted by Chile almost a year earlier. It is clear that the Peruvian Executive, apart from identifying the proposed enterprise as a source of finance, was intent on not only trying to preserve Callao's status as a competing port with Valparaíso, but given the considerable commercial activity between the two, she might have felt that there was no option but to grant Wheelwright the same concessions. Her Government would certainly have been aware from discussions with him that his steam navigation enterprise might probably extend to Panama, thus enhancing her links with the United States and Europe. Such developments, once fulfilled, would certainly have favoured the port of Callao over Valparaíso.

Just as important for Peru's political stability was the need to provide speedier and more reliable transportation systems for the influential élite class. Due to the country's formidable geographical barriers, the latter had tended to congregate in Lima and in Peru's numerous ports. A steamship line, as proposed by Wheelwright and once operational, would have overcome the communication obstacles of unfavourble light winds along this coasgtal region.

Bolivia's decree to Wheelwright authorizing his proposed enterprise to operate within her waters and ports, published on September 12, was finally sealed on November 6, 1836. His acceptance of both the Peruvian and Bolivian navigation licences coincided with the Chilean Congress' decision to declare war to split the Peru-Bolivia Confederation and restore the status quo. Santa Cruz and his deputy, Pío de Tristán, had signed both Wheelwright's Peruvian and Bolivian Decrees in Lima, indicating that the Confederation under Santa Cruz had already become a functioning reality.

It was probably already well known to the Confederation, to Chile, Ecuador and certainly Colombia, that the United States had already focused her attention on the Panama Isthmus, considering it strategically important for her military and economic objectives. Certainly, Wheelwright, as a former American Consul with his high-level contacts in Colombia, of which Panama was still then an integral State, and from his discussions with representatives of other South American Governments, would probably have been aware of an 1835 United States' Senate resolution.

The latter authorised President Andrew Jackson to appoint commissioner Charles Biddle to investigate several different routes on the American continent to ascertain the one best suited for "*inter oceanic communications*". Biddle, advised by Don José Obaldia, a member of the Colombian Congress, eventually secured from the latter, a decree giving him the right to build a railroad across the Isthmus of Panama. Clearly, the construction of such a railroad would have opened-up overland links, not only to the east coast of the United States, but also to the sea-lanes of Europe, Asia and Australia. Peruvian belief that communication with the European and North American spheres of influence could feasibly be strengthened, was fortified by the British Government's increasing complaints at delays in dispatching correspondence to and from South America.

On June 18, 1836, the British Consul General in Peru, circulated letters throughout the Lima and Callao business communities, including copies of dispatches received from London, highlighting the need for a more direct and rapid line of communication between Great Britain and the WCSA, via an overland route across the Isthmus of Panama. United States' discussions on a Panama railroad link had sounded alarm bells within the rival British Government, who would then have wished to be involved in and/or to benefit from any such project.

A meeting of businessmen was convened in Lima on August 12, at which a committee was appointed to investigate and publicly invite proposals for establishing desirable lines of communication. In due course, the committee duly reported the receipt of only one set of proposals, those of Wheelwright. He had indicated that he was not only ready and willing to undertake such a venture on their behalf, but would also formally participate in the enterprise. He had agreed to include in the constitution of his proposed "*Pacific Steam Navigation Company*", a clause guaranteeing the conveyance of all letters to and from British subjects *"from and to whatever source or destination within the Company's permitted operational territory at a rate of six pennies for each letter etc."*

This guarantee was subject to His British Majesty's Government establishing corresponding postal rates for conveyance by steamer to and from Chagres, on the Caribbean coast of the Panama Isthmus. The Lima committee confirmed that three steamships, as proposed by Wheelwright, would be sufficient for the proposed undertaking, provided they were equipped with double the usual quantity of spares. However, the purchase of a fourth vessel to be held in reserve in case of accidents, breakdowns, or other unforeseen events was advised

The original idea of contracting "*specialized*" ships to carry mail is attributed to James MacQueen. Born in Lanarkshire, Scotland in 1778, he had been employed as a sugar plantation manager on the Caribbean island of Grenada. It was said that during his employment there, he had concluded that the delivery of mail, as then undertaken by British Admiralty ships, was often erratic and unreliable. Returning to Scotland in 1830, becoming part owner of a newspaper, he used the latter to publicize his plans for improving the Admiralty postal service. His ideas eventually led to the formation, by Royal Charter, of the Royal Mail Steam Packet Company in 1839. This company, on its formation, did not possess a single ship, but by March 1840, it had contracted with the Admiralty Lords to undertake semi-monthly sailings to the West Indies; its voyages soon extended as far as Halifax in Nova Scotia, New York, Honduras, Cuba, Barbados, Jamaica, and the Caribbean coastline of the Republic of Columbia.

Firm plans for maritime links to an Atlantic-Pacific overland connection via the Isthmus of Panama were, therefore, virtually in place at the time of the business community meeting in Lima on August 1836. The existence of this proposed infrastructure must have contributed considerably to British Government thinking when soliciting opinion through HM Consul in Peru, on the need for a more efficient mail service.

Wheelwright, through his extensive and influential contacts, would also have been alerted to the possibilities of a steamship service being introduced for the West Indies and the East Coast of Central America. His guarantee to the British Government, conditional on the introduction of a steamship connection with Chagres on the Caribbean side of the Isthmus of Panama, effectively ensured the promotion of his own planned undertaking. Both the Pacific Steam Navigation Company and the Royal Mail Steam Packet Company would become heavily interdependent, each supplying the other with cargo and passengers.

Wheelwright had also decided, like the Spanish before him, to make his "*consulado*" or control centre of his proposed undertaking at Callao. This, apart from tradition and its strategic location, would also have been popular with the Peruvian Government and the local and Lima business communities, as an expression of confidence in the struggle for supremacy over Valparaíso. On December 8, 1836, the British Consul, in Santiago, Chile, chaired a meeting similar to the Lima assembly to consider the same scheme. This committee, although indicating strong interest from potential stockholders, followed the lead taken by the Chilean Government and recommended that Wheelwright's proposed enterprise be incorporated in the United States or Europe, probably believing, like their Peruvian counterparts, that stronger links between Europe and the United States would be forged if the enterprise was founded with capital from those nations.

Chile's acceptance of a Panama Isthmus connection was grudging; any successful outcome of the latter operation would have threatened Valparaíso's claim to supremacy as a port over Callao. On the one hand, she appreciated the importance of cultivating stronger links with the Great Powers, but on the other, she had already prepared longer-term plans for introducing steamship services through the Magellan Strait.[68]

Albérdi described Wheelwright as being buoyed by expressions of confidence in him from his South American friends when he set-off for the United States via Panama in search of the financial backing necessary to set the enterprise in motion. William H. Aspinwall, later to become the power behind the Panama Railroad, and the Pacific Mail Steamship Company, together with other New York financiers, examined Wheelwright's proposed scheme.

Maritime historian Arthur C.Wardle[69] claimed that these renowned business people either had proved dilatory in responding to his proposal, or were insensitive to the whole idea. Unknown to Wheelwright, Aspinwall and colleagues had already

A Problematic Venture 1835-1840

drawn-up their own plans for steam navigation services, principally on the West Coast of North America to be served by a railroad connection over the Isthmus of Panama. Professor John Haskell Kemble in *"The Panama Route, 1848-1869"* recorded:

"Just as Howland and Aspinwall were pioneers in the building and operation of clipper ships on the ocean routes of the world, so the[eir business] house envisioned increasing population and trade along the [North] Pacific coast. The line of steamers from Panama to Oregon was only part of the plan in Aspinwall's mind. He saw the need for facilitated travel across the Isthmus of Panama and projected a railroad there in 1848. There is also evidence that the original project included the operation of American steamships along the west coast of South America in competition with the British ships of the Pacific Steam Navigation Company" [70]

Aspinwall's proposals were not implemented until 1848. This delay, fortuitous for Wheelwright, arose because such North American schemes were often subject to prior and lengthy periods of lobbying in Congress and the US Admiralty, especially when petitions and tenders for mail contracts were involved. It was likely, therefore, that Wheelwright's unsuccessful attempt to raise interest and financial backing in his native land had occurred as a result of Aspinwall's own competitive vision and, probably, the latter's greater influence within the United States' Government. Failure to attract US business capital caused Wheelwright to finally head for England.

"He set forth his ideas in a well prepared pamphlet with maps of the Pacific Coast. He was amply provided with the highest testimonials and in addition to all, his commanding personality, dignified bearing and courteous manner gave him a favourable *"entrée"* into influential circles." [71]

Wheelwright attracted significant support in Liverpool and Glasgow; in London, he was able to rely on practical assistance from Lord Abinger's son, the Honourable Peter Campbell Scarlett, with whom he had already discussed his project in South America. Scarlett, a highly influential figure, was to prove extremely valuable to Wheelwright's plans. Having already met in Valparaíso, they shared the same visions for introducing merchant steamships into the Pacific and for constructing railroad connections between the East and West coasts of South America. Scarlett, as a British diplomat, was a seasoned traveller, having crossed South America from Buenos Aires to Valparaíso, passing through the Pampas and over the Andes. He had then proceeded to Panama, describing these voyages in his two volumes *"South America and the Pacific"* published in 1838.

He had also highlighted the need to quickly establish a trans-Andean rail system linking the East and West coasts of South America, and to construct a canal

Ploughing The South Sea

and rail route across the Isthmus of Panama. Additionally, he had painstakingly set out the case for the introduction of railroads connecting with steamship services operating along the Pacific coastline of South America.

Juan Bautista Albérdi reported that debate had arisen as to whether Scarlett or Wheelwright should be credited with the idea of introducing merchant steamships into the Pacific. It is clear that there had been informed discussion between the two, which, most likely, had resulted in a joining of minds to assess the feasibility of their proposals. Scarlett, in an appendix to his book, clearly acknowledged Wheelwright's ideas and plans, and subsequently described them in a separate section entitled "*General Plan of Operations considered by the Pacific Steam Navigation Company*". They were the very same as those proposed by Wheelwright in a paper dated in London July 31, 1837.

However, neither Wheelwright nor Scarlett was the first in this field. Another North American, Daniel S. Grisnold, had broadcast the idea of a merchant steamship service on the Chilean coast in 1821. Having applied to the Chilean Government for the exclusive rights for fifteen years to establish such an operation, he had solicited the support of then President Bernardo O'Higgins. In submitting his proposals to the latter, Grisnold detailed the advantages that his proposed undertaking would bring to the Chilean nation:

"[The introduction of] steamships would prove to be of particular benefit in the two provinces which mark Chile's southern and northern boundaries. It is an established fact that many of the rich mines in Huasco and Coquimbo have been paralysed as a result of the shortages of timber, coal and other stores, all of which are readily available in the province of Concepción which, in turn, depends on supplies of a wide range of mineral ores. Steamships would eventually create a new kind of business trade in Chile, by transporting coal and timber from the South to the North and returning from the latter with ore for the South".[72]

O'Higgins, finding Grisnold's plans highly acceptable, referred his petition to Government Attorney Vial to prepare a report on the scheme's merits, but Vial concluded that Grisnold's proposals, as detailed, were prejudicial to Chile, and gave three reasons for his decision. Firstly, he submitted that they militated against Chile's own laws for the protection of her economy and her own business nationals; these reserved coastwise trading between minor ports to Chilean vessels. Secondly, he claimed that because steamships required less crew to operate them, they would only tend to reduce the eventual pool of available maritime labour with deleterious affects on Chile's Naval Defence policy.

The weakness of Vial's arguments probably reflected signs of growing opposition by the élites to O'Higgins; the latter's star had been clearly waning. Vial had commented:

A Problematic Venture 1835-1840

"Because these steamships are not dependent on winds and currents, they will be able to take the shortest coastal routes and due to their need for coal and wood, they can use this as an excuse, whether true or not, to make for any cove or other spots on the coast and once there, deal in contraband foodstuffs and manufactured goods from Europe..."[73]

O'Higgins, understandably, found Vial's reasoning unacceptable and sought further information from the Consular service to provide support for the steamship scheme. Shortly afterwards, O'Higgins signed a decree granting Grisnold:

"Or others interested in operating 750 tons steamships, an exclusive privilege for ten years to operate this or any other Chilean registered steamship along the coasts and waters of Chile."

Other conditions attached to this concession required steamships operating under this privilege to engage a Chilean national as her first officer, and at least a quarter of her crew had to be Chilean to enable them to gain valuable experience of steamship operation and maintenance. Chilean historian Claudio Veliz reported that there was no record as to why the Grisnold concession was not used and assumed that negotiations had simply broken down.[74]

Fourteen years later, when Wheelwright planned the scheme detailed in his London paper of July 1837, he had carefully listed the Company's aims and objectives, types of steamships to be used, the most suitable machinery and boilers to be fitted, the sailing itinerary and the route that was to be followed on the outward voyage from Liverpool to the Pacific.

Scarlett's influence within British Government circles and throughout the London business community was to prove invaluable. Wheelwright probably appreciated his prestige and influence from the onset; a measure of Scarlett's political weight and commitment to the project was indicated by his subsequent appointment as one of the first Directors of the Pacific Steam Navigation Company. What Grisnold lacked was that considerable influence exerted by Wheelwright within a circle of contacts more powerful than the eventually ousted President Bernardo O'Higgins. Had Portales been the Minister of War and Navy at that time, Grisnold's proposals, which were in accordance with Chilean needs, might have been adopted. Moreover, Wheelwright, could also count on the backing of Chile's national hero Lord Cochrane, Captain Fitzroy, and other leading London figures with whom he had associated for some years on the West Coast.

In spite of this valuable support, the task of raising sufficient finance turned out to be more difficult than Wheelwright could ever have imagined. The affects of a financial depression were still being felt in Great Britain and, until the emergence of the *Great Western*, there had been very little investor confidence in foreign steamship ventures. Purchasing stock in this scheme would then have appeared even more doubtful, especially when found to be dependent on services confined to a distant coast. The proposed area of operations was widely, but erroneously, perceived to be lacking both in coal and servicing facilities; many thought such an enterprise would end in complete financial ruin. The general view of South American investments during the first half of the 19th Century was, accordingly, very cautious, particularly when news had been rife of disastrous speculation in mining stock issues, bonds and the Peruvian Government's rescission of contracts with foreign business houses. The public was also aware of the ravages caused to that region of the sub-continent by war with Spain, civil wars and general political unrest. It was likely that these uncertainties contributed more to investor resistance than the principle of operating merchant steamships on the WCSA.

Investors in the United States and Great Britain had also been especially wary of committing scarce capital to fledgling projects in the Americas. The success of the Erie Canal had sparked a boom similar to "*canal mania*" in the closing decades of the 18th Century in England. The North American project had been financed by credit from the State of Pennsylvania as part of her scheduled improvements. British investors regarding the latter State's bonds as a safe haven for their cash, invested $US35,000,000 (£19,500,000 approximately), but after the financial crash of 1839, their investments became virtually worthless. In the following 1842 depression, Pennsylvania State refused to honour her debts; European investors, understandably, concluded that American securities, even Federal issues, risked being worthless.[75]

An additional negative impact on investment in Wheelwright's venture arose from the general belief that travel by steamship was viewed as hazardous. One third of steamboats on the Mississippi, for example, had been lost in river accidents. Paul Johnson in "*The Birth of the Modern-World Society 1815-1830*" revealed that steamship boiler accidents were common; 150 explosions had been recorded up to the year 1850 with 1400 recorded fatalities, although he believed the total to have been much higher. Boiler accidents continued well after 1850, although the rate of incidents reduced as technology improved.

One of the most tragic accidents, sparsely reported at the time, occurred on April 27, 1865, after the ending of the American Civil War. The 260 feet wide wooden-hulled steamboat *Sultana* carried, to the point of severe overcrowding, approximately 2300 passengers, mostly Union soldiers on their way home after being released from Confederate prisons. A leaky and defective boiler exploded, hurling hot coals over the vessel causing flames to envelope her. Estimates of the numbers who perished ranged from 1550 to 1900 persons.

Typical of the general lack of confidence engendered by steam ships was the advice a friend had given Charles Dickens that when travelling by steamship, one should always sleep in the stern. In February 1830, steam riverboat *Helen McGregor* was leaving Memphis when the starboard boiler was heard to crack;

the resulting explosion killed 50 persons who were either flayed alive or suffocated by inhaling steam.[76]

The overcrowded *Sultana* embarking on her fatal voyage
Photo: US Library of Congress

The potential dangers of steam-operated craft cannot have been the main reason for lack of investor acceptance; accident rates by the time Wheelwright had arrived in London had already begun to decline and some impressive voyages had been undertaken. Steamboats had appeared as early as 1775; the French, with Fulton's involvement, had constructed such a craft, but trials on the Seine indicated that she was too underpowered ever to be successful. In 1780, a 182 tons paddle steamer, the *Pyroscaphe* is recorded as having sailed up the River Loire near Lyons. On August 9, 1807, Fulton himself patented a steamship, which was subjected to trials on the North American East River. A contemporary report described it as *"an ungainly craft looking precisely like a backwoods sawmill mounted on a scow [flat bottomed boat] set on fire."* [77] Despite this unflattering comparison, the steam-powered boat successfully sailed 150 miles upriver to Albany in thirty-two hours and returned downriver in under thirty. Fulton was justified in remarking:

"The power of propelling boats by steam is now fully proven. It will give a cheap and quick conveyance to the merchants on the Mississippi, Missouri and other great rivers which are now laying open their treasures to the enterprise of our countrymen." [78]

Fulton improved upon this success and, in 1816, began operating the *Chancellor Livingstone*, a steamboat fitted with luxurious passenger accommodation that became the benchmark for ship design and railroad carriages, and was one of the earliest steam powered craft to use coal. Fulton had already been granted a monopoly license for the New York region leading to the founding of the highly successful Hudson Steamboat Company. The latter's success led to a proliferation of competing steamboat enterprises on American waterways. By 1839, there were claimed to be around 400 steamships operating on the Mississippi and Ohio Rivers.

In 1809, Colonel John C. Stevens, prohibited by Fulton's monopoly licence from operating in the New York area, constructed a small sea-going vessel, the *Phoenix*. She was the first steamer to actually put to the open sea, but had taken 13 days to travel from New York to Philadelphia. Nevertheless, she continued to operate a commercial service between these two locations, the very first sea-going steamship enterprise. Despite the extremely slow time of the *Phoenix's* first voyage, it was a sufficient achievement to suggest that ocean-going steamships would eventually be a practical proposition. When Wheelwright's proposals were announced, similar steam-powered craft had already been operating in Britain for almost 15 years. Paddle steamers had been built for the Royal Navy on the advice of Brunel, and were first noted in the 1827 Navy List. The Admiralty used early steam-vessels as tugs, fitted with propellers rather than paddle wheels.

The first paddle wheeled steamers were generally restricted to sheltered water tasks and considered useful only for sailing short distances because early engines consumed huge quantities of wood and coal. Typical of such inland steam-powered craft was the Owston Ferry on the River Trent in Lincolnshire, which provided daily services in the 1830s to the port of Hull and return up-river. Steam-powered craft had also operated successfully on the Scottish Forth-Clyde Canal between 1790 and 1803, but the waterway's owners, concerned that damage would be caused to the canal banks by the wash from the paddle wheels, later prohibited their use. In 1812, the Glasgow-built *Comet*, operating on the Scottish Clyde, became Europe's first commercially successful steamship. Five paddle-steamships, operated by the General Steam Navigation Company, were recorded in use on the River Thames in 1815, two of which had sailed down from the Clyde.

There is, moreover, a recorded English Channel steamship crossing in 1816 from Brighton to Le Havre, and a steam-assisted transit of the Atlantic in 25 days from Savannah to Liverpool in 1819. In 1825, the paddle steamship *Enterprise* (470 tons), powered by 120 horsepower engines, undertook a voyage from Falmouth, on the English south coast, to Calcutta in India in 103 days, 64 of which were under steam. In 1827, the paddle steamer *Countess of Lonsdale* operated a regular service between Whitehaven, Isle of Man and Liverpool. From 1833 to

A Problematic Venture 1835-1840

1848, the paddle steamer *John Moore* provided the Liverpool-New Brighton Ferry service on the River Mersey, catering mainly for holiday and residential traffic.

Steam-powered engine units emerged gradually as auxiliary components to sail, and although the time taken to complete voyages was greatly reduced when compared with non-assisted sailing ships, the average speed in 1838 was still only 10-11 knots. Early steamships for a long time were considered unreliable and very uncomfortable; engine compartments, water tanks and paddle wheel housings took up a lot of space. They were also very dirty, prompting Sir George Cockburn, British First Sea Lord, to complain that: "*since the introduction of steamers, he had never seen a clean deck, or a captain, who, when he waited on him, did not look like a sweep.*"

Despite the successes of American steam riverboats and the many established British operations of the type already described, many technical and engineering experts of the day concluded that because steamships would have to carry so much coal to complete their voyages, there would be too little space left for cargo and passengers. With this kind of attitude, it was not surprising that UK business communities were reluctant to invest in Wheelwright's well-publicized operation. In their view, it bore all the trademarks of previous financial disasters.

It would not have been unreasonable, at this stage, for Wheelwright to withdraw from his crusade to raise capital, given the mostly hostile reactions to his proposed scheme. He wrote in Liverpool on January 1, 1839:

"It was criminal of me to be so far apart from my family for such a long time, but my situation has been such that my absence from England would have meant totally abandoning my plans. If I could have imagined for one moment, the time and the money this business has cost me, I would not have dreamed of ever undertaking it; my duty to my family and my self should have forbidden it."

His continuous and unrelenting efforts finally won him the practical support of some Glasgow, Liverpool and Manchester merchants. Importantly, he retained the backing and loyalty of Scarlett and friends. On September 6, 1838, his Pacific Steam Navigation Company was formally established in London. The following prospectus appeared in the following November editions of the London Times and other English newspapers. It clearly underlines the climatic conditions conducive to steamship navigation and draws attention to the potential demand for the company's proposed services:

""PACIFIC STEAM NAVIGATION COMPANY
To be incorporated by Royal Charter. Capital of £250,000 in the form of 5000 shares of £50 each; 1000 shares to be reserved for floating in South America.
There is no other part of the world that is so favourable to steamship navigation than along the Pacific coastlines of South America. The distance between Valparaíso and Panama

is approximately 2500 miles. The population of the West Coast comprises more that 4 million; land communications are difficult and in some areas, impracticable. Voyages by sailing ships are usually monotonous and unreliable whatever the time of the year. In spite of this, approximately 9000 persons travel in this way up and down the coast every year. On the other hand, Pacific coastal waters are calm and serene with a good number of ports accessible all year round; gentle southerly winds with frequent calm periods give rise to an invariably tranquil sea. These are all eminently suitable conditions for steam ships. Voyages that normally take 20 or 30 days can now be completed in 40 to 50 hours by steamship.[79] His Majesty's Government, having already decided to establish steam shipping services between Britain and the West Indies, will in conjunction with the Pacific Service, ensure the speeding-up of communications between Europe and the West Coast of South America. The voyage to Lima, via the Isthmus of Panama, will thus be reduced by approximately 30 days; by way of Cape Horn, the journey would take 4 months. Voyages by the new route between Britain and Australia will be reduced from 4 months to 65 or 70 days".

Importantly, the London press was favourably disposed to the advertised prospectus; the Times referred to Wheelwright as *"the father of the Company"* and mentioned his name alongside that of Scarlett. The London Morning Post wrote in similar vein, emphasizing that the Pacific Steam Navigation Company planned to reduce voyage times to and from the West Coast of South America by up to two thirds of the time normally taken for such travel, due to the lengthy and stormy crossings to the Pacific via Cape Horn.[80]

Describing Wheelwright as an extremely valuable link in a huge enterprise committed to steam shipping, it detailed his financial estimates for operating four steamships of between 400 and 500 tons each, as amounting to 236,000 pesos (approximately £47,200 or US 85,000 dollars); one of these vessels would be held in reserve. Envisaged earnings from three operating vessels were given as 466,950 pesos (£94,000 or US 168,100 dollars), leaving an estimated profit of £46,000 (US 83,100 dollars) per annum to the Company.

It is clear that there was a ready-made passenger market for a steamship line and one that would probably expand once regular and speedy schedules were seen to operate. The enterprise, thereafter, began to be more sympathetically received by the public, although its take-up of stock was still slow, obliging Wheelwright to spend much of his time in Liverpool and other northern cities, trying to talk-up his Company's merits and prospects. Agents were even appointed in Paris and Hamburg to sell stock in Europe.

Although investor interest was beginning to stir, there was still some distrust of the feasibility and soundness of the new enterprise. It was claimed that the public had been unwilling to invest in the scheme, mostly because doubts had been expressed as to whether the British Government was really prepared to grant the

Company the status of a Corporation. Finally, on April 23, 1839, it conceded the principle of limited corporate responsibility, and PSNC received its Royal Charter resulting in a new wave of investor confidence in that company.

Wheelwright continued his efforts to place PSNC on a solid footing. To allay any concerns at the deteriorating military situation between the Peru-Bolivia Confederation and Chile, with the real prospect of Ecuador and Argentina becoming involved, he secured from the British Admiralty, an undertaking that the intended steamships on the Pacific coast would be afforded the full protection of HM Naval Forces, including the assignment of an armed officer to each vessel. In trying to widen PSNC's client base, Wheelwright unsuccessfully petitioned the US Navy Secretary for the grant of a mail contract.[81] The negative response probably arose from US preferences for the formation of US national steamship mail lines, because not only would these provide specific and efficient mail carrying services, but also because they considered such vessels would be useful for military and naval operations. Professor John Haskell Kemble in support of this conclusion, comments in his "*Panama Route 1848-1869*":[82]

"The difference between the steam and sailing warship in the middle nineteenth century amounted to little more than varying methods of propulsion, and since the sailing merchant ship had always formed an effective auxiliary naval vessel in time of war, it was expected that the steam merchantman would be as useful. The subsidizing of lines of ocean steamers by the navy was, therefore, not unreasonable, for by this means, the mails would be carried and additional naval units for service in times of war would also be provided."

In any case, the carriage of US foreign going mail was not properly considered until the emergence of an 1845 Act of Congress. It was likely, given that Wheelwright's steamships were to be confined to the WCSA, that the US Navy would, reasonably, have wanted to favour its own national steamship companies operating vessels nearer to national ports on the Atlantic and Pacific coasts. The refusal might also have been induced by proposals from the influential Aspinwall and his associate New York financiers for the introduction of steamship lines to operate on both Central and North American coasts with connections via the railroad across the Isthmus.

On July 27, 1839, Wheelwright was ordered to take whatever measures he thought suitable, subject to Directors' approval, to conclude contracts for the building of two steamships. The time limits for establishing a steamship service on the Chilean coast imposed by the original decree were about to expire, although subsequent legal representations to the Chilean Government resulted in a time extension. Some historians have taken this latter act as a sign of Chile's good faith. There is no doubt that her Government held Wheelwright in high esteem, but it should not be forgotten that Chile needed PSNC to stimulate trade and communication with Europe just as much as that company required her support. In fact, there had been a strong possibility that the whole venture would fail to get off the ground. Certainly, any delay in refusing to extend the time period allowed by the original permit would probably have caused the enterprise to be abandoned to the detriment of Chile and the other licensing nations. She was not then in a position to introduce a similar operation on the scale proposed by Wheelwright.

It is notable that when Chile granted him the exclusive privilege, she had also made a second back-up grant to a Pedro Allessandri, who operated a small sailing packet service between Callao and Valparaiso, for a period of eight years but:

"The existing concessions [to Allessandri] will not take effect, nor will they prejudice in any way, the rights of the afore-mentioned Wheelwright, if the latter manages to establish the subject steam navigation service before the relevant expiry time." [83]

A shareholders' meeting in Liverpool set the operation in motion by authorizing Wheelwright to contract with Thomas Wilson, a highly renowned ship builder in that city, for the construction of two iron-hulled ships of 700 tons each. The order was conditional on their being launched within 6 months of the contract being signed, at a total price of £18,000 (approximately US 32,400 dollars). The contract had actually been signed on August 31, 1839 and when Wheelwright returned to London to report to his Board of Directors, he was astounded to hear their rejection of the arrangements he had concluded. His response was to request that Board of Directors' meetings be transferred to Liverpool[84] from London, but this was refused. Wilson, the Liverpool shipbuilder, originally contracted to build the two iron vessels, understandably, resolved not to have any more undertakings with PSNC and withdrew from further negotiations.

The Board had not agreed with Wheelwright's requirement that the two proposed vessels be built of iron rather than wood. He believed that using the former material would not only have been cheaper than timber vessels, but would also in the long term, have been more economical to maintain. Fortunately, those differences of opinion did not completely hinder progress. Tenders for the construction of two ships' hulls were re-invited and on October 10, 1839, the Board accepted an offer from Curling, Young and Company for the building of two vessels with wooden hulls of 700 tons each at a total cost of £24,150 (approximately US 43,500 dollars). The contract had been subject to a condition that the builders guarantee both vessels to be certified as class A1 on Lloyds Register for 12 years, and be launched within 12 months of the contract date. The cost of this arrangement was £6150 (US 11,100 dollars) more than that previously concluded for the provision of two iron-hulled vessels. Logic supported the use of wooden-hull vessels rather than iron.

The proposed steamships had been designed to operate specifically along the WCSA where proper facilities for fabricating or repairing iron plate were, in the early years of PSNC, few if any. On the other hand, the availability of timber and the skill to work it was relatively widespread, given the number of shipwrights and carpenters in Callao and Valparaíso. The reasoning supporting the decision to construct the two vessels of wood was soon to prove justified.

4. First Steamship Line. 1839-1845

By November 1839, Wheelwright, was still trying to ship coal to the West coast prior to the new Steamships' arrival, and to dispatch suitable vessels for hulking and conversion to coal storage, ship's spares and provisions. These hulks were also intended to act as unloading pontoons in ports lacking wharfage and storage facilities. Vessels visiting Callao and Valparaíso still had to use lighters in the open bay for loading and discharging cargo.

It was clear to PSNC's Directors that one of the first priorities was to ensure adequate coal supplies on the West Coast. During this period of preparation, the Board, acting contrary to the advice given to them by a Lloyds' Inspector, had already purchased a wooden sailing vessel, the *Elizabeth*, loaded her with coal and instructed her to be sailed out to Valparaíso. At the last minute her crew, claiming that the ship was unfit to sail, refused to put to sea. Following an inspection of the vessel, Wheelwright confirmed the crew's worst fears. The *Elizabeth* and her cargo, therefore, had to be sold in the very same condition in which she was acquired, and without even leaving her berth at London's East India Dock.

A replacement sailing ship, the wooden built *Portsea*, was loaded with Welsh coal and readied for the long voyage to the Pacific. Whether an inspection of the coal's quality was ever undertaken is not known, but this particular batch was to cause unfortunate results. These actions prompt the question as to why so much trouble was taken to send out coal supplies to the West Coast, when highly credible sources, Wheelwright included, had already confirmed the existence of this fuel in southern Chile. If its quality had been suspect, its effectiveness should have been ascertained before announcements were widely broadcast on its claimed and extensive availability in the latter country. If the coal was suitable, as seemed to be the case, then one must assume that there was no mining strategy in place before the two pioneering vessels were launched, a clear management failure on Wheelwright's part.

The PSNC Board, at this time, had decided to introduce an operational and management structure prior to the steamships' arrival on the West Coast. A staff manual entitled "*General Rules and Regulations*" for the conduct of the company's affairs on the Pacific Coast had been rushed into print. Undoubtedly influenced by the recent military turmoil in the region, it hinted at the military and political problems that management and captains on the West Coast of South America (WCSA) were likely to encounter. Captains of PSNC vessels had been specifically instructed to maintain strict neutrality of their respective steamships to avoid the possibility of providing any West Coast Governments[85] with an excuse to take action against them; such was the concern at political storms erupting between any of the West Coast South American nations.

Wheelwright's original plan was to have made Callao alone the centre of operations. However, it was likely that Chilean pressure was applied to oblige PSNC to establish Valparaíso as an additional control point, or else that company thought it prudent to do so, given the still evident hostility between Peru and Chile over the supremacy issue of their respective principal ports, and their bitter struggles over trade agreements. Wheelwright, undoubtedly aware of Chilean sentiment on the proposed trade link across the Isthmus of Panama, and of Chile's determination to introduce steam ship services through the Strait of Magellan, might have considered it appropriate not to place all his eggs in one basket.

PSNC, in any case, had decided to extend the operational area of its activities from Panama to any port in the Republic of Chile, but no further south than Chiloé, despite the Chilean constitutions of 1823, 1828 and 1833 declaring that her territory extended from the Andes to the Pacific and her southern boundary reaching to Cape Horn. The indigenous Araucanians had, up to that time, successfully resisted any Chilean settlement or exploration in the extreme southern regions of the country, and the Chilean Government had been too occupied with internal matters to concern itself with penetrating and developing that bleak territory around and beyond the Strait of Magellan.[86]

It was not until 1843, that the Chilean schooner *Ancud* sailed south from Chiloé Island and established a settlement called Bulnes at Puerto del Hambre (Port Famine), which in 1849, was relocated to Punta Arenas on the eastern shore of the peninsula. Argentina, being preoccupied with internal conflicts, did not officially protest against the settlements until December 15, 1847. The Chilean Government, in the intervening period, planned to establish regular steamship services through the Strait:

"...In order to broaden and strengthen the advantages that Chile has by virtue of its geographical position, making it the emporium of European commerce on the Pacific" [87]

However, a treaty of friendship, commerce and navigation between the Argentine Confederation and Chile was signed at Santiago on August 30, 1856,[88] whereby both countries accepted that the boundaries of their respective territories were to be construed as those existing at the time of the surrender of Spanish control in 1810.[89] Questions that had arisen on the frontiers since that year were:

"...To be postponed and discussed peacefully and amicably without recourse to violent measures and in the event of complete agreement not being reached, to submit the decision to the arbitration of a friendly nation."

Agreeing the dividing lines as those believed to be in existence at the time of their separation from Spanish colonial control, did not allow for a permanent

Ploughing The South Sea

solution and recurrent conflicts were to emerge. No Spaniards had actually inhabited the disputed territory and neither the Viceroys of Buenos Aires nor the Captains-General of Chile had been concerned about them.[90]

PSNC, initially, had only intended to operate two steamships in the Pacific, its first objective being to establish regular services between the ports of Callao and Valparaíso and any intermediary ports that might, from time to time, be included in the ships' itineraries. Although, in practice, the steamships were restricted to sailing between Callao and Valparaíso, the control centres were empowered to occasionally direct them to make for Panama, if required, or to ports north of Callao and south of Valparaíso. In reality, all that was being done by introducing the steamships to this region was to provide an alternative but far superior form of sea transport on already well established sailing ship routes; the main advantages being speed and punctuality.

Wheelwright had intended to arrive on the West Coast before the coal-carrying *Portsea*, and immediately after the launch of PSNC's two pioneering vessels. Having boarded the paddle steamship *Great Western* at Bristol, he arrived at New York on May 4, 1840. His dream of a merchant steamship line was then on the point of realization, but it would develop and progress further than he had, perhaps, ever dreamed. For the next 60 years, this small pioneering steamship company, virtually having the field to itself, would come to dominate all passenger and general cargo trade on the WCSA, making major impacts on both world shipping, South American and Australian trade in particular.

ss. *Chile* **with ss** *Peru* **in right background**

The two steamships were "*christened*" the *Chile* and the *Peru*. The latter was launched at Limehouse, London, on April 18, 1840, the Hon. Peter Scarlett acting as "*Godfather*". Three days later, the *Chile* was launched from the same shipyard. Both vessels, constructed of timber, bottomed with copper and with gross weight of 700 tons each, were designed to carry 200 tons of cargo, 40 passengers and 60 crewmembers. At a reception to commemorate the departure of the two pioneering vessels for South America, the Hon. P.C.Scarlett underlined the advantages the shipping line would bring to the WCSA:

"...It will take only hours to travel from Valparaíso to Coquimbo, whereas it currently takes days [by sailing ship]. Moreover, owing to the calm ocean waters along the entire coast, from Chile up to Mexico, and the abundant coal resources, these conditions and facilities are so very suited to steamships that the success of the Company's operations will certainly have a highly influential outcome [on the Pacific Coast nations], both from a political and social point of view."

Scarlett, notably, confirmed the existence of abundant coal resources; it is, therefore, surprising that lack of such supplies would eventually cause severe operational problems for PSNC. The *Chile* left Falmouth on June 27 and the *Peru* on July 4, 1840. Although not quite capturing the same kind of public attention as the maiden voyage of Cunard's steamship, the 1154 tons *Britannia*, the departure of the two pioneering paddle steamships, while not being the first merchant steamships in the Pacific, did open a new chapter in the history of steam navigation.

Steamships such as the *Great Western*, *Royal William* and the *Liverpool*, had demonstrated in 1838 the practicability of North Atlantic steamship crossings. Before the emergence of Cunard Line, the only vessels regularly sailing on the North Atlantic crossing were North American. British ships, typically, did not operate to fixed schedules, generally remaining berthed in port until sufficient cargo had accumulated to make a voyage worthwhile. This practice often meant vessels stayed docked for weeks.

The British Government of the day, being extremely concerned at this unproductive custom, and fearful that the United States would continue to dominate the North Atlantic, invited tenders for the operation of a monthly steamship service between North America and Liverpool. Samuel Cunard, having convinced the Government of the worthiness of his proposed scheme, actively sought investors to provide the necessary financial capital. In a sideswipe at those who had blindly rushed to invest into, often suspect, railroad companies' shares, Cunard proclaimed to prospective backers:

"We have no tunnels to drive, no cuttings to make, no roadbeds to prepare. We need only build ships and start them to work."

This type of oratory greatly impressed investors, and in 1839, sufficient capital was raised to launch the British and North American Steam Packet Company, principally, to carry the Royal Mail to the USA and Canada. Cunard Line evolved from the latter enterprise, clearly established on a very sound financial footing. It had, importantly, been supported by British Government grants for the conveyance of mail

By comparison with the favourable circumstances prevailing at Cunard, the nascent Pacific Steam Navigation Company had insufficient resources. According to Arthur C. Wardle, marine historian, the latter received no financial support whatsoever from any quarter,[91] but, nevertheless, managed to construct and deliver two ships, small in comparison with Cunard's *Britannia*, safe and sound to a coast 10,000 miles from England. To accomplish this, the two steamers had to sail through the most southerly and threatening seas of the Atlantic and the Magellan Strait, negotiating far greater hazards than the worst conditions ever likely to be encountered on a North Atlantic crossing.

Wardle claimed that the Pacific Steam Navigation Company received no direct financial support from the British Government other than a subsequent annual US 36,000 dollars fee (about £20,000) for carrying mail between Valparaiso and Panama. Chilean Ministry of Finance records[92] reveal that in October 1853, PSNC was granted an annual subsidy of 60,000 pesos, equal then to about US 21600 dollars (about £12,000). Although a usefully large sum at that time, it was not a huge amount in view of the risks involved, and problems of identifying and then exploiting coal resources on the West Coast; the enterprise was more speculative than any attempted by other shipping lines of the period.

Because of the demand for regular and rapid passenger services on the WCSA, it was hardly surprising that both vessels, eventually, fully justified the hopes and aspirations of PSNC stockholders. Despite its initially weak structure, this steamship company was destined to influence the entire future of the world's merchant marine, even national navies, and the ambitions of the young West Coast South American nations. One obstacle that Cunard never had to confront was that constant inertia generated within the Civil Services of these Pacific Coast states. It was a trait inherited from the very restrictive and corruptive influences of former Spanish colonial administrations and, not least, born of the strong and lengthy relationship between the Catholic Church and State. Edwin Williamson commented in his History of Latin America[93]:

"No other issue gave rise to greater disputes between liberals and conservatives than that of the role of the Church in the life of the independent nations. For liberals, the matter was clear-cut; the Church should be entirely separate from the state so that all citizens might enjoy equality before the law irrespective of race, status and creed. The enormous wealth of the Church in land, property and capital from tithes[94] and donations was regarded by liberals as a massive obstacle to the formation of a modern free-market economy. Church control of schools and universities prevented the state from disseminating the rational, scientific and utilitarian education, which liberals believed to be necessary for progress".

The Catholic Church, during the 19th Century, vigorously defending itself against onslaughts from liberal republicanism, had done all it could to prevent attacks on its wealth, influence and exclusion from affairs of state. The controlling conservative élites, mostly the Spanish-descended Creole[95] land-owning element, sided with the Church hierarchy in those bitter struggles. The Church was, therefore, identified by the majority of the landless and indigenous population as being linked with the corrupt Spanish colonial past, and perceived to be acting against their general interest by its opposition to most forms of modern development. It was to be a losing battle for the Church but one, which caused Wheelwright some major headaches and difficulties in his efforts to obtain support and concessions for his steamship service.

Wheelwright's efforts to overcome resistance amongst administrators and supporters of the Catholic Church appear to have had a more bitter and lasting affect than was probably realized. They certainly influenced the content of his last Will and Testament proved in November 1873, whereby it provided for the setting-up of an Educational Trust to assist deserving Protestant young men of Newburyport to obtain a scientific education, remarking that: [96]

"...It was better for young men generally to begin well equipped both in scientific training and in solid character. His experience in South America had given him an unfavourable impression of that country. They were such men as Spain had elevated to that office from the illiterate and degraded masses. They were out of sympathy with the real welfare of the people, and enemies to true elevation. Had the Roman Church there been what it is in Massachusetts, he would have undoubtedly never have restricted his benefaction to young men of the Protestant faith. It was with a view only to avoid any handicapping of its influences that led him to introduce that clause".[97]

Juan Bautista Albérdi, in his biography of William Wheelwright,[98] provided a vivid example of the disorganization that arose when "*progress*" collided with inertia inherited from the colonial past. The concept "*time is money*" was, he claimed, never properly understood by the South American. He related the example of telegrams taking one minute to cover a thousand leagues, (one league equals 3 miles approximately), might require 10 days to be delivered from the post office to its final destination, a distance of only 10 metres. He further lamented:

"Today in Valparaíso, news can be received from Paris in six or seven hours but from Caldera or Concepción, the State telegraph system is unable to provide a service in less than six or seven days".

Albérdi (1810–1884), a former Argentinean diplomat and political commentator; his open opposition to the Government of that country in 1838, obliged him to seek exile in Chile where he wrote his greatest work in 1852; "*Bases y Punto de Partida Para la Organización Política de la República Argentina*" (Bases and Starting Point for the Organization of the Argentina Republic). In this epic, he detailed the case for strong federal government, which later formed the basis of Argentina's constitution. He was also a member of the Asociación de Mayo, the group that first promoted the modernization of Argentina by espousing European style progressive policies, such as attracting immigration from Europe, international investment to develop railroads, industrialization, and foreign trade. He had based his envisaged grand plan on order, wealth, liberty, and civilization; ideals that Wheelwright readily embraced. In a Memorial address given by the Reverend John Webster Dodge, and delivered at Corliss Memorial Hall, Newburyport on December 8, 1898,[99] Wheelwright was described as having:

"True Yankee grit. He would not give up, even in the presence of seeming impossibilities. He could not be deflected from the honourable line by the corrupt examples of those about him. His character was the root of his success. He would tolerate nothing that was not transparently honest."

On one occasion, Wheelwright after visiting Washington with a view to securing mail contracts between the United States and South America, recalled:

"I found other parties interested[100] and that some political lobbying must be brought to bear besides the payment of a considerable sum if successful. This I set my face against. If any bribery is involved, it shuts the door, as far as I am concerned. Kind Providence has upheld and preserved me".[101]

PSNC's two pioneering steamships duly arrived at Cape Posesión at the tip of South America on September 14, and then proceeded to sail immediately through the Strait of Magellan to reach Puerto Famine (Puerto del Hambre). The *Peru* had taken 44 days on the high seas from Plymouth, England, to gain the latter rendezvous while the *Chile*, had taken 47 days from Falmouth. Both had called-in at Río de Janeiro to take-on coal, of which fuel each steamship, between their departure points and that port, had only consumed 350 tons. Both vessels were reported to be in the same good and sturdy condition to sail as on the day they left England and as having sufficient coal for 12 more days of sailing.

The two steamships continued on their voyage through the Strait, but on reaching the Pacific Ocean a storm whipped-up a heavy sea, taking them out of sight of each other. The extremely bad weather lasted 24 hours, during which, the *Peru's* captain recorded her "*excellent sailing capabilities*", but on one occasion, he feared that the strongly pounding waves would smash through her superstructure. After the storm subsided, the ship having suffered no damage, continued on her way to Talcahuano where she dropped anchor on September 29 to wait for the *Chile* to catch-up. For the next few days, the *Peru's* captain, George Peacock, waited anxiously; he was greatly relieved when, on the seventh day, the *Chile* arrived safely. The storm had carried her along a different route where she encountered even worse weather than the *Peru*, but fortunately, like the latter, had suffered no damage.

Whilst at anchor, locally extracted coal had been loaded. Despite being unfavourably compared with Welsh fuel, Peacock reported that it had burned sufficiently well to maintain effective steam pressure. This not only confirms the coal's suitability and availability, but also suggests in the light of later incidents, that there was either then no large-scale mining of this local source of fuel, or if it was being exploited, then its operation had been co-ordinated insufficiently well to service regular voyages of the two vessels. On October 14, 1840, the two steamers left Talcahuano and within 24 hours arrived within sight of Valparaíso. A small launch came out towards the vessels to hand the *Peru's* captain a chart of the bay, together with a long programme of celebrations to commemorate their arrival. Albérdi reported that at the Port Authority's request, Captain Peacock hove-to at the Bay's entrance and on a given signal, a flotilla of small, flag bedecked craft, sailed out to welcome the two steamships.

The *Peru* immediately hoisted the Chilean flag and fired a 21-guns salute. After negotiating a few turns around the bay together, both ships headed towards the quay passing between the Royal Navy flagship *President* and the Chilean warship *Chile*. The two steamships were given a rapturous ovation. Surrounded by this flotilla of colourfully decorated small craft, many of them carrying musicians, they rounded the end of the quay. The shores of the bay, from one end of the Almendral[102] to the other, were a huge mass of spectators enthusiastically cheering this novel spectacle.

Owing to an unforeseen delay in Rio de Janeiro, the Chilean franchise granted to PSNC had expired just two days before the steamships' arrival on the Pacific coast. The enterprise, with its two vessels safely anchored in Valparaíso, was ready to swing into action and, unsurprisingly, the Chilean Government immediately extended the concession for another 10 years, such was the benefit that it envisaged for the nation. Little time was lost in preparing the steamships for their respective missions; PSNC placed its first advertisement with El Mercurio, Valparaíso's daily newspaper, which appeared on October 21, 1840.

"STEAMSHIPS. Destination Callao, calling at Coquimbo, Caldera, Cobija, Arica, Islay, and Pisco. The very beautiful Packet Steamer PERU, 700 tons gross weight and captained by George Peacock, will set sail for the scheduled destination next Sunday 25th October, at 5pm. Cargo will be accepted for Callao only. First class passenger accommodation can be reserved for any of the above listed ports. Any person wishing to make reservations, please contact Messrs. Naylor, Boardman and Company or Lyon Y Santa María. N.B. The above ship will leave Callao, returning to this port on the 15th November next."

The Peru left Valparaíso as advertised, laden with general cargo and a full complement of 40 passengers for Callao. Thus was the inauguration of PSNC's coastwise service, an operation that continued without interruption for over 140 years, except for a three months' lay-up of the two vessels in the early months of their history due to coal shortages. This company's Pacific coastal run was, in 1840, the longest steam-ship route in the world.

5.   Growing Pains   1845- 1849

Wheelwright awaited the arrival in Callao of the *Peru*, the first merchant steamship from England, which had left Valparaíso under the command of George Peacock. Meanwhile, the Peruvian Government, according to Albérdi, complying with a request from Wheelwright, had ordered all its Provincial Governors to survey their respective territories for coal. This not only indicated the degree of his concern at his inability to locate sufficient sources of this fuel, but also demonstrates the high reaches of Wheelwright's influence.

The Lima newspapers had already given extensive coverage of the steamship's anticipated arrival; people from all walks of life whenever an opportunity presented itself, would discuss the benefits that PSNC's operations would create. Consequently, enormous interest was generated at the *Peru's* historic and imminent appearance in Callao. Wheelwright, at this time, was preoccupied with the problem of securing essential coal supplies to maintain continuity of the service inaugurated by the *Peru's* arrival. The question that needs addressing is why Wheelwright had not ensured that sufficient coal supplies were stockpiled from Chilean sources before implementing his planned steamship line. His biographer, Juan Bautista Albérdi, confirmed the existence of coal resources on the WCSA, and Captain Peacock reported that the *Peru* and *Chile* had taken-on locally produced coal of satisfactory quality at Talcahuano in southern Chile.

Given Wheelwright's later actions in securing the lease of a coalmine in the latter area, he must be considered to have badly mismanaged the operation by not making provision to create coal stocks before the start of the steamships' service. The reason he had sought the Peruvian Government's assistance in the search for this valuable fuel arose from information received that a rich coal seam had been discovered on the island of San Lorenzo off Callao; an immediate survey of the entire island, however, proved fruitless.

On November 4, 1840, the *Peru* dropped anchor in the bay of Callao, after an eight days' run from Valparaíso. A gun salute welcomed the vessel as she moored at the dockside to disembark her passengers. Crowds of people wanting to visit the ship had been so numerous that the times the vessel was open to the public were restricted to two days. On November 7, Peruvian President General Gamarra was officially welcomed aboard together with his entourage and members of the Diplomatic Corps.

A measure of the importance that Peru attached to the steamship service was demonstrated by her President's previously expressed intention to visit the ship, invited or not. A public relations disaster was averted when the Company's agents, forewarned of the visit, pre-empted the action by extending an official invitation to the President together with ministers and various other dignitaries, to formally inspect the vessel. Lima's daily newspaper, El Comercio, recorded that the Presidential procession arrived at 12.30 pm amidst cannon salvoes fired from the Plaza del Callao in concert with the ship's own two cannons; a group of musicians, specially engaged for this event, played throughout this presidential inspection.

The guests were reported to have visited the sumptuous passenger accommodation and to have made a detailed inspection of the engine room "*with its awe-inspiring machinery*", and were seen to be very excited when the ship's engines stirred, lurching the vessel forward as it set off on a short trip around the bay to the sound of further gun salutes. Crowds lined the dockside; people packed the balconies and climbed onto the many flat-topped roofs to gain a better view of the ship's manoeuvres in the bay as she headed out towards the isle of San Lorenzo.

The report in El Comercio de Lima, described the proceedings in extremely fine detail; one hundred and two guests had sat down to a splendid banquet laid out in the *Peru's* main salon. Toast upon toast was proposed, the PSNC's virtues being repeatedly extolled. William Wheelwright and George Peacock were singled-out for special praise and interminable discussions dwelt on the Company's prospects and the benefits that would accrue to the Peruvian nation from its steam ship services. The newspaper confirmed that crowds of spectators had travelled to the dockside on foot, and by any available means of transport; buses and carriages were packed; not a seat on them could be had as they headed towards the port. From eleven in the morning to five in the afternoon, there had been a constant stream of visitors, with never less than 200 persons on board at any one time.

Throughout Callao, the main topic of conservation continued to linger on the steamship *Peru* and the Pacific Steam Navigation Company. News that it was to locate its South American control centre there generated even greater interest. The newspaper also expressed the hope, shared by many in Callao and Lima, that the proposed railway connecting the port and the capital be subjected to the same vigorous application displayed by the PSNC Directors. If that was possible, it remarked, then Lima could quickly establish itself as an important link with the rest of world.

The proposed Callao-Lima Railway had been a controversial issue for some time. In May 1826, a request had been submitted to the Peruvian Government for permission to construct a railway between the capital and the port. Tenders had been invited but eighteen months had passed before these offers were whittled down to three prospective contractors. Despite the Government's relaxation of contractual conditions, the scheme did not progress. The War of Independence prevented any movement in the project. Even when it had ended, no funds were forthcoming because Liberator San Martin, together with his relentless minister Monteagudo and then Bolivar, had emptied the State coffers during the struggle.

In 1847, William Wheelwright even attempted to advance the railroad using his own construction methods, but was unable to meet the deposit demanded as a guarantee of good faith to commit to the project; he had already financially compromised himself with the construction of the Caldera-Copiapó Railway in Chile.[103] Finally, in March 1848, Pedro Gonzales de Candamo and Manuel Vicente Oyague were granted the concession and the railway was completed in 1849. This was the second railway service in all of South America, the first being laid down earlier in that year in British Guiana. Several hundred convicts had carried-out much of the grading work for the Lima-Callao railroad, but local opposition to the building of the line had caused considerable delays until the Government clamped down on those trying to hinder the Engineers.

Captain Peacock, prior to leaving Valparaíso on the *Peru's* inaugural voyage to Callao, had instructed the *Chile* to leave on November 15 and to head for the Peruvian main port. The ship had sufficient coal on board to make the voyage north and the return trip to Valparaíso. The following extract from Peacock's Logbook, describing the *Peru's* first voyage out of Callao, provides useful insights into passenger/cargo levels and the tensions evident in port bureaucracy. The *Peru* was constructed with passenger accommodation for 40 persons; numbers in excess of this must have travelled as "*deck passengers*":

SUNDAY 15th NOVEMBER. 1840. We received one hundred and sixteen passengers on board. The ship's cannon was fired signalling the weighing of the anchor. At five o'clock in the evening, we set sail and by six o'clock, had already passed El Boquerón, reaching a speed of 9 knots in a following sea.
MONDAY 16th. At quarter past eight in the morning, we arrived at Pisco. The Port Captain boarded and fresh stores were brought on board. Twenty-seven passengers and seventy items of baggage were also embarked. These had been ferried to the ship by launch. At 10 o'clock in the morning, we departed for Islay.
WEDNESDAY 18th. Entered the port of Islay at 9 o'clock in the morning. Forty-one passengers disembarked and we unloaded one hundred and seventy items of general cargo and baggage. Six passengers boarded and at quarter past eleven, we continued on our way to Ilo where we arrived at 6 o'clock in the evening. Here we set down eleven passengers and thirty loads of baggage using one of our own boats. At 8 o'clock, we continued on our way to Arica. [104]
THURSDAY 19th. At daybreak, we sighted the Arica headland and entered port at seven-thirty. Nine passengers disembarked and we discharged thirty-four items of baggage. Eight new passengers came aboard and we took on twenty-five pieces of baggage. At eleven minutes past one, we set sail for Iquique[105]
FRIDAY 20th. At three in the morning, we reached the outskirts of Iquique. We sounded the cannon and fired a rocket. These signals were answered by the setting alight of a bonfire on shore. We landed one passenger only and one thousand two hundred assorted small items of cargo. At half past five, we continued towards Cobija.[106] At one in the afternoon,

we sighted the steamship *CHILE's* smoke plume and at three o'clock, we were able to communicate with each other by small boat.

SATURDAY 21st. At twelve thirty in the morning, we shut down the engines to ensure our daylight arrival at the port of Cobija; a storm appeared imminent. Nevertheless, we saw a light, which we supposed, emanated from the port and entered it at a quarter past six. Six passengers disembarked; we welcomed another nine on board and loaded two hundred and seventy items of cargo. The Governor of this region, and leading associates, visited the ship. At twenty-five to three in the afternoon, we continued on our way to Caldera, [the Chilean port serving Copiapó].

MONDAY 23rd. The night was dark and very foggy, delaying our entry into the port until a quarter past six in the morning. We waited a good while before a small boat came out from the shore. Finally, the Port Captain arrived but instantly placed the ship under guard, forbidding any communication with the shore, even refusing permission for passengers to land. Only those destined for Valparaíso were allowed to come on board.

Eventually, but only after a great deal of difficulty, two passengers, scheduled to disembark here for Copiapó, were allowed to go ashore. We realized that we were now running short of coal. Luckily, the Captain of the HM Royal Naval vessel *FRANCES* kindly supplied us with some. Unfortunately, Chilean Customs withheld consent to transfer the fuel. Accordingly, we felt obliged, because of the coal shortage, to take the most direct route to Valparaíso and in the process, omit the ports of Huasco and Coquimbo from our schedule. We took a further 16 passengers on board and at twenty minutes past ten, left Caldera sailing through the narrowest channel of the Baja Grande with heavy seas coming from the south west.

WEDNESDAY 25th. Very strong southerly wind with heavy seas off the bow. These unfavourable conditions hindered our progress. At half past nine in the morning, we rounded Pichidangui Point in heavy seas as the vessel strained to make way. At six o'clock in the evening, we finally reached Valparaíso, the voyage having taken 10 days."

From 1839 to 1841, Chile's Government was concerned that General Santa Cruz, then exiled in Ecuador, might successfully regain power in Bolivia and restore her union with Peru. Chile perceived that her best defence against such action was to ensure that strong and stable government operated separately and independently in both the former confederated countries. Crisis was the normal state of affairs in Peru and Bolivia after the collapse of the Confederation, but Peruvian President General Agustín Gamarra, remaining wedded to a political union of the two nations, worked unceasingly to bring this about, notwithstanding his own earlier participation in Chile's Expedition of Restoration. Consequently, Chilean concerns at Gamarra's intrigues would have been sufficient to make the authorities of the Chilean port of Caldera extremely nervous and suspicious of passengers disembarking from Peru. This might, therefore, have accounted for Peacock's vessel being delayed by the Port Captain.

On returning to Valparaíso, Wheelwright was pleased to learn that the *Portsea* had already arrived from England with 600 tons of coal but was soon disheartened to discover that it was useless. Not only had it been unable to raise sufficient

Growing Pains 1845- 1849

steam pressure, but it had also seriously damaged the steamships' boilers. When the *Chile* arrived on December 15, her Captain confirmed that steam could only be maintained with the greatest of difficulty due to the coal's inferior quality and also reporting that his boilers and engines were in poor condition as a result. Fortunately, another small vessel had arrived from England with a cargo of high-grade coal. The *Chile*, having been supplied with this, was instructed to depart for Callao, as scheduled, and await further instructions on arrival.

PSNC at one stage, looked as though it would collapse from the affects of coal shortages. The two ships were, in fact, laid-up for three months. The economics were clear; if coal could be produced in South America, the operation of the steamships was practically guaranteed, but Wheelwright must have surely realized that if the cost of transporting fuel from England could not be avoided, operating costs would be considerably higher. It makes the queries relating to the Chilean coal mining inactivity all the more intriguing.

In his after-dinner speech following the *Peru's* mini trip up and down the Thames to celebrate her launching, Lord Scarlett asserted that there were plentiful coal resources in Chile. Darwin on his surveys of southern Chile had also confirmed such an abundance, but believed that its quality was substantially inferior to that mined in Great Britain. Daniel S. Grisnold who, in trying to launch a Chilean coastwise steam operation in 1821, had supported his case to Bernado O'Higgins by claims that coal could be obtained from the province of Concepción in southern Chile.

Juan Bautista Albérdi had also stated[107] that there were plentiful natural coal resources all along the West Coast, specifically citing Panama, Guayaquil, Callao[108] and, above all, the south of Chile. He admitted that its quality was unknown; nobody, he remarked, had any experience of using it for the simple reason that in tropical climates, wood and vegetation, being in abundant supply for domestic use, had precluded the need for this fuel. He explained that the latter had never been used for industrial purposes on the West Coast due to the restrictive and suffocating influences of the former Spanish administration. Spain had feared that the creation of industry in her colonies would eventually lead to competition against her own homeland manufacturers and had not encouraged such development.

At the beginning of the 19th Century, railroads, gas works and street lighting had not then been introduced to the West Coast and until the arrival of steamships, nobody in that region had had any use for this undeveloped coal resource. According to Albérdi, Wheelwright was its great discoverer and developer, yet on October 20, 1841, Wheelwright wrote:

"Lack of coal was the first real obstacle facing the Company when our two vessels arrived in the Pacific. After such a brilliant start to our enterprise, it was painful to see those two beautiful ships laying at anchor and inoperative for nearly three months. I eventually went directly to the South of Chile and was fortunate to secure good quality coal at a very low price. The coalmine had never been previously worked and what coal that had been produced was surface material and poor quality. I have not the slightest doubt that we will find coal just as good as that produced in England..Southern Chile contains unlimited quantities of coal".

This statement by Wheelwright confirms his earlier neglect in either not undertaking to develop the coal resources in southern Chile, or by not ensuring that proper contractual arrangements had been concluded with the mines' private owners before the two steamships reached Chile.

Coal shortages were quite common among contemporary and pioneering shipping companies for many years. In 1849, the North American Pacific Mail Steamship Company's steamship *California*, on her first voyage from Panama to San Francisco, was reported to have consumed all her coal supplies well before reaching port. Spars, bunks, transoms, cabins ornaments and a variety of other items had had to be collected and used to fire the boilers. This strategy was found to be insufficient for the steamer to reach Monterey, but the crew, fortunately, discovered that approximately a hundred sacks of coal had unknowingly been stowed along the keel as ballast. This was just enough to take the vessel into port. She lay there for five days while her crew and some passengers worked ashore for five dollars a day to cut timber to fuel the remainder of the ship's voyage to San Francisco.[109]

When the *California* did eventually reach her destination, there was still no coal available, resulting in a further delay of some weeks. On her return voyage to Panama, having again exhausted all her coal supplies, she was once more reduced to burning spars, bulkheads, berths and boats at a replacement cost of approximately $US 4000 (£2200 approximately) in order to reach the Island of Taboga in the Bay of Panama.[110] Another of the Pacific Mail Steamship Company's vessels, the *Oregon*, had left San Francisco with only seventy tons of coal on board, but when all her coal was consumed, she continued her voyage under canvas.

Steamships of the mid 19th Century were nearly always rigged for sail; steam engines then being considered merely auxiliary units. When the *California* had remained at length in San Francisco due to lack of coal, William H Aspinwall, President of the Pacific Mail Steamship Company complained to Alfred Robinson, his San Francisco agent, that:

"[The *California* would] have been better to put to sea under canvas...or else all the spars and rigging carried by these [steam] vessels had better be removed for, if not to be counted on in an emergency like this, it is useless to be encumbered with them when under steam.[111]

It is surprising that since both PSNC steamships were also rigged for sail, why Wheelwright did not attempt to use the latter to operate at least some form of limited service. He was, like Peacock, an expert navigator and had proved his mastery of sail by the earlier and very successful operation of a sailing packet service out of Valparaíso, earning himself widespread respect in the process. Even when deprived of coal for his steamships, he had resorted to sail by using his own resources to purchase the wooden schooner *Lord Abinger*,[112] 120 tons gross weight, to head to Talcahuano in the south of Chile in search of that fuel. In assessing whether it was feasible to "*sail*" the two ships, it is accepted that he would have had to balance the fact that, given the light winds on the West Coast of South America, such voyages to Callao from Valparaiso could have taken around thirty days.[113]

Eventually arriving at Talcahuano on January 15, he contracted a local mine owner to begin coal production under new working practices, thus securing supplies to allow the resumption of the long delayed steamship services. According to the newly advertised schedules for the two vessels, one was required to leave Callao for the South on April 15, 1841, and the other to sail northwards from Valparaíso on the same date; this was to have been the pattern for future sailings. Describing his coal mining success in a letter from Talcahuano on September 11, 1842 to the National Institute of Washington, of which he was a member, he wrote:

"As Chief Superintendent of the Pacific Steam Navigation Company, I have been obliged to work mines in this region for about 18 months now to ensure coal supplies for its steamships. I chose El Morro mine in Talcahuano as being the one likely to be the most satisfactory; coal mined here has been used very successfully in our ships for the last 18 months and up to today, we have produced 4000 tons. This coal is not as strong as the English variety. It burns strongly, produces a lot of clinker, is light textured but does not stick to the fire bars."

This letter indicates that Wheelwright had not started mining operations until March 1841; the Peru had dropped anchor in Callao on November 4th, 1840 approximately three months earlier. Why Wheelwright had not acted before March 1841 to commence mining operations in the Talcahuano district or elsewhere, has still not been established. He was well aware that Southern Chile had plentiful coal deposits; he had actually discovered some resources well before launching his steamship enterprise.

Chile's Admiral Cochrane had also informed him that navy vessels in the Pacific were already using this fuel. It surely would have been a simple task to ascertain the source of their supplies. In fact, Wheelwright, according to Albérdi, had, even before PSNC's formation, demonstrated to Chilean statesmen how to produce coke from their own coal deposits. Allegations by this company's London Directors of Wheelwright's mis-management of the organization of coal supplies do appear to have had some foundation. Nevertheless, on March 24, 1841, Wheelwright left Talcahuano aboard the *Peru* and returned to Valparaíso to purchase a small hulk for storing coal. Having instructed Peacock to sail to Callao from Valparaíso on April 15, he booked passage on a sailing ship also headed for the Peruvian port. Arriving on April 4, he received the disconcerting news that the Company's agents, Messrs Templeman, Bergmann & Co., had already ordered the *Chile* to return to Valparaíso, contrary to his instructions.

Understandably, this state of affairs caused a great deal of consternation, especially as he had already informed prospective shippers and agents in other scheduled ports of call, that the two vessels would leave their respective departure points simultaneously on April 15. In other words, Wheelwright's already widely advertised voyage timetables had, overnight, become a complete shambles. In trying to re-schedule, one of the *Chile's* intended sailings had to be sacrificed, causing great difficulties for shippers and evoking strong criticism from all along the West Coast, especially after the long period the two vessels had been out of commission due to coal shortages.

On returning to Lima, Wheelwright suffered another setback, and one that had caused an angry public outcry. PSNC's agents, Templeman Bergmann & Co., had refused to accept passenger reservations on the *Chile* for the voyage to the then Peruvian port of Arica, made on behalf of President Gamarra and his retinue. Permission had been withheld despite the fact that the voyage to the latter port would have only taken a few days without greatly affecting the advertised timetable. Moreover, the vessel's arrival there, with the President on board, would have generated a great deal of favourable publicity for PSNC.

No reason was forthcoming for Templeman Bergmann's refusal of passage to Gamarra. They may have been wary of losing the agency given the furore over the despatch of the *Chile* contrary to Wheelwright's instructions, and accordingly, may have felt obliged to adhere strictly to the published itineraries. On the other hand, and in view of Gamarra's threatened invasion of Bolivia, the resentment of the Creoles in southern Peru and Chile's opposition to her confederation with the latter, the agents might have been persuaded that his proposed voyage to the then Peruvian port of Arica was subversive. They might, therefore, have interpreted the Company's regulations far too rigidly, or even succumbed to pressure from those who held this view. Gamarra eventually invaded Bolivia in November 1841, but was killed in the battle of Ingavi by Bolivian General Ballivián.

Having being denied passage on PSNC's flagship, the President of Peru angrily departed for Islay on a sailing ship from Callao. On hearing this, Wheelwright immediately set off on the steamship *Peru* in pursuit of the Government party to try to repair his enterprise's increasingly damaged reputation. On arrival in Islay, he sought out the President to express his deepest sympathy and regret for what had happened, explaining that that while PSNC was always willing to assist any West Coast American nation, in any way possible, it could only provide such help if it conformed to its strict code of neutrality. That Wheelwright should mention this latter issue suggests that there may have been some political pressure applied on the agents, but the company's neutrality was to be sorely tested, if not completely abandoned, during the later War of the Pacific.

Another disturbing incident again required all Wheelwrights' attention; the Peruvian Government, seeing the need to quell an insurrection in the southern part of the country, had asked Messrs. Templeman, Bergmann & Co. to instruct the *Chile* not to call at the port of Islay. The company's agents promised to comply, but were induced to withdraw their assurances and the vessel proceeded to that port where it was unfortunately detained. This episode caused considerable resentment within the Peruvian Government, raising tension between the latter and PSNC even further. Wheelwright, once again, having to call upon all his renowned diplomatic skills to restore normal relations commented:

"It is now clear that if steamship navigation is ever to be successful here, it must be at the cost of overcoming innumerable difficulties. Whenever I am faced with obstacles at every turn, I almost regret having being so successful".

Even more difficulties awaited the overburdened Chief Superintendent. Having removed Captain Glover from the command of the *Chile* for breaching his orders, he appointed a new Captain[114] and instructed him in the proper navigational procedures for that ship. PSNC's regulations had clearly stipulated that the Marine Superintendent on the West Coast had jurisdiction over personnel; Captain Glover had deferred to the Company agent's instructions instead of those of Wheelwright. The latter's action in ending Glover's command was subsequently endorsed by the London Board of Directors.

On June 15, 1841, after re-compiling the schedules for the two vessels, Wheelwright received the disastrous news that the *Chile* had struck a reef about 35 miles north of Valparaíso; she had just managed to reach port but had been almost on the point of sinking. This was a serious setback; the nearest port where suitable major repairs could have been undertaken was Guayaquil, 2500 miles to the north. Having been assured by Peacock that temporary repairs could be undertaken, sufficient for her to sail to Guayaquil, Wheelwright loaded the schooner *Lord Abinger* with coal for discharge at the latter port to supply the *Chile* when she arrived. He then set off for Valparaíso to inspect the crippled vessel. This incident was a bitter blow; half of his company's schedules was again in ruins and it highlighted the shortcomings of Valparaíso as a port in not possessing major ship repair facilities; certainly, it prompted a re-evaluation of his management strategy.

Ploughing The South Sea

Fortunately, Peacock saved the situation by effecting repairs in the open bay. Having removed the *Chile's* engines, storing them on a pontoon, he was able to confirm that the main damage had been taken on the bow. Ordering a watertight bulkhead to be constructed within the affected section of the vessel, he set about the dangerous task of careening the vessel to starboard to expose the damaged port section above the waterline. Once this had been accomplished, he arranged for temporary repairs to be made to the damaged hull and on completion, re-installed the engines and other machinery. The *Chile* eventually left Valparaíso on September 21, 1841, arriving at Guayaquil 17 days later. Once there, a much-relieved Wheelwright supervised the required permanent repairs.

Shortly after his emergency patching-up of the *Chile*, Peacock, justifiably proud of his achievement, sent a letter to the Editor of the Nautical Magazine in which he described, in fine detail, the procedures used, and the equipment he had assembled to enable the vessel to be listed in the open bay of Valparaíso. The remainder of Peacock's letter is revealing in that it not only indicates the extent of the public demand for the service provided by the two vessels, but also outlines proposals to expand it.

René De La Pedraja commented in his "*Oil and Coffee*"[115] that the PSNC service was not profitable at this time. While it is true that the Company's final account for its first year as a trading concern showed an overall loss, this was mostly attributed to the lengthy periods the two vessels had been laid-up due to coal shortages, the time the *Chile* was out of action for the emergency repairs in Valparaíso and her subsequent overhaul in Guayaquil. De La Pedraja's claims appear to be based on Wheelwright's own calculations of losses made at the time of his spat with his London based Directors' attempts to remove him from his post. In order to bolster his case of the Board's negligence, he had included the cost of the vessels' construction and other capital costs, setting them against income generated, thus grossly exaggerating the deficit. In later standard accounting practices, such capital expenses would have been depreciated over a period of years with proportional annual sums being charged against gross profit. Not to acknowledge these facts misrepresents the popularity and viability of the West Coast steamship service when it was actually operational.

It is clear from previously mentioned log book entries maintained by Peacock and references to earnings from particular voyages in the following extract of his letter, that not only was there evident demand for the steamship service but each normally completed voyage was also hugely profitable on its own account:

"It will please you to learn that the Company continues to flourish. From the *Chile's* last voyage, we received almost 18,000 dollars (£10,000) in a month, leaving us profit in hand of £2,000 (US 3,600 dollars). I think we will do even better but we will need more and bigger ships. The Company is one of the safest investments available and in spite of

Growing Pains 1845- 1849

experiencing a thousand difficulties; people can see progress and have greater confidence in these steamships. The West Coast of South America is ideal for these vessels. A trial run to Panama is to be undertaken; our proposed operation is to extend the service presently provided by these two vessels, which will have to operate between Guayaquil and Talcahuano until two extra ships are acquired.

The coalmine that I am working is producing good results. We have already gone through some thousands of yards of galleries and have almost extracted four thousand tons of coal; this has more than exceeded our expectations and is even more appreciated considering that its cost to us is no more than three dollars a ton.

I have never attempted this type of work before, but as I lived for some years in Sunderland, I found that the little knowledge of mining I did acquire there has been very useful. Nevertheless, we still had to train the workers how to work the coalface, given that they had never been in a mine before. I left one of the ship's stokers in charge of mining operations with instructions on how to proceed. He is an intelligent enough man and we are making good progress. I am in the course of laying a railway line from the mine entrance along the wharf I am currently constructing, thus avoiding the very expensive cost of hauling coal by oxen drawn carts. Since the *Peru* left England, it has sailed more than 50,000 miles and earned in a period of 14 months, including the trip out here, a total of 120,000 dollars (£67,000 approximately), an excellent start. The increase in earnings for the last three months has been extraordinary." [116]

Six years later, Peacock received a cheque for £200 from the Company's insurers for his actions in saving the *Chile* from total loss. The benefit to the Company was very much greater, given the long and unproductive delay that would have arisen during the wait for a replacement vessel.

Just as fortuitous, perhaps, rather than resulting from any informed decision by the Directors, was their action in ordering wooden hulled ships instead of the iron version recommended by Wheelwright. No information is available on the method that would have been used by Wilson shipbuilders of Liverpool if Wheelwright's contract with the latter had been honoured. It is assumed that, had this firm been allowed to complete that contract subsequently overturned by the London Directorate, then the *Chile* and *Peru* would, in 1840, have been constructed of iron plate, a relatively new technology at that time, and which metal was considered quite brittle.

In refusing to construct their vessels of this material, the London Board, apart from exercising caution, might have been influenced by contemporary British Admiralty attitudes. Despite available evidence to the contrary, the Admiralty, remaining wedded to its established and proven policy of wooden hulls, saw no reason at the time to depart from this practice. In support of its contentions, it had let it be known that, in its view, iron-hulled vessels would sink, would not be as durable as wooden ships, and would be difficult to repair. It did, however, correctly forecast that iron hulls would strongly interfere with compass accuracy; this latter disadvantage was not completely overcome until the early 1850s when

Ploughing The South Sea

the distorting affects of iron ship environments on compasses were remedied by positioning magnets in appropriate positions to counter local attractions acting upon them.

If the *Chile* had been constructed of iron plate, and taking into account the 10-11 knots speed at which she struck the reef, a far more extensive area of the vessel's port side might have been damaged than was actually sustained by her wooden hull. Moreover, facilities for major ship repairs on the WCSA were practically non-existent, except at distant Guayaquil in Ecuador. It is supposed that Peacock would have concluded that emergency repairs to an iron-hulled vessel in Valparaíso would have been impossible to undertake. This hypothesis is largely supported by the state of Chile's shipbuilding industry as late as 1852. In that year, despite her Government's moves to assist the national shipbuilding industry, for example, by exempting from import duty all relevant strategic materials,[117] 170 vessels of all types had been launched in that country producing a total of 2,312 tons. This may seem a respectable figure, but it averages only 13.6 tons per vessel, and only three of the 170 craft exceeded 150 tons. The assorted ships comprised small wooden fishing boats, sloops, and wooden launches.[118]

Apart from working with wood as the main, if not the only hull material, it is apparent that the technology and expertise to undertake extensive repairs to iron-hulled vessels did not exist even twelve years after the *Chile's* accident. The question of whether more attention should have been paid much earlier to establishing repair, fuelling and provisioning facilities on the West Coast, would later form the basis of accusations and counter claims between Wheelwright and the London Board of Directors.

When the *Chile* had completed major repairs at Guayaquil, she sailed for Callao on December 1, 1841. The two ships then finally resumed their normal monthly services between the latter port and Valparaiso. Thereafter, these merchant paddle steamships completed their scheduled voyages without further mishap until the *Peru* was lost after running aground in 1852. Both vessels had, in any case, been scheduled for withdrawal from service later in that year, the *Chile* being sold to the Chilean Government. Wheelwright boarded the *Chile* in Callao for her trial run to Panama; she departed for the Isthmus "*along with a good number of passengers*". He had wanted Peacock to familiarize himself with the voyage to that port with a view to extending PSNC operations as originally proposed. The steamer arrived in Panama on February 19, 1842 when Wheelwright decided to take the opportunity to cross the Isthmus to the open bay port of Chagres on the Caribbean coast to collect important mail expected from England.

The *Chile* returned to Callao to resume normal operations. Wheelwright found no mail waiting for him on arrival at Chagres but fell ill there and was hospitalised on board HM sailing ship the *Charbydis*. After a month's convalescence, and having set off from Chagres for Panama, he claimed to have crossed the Isthmus in 21 hours, a record at that time. Joining his schooner Lord Abinger, he continued with her on the voyage to undertake a survey of possible coal deposits in the Chiriquí region of Panama. From there, the vessel continued on to Guayaquil. At the latter port, in the light of previous experiences, he arranged for a ship repair yard to be built specifically to serve PSNC ships; soon after, other companies began to make use of this facility, continuing to use it for many years, including Aspinwall's Pacific Mail Steamship Company.

Wheelwright then turned his attention to the provision of similar repair and maintenance facilities at Callao. Having obtained a lease of land from the Peruvian Government, he proceeded to reorganize the PSNC base by creating coal storage facilities, erecting warehouses for the safe keeping of machinery spares, ships' provisions and other related articles. The buildings were to comprise workshops for boiler construction and repairs. Valparaíso also benefited from a review of her repair and storage facilities and Wheelwright, having secured an extension of the lease for the Talcahuano coalmine until 1850, arranged for three Newcastle miners to travel out from England to work it.

Arthur Wardle asserted in his "*El Vapor Conquista El Pacífico*", that never had the PSNC owed so much to one man's energy and personality. The Chilean business community certainly held Wheelwright in the highest regard, a fact confirmed by the many tributes paid to him at a meeting of Commercial Exchange members, held on February 15, 1842, and attended by other influential residents of Valparaíso. It had been convened by the Exchange's Directorate and chaired by the Honourable John Walpole, HBM Chargé d'Affaires in Chile. The French Consul had also been present at the assembly, which unanimously approved the following grandly worded resolutions, compiled with a considerable degree of flattery; a reflection perhaps of the influential circles in which Wheelwright moved:[119]

"Considering that Mr. William Wheelwright, Chief Superintendent of the Pacific Steam Navigation Company, is going to be absent from this country for some time, our business community, along with other leading citizens of this area, intends to express in the most explicit and decisive way possible, their highest regard for the way in which he has promoted such a useful and important enterprise:

1. That this meeting renders a vote of thanks for the business-like manner in which he launched his project, and for the untiring zeal and perseverance with which he overcame almost insuperable odds to establish steamship navigation in the Pacific.

2. That this meeting expresses its admiration of Mr. William Wheelwright for the way he has managed the steamships' operations since their arrival on this coast, especially, for the exemplary conduct demonstrated in his dealings with Governments of Pacific coast nations; conduct based on such wise judgment and fairness, justifiably earning him the very reputation and respect which he originally set out to acquire.

3. That this Assembly is of the opinion that, in view of the frequent political disturbances taking place in some [South American] countries in which thousands of their inhabitants are

compromised in one form or another, it should consider as perfectly proper those measures adopted by Mr. Wheelwright, whereby any passenger presenting a valid passport at the point of departure will be admitted on board the Company's vessels without distinction. Every time these procedures are seen to be operating at different ports, they increasingly win the support of their respective citizens. Attempting to generally exclude certain classes of people or particular persons, will not only prejudice the Company's interests, but will only succeed in alienating them and incurring the wrath of all.

4. That this meeting recommends all shareholders who have not yet appointed agents in England, to give Mr. Wheelwright power of attorney so that he can vote in their interests at any stockholders' meetings there. This meeting has already been convinced by his past record, which bears all the hallmarks of success, and makes it likely that there will be a profitable outcome to the Company's business.

5. That a Commission be appointed comprising four persons, charged with the task of producing a lasting and fitting memorial to Mr. Wheelwright, by having his portrait painted and hung in the Exchange Hall. Furthermore, that he be presented with a gift, worthy of the respect and high regard in which he is held by this meeting, to mark members' appreciation of him, and his actions will, hopefully, encourage others like him to introduce useful and beneficial European inventions into the New World.

6. That this Commission be authorized to use funds so far collected from the present membership and other contributors for this purpose.

7. That the award to be presented to Mr. Wheelwright be suitably inscribed with a description of the reasons for which it was being made."

The afore-mentioned resolution number five conforms with the belief that the élites' objective in eulogising their heroes was mainly to encourage other like-minded European entrepreneurs to relocate to the American sub-continent. Resolution number three clearly implies that PSNC did not operate any official discrimination policy, at least not in Chilean ports, although it indicates that it was practised in another West Coast country. This reference to "*discrimination*" most probably would have referred to "*political*" identification emanating from the tumultuous disorders in Peru rather than racial segregation or racism generally.

However, Jorge Guzmán, a university lecturer, when delivering a talk[120] at Santiago University in 1996 concerning feminine/masculine issues, highlighted two specific literary texts, one of which accused PSNC of practising class, if not racial discrimination. The subject publication dealt with racial issues regarding the Creoles,[121] who were alluded to in the text as "*whites*" and the "*Criollos*"[122] as blacks, i.e. the indigenous population or the landless peasant or labourer. The actual work cited as containing this claim of racial discrimination by PSNC was a novel set in the port of 19th Century Valparaíso, entitled "*En El Viejo Almendral*"[123] and written by Joaquin Edwards Bello. Guzmán claimed that throughout this book, Edwards-Bello's underlying theme concerned the discrimination by the Creoles and their European counterparts, particularly the British and the Germans, of the native "*Criollos*". He wrote:

"The British in [their Chilean based] schools, in business and throughout [Chilean] society, keep themselves apart from the native population. Their dining rooms, their bedrooms, their toilets and so forth, were all carefully kept isolated [from the Criollos]. At school, pupils, although mingling with their teachers, did not associate with indigenous children just as [passengers were wont to do] in Pacific Steam Navigation Company ships, where there were only two classes [of accommodation], English and Criollo."

Such discrimination may have indeed occurred but no proof has yet emerged to confirm the deliberate deployment of such a policy on PSNC ships in Chile. It is supposed that, if a prospective passenger had had the financial means to travel first class, whatever his/her background, then he/she would have been permitted to do so, given that a person's status was then judged, according to Creole standards, on either the extent of his/her property and/or financial wealth. Considering the general economic and social situation prevailing in the 19th century, it was unlikely that individuals from the alleged "*discriminated*" sector would have then possessed sufficient financial means to travel in "*first class accommodation*" style, nor, probably, would their upbringing and background have suited them for it. The only realistic alternative would have required the "*criollos*" to travel as deck passengers.

Dr. Robert Robertson, Surgeon on PSNC's *ss Araucania*, recorded the following entry in his diary for May 1, 1871 [124]. He was aged 24 at the time and had not been at sea for many months, having until then served as a local medical practitioner in Doncaster, England. The attitude he displays in his writing could be taken as that then prevailing among British and European élite classes:

"Left Valparaíso at 6pm with 800 peons [labourers] on board for Callao. The ship is perfectly crowded now and they are a filthy class, I think worse that the very lowest of the Irish."

Dr.Robertson wrote a follow-up entry after the disembarking of passengers at Callao, to the effect that it was found necessary to hose down the decks after the deck passengers had left the ship. Conditions for such passengers appeared not to have changed much over the next 50 years. Wallace G.Carter recalls being transferred at Antofagasta in 1920 from Assistant Purser of the ocean-going *Orca* to fourth Assistant Purser of the *ss Chile (III)* operating on the West Coast. It was normal practice then for PSNC's Pursers to undergo three years' training on the company's vessels plying the WCSA routes. The *Chile* (3225 tons) operated on the Talcahuano to Cristobal service using Valparaíso as her homeport. She had accommodation for 150 first class passengers and approximately 60 on deck. Carter recalled:

"Food for the deck passengers was provided in large pots and bowls placed on the open deck and around which, groups of men, women and children squatted and dipped into at will. It consisted briefly of stewed meat and vegetables or stewed codfish. They ate lots of beans and bread but preferred their own cheap wine to ship's coffee. Hour after hour, they sat on deck with their scanty belongings and wretched chickens tied together by the legs strewn around. Dejected and dirty, they were often too seasick or frightened to properly attend to personal hygiene of which they appeared entirely ignorant or careless of.

One writer states: "*it can be safely said that the majority of the working classes or country people apply water sparingly to their hands and faces only, and never to their bodies, and many of them are utter strangers to its personal application*". Lack of education and the absence of effective sanitary services in the mountain communities and small towns, accounts for much of this deplorable ignorance of the simple rules in cleanliness". [125]

While accusations against PSNC of deliberate racial discrimination may appear unfounded, there was, nevertheless, a clear and general perception in Chile by the majority of the native and landless population, that the Creoles, and their European and North American associates, derived all the benefits of trade and increased economic well being at their expense. PSNC, and other contemporary European and North American enterprises, were clearly identified by the latter underclass as embracing the élite Creole system.

Quite naturally, British entrepreneurs tended to socialize with each other. Executives of leading companies such as PSNC, Gibbs y Cia, Banco de A. Edwards and the then English published newspaper, El Mercurio de Valparaíso, occupied luxurious residences in salubrious and picturesque locations on the hillsides overlooking the port and known as Cerro Alegre, or at other much sought-after locations at nearby Viña del Mar. Socializing often meant frequenting the English Country Club at Santiago and the Valparaíso Sporting Club, which were also associated with and visited by PSNC executives. There was nothing untoward about this, but from the perspective of the non-Creoles class, such establishments stood-out as brightly burning beacons denoting the differences between the "*haves*" and the "*have-nots*".

The most sacred word in the élites' vocabulary was "*progress*" which modern scholars now take to mean "*modernization*". The ruling Creole class had always wanted to adopt rather than adapt the latest concepts, modes, inventions, fashion and living styles from Europe and the United States. Their concept of "*progress*" was to persuade their respective nations to mimic. as closely as possible, the European and North American models. Of course, the Creoles believed that the entire nation would benefit from such changes, but they tended to confuse "*nation*" with the well being of their own élite class, generally ignoring the plight of the indigenous poor and uneducated. The understandable perception emerging from within the majority native sector on comparing their situation with that of the ruling élite was that their own country was truly ruled by the Creoles solely for the Creoles. In Chile, for example, between 1820 and 1860, about 80% of the population had worked in the countryside as "*inquilinos*", that is as tenant labourers or tied peasants.

In the 1850s, there were about 1000 haciendas or large estates, of which about 200 were exceptionally extensive, comprising about 75% of all that nation's arable land. Agricultural producers had prospered during this period, particularly during the gold rushes in Australia and California when Chile was the only effective wheat producer on the West Coast. Accordingly, the land-owning Creole's prosperity increased, but the growth in their wealth did little to improve the lot of the peasant class. The Creoles were not encouraged, nor did they aspire to modernize their traditional agricultural practices; the emergence of new farming equipment was spurned or ignored, prompting some newspapers to denounce the landowners "*for their habits of idleness and unthinking routine*".

Most of the business community owned land in Chile, the larger its extent the greater the status of the owner. Unfortunately, this class of property was generally not actively productive. As long as their wealth continued to accumulate, and was not threatened, the agricultural Creole class was disinclined to change its ways. The great ambition of the élite land owner in Chile was to acquire capital wealth, not generate it by productively applying efficient use of capital; any significant riches accrued would enable them to relocate to the capital Santiago to live and tour in style, specifically to Europe to undertake the Grand Tour, especially as the steamship facilitated such travel.

The élite Creoles, generally, displayed no thought or concern for the majority poor. After the West Coast republics had achieved independence, titles of nobility had been abolished, although older South American families still harboured pretensions of grandeur. Persons without such venerable ancestry were accepted into the upper class merely because of the fortunes they brought from marriages of convenience. The élite's lifestyles were centred on fashion; in Santiago, a taste for all things French; novels and historical works were often serialized in the capital's newspapers. Valparaíso, on the other hand, was more attuned to the English élites' way of life.

The core of Edwards-Bello's complaints against the Chilean Creole sector was the laissez-faire attitude of the latter with regard to the underprivileged class. This had provoked one of Santiago's newspapers to remark, in 1859, that the reason the nation's poorer elements barely attracted the attention of Society, derived from the fact that nobody was actually perceived to have died of hunger, and that caring for the people was generally lacking. Few members of the upper class were interested in the poor, a notable exception being the business house of Balfour Williams in Valparaíso. Wallis Hunt in his "*Heirs of Great Adventure: The History of Balfour Williamson and Company*" records:

"Their [the partners of Balfour Williams Co.] aims in business had been clearly stated. If they made money, it was not to be used for their own aggrandizement, but for religious and secular education and for the amelioration of poverty and suffering. In South America, they foresaw great opportunities for doing good. Their profits, if they made any, would not be wasted."

It is accepted that Wheelwright had donated to churches and schools in Callao, but these seem to have benefited PSNC employees and their children at that company's extensive ship repair facility. Care must also be taken to identify which sector the donations were directed; Balfour William's charity may not have extended to the South American indigenous population. Moreover, *"Poor"* in 18th and 19th Century Britain actually meant *"not owning land or other property"*, although there were extreme examples of landless individuals, e.g. owners of travelling theatres or circuses who were sometime monetarily quite wealthy. Similar treatment and definition of *"poor"* applied by the British to their landless citizens, and the related components of some of the harsher and more callous English Land Enclosure Acts, would most certainly have been exported to the WCSA during the *"Enlightenment"* era.

There existed, during this period, various European-originated philosophies, often at odds with each other, and which in their own convoluted way, sought to suppress any possibility of the poorer classes becoming financially independent. In the immediate post independent years of the new republics, the liberals had, at first, striven to strengthen their nation through egalitarianism, but as the century progressed, they became increasingly pessimistic about the potential and ability of the majority of the landless population to make positive contributions to the new republic.

In very simple terms, there were two identifiable schools of thought. The first group wanted to adopt a policy of *"Social Darwinism"*, that is from the start, the ruling class would be obliged to admit that the South American masses were, inherently, racially inferior; the proper way to deal with them, it was commonly believed:

"Was to stop pampering them in a spirit of paternalism and let them die out in unrestricted struggles with the fitter elements of society." [126]

This view was complemented by the belief that immigration from the European advanced countries should be encouraged so that the goal of national economic growth could be achieved. The previously mentioned newspaper criticism of the élite landowners seems to suggest that most of the latter belonged to the *"Social Darwinism"* set. The second group comprised *paternalistic positivists* who, in postulating their brand of charity, always emphasized that the need to maintain harmony and social order took priority over economic progress [127]:

"This group realized that national development based upon [a policy] of awakening the competitive instincts of the masses would bring about the collapse of traditional society [i.e. one controlled by the élite class]. The aim was to prevent such a collapse by inducing the masses to accept their place in a pattern of existence characterized by dependence [i.e. on the élites]".

In other words, the privileged classes, the paternalistic positivists, should provide the masses with those non-material rewards that would afford the "*criollos*" spiritual contentment within their lowly environment and poor economic status; the masses should, at the same time, be taught to know their place in society. Later in the 19th century, education was provided for the children of these "*lower classes*", but their teachers were appointed from amongst the élite and, accordingly, were accused by liberals of attempting to imbue their pupils from the onset with the belief that they were dependent on and inferior to the ruling class.

It is evident from the praise and congratulations extended to Wheelwright by the Valparaíso business sector, that the latter was adopting, unconsciously perhaps, those progressive ideas for wealth creation identified as successful in the European and North American economies. Business communities, generally, in Latin America then principally comprised mine owners, bankers and élite land and property holders, either European or of European descent who, because of their skills, contacts, powers, adaptability, intelligence, birth, and/or wealth, exercised an unusual degree of authority. Such individuals controlled Governmental institutions, as well as commerce, banking, agriculture, and the arts.[128]

These men, Wheelwright included, represented the minority of the population; they were entrepreneurs in the strictest sense, they were capitalists; their sole purpose was to make money, not to provide for the well being of the majority poor whose existence they were wont to ignore. That some benefits gradually filtered down to the indigenous populations was probably true, but these would have been only fortunate by-products of profit-seeking enterprises gaining from cheaply available indigenous labour, and the abundant but non-renewable mineral resources of South America.

It is accepted that the young South American nations raised much needed revenue from taxes on such exports as copper, guano and nitrates, but these were often used to fund further infrastructure improvements to facilitate the European and North American operations that originally generated that income. In Peru, such earnings were used to repay huge foreign debts, but much was wasted on military expenditure. The new republics had welcomed new railroads, highways, gas, electricity, and water works in the national interest, but again, they were all primarily undertaken with an eye to profit, and one that was eventually repatriated out of the country to the accumulating detriment of the latter.

Wheelwright, described as the "*George Stephenson*"[129] of South America, had convinced many other influential people on the southern part of the continent, of the necessity of providing railroads for the development of their nations. The following are the words spoken at the inauguration of his Caldera-Copiapó railroad project:

"Its object is the regeneration of the provinces, which will be attained by giving to the population, spread over the ocean of this land, the merchandise of the world in exchange for the products of the soil; in unbosoming the rich treasures of mineral wealth so long hopelessly buried; and above all, in disseminating light, knowledge, education and refinement among the masses, and teaching them the value of peace and order, respect for the laws and institutions of government" [130]

He had started this project only after consultation with the President of Chile and business interests in that area; the scheme's objective was simply to harness the resources of the copper and nitrate mines in the inland regions and to facilitate their access to Pacific Steam Navigation Company ships:

"The copper had been brought down to the harbour for shipment on the backs of mules- the old hard slow way familiar to that latitude. With the same energy and tact he addressed himself to the removal of the gigantic obstacles in the way, secured the necessary government concession, and formed a company with eight hundred thousand dollars capital..."[131]

Whether PSNC, together with other European enterprises, operated in an atmosphere of widespread prejudice against Edwards-Bello's "*Criollos*" is true or not, the perception of the indigenous masses was that the English Company was clearly and extensively part of the privileged class. It was evident from the introduction of voting procedures based on European models to disenfranchise the indigenous and non-Creole population, that such discrimination could have only served to exacerbate the latter's bitter claims that the whole system of government was established exclusively for the Creole class. The latter, according to Bradford E.Burns in his "*Interpretive History of Latin America*", represented less than five per cent of the total population that had remained spiritually linked to Iberia, culturally dependent on France and economically subservient to Great Britain.

The Enlightenment or the European way, as recommended by the intellectuals in Buenos Aires during Wheelwright's brief stay there, had clearly spread to Latin America generally, although such thinking was probably already predominant in Chile and Peru, given the large number of British and other European émigrés then resident there. The majority of the South American population, as in Europe, had no say in the government of their countries, a situation inevitably leading to conflicts and revolutions that would long dog the sub-continent. In 19th Century England, only property holders were allowed to vote. This injustice was similarly introduced to Chile as part of the Europeanization process, but with added literary requirements that the Creoles knew were not only mostly absent in the indigenous majority, but were also clearly aware that the *"Criollos"'* means of acquiring them were unattainable, thus ensuring that the élite land and property owners would continue to remain in power. There may have been some truth in Edwards-Bello's assertions of specific racial discrimination by PSNC. if it had actually occurred, there then it would have arisen more probably in Peru.

In resolution three passed by the Assembly of the Valparaíso business community, the reference made to *"political disturbances taking place in other countries"* would have, undoubtedly, referred to Peru and Bolivia. Given that the only other countries visited by PSNC ships at the time of the business community meeting, the reference is clear. There were certainly racial tensions amongst the different elements of the various castes comprising the then Peruvian population. These consisted of the Spanish race, the Indian, the Negro, the Oriental and the mixed-blood (mestizo) or *"cholo"*. Each group or caste had its own supporters and detractors, and each felt superior to the other four. According to the Spanish Authorities' own calculations in 1796, there was, in the Vice-Royalty of Peru, a total population of 1,076,122 of which 135,755 were Creoles or *"peninsulares"* (those originating from the Iberian peninsular), 608,894 Indians, 244,436 mestizos, 41,256 free Negroes and 40,336 slaves.[132]

Typical of the support for the group comprising Spanish colonial peninsulares and Creoles was Bartolomé Herrera's appraisal in 1846, the leading clerical spokesman of 19th century Peruvian conservatism, mostly the traditional élite class:

"The work which the Spaniards accomplished...was the greatest work which the Almighty has accomplished through the hands of men. To conquer nature, to master inward fears, to dominate far-off places through the formidable power of the intrepid heart, to accomplish all of this as the trophy of victory a new section of the world with Christianity, to introduce the fire of life into millions of moribund souls, to broaden by millions of leagues the sphere of human intelligence, was an accomplishment of unparalleled splendour"[133]

Among this élite-class, an anti-Spanish element had blamed Peru's backwardness on the Spanish colonial institutions. This liberalizing sector took the view that the nation could never progress until:

"every lingering and pernicious effect of colonial customs and values had been totally eliminated from the intellectual, spiritual, economic, political and social milieu" [134]

Typical of this mode of thought was Alejandro O. Deustua, who finding little to admire in the latter class, contended that the colonial regime in the Americas was "*an organism sick by nature*" because:

"In religion it favoured fanaticism, in Government a sorry mixture of weakness on the one hand and on the other, a total lack of limits on the exercise of civil power; in politics, intrigue and anonymous accusations; in the moral order the perversion of customs, and in economics, the most absurd practices of exclusivism, monopoly and ruinous privilege." [135]

It is evident from these two different schools of thought that the main areas of disagreement between the supporters, the Creole conservatives, and the detractors, the Creole liberals, during a period when the Executive was administered by the Spanish ancien regime, centred upon the latter's affects on politics, economic policies, administration, religion and culture. The supporters clearly wished to retain the old ways under which they had accrued substantial benefits, but by 1820, not all liberal intellectuals had recommended a complete break with Spain; some saw themselves as successful entrepreneurs in an economy that would expand vastly from more tolerant legislation and Spanish investment. These liberals were still wedded to the old colonial practices, but the economic success that they desired was intended for themselves rather than for the good of the entire nation.

Considerable destruction had occurred during the four years' struggle leading to independence in 1824. The port of Callao had been reduced to ruins and many coastal and highland agricultural estates laid waste by foraging armies. The climate of opinion after the attainment of independence was such as to cause many *peninsulares* to leave Peru, in the process, mostly removing a trained bureaucratic corps. Peru had entered a period of commercial isolation in the closing years of Spanish imperial rule, which continued until the late 1840s.

When political stability was established for a short period, Peru began to enjoy significant commercial interchange with foreign countries, especially England and France. In the South of the country around Arequipa, liberals were opposed not only to any attempts by Gamarra to draw Peru into confederation with Bolivia, but also to the increasingly centralist style of a Government controlled by the Lima élite. Gamarra contributed to the country's stability by the framing of a constitution in 1839, which lasted for twelve years. It was compiled by politically motivated and business oriented men rather than by theoreticians, and was the first to stress the need for order over liberty. It called for a strong Executive with a six-years' term of office. The powers of the bicameral Congress were somewhat curtailed in comparison with earlier forms of government; the Council of State, comprising fifteen men chosen by Congress, either from within or without its membership, was expanded and besides being authorised to bestow extraordinary powers upon the President, they acted as his advisory body.

The Peruvian Constitution then stipulated that only literate male citizens of 25 years or more could vote, although illiterate Indians and mestizos were permitted to continue to register their vote until 1844; eligible deputies and senators had to be 30 years and 40 years old respectively. The main affect of this Constitution was a strongly featured centralism benefiting Lima, but disastrous to the economic and political life of the rest of the country.[136] Accordingly, the seeds were ripe for discrimination, not only between different classes and those who espoused different political beliefs, but also between those regions far-removed from the controlling bureaucracy in Lima.

Given the honours bestowed on Wheelwright by a grateful Chilean Creole nation, and the sympathy, respect and co-operation extended to him by the Peruvian ruling class, there is a tendency to view his accomplishments and the growth of the Pacific Steam Navigation Company through rose-colored spectacles. Similar assessments have no doubt been made of other European business houses in South America that project heavily romanticized histories of their operations. It should not be forgotten that Wheelwright, like contemporary entrepreneurs in South America, was a renowned businessman, operating in a European-charged commercial atmosphere, mostly to the benefit of the privileged class. The main danger in interpreting 19th century events on the WCSA from current perspectives is that contemporary assessments of Wheelwright, the PSNC and other business houses, were compiled and delivered by a very self-sympathetic élite class and have, unfortunately, since been generally accepted as representative of the West Coast population.

There were, of course, stark contrasts among those profit-seeking businessmen. On the one hand, there was the exemplary Balfour Williamson business house. At the other extreme were opportunists such as "*Colonel*"[137] Thomas North, dubbed the "*Nitrate King*". He had one purpose only throughout his entrepreneurial career in Chile, and that was to make enough money to live-out the rest of his life in Britain in magnificent style but, more importantly, was his insatiable desire to be accorded the status and recognition he felt was owed to him. After his death in 1896, much of his financial activities and enterprises were considered fraudulent and respected contemporary biographers distanced themselves from his life-history.

It is tempting to place the entrepreneurial Wheelwright towards the end of the scale occupied by the philanthropic Balfour Williams family. On the other hand, Wheelwright had formed his Pacific Steam Navigation Company with the clear objective of making money by developing further trade along the West Coast and to integrate it with trans-Andean railroad links to the West Atlantic ports and Pacific sea routes to Australia. One must conclude, therefore, that his project was never pursued simply for the general good of the people in South America.

As evidence of Wheelwright's success in maintaining influential contacts within West Coast Governments and business communities, is the widely related anecdote that General Salaverry considered Wheelwright such a close friend, that after the General's death, he left all his personal papers and correspondence to him. Wheelwright had been widely respected for conducting business fairly and justly, but he was judged on the élites' accepted terms of moral conduct. He was reported to have abhorred the corruption that was endemic throughout Latin America, and was said to have been a very moral and religious person. Although profiting by his works such as gas, water distribution networks and brick making factory, opportunities benefiting the non-élite population were created in the employment process, albeit not deliberately so. The members of the Commercial Exchange eventually made their presentation to Wheelwright, and his oil portrait was hung in the office of the Exchange's Director in Valparaíso. When that establishment was eventually dissolved, it was presented to the Chilean Naval Club where it remains.

The year 1840 had been a volatile period for PSNC; its London Directorate had had to deal with extensive financial problems. The Board's minutes of those early years frequently referred to loans negotiated by the Company to meet shortfalls in emergency expenditure, and to compensate for revenue losses resulting from the upheavals in the normal steamship service. These arose firstly, following the *Chile's* accident and secondly, due to the laying up of the two vessels for three months because of coal shortages.

Wheelwright returned to London in May 1842 to attend a special Board meeting. After briefing the Directors on the situation on the West Coast, he was described by Wardle as being surprised to hear some of them speak disapprovingly of his decisions and actions. At the following meeting, they censured him for ignoring the Company's Rules and Regulations and accused him of certain administrative irregularities. Wheelwright, not reputed for quitting so easily, responded by sending a letter to the Board emphasizing his strict adherence to the terms of his contract. In the letter, ever business-like, he took the opportunity to ask that shares to the value of £3500 (US 6,300 dollars) at a purchase price of £40 (US 72 dollars) each totally paid up, be transferred to him as previously contracted.

The Board's first report detailed PSNC's business affairs on the West Coast. Having announced that the *Peru* and the *Chile* had proved their worth as efficient steamships, the Directors then recorded their appreciation of the Pacific Republics for promptly renewing the decrees granted to the Company before the steamships' arrival on the West Coast. They also referred to the problems of supplying the Pacific coast ports with coal and then focused on the Company's coal mine in

Growing Pains 1845-1849

Talcahuano, reporting that 5000 tons of that fuel had already been produced with prospects of even greater yields. The cost of mining the coal was 15 shillings 3 pence per ton (76p approximately or $US 1.37).

The Directors confirmed that with regular operation of their steamship service, the voyage from Callao to Talcahuano and return was then taking 40 days, with calls being made at Pisco, Islay, Arica, Iquique, Cobija, Caldera, Huasco, Coquimbo, and Valparaíso. The Board emphasized that in every port visited, there had been demand for cargo space and passenger berths. On that basis, they indicated that each vessel could undertake nine voyages a year. The Board, however, was obliged to highlight PSNC's dire financial situation. Subscribed capital was found to be insufficient to cover outgoings, and after a loan of £20,000 (US 36,000 dollars) had been taken into account, total debt had reached £111,630 (US 201,000 dollars). Estimated revenue from operating Company vessels until the end of the financial period projected a loss of £13,695 (US 24,600 dollars).

Nevertheless, the Directors asserted that the Company's prospects were still good, explaining that most of its past expenditure had been non-recurring. The Directors also explained their decision to build a third vessel; announcing that estimated costs of construction would be £20,000 (US 36,000 dollars), but reasoning that the new vessel would enable the *Chile* and the *Peru* to undergo overhauls and, thereafter, would be assigned to the Panama-Guayaquil service. At the Board's meeting on October 5, 1842, for reasons unknown at the time, they resolved to remove Wheelwright from the post of Chief Superintendent. On November 6, a minute confirmed the appointment of a committee to investigate the Company's management and operations on the West Coast "*in view of the departure of Mr. Wheelwright*".

The precise events leading to this dispute are unknown; according to Wardle, much of the Company's records relating to this period were reported lost, but it is significant that Albérdi's biography of Wheelwright omitted any reference to his spat with the PSNC's Board of Directors. The absence of even a token defence of Wheelwright might suggest that there was some foundation in the Board's criticism. Historian Arthur Wardle, on the other hand, claimed that Wheelwright vigorously defended himself by providing detailed accounts of events and his actions on the West Coast during the years 1840/2. In an extensive document circulated to all stockholders, he had firmly criticized the Directors' attitude and described in some detail, the Company's organization on the Pacific Coast. Submitting his own reasons as to why the Board had incurred large amounts of unnecessary expenditure, he cited their rejection of Thomas Wilson's offer to construct two iron-hulled vessels at a cost of £6000 (US 10,800 dollars) less than the price paid for the two wooden steamships.

Ploughing The South Sea

Having itemized the Company's losses, Wheelwright proceeded to highlight the Directors' inexperience when purchasing coal and produced a statement showing that £23,000 (US42,000 dollars) had been wasted in these circumstances. He suggested that a further £6000 (US10,800 dollars) should have been added to this figure, due to the decision to build the *Chile* and *Peru* in London rather than Liverpool. Wheelwright also urged stockholders to take into account the £9,000 (US 16,200 dollars) revenue "*lost*" due to the *Chile's* accident, although this clearly was not the fault of the Directors. He calculated that a total sum of £38,000 (US 68,400 dollars) had been wasted, representing about half of the Company's share capital.[138]

Significantly, there is a complete absence in Wheelwright's combative report of any references to the matter of coal mining in Chile and his lack of foresight in this respect. It was clear that there had been ill feeling between Wheelwright and the Directors for some time; difficulties had arisen before the Company's Annual General meeting, when he remarked in a letter to the Board that the treatment meted to him on his return to England was so unacceptable as to make him stay away from the Company's offices. He attached importance to the fact that he had refrained from publicly making his opinion known until after the Annual General meeting had taken place. The Directors responded by commenting that they had observed his attitude with the utmost distaste and had pointedly asked him if he intended to board the *Great Western*, presumably as the first stage of the return journey to the West Coast. More correspondence was exchanged with Wheelwright receiving a reply to the effect that he was considered "*dismissed and removed from the Agency and Administration of the Pacific Steam Navigation Company*"

Wheelwright concluded his counter attack by asserting that he had always carried out his duties towards shareholders to the best of his ability, only to find that the Directors had now impugned his past accomplishments and character. The complete set of correspondence was circulated to all shareholders and resulted in Wheelwright being reinstated. On December 11, 1844, the second Annual General meeting took place when those Directors opposing Wheelwright were obliged to account for the fact that, from an initial capital base of £93,905 (US 169,000 dollars), a loss of £72,011 (US 129,600 dollars) had been incurred over the first four years of the Company's operations.

A Committee was immediately appointed and charged with investigating the Company's affairs and the Annual General Meeting was deferred until January 15, 1845. At this meeting, the Investigating Committee duly presented its report and the Board of Directors resigned. Lord Abinger (P.C.Scarlett) and George F.Dickson were authorized to recruit a new Directorate. The postponed meeting was delayed until May 6, 1845, when a majority of stockholders proposed that it would be better for the Company to relocate its offices to Liverpool where most of them resided. A vote of thanks was also passed on Wheelwright's behalf for his efforts in negotiations with the Postmaster General for a new mail-carrying contract. He had clearly made a strong and favourable impression, not only on most of the shareholders in England and South America, but also on their respective business communities. For him, this was only the beginning of a great adventure; the time taken-up in spats with the Board had only served to delay the inevitable progress of steam navigation on the West Coast of South America.

6. Political Developments 1845-1848

In August 1845, British Admiralty officers inspected the *Peru* and *Chile* to assess their suitability to operate mail contracts. Unlike other contemporary postal agreements, no public tenders were invited prior to Wheelwright's contract to maintain regular postal services between Valparaíso and Panama with intermediate ports of call at Coquimbo, Huasco, Caldera, Arica, Islay, Pisco, Callao, Huanchaco, Lambayeque, Payta, Guayaquil and Buenaventura. The fee paid to the Liverpool shipping company for providing this service was £20,000 (US36,000 dollars) annually for a period of five years.

Having undertaken to provide monthly services between Valparaíso and Callao, using the *Chile* and the *Peru*, PSNC decided to commission a new paddle steamship, this time with an iron hull, to operate between Callao, Guayaquil and Panama. The new vessel, *Ecuador*, built by Todd & McGregor Company of Glasgow, was launched in October 1845. She set sail for the West Coast on December 10 to join PSNC's small steamship fleet. Arriving in May 1846, she immediately extended the Valparaíso-Callao postal contract provided by the *Peru* and the *Chile* to embrace Panama. Strict adherence to publicized schedules was the backbone to this service, allowing sufficient time for the new steamer to discharge and take-on passengers and freight at Panama, and dovetail with those operations of the Royal Mail Steam Packet Company; the schedules also had to allow for cargo and passengers crossing the Isthmus from Chagres to Panama and vice-versa. Such transits were undertaken under conditions that would appear both unhealthy and extremely risky by today's standards. In 1838, Wheelwright, drawing upon his own experiences, advised:[139]

" It will undoubtedly be helpful for travellers thinking of crossing the Isthmus to know that, on arrival at Chagres, they should immediately hire commonly available canoes, and set forth on the river journey without delay. For single travellers, the smaller version, known as a "*cayuco*" is advisable due to its faster speed. Moreover, passengers can take one trunk and camping bed with them. These usually constitute the normal load carried by mule. For luggage in excess of this, travellers are advised to hire a second cayuco. For family travel, larger canoes are advisable; these can be fitted with canopies made from plantain tree leaves to protect passengers from sun and rain. Fowl, fruit and eggs can be purchased from the innumerable small makeshift shops lining the riverbank.
During periods of drought, beginning in December and ending in June or July, the cayucos take around 18 hours to complete the trip to Gorgona whilst the larger canoes take up to two days. However, during the rainy season and at the onset of the violent and stormy weather, which reaches its height anytime during the period August to October, the time taken can be doubled. The cities of Gorgona and Cruces are situated in magnificent settings, high

up on the banks of the River Chagres. They are both very pleasant communities; their residents kind and friendly, charge the traveller the lowest possible prices for stores. Two pack routes or mule tracks cross Panama, one leading from Gorgona, the other from Cruces. Travelling along the former route takes rather longer, but in the dry season, the ground is firm enough to allow horses to gallop and they can easily cover this journey in six or seven hours.

During the rainy season, however, the track becomes almost impassable from heavy mud. The other route is uneven, stony and at times very steep. This road was, at one time, stoned, but has now fallen into such disrepair that the surface has become dangerous. Nevertheless, the mules are sufficiently sure-footed to overcome this. Because the men in charge of the mules have friends and family in Cruces, they are inclined to persuade travellers to follow the road to Cruces rather than to Gorgona.

The traveller, on arrival at Cruces or Gorgona, should instantly hire the appropriate number of mules. If none can be found, a message sent to Panama will ensure they are provided on the following day. It is always best to send baggage on ahead by some six hours, thus ensuring its arrival in Panama before the traveller, and where it will be kept safely at the Customs House. One can always find good lodgings in Panama. This rather pleasant city is situated on a promontory almost surrounded by the sea. Its residents are also both kind and friendly."

Wheelwright considered that postal costs on the Isthmus before the arrival of steamships were excessive; persons sending mail to more distant destinations had to retain the services of an agent in Panama to pay the ongoing postal costs, otherwise their letters would have been detained there. Security for transporting bullion and merchandise between Chagres and Panama had been good. For centuries, ever since Spain had conquered Central and South America, specie had been conveyed from Peruvian and western Mexican mines across the Isthmus en route to Europe; in all that time, there had only been one reported robbery.[140]

Before the construction of the Panama railroad in 1855, crossing the Isthmus was not as favourable as Wheelwright had described. Whether certain difficulties encountered on this daunting transit were deliberately omitted to avoid deterring potential passengers, or whether he considered them insignificant in his overall assessment, is debatable; many considered them major hazards. It is also interesting to note that Wheelwright claimed in 1838 to have crossed the Isthmus in 21 hours, a record at that time. It is highly unlikely that Wheelwright would have knowingly made improbable or fabricated claims. It is just possible that because he was already well known to local residents, his fame as a businessman, his reputation as former American Consul in Guayaquil and the widespread knowledge of his proposals for a link-up with Royal Mail Steam Packet Company, might have singled him out for particular and favourable attention.

This could have involved making special arrangements, for example, to have mules ready for his onward journey to avoid wasting time haggling over the costs of hire and/or the reservation of canoes for his use. Such instances might simply have been a case of potential traders touting for future business, eager to give Wheelwright the right impression of their services. These actions would have undoubtedly allowed him to proceed more speedily on his journey, and he might have accepted such treatment as either standard practice in the area or capable of becoming so.

When PSNC held its third Annual General meeting in London in December 1845, Wheelwright and William Just were appointed Joint Managing Directors. The latter had been previously employed with the Aberdeen & London Steamship Company and was also to play a truly important role in the development of West Coast merchant shipping. Wheelwright was ordered by the Board of Directors to remain on the West Coast where, "*armed with full powers*", he was to completely re-organize the Company's operating structure. He was specifically instructed to (a) ensure the regularity and punctuality of the mail ships, (b) investigate the possibilities of creating storage facilities at various ports, (c) maintain supplies of between 3000 to 4000 tons of coal at Payta and Coquimbo (d) obtain extensions to the Chilean and Peruvian decrees already granted and (e) obtain from the Ecuadorian and New Granada Governments similar privileges to operate in those countries.[141] Wheelwright was also asked to advise on the conveyance of bullion and valuables across the Isthmus of Panama, bearing in mind that, having already established regular shipments via the *Ecuador*, it had become public knowledge when and where such cargo was being transported. Accordingly, the risk of shipments being stolen had increased.

After the departure of the *Ecuador* from Liverpool, the Editor of the Mining Journal wrote:

"We must now say a few words about the Pacific Steam Navigation Company, first conceived from ideas and plans submitted by Mr. William Wheelwright, the Managing Director, and later brought into existence by Mr. Boardman of Liverpool along with other Directors and shareholders. It now provides regular steamship services out of Valparaiso, the Chilean Republic's great commercial port and serves the entire length of the Pacific Coast up to Panama. We have been informed that due to the Company's revised arrangements, their steamships will adhere to a monthly schedule requiring calls at the following ports: Coquimbo, Huasco, Caldera, Cobija, Arica, Pisco, Callao, Huanchaco, Lambayeque, Payta, Guayaquil, Buenaventura and Panama." [142]

Such was the increase in the volume of PSNC business that a fourth steamship was soon ordered from Rodgers & Co. of Govan, Scotland. She was of iron-hull construction, propelled by paddle wheels and named the *New Granada*. Gross weight 649 tons with 200-horse power engines. Completed in August 1846, she reportedly had the appearance of a schooner. PSNC's expanding operations eventually alerted the Republic of Chile to the vulnerability of her coastline and the need to strengthen her navy. She had acquired extra shoreline by virtue of Bulnes' unopposed military occupation of the southern region, including the all-important Strait of Magellan in 1843, and required to protect her commercial interests in the Atacama Desert. The beneficial affects steamships had brought to the nation by the considerably reduced voyage times between other countries on the West Coast and her own ports located along an extremely lengthy coastline, had revealed that steamship technology also posed dangers from potentially hostile naval action. It was clear that Chile needed to expand and fortify her navy. In 1844, her Minister of War and Navy had also advised the Chilean Congress that the nation's extensive coastline laid her open to attack from the sea.

This scenario prompted objections from within the Congress on the grounds of cost, and especially because there was, at that time, no perceived threat from any other country. However, Chile's Commandant-General of the Navy, exemplifying the nation's tendency to model herself on the great industrial powers, vigorously promoted naval expansion by commenting:

"If you cast a glance over the rest of the world and observe that the two most free and industrious nations are precisely those that possess the greatest naval forces, you would be tempted perhaps to study the intimate relationship between their merchant fleets and the greatness of their people." [143]

Heeding the Commandant-General's advice, the Chilean Congress authorized the addition to the Navy of a 900 tons steamship, and the replacement of two small existing schooners by two sailing ships of 240 tons each.

It was essential for Chile to continue enjoying peace and stability; from 1845 onwards for the next 20 years, she enjoyed rapid economic growth, witnessing an expansion of her silver and copper mining production, and a short-term increase in her wheat and flour trade to meet the demand created by the gold rushes in Australia and California. During this important period, her Government's revenues increased by 75 per cent and foreign trade by approximately 225 percent.[144] In the early 1840s, the Peruvian Government's monopoly of the guano industry had begun to generate significant revenue for the national exchequer, although much was diverted unproductively to military expenditure. Revenue receipts of 4.2 million pesos in 1846 and 1847 had grown to almost 10 million by 1854,[145] the equivalent of £800,000 (US1,440,000 dollars) and £1,916,000 (US3,449,000 dollars) respectively.

Ramón Castilla had also identified the need for a period of internal calm in Peru. Having seized power in 1844, this former caudillo imposed order on the warring Peruvian factions during his Presidency from 1845 to 1851, and again from 1855 to 1862. Throughout this period, he restructured the nation's finances and resumed repayment of outstanding loans to Great Britain, Chile and New

Granada. Educational and military reforms were introduced, a national navy created and importantly, merchant shipping was encouraged to develop.

Chile regarded Peru's increasing wealth and national stability as a potential threat, not only to her influential position in South America, but also to her northern borders. Peru, however, was still embroiled in other international arguments, principally her continuing and bitter conflicts with Brazil over territorial disputes in the Amazon and, to a lesser extent, in struggles and problems in Ecuador; her relationship with New Granada had also deteriorated. Chile, on the other hand, was relatively free of this degree of resource-sapping distraction, although she was still involved in unresolved boundary disputes with Bolivia and Argentina.

The benefits derived from Chile's free trade policy, resulted in a steady increase in Peruvian demand for Chilean goods, and accordingly, the threat of bitter economic war re-igniting between the two nations was substantially reduced, at least for a time. In any case, the possibility of Peru wanting to rekindle former claims was diminished by what was then perceived as a threatened invasion of the WCSA by General Juan José Flores, the former Ecuadorian President then, significantly, exiled in Europe.

Towards the end of 1846, Peru had learnt that Flores, having solicited the support of the Spanish Government, was preparing to re-enter Ecuador to re-assume power. Had he been successful, an Ecuadorian monarchy under a Spanish Prince might have been established.[146] This threat acutely alarmed Peru; she had known that General Andrés Santa Cruz was, at the same time, also exiled in Europe and believed to be conspiring with Flores. More alarmingly, the latter was considered by the West Coast nations to enjoy the wide support of Great Britain.

The idea of any European power gaining a foothold in South America presented a terrifying prospect for Chile, and undoubtedly, for other nations on the sub-continent. Chile perceived that the already delicate balance of power she had struggled for so long to cultivate and preserve could be threatened by a resurrection of the Peru-Bolivia Confederation. Chile saw no alternative but to join with her West Coast neighbours in resisting any potential invasion by Flores. At that time, ill feeling, rivalry and mistrust clearly existed between the Great Powers, which Chile sought to exploit. She accordingly invited France and the United States to oppose Spanish and British actions in supporting Flores' invasion campaign. In addition, she adopted a more enlightened and skilful diplomatic strategy. Given the rapport she enjoyed with British commercial enterprises and banks based in Chile, she solicited their support in influencing their own Government to oppose Flores' threatened incursion into South America.

No doubt, the British business sector in South America was intimidated by the implied adverse reactions that would arise following any refusal to co-operate. The possibility of retaliatory action on the commercial sector was clearly signalled

Political Developments 1845-1848

by the Chilean Government's proposals for a complete halt to trading relations with Spain. The implications of resisting Chile's request would not have been lost on Wheelwright, PSNC and the British business community, particularly as Chile had already and openly advertised her willingness to resist any invasion by force of arms. The Chilean Navy was also reinforced and her Army placed on full alert. Eventually, pressure from the highly influential British business community in South America was such that the British Government was obliged to take steps to thwart Flores' plan. Clearly, Chile and the British commercial sector then needed each other more than ever; their interdependence was one of the most important factors in the development of West Coast trade.

By the end of 1847, there had been a noticeable and general improvement in West Coast commerce, principally because of Chilean and Peruvian Free Trade policies. On February 8, 1848, a Confederation treaty had been signed in Lima, providing for a permanent Congress of "*Plenipotentiaries*" endowed with major peace and security responsibilities.[147] The accord required that all disputes between confederated or member nations would have to be submitted to arbitration by this Congress, which had been empowered to enforce its decisions by the imposition of sanctions.

The formation of this peacekeeping body was motivated by its members' deep longing for international order and stability with all the concomitant trade benefits. Each nation's security was to have been protected by the Congressional requirement to unite the separate military forces of its constituent nations under a single command structure to defend their territorial integrity and independence against foreign aggression. It obliged member nations, by majority vote, to commit this unified force.

Some historians have suggested that had this treaty been in place before 1835, the Peru-Bolivian war might have been prevented. On that basis, one would have thought that the Lima Congress treaty would have been welcomed unreservedly by Chile. However, it became clear that only one clause accorded with her long-standing basic policy. The treaty stipulated that if any attempt was made to unite two or more of the confederated republics, or to detach from one in order to add to another nation, one or more ports, cities or provinces, it would require a prior and express declaration from the other member Governments that such a change was not prejudicial to the interests and security of the Confederation itself.

Chile's assessment of that treaty indicated that its terms would limit national sovereignty and freedom of governmental action. She was also concerned that some clauses were openly hostile to the Great Powers, and regarded the Confederation of republics as being too lightweight to confront the military and economic might of any of the great industrialized nations. Chile, realistically, envisaged that if offensive action was taken against Great Britain, in particular, then she herself might be on the receiving end of ruinous retaliatory economic sanctions. There were also similar objections from other Congress member-states, but as the threat from Flores lessened, the spirit of co-operation subsided and gave way once more to rivalry and competition among the West Coast nations, provoking concern throughout Chile of Peru's increasing military and naval capabilities.

At the end of the Peru-Bolivia war of 1839, Peru's Navy had been virtually non-existent. During the first year of Castillo's Presidency in 1844, it comprised just one frigate, two brigantines, two schooners and a transport vessel. In 1847, a period of modernization enabled the Peruvian Government to raise finance to purchase the war steamship *Rimac*.[148] Chile's Navy, by comparison, had not benefited from any such additions, despite her Government having granted authorization in 1845 to do so, the Chilean Congress failing to provide the necessary funding. The view, in 1847, was that the Flores threat and the Argentinean protests against Chile's occupation of the southern region of the sub-continent, including the Strait of Magellan, were not sufficient reasons for Naval expansion. Nevertheless, the Chilean Congress' identification of Peru's growing military and economic strength led to a decision change, especially as it was again suspected that Chilean nationals, resident in Peru, continued to suffer discrimination. In 1848, a Frenchman, living in Valparaíso, was awarded the contract to construct the first warship to be built on Chilean territory.

Wheelwright returned to Chile in August 1848. His subsequent report to PSNC's Directors reminded them that, in 1845, he had emphasized the importance of introducing a twice-monthly service. He submitted that had the Company then taken his advice and commenced operations in 1840, they would at the time of his report have been in a position to have already introduced *"two or three times the number of ships that we now have"*. Importantly, he also strongly advised the Company to maintain cordial relations with the West Coast nations at all times, commenting:

"Each Government claims that it wishes to ensure the development of its economy under its own national flag. The Peruvian and Chilean Republics will actively encourage investors to do this but unless the company recovers lost ground and succeeds in creating good relationships and understandings with the Governments concerned, it is possible that the current licenses granted under their respective Decrees will not be renewed."

Clearly Wheelwright, having contact with the higher levels of Government in both Chile and Peru, had had their intentions clearly signalled to him; it was, he said, advisable that, following growing opposition within their respective nations to foreign involvement, the company should behave more diplomatically by extending its co-operation. Wheelwright, accordingly, advised the PSNC Board that the only political and acceptable way open to these Governments to deter

Political Developments 1845-1848

competition from abroad, was to satisfy nationalistic demands by using their own resources in concert with the mostly foreign West Coast business sector:

"Rather than providing opportunities and persuading [foreign] competition to set-up in their country, as in our case, they should try to discourage this by introducing their own steamships to maintain rapid and frequent services at moderate charges, and earning in the process, public goodwill and trust. The latter will continue to support us in times of need, by placing themselves between their Governments and ourselves, and by doing so, they will not only protect their own interests but also protect ours. By accepting this policy, we will be seen to behave diplomatically. Such action will also be to our benefit because we could eventually find ourselves in a more advantageous position than we now are, even with all our exclusive rights and privileges. Furthermore, such measures would dispel any accusations of the Company being a monopoly. If the Company has been perceived as being badly managed, then it is our fault alone and not attributable to any policy of those Governments. We are morally obliged, in any case, to do everything in our power to encourage the means of trade and by doing so we will increase our profitability." [149]

Referring to the re-organization of PSNC's operations on the West Coast, Wheelwright highlighted the damaging risks facing the Company in Panama if delays occurred in the arrival of the mail steamships from England. Trying to dovetail operations with the schedules of the Royal Mail Steam Packet Company was difficult. If one of the latter's steamships was delayed by storm or other unforeseen event, the intended PSNC connecting vessel in Panama might have to wait longer than anticipated, resulting in adverse knock-on affects to her schedules. Such an event would have strained the limits of patience of the influential West Coast business community who attached great importance to regularity of service. The same adverse results could also have been generated by PSNC. If one of the company's vessels arrived at Panama behind schedule causing delay for freight shippers and passengers, or to make them miss the Royal Mail connection at Chagres, the ensuing publicity would have been equally unacceptable.

Wheelwright had also indicated in his report that previously acquired coal storage facilities on the West Coast were becoming very expensive and recommended the purchase of replacement storage hulks, the *Portsea*, *Cecilia*, and the *Jaspar*, capable of storing between them a total of 2000 tons. Such was the increase in PSNC's business in Valparaíso, that Wheelwright recommended the internal appointment of a port agent; he complained that he was constantly having to deal with Company business matters, and undertaking work that really needed to be carried out by others, although acknowledging that performing such tasks himself helped to maintain low running costs. He also drew attention to the shortage of stokers and engineers on the West Coast. So desperate was the situation, he explained, that the company had had to employ whomever it could find. The shipyard that he and Captain Peacock had built some years earlier at Guayaquil still provided valuable service for his firm; one was also under construction, at that time, in Valparaíso.

Wheelwright again expressed his considerable concern at the unflattering opinion of PSNC held by some of the West Coast nations. Drawing the Board's attention to the attitude displayed by some of the PSNC Captains, which had contributed to further ill feeling within these Governments, he advised that whilst this situation prevailed, it was unwise to seek a renewal of the steamship licenses; it was a problem, which would rebound on PSNC and other foreign business houses. British arrogance, in particular, probably born out of a sense of superiority as a result of accomplishments achieved in the Industrial Revolution and advances in empire building, was a trait identified particularly by the indigenous West Coast populations and was to last well into the 20th Century. The North American William Grace, whose great business empire was founded from early beginnings in a Callao chandler's store, commented:

"...The English in foreign lands I have never liked; they are in my experience, presumptuous and self opinionated.... I know [business] houses in Peru that were in my time hated as haters of Peru.... if you educate your mind.... to think kindly of the people of the country and to sympathize with them, you are received and treated as a friend" [150]

Developments within PSNC led to an interesting philatelic event in 1847. William Wheelwright was a cousin of Joshua Butters Bacon of the firm Perkins, Bacon & Petch, printers and stamp engravers. On his return to England, Wheelwright informed his cousin that PSNC intended to produce a batch of postal stamps for use on the West Coast. On August 17, he submitted two proposed stamp designs for the Board's consideration. Neither of the two was accepted and the Secretary was instructed to send the printers two alternative layouts depicting the Company's ships. The printers complained at having to engrave a ship in such a small space, explaining that to do so would provide insufficient security against forgery.

Nevertheless, the Directors were adamant that the stamps should depict one of their vessels and accordingly, printing-dies were cast and the stamps printed. 57,280 stamps were dispatched via Royal Mail Line on November 17, 1847 to Alexander Hutchinson, the Company's Agent in Panama. A second batch of the same quantity was sent on January 15, 1848 to the Company Agents in Callao. Larger amounts were subsequently printed but there was little demand for them and many were destroyed in a fire at the printers' workshops. There were two varieties of stamps, a crimson 1 ounce-2 reales, and a blue ½ ounce-1 real. They remained under the control of the Company's Manager on the West Coast until 1851 when the Director General of the Peruvian Post Office, authorized by his Government to introduce postage stamps for a limited trial period in Lima and some other cities, acquired the Company's remaining stocks depicting the *Chile* and *Peru* for this purpose.

The experiment lasted from December 1, 1857 until March 1, 1858 and was so successful that the Peruvian Government issued its own stamps. The Pacific Steam Navigation Company can, consequently, claim to have been the only steamship line to have had its own stamps printed to its own specification and used in a national postal system. Moreover, these stamps were unique in denoting both the weight allowance and the respective charge. As the printers had forecast, some forgeries were made in later years, taken off printings commemorating earlier editions.

The reliability and punctuality of the PSNC steamships on the West Coast had so impressed the Chilean Government that the latter insisted upon the introduction of a fortnightly service between Valparaíso and Callao. Wheelwright must have derived some considerable satisfaction at this development after thirteen years of continual hard work dedicated to the provision of regular steamship services in the Pacific. In order to maintain this success, PSNC had to continue expanding.

An indication of the extent of its operations in fulfilling mail contracts can be drawn from the testimony of its Managing Director William Just in 1849. Having been obliged to appear before a House of Commons Select Committee appointed to review the Government's postal contracts, Just confirmed that the total distance covered by the present British Government contract amounted to 75,216 miles annually. He advised that in order to meet the demands of the West Coast countries, the subject steamships had been obliged to travel a total annual distance of 100,887 miles. He complained that on these figures, the British Government's subsidy barely amounted to 3 shillings and 7½d (approximately 17.5 pence or 32 US cents per mile). Moreover, to conform with the contract, the mail carrying steamships were obliged to install engines with a minimum 150 horsepower. Just revealed:

"At present, there is only one vessel with 150 hp engines, the *ECUADOR*, two with 180 hp engines, the *CHILE* and the *PERU*, and the *NEW GRANADA* with a 220 hp unit. The company has a fifth under construction of 750 tons gross and 265 horsepower engines."

He emphasized that, during the first five years of its existence, PSNC had been unable to obtain a single British Government postal contract and that during this period, the enterprise had suffered losses equivalent to two thirds of its paid-up capital, resulting in the distribution of only two dividends in nine years. The Select Committee heard that PSNC's mail volumes had increased and that when HM Consul in Panama received the Company's mail it was redirected across the Isthmus for onward shipment to Europe. Although warning of the dangers involved in transporting currency and bullion, Just gave assurances that both PSNC and

Ploughing The South Sea

partner Royal Mail Steam Packet Line had transported increasing amounts of this valuable cargo for some years without mishap. For year 1848, he announced that bullion to the value of 2 million US dollars in American gold, more than that carried in 1847, had actually been conveyed across the Isthmus. He also highlighted the ¼ percentage saving in insurance premiums charged for not transporting the same cargo via Cape Horn.

7. Panama and The Railroad 1849-1860

Wheelwright's description of his Isthmian transit is a world apart from the conditions detailed in Robert Tomes' book "*Panama in 1855*", published after the inauguration of the Panama Railroad. It is accepted that Tomes might have been tempted to exaggerate the difficulties present in previous conventional crossings of the Isthmus in order to elicit further support for the new rail enterprise, of which Wheelwright's former competitor Aspinwall was then President. Tomes' account was written on completion of a specially arranged excursion undertaken at the invitation of the Panama Railroad Company and extended to him and sixteen others comprising an assortment of journalists, clergy, lawyers and businessmen. The costs of the voyage to and from Aspinwall (Colón) in Panama, hotel accommodation, wining, dining and excursions had been met entirely by the Railroad Company.

Tomes openly admitted to the liberal and extravagant gratutuities heaped upon him, but claimed that he was alert to the fact that while he and his fellow travellers had been ostensibly invited to celebrate the laying of a memorial stone commemorating the inauguration of the Panama Railroad, he was conscious of the Railroad company's real intentions. His appears to be an honest and, at times, humorous account of the voyage. Highly critical of the Railroad's construction work and the tendency of the trains to de-rail, he was not reluctant to set out the real objective of the arranged excursion:

"The enthusiasm [for the Panama Rail-Road] of the public required to be stimulated, as was clearly proven by the fact that the stock stagnated in Wall Street at the dead level of par, when if justly appreciated, it could not fail to rise to a premium of 50 per cent, at the lowest calculation. Europe too, was either in a state of profound ignorance of its own interest, or in such a complete deadlock at Sebastopol, that it was felt necessary to disperse the financial clouds in that country, and quicken enterprise with an electrical shock from the brisk battery of American energy. The proposal to borrow a million or so, which had been generously tendered to the London bankers, that they might be made sharers with their American brethren in the profits of the great enterprise, was not responded to in the same free spirit with which it had been proffered, and it was determined that reluctant Threadneedle Street should be aroused to a more lively sense of its own interest, as far as Panama Bonds were concerned." [151]

Tomes' following account of the pre-railroad transit does accord with a wealth of contemporary historical data, and is in sharp contrast to Wheelwright's experiences:[152]

"The railroad will be appreciated by the traveler who has once undergone the trials across the Isthmus during the days of the now obsolete mule and canoe. He will recall the long days on the Chagres River and the hard ride over the rough road to Panama. He will think with a shudder how, swinging from the tall sides of the great steamer, tossing miles away in the swell of the open roadstead, which dashes its waves against the steep foundations of the rock-built fort of San Lorenzo, he timidly dropped into the slight canoe, which rose and fell like a bubble on the waves, and was finally cast ashore at the hazard of his life.

He will recollect how, alternately chilled in the cold sea-waves, and broiled in the hot sun, he shuddered with a dread presentiment of Chagres' fever, as he went up the hot beach, and thence into the inhospitable pine-board settlement of Chagres. He will recollect how he shrunk from the gaunt specters of Yankees who haunted the place, and who only reminded him of their humanity by their eager demands for his dollars. He will recollect the struggle with his thronging fellow travelers for the scant boats; and if he had the good luck to secure a footrest in a crowded canoe, he will not forget how eagerly he sprung from the shore infected with pestilence and vice.

He will recollect the three days and nights of his wearisome ascent of the ever-bending river, the never-ceasing monotonous cries of the Negro boatmen, as they toiled along the banks, tugging at the overhanging foliage, startling the chattering monkeys, putting to flight the noisy parrots, and disturbing the sleepy alligators, which slid their huge black slimy bodies from the mud-reefs into the water. With the tedious monotony of his slow progress by day, and no rest at night, in this contracted canoe, shared with coarse adventurers, and no relief in the exorbitantly-paid entertainment at the hovels which stretched their mud-floors, and dispensed their stringy pork, muddy coffee, and wretched brandy by the wayside, for the refreshment of the traveler, he will recollect how spiritedly he took to mule at Cruces, and sped joyfully on until, soon jaded by the hard ride, he at last reached Panama, fatigued and dispirited, where, perhaps, if with powers of endurance equal to every trial, he slept, or if not, tossed restlessly about on his hard cot in the early agonies of fever. The old traveler will recollect all this, and rejoice in the comforts of the Panama Railroad."

Tomes' assessment of the Isthmian transit prior to the introduction of the Railroad may have also been influenced by earlier events in 1848, which although having a worldwide impact, significantly affected the development of shipping on the West Coast South America (WCSA). In January 1848, gold was discovered in abundance in Alta California. The extent of the buried riches in the Sierra Nevada was only rumoured at first, but then news spread rapidly when official notice of its richness and availability was finally confirmed in Washington in September 1848.

Any doubts of the gold's existence were dispelled when US President Polk announced the finds during his annual address to the nation on December 5th. From that moment, excitement and greed swept the nation and beyond; thousands of men were immediately drawn westwards towards California. The main US overland route had been closed down by the winter storms and was not normally accessible until the following April or May. In the minds of many, that would have been too late; fortunes could be lost in the long wait.

Apart from an overland passage, there were two alternative routes to California from the eastern coast of the United States, one round Cape Horn, the other across the Isthmus of Panama. The latter voyage with departures from New York or New Orleans to Chagres on the Caribbean coast of the Isthmus was considered, at the time, to be the quickest way to California. However, the transit was only for those with sufficient funds to obtain passage on one of the regular steamship voyages operating from Panama to San Francisco, and only for those with the strength to undertake the gruelling crossing.

In December 1848, the small steamship *Falcon* anchored just off the entrance to the River Chagres on the Caribbean coast of Panama. It discharged nearly two hundred North Americans armed with an assortment of guns, pistols, rifles, knives, shovels and picks. These were the advance guard of the prospectors, otherwise known as the "*Forty-Niners*", striking-out in a desperate attempt to reach California in the quest for gold. On learning of the numerous gold-strikes in this region, many thousands of North Americans had unhesitatingly changed their normal lives, dropping everything to join the blind rush via the Isthmus.

David Howarth in "*The Golden Isthmus*" confirmed the observations made by Robert Tomes in 1855 regarding the pre-railroad crossing:

"The Chagres was the only route they had heard of.[153] Some of the people in the village at its river mouth possessed canoes, and were besieged by these foreigners bidding against each other for a trip up-river to Las Cruces. The boatmen started by asking what was probably the highest price they could think of---ten dollars a head; but more and more ships came in, and soon they were being offered fifty---far more cash for a few days' work than they had ever earned, or ever needed, in a year. It was a situation that brought out the worst in both races. Yankees shouted, threatened and bullied, argued and fought; Isthmians swindled. They hired canoes to one party and then, when the first had gone to fetch his baggage, hired them to another and disappeared - or, after starting up the river they stopped halfway in the heart of the jungle and demanded double pay.........

...At Las Cruces, the pandemonium was worse. Every day for the first few months of 1849, more and more canoe-loads of strangers appeared round the bends of the river and settled like locusts on the derelict little settlement. All of them had to spend the night there and bargain in the morning for mules to carry themselves and their baggage over the 18 miles of trail to Panama. On busy days the natives managed to charge them twenty dollars to hire a riding mule -- enough to have bought a mule a year before. And after the river trip, they willingly paid a dollar for space to lie down on one of the wooden bunks that ingenious natives fixed up in the disused stables and storehouses.

The last part of the crossing, the mule track, was the worst of it all in the eyes of letters home. One would have supposed that that any American in that era could have ridden a mule without any notable hardship. But what impressed them was not the exotic jungles they were riding through, most of these travellers wrote hair raising stories about in it their diaries, it was the mud and roughness and narrowness of the track, the discomfort of the saddles and the animals' jolting gait."

Peru suffered the emigration of many of her merchant ships to San Francisco where passengers, captains and crews deserted them to join-in the crazed rush for gold. In June 1849, the Peruvian Government even announced the dispatch of a warship to San Francisco:

"....to assist the nation's merchant ships which found themselves unable to sail out of the port because of a shortage of hands".

This had been reported in Valparaiso's newspaper El Mercurio on July 2, 1849, as part of a campaign to, inter alia, urge the Chilean Government to follow Peru's example by ordering the frigate *Chile*, along with sufficient additional crew, to bring back the Chilean merchant ships lying abandoned in San Francisco Bay.[154]

The affects of Californian gold seekers pouring through Chilean ports had been profound. Chile's agricultural and mining interests had reacted almost immediately by grossly inflating selling prices of their produce as a result of the growing and voracious demand for food supplies to take to California. The lure to the newly acquired North American state by thoughts of fortunes in gold had been too powerful for hundreds of Chileans to resist; the exodus soon swelled to thousands.

The remaining Chilean merchant fleet was rapidly diverted from normal coastal trading to the transport of impatient prospectors to San Francisco. On arrival, captains, officers and crews, like the Peruvians, immediately abandoned their vessels to join the crazed ant-like processions to the gold hills. Chilean ship owners, who had let their vessels on charter for the voyage to San Francisco, never imagined the affect the gold craze would have on their captains and crews. Towards the end of 1849, those vessels that had sailed away loaded with stores, wheat and other supplies, became part of a contingent of approximately 300 assorted craft lying abandoned in the graveyard of ships that was San Francisco Bay[155].

Many vessels were used as floating hotels; others were dismantled to provide timber for house and shelter constructions in the port; many were left to rot at anchor and eventually sank; some survived only to be destroyed in the great fire of 1851. The Chilean Government realized that the greater part of the Chilean merchant marine had effectively disappeared. It prompted the Commander General of Chile's Navy, Manuel Blanco Encalada, to write to the Navy Minister drawing attention to the dire conditions being experienced at all Chilean ports due to the shortages of national ships, and recommending the temporary lifting of restrictions on foreign vessels wishing to operate along her coast:

"Our [merchant] marine having being enticed to the Californian coast where ships are detained there with no crews to enable their return [to Chile]. [This situation] has transpired because previous crews have deserted at the first whiff of gold and we now find that our coastal trade has been reduced to almost zero because of the lack of ships. I would, therefore, advise the opening-up of our coastal trade to all foreign vessels for six months, to be extended if necessary, but limiting unrestricted navigation to those ships over 200 tons. By these measures, we will avoid our country's goods not being moved due to the shortage of coastal freighters and we will thus enable the southern provinces to comfortably supply the northern areas and mining districts with food..." [156].

Blanco Encalada's proposals were taken-up by the mining interests of Chile's northern provinces and supported by copper magnate Carlos Lambert who subsequently lobbied Congress for the opening-up of Chile's coastal shipping routes to British flagged vessels.[157] Understandably, the petitions met with resistance from Chilean ship owners and associated interests; letters of support and opposition to the removal of the Chilean flag monopoly from coastwise trade were published extensively in Valparaíso's El Mercurio newspaper. Grain producers and ore smelters in the southern province of Concepción, relying on exports of produce to and import of raw minerals from the northern regions, naturally favoured the northern provinces' demands.[158]

Apart from making strong representations to the Chilean Government to take action to move their static cargoes, the northern and southern provinces' pressure groups had a hidden agenda. The Chilean ship owners' monopoly was able to charge much higher freight rates than would have been the case had foreign ships been allowed to ply for coastal trade; letting the latter operate in Chilean waters was a cheaper and more competitive arrangement.

Congress Deputy Jose Joaquín Vallejo, favouring dissolution of that monopoly by opening coastal trading to foreign ships, commented that the Chilean ship owners' coastwise privileges had brought the nation to the point where neither traders, nor mining and agricultural producers could move their goods from one Chilean port to another except by using Chilean registered vessels. He accused these ship owners of applying their own high freight tariffs, safe in the knowledge that they would be unaffected by the involvement or intervention of foreign ships. He highlighted the long-standing grievance of the northern and southern producers that, because of Chile's existing coastal shipping law (cabotage), the northern and southern business communities had been condemned to pay higher freight rates than should have been the case.

Those supporting the removal of cabotage restrictions shared Vallejo's view that the element representing the excess profit in the freight charges then operating, in effect, amounted to an additional tax benefiting only the ship owners of Valparaiso. Vallejo, no doubt encouraged by the Chilean Government, remarked scornfully that the very ships deemed to constitute the national merchant marine actually comprised decrepit and decaying "*sailers*" that had been sold cheaply to the nation's ship owners by merchant ship companies the world over, after being declared surplus to the latter's requirements. He added, caustically, that the only benefit the nation derived from the coastwise shipping monopoly was the all too familiar sight of flapping sails dangling from ships, almost eaten away by woodworm and only floating on Chilean waters by some miracle of Providence.[159]

Expressions of support for the removal of cabotage restrictions had been extremely useful to the Chilean Government in that they prepared the political ground for its inevitable decision. By reading and hearing such comments, the nation was reminded that, despite the long period over which Chilean ship owners and builders had received Government financial inducements, the Chilean merchant fleet, much of whose ships had been constructed abroad, had continued to operate only on a small scale without showing any signs of expansion. The conclusion the Government hoped would be drawn was that the national policy of cabotage had clearly failed. Inevitably, the coastal trading monopoly was withdrawn on September 1849 for four months, the latter period being extended for a further six months in December 1849.

In 1850, Wheelwright returned to the West Coast principally to seek renewals of the decrees and concessions formerly granted by the subject Governments. Due to the difficulties caused by the deterioration and reduction in Chile's merchant shipping, he arrived at the onset of a political and economic period that had and would remain favourable to Pacific Steam Navigation Company (PSNC) for a considerable number of years. The latter company's Chilean licence had been due to expire on October 15, 1850 but, according to Chilean Ministry of Finance records,[160] it had not been intended to automatically renew its privilege. Four days after the lifting of restrictions on coastal trading by foreign ships, the Government appointed a Commission comprising four Valparaíso businessmen, three of whom were ship owners, and three British residents in Chile, to investigate whether the English company's privileges should be renewed.

On September 8, the Commission's findings, published in El Mercurio, concluded that the monopoly concession enjoyed by PSNC should continue to apply for another four years, provided the company operated a monthly steamship service to Chiloé in the south of Chile. The Commission also advised the Chilean Government to reserve the right to enter into contracts with other enterprises to establish a steam shipping operation through the Strait of Magellan to carry mails to Europe, the United States and the West Indies. The British business community in Valparaíso supported the Commission's recommendations, not out of any loyalty to PSNC or because it was a British firm, but rather because their interest was primarily one of having a service introduced that could eventually establish direct links with Europe. In their opinion, PSNC was then the only available enterprise capable of meeting this requirement.

Two days later, El Mercurio newspaper published a copy of a letter submitted by Wheelwright to the Chilean Government when seeking renewal of the steamship privileges. In this petition, he listed the unfortunate disasters and other mishaps that the company had suffered in the ten years' period of the steamship concession. Wheelwright also claimed the financial climate had been so bad in 1845, that the company's shares, previously trading at around £40 (US72 dollars), had subsequently fallen to £9 (US 16.2 dollars). He asserted that if it had not been for the British Government's financial assistance in the form of an annual mail subsidy of £20,000 (US 36,000 dollars), PSNC might never have been able to continue operating.

There was then, however, a strong body of opinion, which believed that the financial misfortunes cited by Wheelwright should not distract from the main thrust of the issue as to whether or not PSNC's permit should be renewed. The predominant view was that the English company was, at that time, already well entrenched on Chile's sea routes unthreatened by competition[161]. In the same newspaper edition, there appeared a related article outlining the case on behalf of Chile's southern agricultural producers and foundry operators. They proposed that the Chilean Government extend PSNC's privileges, but only in accordance with the Commission's recommendations otherwise, they submitted, the southern areas would never, in the next ten years, be provided with a steamship service.

The main objective of the southern business community was to oblige the Government to provide this monthly steamship service to Chiloé. Deep concern had already been expressed that the southern regions would become isolated from the rest of Chile if the PSNC's privileges were not extended.[162] Governmental consideration of the matter lasted for approximately a year until a final decision was made in January 1851. Those opposing the renewal of the grants had previously campaigned against the removal of restrictions on other foreign ships to undertake coastal trading. Surprisingly, Carlos Lambert, the copper magnate, who, as a leading spokesman of the northern provinces' business communities had supported the removal of cabotage restrictions, opposed extending PSNC's licence. This opposition may have derived from his ownership of the small steamship the *Firefly*. Having applied to the Chilean Government for the right to use her to transport his products to the southern provinces, he had been rejected because his vessel was registered under the British flag. In these circumstances, it would probably have been galling for him to support PSNC's application when his had been refused.

In December 1851, following discussions with the Chilean President and businessmen in the region, Wheelwright promoted the construction of a 50 miles long railway from the Chilean port of Caldera to the copper and silver mining region of Copiapó. It was Chile's first railway and it produced a surge in mining operations including nitrates' extraction, eventually generating considerable freight for the PSNC.[163] It was, therefore, likely that Wheelwright's considerable influence within the Chilean Executive and the investors/owners of the mining complexes in the northern region, would have had some bearing on the Commission's considerations.

Indeed, support for the latter body's decision had come from those Valparaíso business interests, not only closely involved with PSNC, but also from those desiring direct shipping links with Europe via the Strait of Magellan. The core support, however, emanated from those who considered that the English company alone was then capable of providing these requirements. Moreover, many of these same businessmen were clients of PSNC, and looked to that company as a means of obtaining and maintaining lower freight charges than those offered by Chilean national ship owners.

The Chilean Government was, once again, faced with a dilemma; there were two groups wanting additional services, one specifically to cater for the southern provinces and the other, the northern group opposed to renewing PSNC's concessions. As a political solution, the Government decided not to renew the English company's exclusive privileges but to open-up steamship coastal trading to all foreign steamship companies for a period of five years. At the same time, it decreed the award of a subsidy of up to 36,000 pesos (approximately £7200 or $US12,960) to any shipping line undertaking a monthly steamship opderation between Valparaíso and the southern provinces by assigning a vessel of at least 300 tons and capable of a service speed of between 8 to 10 miles per hour.[164]

Two months later, the Chilean Government found itself dithering over two identical offers it had received; one from Robert Simpson of Nicodemes Ossa y Cia and the other from a Samuel Green. In order to provoke a decision, the latter had offered to accept a 6000 pesos (£12000 or $US 21600) reduction in subsidy if awarded the contract, whereupon, Robert Simpson of Ossa y Cia immediately countered with the same terms. The latter's offer was accepted on March 24, 1851, on the grounds that Ossa y Cia was not only a Chilean enterprise, but had also specifically acquired the small steamship *Arauco* to operate the southern service.[165]

Shortly after these deliberations on the provision of a southern steamship route, politicians had their attention diverted by a short and abortive revolution during which rebels captured two small steamships, one of which was the *Firefly* belonging to Carlos Lambert, one of the northern mining group protesting against the renewal of PSNC's privileges, and the other, Ossa y Cia's *Arauco*. By September 7, 1851, the rebellion had died, but on September 30, the Chilean Government withdrew the *Arauco's* Chilean registration after classing her as a corsair or privateering vessel because of her capture by the insurrectionists. Both vessels were eventually returned to their rightful owners. A year after the rebellion, a decree of August 1852 ordered the *Arauco's* owners to be fined; on the first two and only voyages she had made to the south, she had not called at the port of Constitución as demanded by the scheduled itinerary detailed in the March 1851 decree.[166]

Access to the latter port on the River Maule was only available to shallow-draught vessels given the presence of a sand bar across the mouth of the river. This physical obstacle had prevented the *Arauco* from making directly for the port as contracted. Ships that could not negotiate the sand bar were therefore obliged to anchor in a small cove near the river mouth. The presence of this physical feature was to assume vital importance in the development of Chile's merchant marine. The little steamship, *Arauco*, was reported by El Mercurio, in its February 3 1853 edition, to have been shipwrecked in Talcahuano Bay causing the vessel's owners to successfully petition the Government to be released from its contract; the southern provinces of Chile, were, once again, without a steamship service.

It was at this stage that PSNC's fortunes began to change for the better. El Mercurio printed an editorial on January 21, 1853, to the effect that the newspaper was opposed to any small or medium sized steamship enterprise being allowed to undertake the desired regular service to the Southern provinces. The editor reminded its readers that experience had already shown one such operation to be very costly and that provision of a regular southern service was never going to be resolved with the introduction of just one vessel supported by insufficient capital.

The main thrust of the newspaper's argument was that it was inexcusable to maintain such a service with so little financial support. El Mercurio's editor detailed two possible solutions, one of which was to establish a Chilean registered company with a capital base of not less than 20,000 pesos (approximately £4000 or $US 7200) to provide a minimum fleet of three vessels. The other alternative, it advised, was to secure such a service from the PSNC by awarding it the maximum possible subsidy. This newspaper's pronouncement must have given great pleasure to Wheelwright, who up to that point had not expressed any official interest in operating the southern service. It had, more likely, reflected the feelings of the Valparaíso resident British business community.

Chilean historian Claudio Véliz considered that El Mercurio's editorial was more probably directed against a later proposal to provide a southern steamship service; the Chilean Government had already accepted an offer from two brothers, Ponciano and Nicanor Dávila, joint owners of the steamship *Caupolicán*. Five days after the publication of El Mercurio's editorial advice, it was announced that the brothers' steamship had left on her first voyage to the south of Chile to demonstrate her capability of reaching the speeds needed to comply with the subsidized contract. On February 3, 1853, El Mercurio published an update following an earlier report that the *Canpolicán's* trials had been unsuccessful. It recommended that, because the question of providing a regular steamship operation to the southern ports was both problematic and difficult to resolve, the contract be awarded to the PSNC whom it believed was capable of undertaking its requirements.

On April 22, 1853, Lyon Hermanos, as PSNC agents, submitted an offer to launch a monthly steamship service to Ancud, making intervening calls at Maule Cove (for Constitución), Tomé, Talcahuano and Corral, but reserving the right to put in at any other port to take on coals. The Chilean Government, three days later, mindful of the breakdown in the effectiveness of its national ship owners, and being influenced by PSNC's announcement that four vessels of 1,100 tons each would be allocated to the West Coast service, duly accepted that company's proposals.

Under the contract's terms, PSNC was required to pay a fine of 500 pesos (approximately £100 or $US 180) for every 24 hours' delay occurring in the list of scheduled departure dates, and 4000 pesos (approximately £800 or $US 1440) if the monthly service was not properly fulfilled. In case of vessel loss by shipwreck or any other unfortunate event, PSNC was required to replace that ship within 90 days. Failing this, the company was obliged to pay 1000 pesos for each cancelled voyage. The contract was to remain in force for two years, renewable for a further year on authorization from the Chilean Congress. PSNC had wisely negotiated for the contract to omit the requirement for direct calls to Constitución, given the presence of the obstructing sand bank at the river mouth. The eventual service provided by this company became so effective, that not only was its licence automatically renewed each year, but the company's operation also evolved into a national institution.

Government subsidies attached to the contract rose from 36,000 pesos (£7200 or $US12960) in 1853 to 50,000 pesos (£10,000 or $US 18,000) in 1857.[167] Ten years after the failure of the *Arauco*, Chile's own merchant fleet, although comprising 267 vessels totalling 60,847 gross tons, could only muster seven steamships;[168] no Chilean shipping enterprise, therefore, was at this time in a position to compete with the expanding English steamship company.

Another generally unappreciated event contributing indirectly to PSNC's fortuitous position occurred after Chile had received notice from the United States that the Trade and Friendship Treaty signed by both nations in 1832, during Andres Bello's leadership, was due to expire in April 1850.[169] The affect of this expiry was that Chilean vessels subsequently entering any United States port would be liable to taxes and dues of one peso for each ton of cargo landed, and 10% of the total value of cargo imported; under the treaty's terms, Chilean ships had previously been exempted from theses taxes.

The ending of the accord occurred just as Chilean exports to the United States were steadily increasing. It would have been a very serious setback for Chilean ship owners if no solution had been found, given that 50% of Chile's exports were then directed to California. The Chilean Government was concerned that this state

Panama and The Railroad 1849-1860

of affairs could have caused some Chilean enterprises to re-register their vessels under the flags of those nations continuing to enjoy reciprocal arrangements with the United States.[170] The obvious political remedy for Chile was either to seek the treaty's renewal or to introduce some measure to counteract or compensate for the obligation on Chilean merchant vessels to pay US taxes.

Navy, Foreign Relations and Treasury Ministries requested, a year after the abolition of coastal trading restrictions, that legislation maintaining differential rights for Chilean ships since 1834 should be repealed. The latter authorities had taken the view that the establishment of reciprocal agreements[171] with other nations, especially the United States, was the only practical solution. The 1849 legislation repealing the 1834 protectionist measures for coastwise trading thus meant that Chilean merchant ships would, thereafter, pay the same import and export duties, anchorage, tonnage and other port dues as applied to all foreign vessels entering Chilean ports. Importantly, if any nation concluded a *"reciprocity"* agreement with Chile to exempt the latter from import and export duties and other taxes when entering that nation's ports, then Chile would respond by withdrawing any tax and duty requirements from that country's ships entering her own ports.

These new arrangements were widely welcomed and became very popular, leading soon afterwards to the disappearance of Chile's old and decrepit cargo vessels. Thereafter, her merchant fleet expanded rapidly, especially in the numbers of foreign-going ships[172]. This increase in the availability of vessels resulted in a general lowering of freight charges, both for foreign and coastal shipping, which in turn, not only led to growth in the quantity of cargo shipments, but also to a reduction in the number of merchant ships sold in Valparaiso due to a collapse in their value. This latter decrease was not confined to the West Coast, but was more extensive, especially throughout California and Europe then suffering from economic depression. Construction of the best quality iron hulls had normally cost between £25 (US 45 dollars) and £35 (US 63 dollars) per ton, but during the depression, prices had plummeted to as low as £15 (US 27 dollars) per ton. Price falls of between 10% and 15% were similarly recorded for the construction of wooden hull vessels.[173]

One would have thought that the mining interests of Northern Chile, the southern foundries' operators and agricultural producers would have taken advantage of their Government's financial incentives to become ship owners and/or shipbuilders themselves without diminishing their established businesses. In that way, they could have benefited by controlling freight charges and guaranteed service operations to ship their products. This opportunity had been there for the taking, especially since there was then a distinct absence of short-term speculators interested in Chilean shipping, and because prices of acquiring vessels had reduced tremendously.

This was attributable to the considerable growth in tonnage then available along the Chilean coast which had dragged down the rate of freight charges to very low levels, with little prospect of them increasing in the short to medium term. Accordingly, speculators generally, only accustomed to making substantial short-term profits, were simply not interested in acquiring shipping concerns or even launching new enterprises that would probably only deliver long term financial gains.

During this period, there had been significant discoveries of copper and silver in the Copiapó district, which might have concentrated the minds of both the northern and southern provinces. Chilean historian Claudio Véliz suggested[174] that entrepreneurs in these latter areas did not then possess the relevant investor knowledge and acumen of the foreign businessmen resident in Chile, especially the British, who predominated the central regions, particularly in and around Valparaiso. These were the long established and resident bankers, the exporters and importers distributing through their shops and stores, the many and varied merchandise imported from Great Britain. They had previously paid freight costs to other non-Chilean shipping firms when importing and exporting goods between Chile and northern Europe; purchasing their own ships and/or shipyards to build them would have meant long-term savings in freight charges. They would also have been able to distribute their imported goods along the many Chilean ports following the removal of cabotage restrictions, as well as being able to attract valuable export cargoes from along the coast. By investing in such shipping enterprises, the objective of these far-sighted entrepreneurs was not to seek short-term financial gains but rather to consolidate and expand their current business interests.

Some of these business houses had long been established on the West Coast. Gibbs y Cia, for example, was a shareholder in PSNC[175] and had even purchased a 25% holding in a large rice, sugar and cotton[176] plantation in Peru along with 135 slaves, with the intention of integrating this type of trade with its normal general merchandise import and distribution business. Soon afterwards, this firm started to deal in metals and it was, therefore, not surprising when, in 1849, it logically diversified into shipping following its wealth-generating consignee involvement in guano.

Gibbs & Cia, like other business houses participating in the guano trade, had no day to day involvement with the digging and loading of this commodity at the Peruvian Chincha Islands up to 1849; such activities were dealt with through intermediaries, but in 1855, Gibbs was given responsibility for its loading.[177] After 1849, Gibbs and other such concerns normally chartered vessels to carry guano to Britain, Europe and the United States The work force needed to dig and load the guano onto ships was always considered inadequate. Up to 1854, it comprised a mixed system of slave labour employed in the workings, but throughout the 1850s,

Panama and The Railroad 1849-1860

Chinese were principally indentured into the work gangs. The insufficient supply of workers numbering well under 1000 by the late 1850s, operated without any mechanical aids; the guano was extracted with pick and shovel, carried in bags and wheel-barrowed or rolled along rails and then placed in large enclosures on the cliff tops. They were then dropped down canvas chutes into the holds of ships waiting below the cliffs or dropped into small feeder launches.[178] Frequent calls were made in the Peruvian Executive for the work force to be doubled, particularly as there were frequent delays in loading.

James Caird, a British agricultural writer, according to W.M.Mathew in the *"House of Gibbs and the Peruvian Guano Monopoly"*, claimed that loading facilities at the Chincha Isles were no better than they had been some seven years earlier when the trade was only about one-tenth of its then size. There was, he said, good reason why a ship would spend more than one week laying off the islands. He contended that a vessel of 1000 tons could be loaded inside two days through the chutes but a shortage of loading positions meant that numerous vessels were constantly waiting in turn, resulting in delays of between two to three months.[179]

Mathew also reported that a British naval officer visiting the islands in 1853 had claimed that he counted as many as 100 vessels waiting at the Isla del Norte (the northern island of the Chinchas). Casa Gibbs confirmed that as many as 128 ships with a combined tonnage of 188,804 tons were waiting at the islands in March 1857; these, he submitted, were capable of carrying about 160,000 tons of guano, which he estimated would take four months to load. Guano ships had to manoeuvre under the cliffs to connect with the chutes; this was often undertaken in a heavy swell bringing its own dangers and difficulties, and not least, contributing to wastage of 16% of total guano extracted. The total imports and sales of guano in Great Britain for the years 1841 to 1880 inclusive had amounted to 4,795,344 tons, valued at approximately £21,579,048 (US 38,850,000 dollars) for the period in question, or an average of £539476 (US 971,000 dollars) per annum.[180] The sum the Peruvian Government received for each ton landed in Britain was £4.50 (US 2 dollars 50) in 1842.[181]

Based on these figures, estimated wastage over the 40 years would have amounted to 913399 tons, and in value approximately £4,110,000 (US 7,400,000 dollars); in terms of actual ships' cargoes, the equivalent of approximately 731 vessel loads.[182] These calculations relate to sales of guano in Britain; one could perhaps broadly double the figure for comparable tonnages wasted for guano shipments to the United States and the rest of Europe.

Inefficiency was not just confined to the extraction and loading of guano, administrative processes were excessively bureaucratic and wasteful. During the period 1840-1880, the Peruvian Government required all guano-cargo sailing ships to observe various commercial formalities by calling first at Pisco and thence at Callao. After being loaded with this commodity, they were again required to re-enter Callao where crews, suffering from a lengthy layover at the Islas Chinchas, tended to jump ship; the vessels, thereafter, were obliged to re-enter Pisco. These requirements were a source of great annoyance and expense to ship-owners and charterers and only added to voyage length. In 1857, 40 guano-laden ships sailing from Callao to Liverpool took an average 18 weeks to complete the homeward journey.[183]

By 1866, no improvements had been introduced in loading procedures at the Chincha Islands; ships still had to wait 70 to 80 days before being loaded, and there was always a queue of between 90 and 100 vessels. A Royal Commission on *"Unseaworthy Ships"* held in London in 1873, heard that sailing ships were deterred from the guano trade due to the many unproductive days spent at the islands waiting their turn to be loaded. These layover days were never fewer than 30 or more than 80; when loading commenced it was at a daily rate of merely 10 tons.[184]

These long delays at the Chincha islands had motivated W.R.Grace to expand his initial ships' chandler business interests from Callao. His wealth accumulated from this and previous dealings with American Railroad pioneer Henry Meiggs attracted him into mining in Peru, nitrates in Chile and rubber in the Amazon. This diversification into various regions and countries enabled the Grace firm to prosper. It tended to charter ships, often purchasing part shares in vessels as a way of minimizing risk, to transport materials from the WCSA to the United States. These shipping arrangements were eventually drawn together in 1882 to form the Merchants Steamship Line serving the Americas, but it was not until the early 1890s that its first steamships were acquired to establish the New York to WCSA line.

Merchants Line's main competitor had been the Fabbri & Chauncey Line also operating out of New York to the WCSA. Lawrence A.Clayton, author of *"W.R.Grace & Co. The Formative Years 1850-1930"* recorded:

"Grace rapidly drove Fabbri & Chauncey out of business by cutting rates, first on the Chile run and then on the extension of the line to Peru. Once Grace had got the lion's share of the business, Fabbri & Chauncey were bought out by Merchants Line and the rates were raised once again to their normal level. [185]

Another business house conducting trade on the West Coast was Ravenscroft, Alston & Co., later to become the famous firm of Duncan Fox. Established there since 1843, it had concentrated initially on selling and distribution of imported merchandise from Britain before extending into the shipping sector in 1851. Thereafter, this company began acting as agents for other British shipping firms as well as undertaking marine insurance. Expansion, at this time, also led to diversification as Ravenscroft & Co. moved into direct exports of guano to Europe using its own sailing ships. The Bolivian ports of Cobija and San Felipe were the principal loading points through which this firm had first contracted to load 25 tons of guano daily.

Many other business houses such as Balfour Williamson and Co. were to successfully follow the example of these two British establishments and occupy the fertile investment ground of Chilean merchant shipping. Chilean historian Claudio Véliz discovered from data in the Chilean Navy Archives of 1854, that foreign, mainly British business houses, then owned 52.8% of all Chilean merchant shipping. Moreover, he established that, including the remaining 47.2%, the majority of their captains and crew of Chilean vessels were foreigners.

Basil Lubbock, author of "*The Nitrate Clippers*" attributed the foreign intake into the Chilean navy and Merchant marine on the fact that:

"The West Coast was a veritable paradise for drunkards...many and many a good British seaman deserted in such ports as Valparaíso or Callao owing to the attraction of cheap drink. He then either drifted into the ranks of the beachcombers or developed a business head and became the successful proprietor of a fandango hall or sailors' boarding house. Numbers of European seamen served for a term in the Chilian Navy. Many of the Chilian warships in the olden days were three quarters manned by wild foreign sailor men of every nationality." [186]

The situation, whereby mainly foreign nations manned Chilean ships, appeared not to have changed over the next eight years; recommendations were made to the Chilean Government in 1862 that foreign captains of Chilean registered merchant vessels undergo some basic form of instruction and examination in Spanish, due to the inability of the majority to speak it.

PSNC advised the Chilean Government that it would introduce four steamships on the West Coast. These appeared shortly after that company obtained an extension of its British Postal contract. The four vessels, acquired at a total cost of £140,000 (US 252,000 dollars), were larger and more powerful than any previous ship in PSNC's fleet. A Liverpool newspaper reporter, at the time, described one of the four vessels:

"The *Santiago* is registered as 1000 tons gross weight. With 400 horsepower engines, she is designed to operate at an average service speed of 10 knots. She will carry mail, bullion and passengers between Callao, Panama and intermediary ports. Captain Hind, a very competent and experienced navigator, is to be given command. She is a beautiful, two funnelled ship with sumptuous passenger accommodation. Three additional, even larger, vessels are already being built on the Clyde for The Pacific Steam Navigation Company. They will depart from Liverpool on their respective maiden voyages."

The other three steamships were the *Lima, Quito* and *Bolivia*.

Ploughing The South Sea

PSNC painting ss.*Santiago*. 961 tons. Built 1851

Since its formation, PSNC had always maintained close links with the Royal Mail Steam Packet Line (RMSPL). Early in 1852, it reached agreement to jointly introduce a mail steamship service between Panama and Sydney, Australia. The outcome was the creation of a new company, the Australia Pacific Mail Steam Packet Company with headquarters in Moorgate, London. PSNC subscribed to the shares of this new enterprise for which five new iron steamships had been commissioned. Management of the new enterprise was to have been entrusted to the Liverpool firm, obliging the latter to relocate its control centre from Callao in Peru to Panama, where huge supplies of coal had been stockpiled in readiness for the new operation. RMSPL was to have received 30% of freight charges for cargo shipped from the United Kingdom via the Isthmus of Panama to Australia.

The first steamship, the *Emeu*, had been scheduled to leave Southampton on February 21, 1853, but suddenly, for reasons unknown, the project was abandoned. It appears that differences of opinion may have arisen between the two shipping companies, because in March of that year, Samuel Cunard was appointed as arbitrator in a legal action launched by the Pacific Steam Navigation Company against the new corporation. Stores and coal supplies stockpiled at Panama to service the new steamships were sold and the Superintendent in Sydney was stood down.

Panama and The Railroad 1849-1860

In 1852, the *Peru* ran aground and foundered. This was the first time that a mail-carrying vessel had been lost. That same year her sister ship, the *Chile*, was sold to the Chilean Government. It also marked a turning point for Wheelwright; aged 54, he ended his active involvement in the management of the PSNC and accepted the position of Company Consultant-Director; he took up permanent residence on the WCSA to concentrate on railroad construction, in particular, the trans Andean route to Argentina.[187]

It was at this time that the two new paddle steamships, the *Bogota* and the *Quito*, sailed from the River Mersey, carrying passengers and mail to Valparaíso. Shortly after this, PSNC commissioned a small iron steamship called *La Perlita*, 140 tons gross and two 2 cylinder 40 horsepower engines from a Warrington firm, to operate as a support craft between Buenaventura (Colombia) and Panama. This small vessel left Liverpool on June 17, 1853, but never reached the West Coast. Nothing was heard from her; it was presumed that she had been overwhelmed and lost. The journey to Buenaventura from Liverpool was over 11000 miles; it was probably asking too much of her to undertake that particular route; she was only 106 feet in length, 17 feet 5 inches in beam and 8 feet 6 inches in depth. By contrast, her tragic loss underlines the sailing capabilities of Sir Francis Drake's *Golden Hind*, in the early 16th Century; she was said to be less than 100 tons gross weight, approximately 75 feet in length and 20 feet wide.

Another small paddle steamer, the *Osprey* (609 tons), built in Glasgow, was purchased from the City of Cork Steamship Company with a view to establishing a service between Callao, Pisco, and Huacho; she was also lost en route to South America. In that same year, PSNC introduced a wooden hulled ship into service, the *Valdivia*, 573 tons gross weight, but for the first time in that company's history, she was propeller driven and the only such wooden hulled vessel. Intended for the West Coast trade, she was eventually found to be too small to be profitable.

The mid 19th century witnessed dramatic changes in the design and propulsion of most types of vessels. From a military point of view, paddle wheel propulsion had posed serious and visible military weaknesses, such systems easily being disabled by shellfire. Moreover, the space occupied by the paddle wheels and their housings could have been more effectively used for the installation of artillery. Propeller or screw propulsion had developed by accident. An Archimedes screw, of the type used in early water pumps, had been fitted to a canal barge in a series of experiments in Britain. The subject screw is alleged to have struck a piece of floating debris causing the major part of it to break off. At that point, the barge was reported to have lurched forward to maintain a much faster speed.

Further research improved the efficiency of this accidental and rudimentary design. The important feature of propeller propulsion was its obvious advantage of operating below the waterline, and hence not presenting as easier a military target as the paddle wheel; it also took-up less valuable space within the vessel, a more important consideration for merchant steam ship operators. Successful developments adopted by the Royal Navy usually found their way into merchant shipping lines, but the matter of propeller propulsion efficiency over paddle wheels eventually had to be earnestly-addressed by the British Admiralty before it was completely adopted. In 1845, the latter conducted a series of trials; two sloops of approximately equal power and weight were selected; the screw-propelled HMS *Rattler* and the paddle-wheeled HMS *Alecto*.

Three tests were set; the first comprised a straightforward race in smooth seas over an 80 miles course; *Rattler* completed this 23 and one-half minutes faster then the competing "*paddler*" *Alecto*. The second test was conducted over a 60 miles course in rough seas with *Rattler* again emerging victorious by 40 minutes. The third and most famous test was carried out in the form of a tug of war. Each vessel had been secured to the other's stern by hawser. After both ships had worked-up to full steam, the screw propelled steamer demonstrated her superiority by towing the paddle-driven vessel in her wake at a speed of 2.5 knots. The issue was, therefore, conclusively decided; the Royal Navy, thenceforth, constructed all their principal vessels with screw-propulsion although paddle steamships continued to be used for sheltered tasks, such as harbour work and also to accompany Royal Navy sailing ships on duty to provide towing and assistance in manoeuvreing.

Operating steamships on the WCSA, at this time, was a much more difficult proposition than providing services on the North Atlantic or Far Eastern routes. The affects of revolutions and political instability in the South American republics caused constant problems in maintaining economic levels of coal supplies. Additionally, the need to carry adequate stores and spares for the whole fleet, far removed from its management centre, demanded a more extensive and de-centralized administration able to take on-the-spot decisions. For example, in March 1852, news had been received of the loss of the newly acquired sailing ship *Hope*, together with her cargo of coal. The following month, the paddle steamer *Lima* carrying mails to Guayaquil had been hit by cannon fire from New Granada's artillery installations in that port; the latter republic allying herself with Ecuador to provide her practical protection against threats of Peruvian expansionism.

A further unrelated difficulty occurred when the PSNC Agent for the mail service in Panama was denied permission to receive bullion, in transit to Europe, already landed by a Company vessel. PSNC suffered another unfortunate event when the new steamship *Quito*, operating on the Panama to Valparaíso service, was lost in August 1853 after striking rocks 12 miles out from the Peruvian port of Huasco.

There were also political pressures to plough through, and not only on the West Coast; there had been a long lasting and bitter rivalry in the Caribbean between the United States and Great Britain. The former, having assessed the importance of the canoe-mule link across the Isthmus established by the two British

Panama and The Railroad 1849-1860

steamship companies, had signed the Mallarino-Bidlack treaty with New Granada. This accord guaranteed the latter's sovereignty over Panama, at that time a State within New Granada, in exchange for certain commercial considerations. It also created a right of passage across the Isthmus for any United States company to provide transportation and mail between her eastern seaboard and the Isthmus of Panama. Two wealthy financiers, George Law and William H.Aspinwall, won the contract offered for this purpose by the United States Government in 1848, resulting in the creation of two separate mail-shipping routes. Aspinwall assumed responsibility for the Atlantic service and Law the Pacific route.

The only way that these two shipping enterprises could be connected at the time was by mule-trains along the Old Spanish trail via Las Cruces. The launch of this North American steamship service, had importantly, coincided with the onset of the Californian Gold Rush, highlighting the need for an Isthmus railroad. The establishment of the Panama Railroad Company by United States' interests in 1850 was one of the most significant events in the development of maritime trade on the WCSA; it was destined to play a major role in many ways in the growth of North American and European steamship traffic.

British and French capitalists had previously, and separately, investigated the feasibility of constructing similar railroad schemes across the Isthmus. In his "*History of The Panama Railroad*", F.N.Otis, echoing the remarks made by Robert Tomes in his "*Account of the Panama Railroad in 1855*", commented:

"England had looked toward the project with longing eyes but quailed before the magnitude of the labor. France had done more, she had surveyed and entered into a contract to establish it but too many millions were found necessary for its completion and it was lost by default".

Although petitions for the Isthmus transit concessions had been lodged by the United States with New Granada as early as 1837, a formal contract was not delivered by both nations until April 1850. This required that a railroad be built within eight years and designed to link the old colonial city of Panama on the Pacific coast with a then unspecified location on her northern shores on the Caribbean. The United States had also been required to deposit 120,000 US dollars (£66,700 approximately) at the commencement of the project, to be returned with interest on completion of the railroad. The appointed contractor was allowed to operate the service for a further 49 years. Of important benefit to New Granada was her contracted option to purchase the railroad after 20 years for $US5,000,000 (£2,800,000 approximately), this being the amount of the initial stock offer and the estimated total for development and construction costs.[188]

Other important privileges granted to the United States were to have a later and major impact on the Isthmus. All public lands lying on the line of the proposed railroad were to be used free of charge by the eventual railroad company, together with an outright gift of 250,000 acres of land to be selected by them from the public ownership register. In return, the New Granada Government was to receive 3% of all dividends declared by the Railroad Company.

The Caribbean coast terminus was originally proposed as Porto Bello with the railroad following the route of the old paved highway, the Spanish Camino Real. George Law, who had been awarded the contract for the Atlantic section of the overall US mail service from New York via Panama to California and Oregon, having discovered PRC's originally proposed route plans, set about acquiring all available land around Porto Bello at very low cost. He had then offered it to the PRC at a highly inflated price but was never able to secure that company's agreement to purchase. A number of alternative locations had been considered before PRC engineers finally designated a site on the island of Manzanillo in Limon Bay.

A little known element in the chapter of PRC's creation was PSNC's purchase of a large but not controlling part of PRC's $US 5,000,000 fixed capital. At $100(£55.56) a share, the entire stock had been fully subscribed. Although no record has emerged to establish any British Government prompting or encouragement of PSNC to provoke a spat with PRC, historically such understandings in other areas have been informally reached between company executives and Government officials. For example, unofficial discussions between the influential Chilean Government-linked Portales and Wheelwright had taken place in Valparaíso concerning the licences for steamship navigation in Chile, well before Wheelwright had officially petitioned for them. Wheelwright and interested business parties had also held informal talks with the Chilean President prior to the later construction of the Caldera-Copiapó railway. If the British Government or particular members of it had held similar informal conversations with PSNC, they were unlikely to have been officially recorded or referenced in Boardroom or Government minutes.

An earlier 1850 agreement, termed the Clayton-Bulwer Treaty, between the United States and Great Britain, both maintaining rival interests in the Caribbean, required either nation not to extend her territorial possessions in Central America. Importantly, they had agreed to joint control of "*any inter oceanic canal*" that might be constructed. The agreement stipulated the word "*canal*" and not "*other means*" so that a British, albeit private, interest in the Railroad could have provided a legal excuse for British Government involvement in times of conflict. as was the case when Britain involved herself with military action in 1848 in the dispute of the River San Juan in Belize, formerly British Honduras, the river was then part of the United States' envisaged Nicaraguan canal route

On the other hand, PSNC's purchase of part of PRC's share capital could simply have arisen purely from investment considerations. The railroad company was, at the time, likely to have derived substantial earnings from PSNC's and Royal Mail Steam Packet Company's passenger and freight traffic, as well as similar revenue from the Pacific Mail Steamship Company, the Atlantic Mail Steamship Company, the latter's bitter rival, and from shipping concerns of other nations. A stockholding in PRC, therefore, would have been one way of recovering costs contributed to the railroad's freight and passenger revenues, as well as allowing a more direct line of communication with the PRC's Board of Directorate concerning its operations.

The need for a railroad transit of the Isthmus had become more apparent following the United State's acquisition of the new territories of California and Oregon. Extending over 45 miles, the railroad was completed in 1855 at a cost of $US8,000,000 (£4,500,000 approximately), but at a huge cost in construction workers' lives. However, the story that there was one death for every railroad tie or sleeper is a complete myth. No exact figures appear to have been recorded but correspondence between the Board of Directors and the Railroad Company indicated that, out of a complement of approximately 6000 white construction workers, there were 293 deaths throughout the entire building period.[189]

Kemble, in his *"The Panama Route 1848-1869"*, although adamant that there were never more than 15,000 people employed on the railroad, offered no figures on the total deaths other than his assertion that claims of 50% or 80% mortality rates were fantastic. The true figure may never be known, but it is certain that the death rate was very high and that on some occasions, labourers were dying faster than they could be replaced.[190]

The Panama Railroad was built and opened in stages, earning two millions US dollars (£1,111,000) even before its final inauguration from coast to coast. Such was its popularity that by 1859 it had recovered, according to figures provided by F.N.Otis in his *"History of the Panama Railroad"*, nearly all of its building costs. By January 1865, it was producing profits in excess of 11 millions US dollars (£6,111,000 approximately). According to Ira E.Bennett, author of *"History of the Panama Canal"* published 1915, the volume of traffic in 1855 had been far greater than the PRC could then accommodate or had even anticipated. It, therefore, introduced a supposed deterrent charge of 25 US dollars (£13.89) for the one-way passenger journey between Colón on the Caribbean coast, and the Pacific port of Panama and 50 cents per cubic foot of freight per mile.

Bennett confirmed that, although these rates remained in force for more than 20 years, freight and passenger traffic still increased. Furthermore, the PRC then enjoyed a monopoly of the trade emanating from the Atlantic, together with that generated from the entire western shores of North, Central, and South America.[191] It is not surprising that the Railroad Company became one of the greatest dividend earners in the world. In 1852, a 10% dividend was declared followed by a 7% distribution for each of the years 1853 and 1854, and a 12% annual payout between 1855 and 1859 inclusive. Stockholders, at one stage, received as much as 24% annual yield on their investments. The completion of the Railroad in 1855, and the introduction of direct passenger and freight services across the Isthmus to connect with ships sailing to and from Europe, North America and the West Coast South America, considerably increased the workload at PSNC's Liverpool headquarters. Up to December 1867, more than 400,000 passengers had been carried across the Isthmus by the PRC and between 1855-57, specie to the value of over $US 750,000 (£417,000 approximately) without any loss whatsoever.

The Railroad Company was awarded the Isthmian transit concession by the New Granada Government following the forfeiture by the French of the right to continue with the project. Kemble[192] submitted that the Railroad Company President, William Aspinwall and the New Granada Government had already agreed informally before 1848, to transfer the rights to the North American owned Railroad Company. Aspinwall had, by then, purchased the Pacific Mail Steamship Company which, many of his contemporaries thought was an ill-judged investment, but he was confident that that it would profitably dovetail with his Panama Railroad operation.

The New Granada Government had prudently retained the right to purchase the Railroad enterprise in 1875 for 5 millions US dollars (£2,800,000 approximately). This eventually proved to be an unacceptable deal for the United States; the project had cost 8 millions dollars (£4,500,000) in 1855 and was, shortly afterwards, paying dividends of 24%. A US representative was duly dispatched to Bogotá in 1867 to conclude a new arrangement, whereby the New Granada Government received an instant payment of one million US dollars in gold (£555,000) and 250,000 US dollars (£139,000 approximately) annually thereafter. In addition, she was to have her mails transported free of charge, and her request to have the Railroad extended to certain islands in the bay of Panama was also met. The PRC, as well as securing a new franchise, retained the benefit of large grants of public land on the Isthmus, later to prove invaluable to the United States.

The port of Colón, originally named after Columbus, was re-christened "*Aspinwall*" by the Railroad Company after its founder President. This action was taken without consulting the New Granada Government, which refused to recognize it. For a long time, both names continued to appear on maps and charts causing a great deal of confusion. There exists an unconfirmed tale of a ship's captain, navigating towards Colón, who saw and passed the port of Aspinwall and then ran aground believing that Colón would shortly be sighted. Use of the Aspinwall name for this latter port eventually faded away.

The Pacific Steam Navigation Company, not only profited from this Railroad as a minority stockholder, but for the first time, the "*English Company*" was able to issue return tickets from the West Coast to Europe in conjunction with Royal Mail Steam Packet Line. In 1855, PSNC ordered three new ships, the first of these was the *Panama*, a small propeller driven iron steamship, built by John Reid of Glasgow for the service from the New Granada port of Buenaventura[193] to

Panama. She had set sail from Liverpool in April 1856, but was lost on the rocks at Punta Tamar in the middle of the Strait of Magellan.

The other two new iron vessels were the paddle steamer *Inca* of 290 tons gross weight and the paddle steamer *Valparaíso* of 1060 tons. These steamships performed much more efficiently due to newly introduced engineering developments in the form of high and low-pressure engines fabricated by John Elder & Co. Glasgow. PSNC ships had made use of this type of marine engine well before they were in common use in other Atlantic going vessels; their introduction spelt the end for many sailing ships on the West Coast.

The paddle steamer *Valparaíso's* engines had been fitted with two high pressure and two low-pressure cylinders, producing 25 lbs to the square inch. To test the superiority of this new type of engine, she had undertaken a run from Glasgow against the *Pride of Erin*, powered by the traditional and commonly used marine engine. The *Valparaíso* made this short trip in five and half hours consuming one third less fuel than the latter vessel. This was a huge saving given that the cost of coal on the Pacific Coast varied from between 50 to 80 shillings (equivalent to £2.50 to £4 or $US 4.50 to 7.20) per ton. On the *Valparaíso's* first voyage from her namesake port to Panama and back, her fuel consumption was only 640 tons compared with the 1150 tons normally used by PSNC's older vessels, an approximate fuel saving of 44%.

PSNC painting of Paddle steamer *Valparaíso* 1060 tons. Built 1856

Towards the end of 1854, the paddle steamer *Lima* was dispatched to England to have her engines replaced with the same modern high-low pressure type and her hull lengthened. It was the first time that one of the Company's vessels had made a return voyage to England. The successful installation of these new engines produced much-improved performances, as was demonstrated after the fitting of this new type of power unit in the *Arica* and *Valparaíso*. Collectively, they achieved considerable fuel economies and it was, therefore, unsurprising when PSNC comprehensively adopted this new machinery. In doing so, it commenced a long and friendly association with their builders, John Elder & Co, marine engineers.

In 1857, an agreement was struck with the Peruvian Government to provide a postal service between Callao and Chala, a small port approximately halfway between Callao and Iquique, utilizing the small steamship *Inca*. The port of Panama, meanwhile, had developed as the most important place in the PSNC's sphere of operations and competition between visiting steam ship lines was bitter. Charles T.Bidwell, American consul in Panama, had, during his term of office, publicly written that Aspinwall's Pacific Mail Steamship Company had the largest and probably the best-paying steamers in the world, and that *"finer ships and better accommodations for passengers would be rare.*"[194] These remarks were produced to contrast the conditions of the Pacific Mail Steamship Company's competitor, the Atlantic Mail Steamship Company, operated by Cornelius Vanderbilt. The press on both North American coasts, highly critical of the Vanderbilt company, described the latter's ships as floating pigsties, sailing with insufficient crew for the type of vessels used and portraying Vanderbilt as the "*Nero of the sea*". The Panama Star and Herald newspaper remarked that in spite of improvements then being carried out in Atlantic Mail Company's ships, nothing would be achieved as long as he had anything to do with them.

For many years, PSNC, conscious of how competitors could easily provoke the strongest adverse public criticism, employed a company doctor on the island of Morro to care for the large numbers employed in that firm's island workshop and stores and the considerable number of company ships passing through. Lady Emmeline Stuart-Wortley, a passenger on the *Bolivia*, once, after a visit to the island, reportedly described it as Panama's answer to Merseyside's New Brighton.[195] This island was separated from the neighbouring island of Taboga at high tide, but when this ebbed, a narrow connecting beach was revealed. It was purchased in 1859, and in 1940 was still owned by PSNC together with a small part of the Isle of Taboga, acquired in 1866. PSNC was then the only shipping company to possess such territory with full sovereign rights although Pacific MAIL Steamship Company had bought four islands in the Bay of Panama to serve and maintain her own fleet.

In 1857, PSNC's earnings from its West Coast operations fell drastically, resulting in severe cutbacks while the financial crisis continued for some years. Other firms on the West Coast evidently experienced similar trading problems. Wallis Hunt described the situation within the Valparaíso branch or "*House*" of Balfour Williamson & Co[196]:

"The bubble burst in November 1857. Stocks [of merchandise] began to stick in Valparaíso and remittances fell behind maturities All Britain seemed short of money and in the crisis, it was impossible to renew some of the bills drawn against shipments by the original sellers."

Throughout 1857, the Chilean market economy became saturated, resulting in many commercial failures. The Chilean Merchant marine experienced considerable falls in tonnage, from 62659 tons in 1857 to 58877 tons in 1859. During 1858, the financial crisis had begun to dissipate and the fortunes of PSNC and other establishments such as Balfour Williamson Company changed for the better. By 1860, the outlook was much brighter generally, and PSNC entered into a provisional agreement with the Panama Railroad Company to transport goods across the Isthmus on through bills of lading for direct onward shipment.

8. War With Spain. Panama Railroad Dispute 1860-1871

The outbreak of the 1861 American Civil War prompted British ship owners to express disquiet at the lack of security for their unarmed vessels plying American territorial waters. A detachment from a United States warship had already stopped and boarded the British merchant ship *Trent*, and hostilities had broken-out as a result of blockade-breaking ships. It was widely believed that Great Britain would be drawn into the conflict; Royal Navy protection, therefore, was sought for the PSNC's fleet. The Admiralty obliged by arranging for ten officers and one hundred armed marines, including a number of Royal Navy Reserve gunners, to sail with the newly acquired *Peru (II)* from Liverpool. Three rifled cannons were also installed on the vessel, this being the first time that a PSNC ship had been specifically armed for its own defence, although the *Chile* and *Peru* of 1840 had each been fitted with two small cannon to deter pirates.

The American Civil War between the Northern and Southern states lasted from 1861 to 1865. It was a severe setback not only for that young nation, but also for the development of West Coast South American countries. Wallis Hunt in his history of Balfour Williamson Company Ltd wrote:

"Whilst the Americans were preoccupied with their internecine conflict, British privateers drove their shipping from the seas and paralysed their foreign trade. In the inevitable financial crisis, the value of greenbacks, the legal tender notes issued in 1862, fell as low as 39 cents (£0.22) on the gold dollar. Between 1860 and 1866, the National Debt rose from 20.06 (£11.14) to 77.69 dollars (£44.27) per person."[197]

Wallis Hunt also reported that in October 1865 the *Chile (II)* was the last vessel to leave Valparaíso harbour before the Spanish blockade began:

"This was a reprisal for Chilean aid to Peru in defence of the Monroe Doctrine[198], but had no lasting effect on Chile's economy. The bombardment of Valparaíso on March 31, 1866 did damage worth £2,000,000 (US 3,600,000 dollars). Williamson Balfour[199] had goods worth £2,000 (US 3,600 dollars) burnt in storage"

No records have emerged to explain what affect the Spanish blockade had on PSNC, but from 1963 to 1869, the number of ships entering Chilean ports increased steadily from 2596 vessels to 4008, and in terms of growth in ships' tonnage, from 820,014 tons in 1863 to 1,872,474 tons in 1869[200]. Although two deaths occurred during the bombardment and considerable damage was inflicted on the Customs House and the adjoining port facilities, the attack did not affect later movements within the port; war with Spain seemed to have had only a minimal impact on Chilean trade.

Chile's merchant marine, in 1865, comprised 259 ships, the bulk of which had been constructed in either the USA or Great Britain. The number of vessels actually built in Chile amounted to only 26 and most of these were small craft. Of the 259 total, only one had actually undertaken ocean crossings to Europe, although 32 sailing ships had voyaged to California, 11 to Australia and Polynesia, leaving 170 small ships to operate on coastal trade. The remaining craft were used as auxiliaries within individual ports or operated as fishing boats. Out of 259 vessels, only nine were steamships with a combined tonnage of 1,633 and an average of 181.4 tons compared with an average of 221.94 tons for sailing ships.[201]

Of more concern to the Chilean Government was the age of the 250 sailing ships, 21 of which were less than five years old; 33 were between 5 and 8 years old and 42 vessels aged between 10 and 15 years. The remainder were built well over 40 years previously when 10 years was the average lifespan for contemporary sailing ships. Many of these "*sailers*" were clippers purchased in the USA after the Gold Rush; built for speed, they incorporated the very best in naval architecture and design. They were, however, constructed mainly of soft wood, unlike the hard timbers employed by English shipbuilders, and only enjoyed an average lifespan of around 4 to 6 years. After this period, their structures became so stressed by the forces generated on the masts from the huge expanses of sail, especially during storms, that they tended to weaken rapidly.

The following article, highlighting the poor condition of Chile's merchant fleet, appeared in El Mercurio on July 10, 1860; it reported the shipwrecking of the *La General Lastra* in that year:

"*The General Lastra* was a very old and decrepit ship and in too dangerous a condition to have been taken out onto the open southern seas in winter. She had been chartered in Valparaíso to transport 400 tons of coal to the former port from Lota...and had set sail for the latter in light winds. After three days' sailing, she had not even cleared the parallel of latitude from where she had left port, clearly highlighting her suspect sailing qualities and overall damaged condition, the result of being caught in a severe storm in the Gulf of Arauco, ...she had had to make for the port of Coronel to sign-on crew to man the pumps and undertake rigging repairs.

Having secured these objectives, and the weather having become calmer, her bold and zealous captain, William Jones, had set a course for Valparaíso on June 10th after taking advantage of favourable breezes. Ceaseless manning of the pumps on board was, however, unable to reduce water levels in the cargo holds. Eight days into the voyage, the crew were exhausted and, seeing little hope of being saved, began to jettison cargo to prepare for the worst."

The ship was eventually wrecked, but crewmembers managed to save themselves and on reaching shore, proceeded to make the long journey back on foot to Valparaíso from Llico. El Mercurio's Editor commented that such shipping abuses would continue to prevail unless existing laws were implemented, not only to condemn ships not meeting prescribed sea-worthiness standards, but also to prevent them from leaving port. Chile's merchant marine really was in a lamentable state on the eve of war with Spain, with no sign or prospects of improvement, either in quality of ships or in quantity; this at a time when other leading nations were modernizing and expanding their fleets

Before the war, the reign of Queen Isabella II of Spain had been chaotic; her ministers were weak and her nation divided. Her Administration, steeped in corruption, had allowed the country to slide inexorably into Civil war. In an attempt to restore national confidence and prestige, Spain ostensibly sought to regain her lost Central and South American colonies. Peru had been the jewel in her crown and the former's winning of Independence in 1824 had been a severe loss of face to Spain, a nation that placed honour above all else. Peru's statehood had been widely recognized internationally, but not by Spain, although the latter had, by this time, accepted Chile as an independent nation.

South American concerns at European involvement in the sub-continent were well justified; Spain had already "*reannexed*" Santo Domingo. France, Great Britain and Spain had also intervened in Mexico in attempts to secure repayment of the latter's foreign debt. France's prolonged and tragic attempts to impose a monarchy on Mexico deeply shocked the South American nations; they reasonably perceived the European countries as a threat to their independence.[202]

There had also been considerable pressure from the British farming sector on Parliament for Britain to take possession of the guano-rich Lobos Islands; it was suggested in some political quarters that because Peru had never legitimately occupied them, Britain was legally entitled to do so.[203] Even the London Times newspaper in April 1852 published a lengthy call to take action to acquire the vast guano resources of the Lobos islands and bypass Peru. Landowners all over Britain repeated the call for the reluctant British Government to take possession of these Islands, but in June 1852, it judiciously announced its recognition of Peruvian sovereignty over them; the clamour for naval and military action eventually died down.

As early as 1840, the United States Government had also cast covetous glances at the Islands and had even supported a plan by a group of US entrepreneurs to seize the Islas Lobos de Tierra and Lobos de Afuera using a US gunboat. The rationale supporting this action was based on these guano-rich islands being "*unoccupied*". Their enormous guano deposits were then the source of the most valuable fertilizer available, and a potential asset not then being exploited by Peru. Accordingly, the US believed that it had every right to occupy the islands because of their state of "*un-occupation*". This thinking later formed the basis of her Guano Island Act of 1856, which legalized, in US terms, the proposed occupation of the Lobos Islands and their integration into US territory, islands previously claimed by the Spanish Empire and occupied from time to time by Peruvian fishermen.[204]

The Great Powers' territorial ambitions, therefore, provided Spain with the very justification to recover her former colonies. In order to provoke war with both Peru and Chile, she contrived to manufacture a number of incidents within the new republics, believing that these would provide legitimate excuses for landing her armed forces on their shores to join with local sympathizers to foment discord and eventually overthrow the republics' Governments. In 1862, Isabella had been persuaded by her advisors to dispatch two frigates and a schooner to WCSA waters, under the guise of a scientific research expedition.

Many historians consider that Spain's campaign to recover her former colonies was a subterfuge for her more realistic objective of securing the guano-rich Chincha Isles. The latter aim may have been prepared as a back-up arrangement in case of failure of the mission's main "*military*" purpose of supporting so-called claims of Spanish citizens resident on the West Coast. On this pretext, her forces and resident supporters were expected to make military inroads into her former colonies. Spain eventually did occupy the islands for eight months, perhaps in the vain hope that her actions would eventually generate international recognition and acceptance of her occupation. Nevertheless, during her military stay, production and transport of guano proceeded without interruption and continued to provide valuable revenue for the Peruvian Government.[205]

The Chilean authorities had cordially welcomed the expedition on arrival at Valparaíso in 1862; the Spaniards happily exchanged courtesies; the squadron later proceeding to Callao under the command of Rear Admiral Luis Hernandez Pinzon. Nothing of significance occurred there until the Spanish fleet departed that port. Shortly afterwards, violence erupted on the Peruvian Hacienda of Talambo when immigrant Spanish workers, in conflict with the hacendado over working conditions, took their disagreement to the Peruvian Court of Justice which, unsurprisingly, found in favour of the landowner.

The Peruvian Government, anticipating strong protests from the Spanish Consul, tried to reconvene the Lima Congress of South American nations in an attempt to secure support and establish common defence policies against Spain's bellicose posturing. Before the Congress could assemble, the Spanish Fleet returned to Callao to display a highly visible show of force in support of a recently arrived Spanish Commissioner, sent by Madrid to seek justice for the Spanish émigrés in the "*Talambo affair*". The reasons why the latter occurred are unclear, but violent incidents certainly took place; some historians claim that these were orchestrated by Spain to justify committing her armed forces in Peru. One Spaniard was killed in the fighting and several others injured, prompting Spain to lodge an official protest and appoint an emissary to treat with the Peruvian Government.

The crucial element in the appointment of this Spanish envoy was the fact that he had been dispatched with the rank of "*Comisario Regio*" [Royal Commissioner]. This was an intentional slight to the Peruvian Government because this position was normally a title associated with Spanish Colonial representatives, and not with the higher status of Ambassador as diplomatic protocols demanded when leading envoys were dispatched to independent sovereign nations.The Spanish, by delivering this procedural insult, had conveyed the warning that they still regarded Peru as their colony. Peru refused to enter into discussions with Madrid's envoy until her Independence had been officially recognized by Spain. Inevitably, talks between the Commissioner and the Peruvian Government broke down in April 1864.

The Spanish expeditionary force departed Callao but only as far as the Chincha islands, then the largest generator of Peruvian wealth. The defending Chincha garrison was forced to surrender to Spanish occupation and Peru's major ports were blockaded. Spain's representative justified his country's action by alleging that because Spain had never recognized Peruvian Independence, and by her action of occupation, she was simply recovering her own territory. The Peruvian Government reacted by seeking emergency powers from Congress, as well as authorization to acquire arms and naval vessels from Europe and the United States, together with the necessary means to finance their purchases. However, faced with a superior armed force, Peru concluded that she had no option but to negotiate a settlement directly with the Spanish Government.

The Spanish presence on the Chincha Islands created more alarm throughout South America; Chile, in a note to all South American nations, strongly denounced the re-occupation, portraying Spain's action as a "*reconquest*" and simultaneously declaring that she would never recognize any sovereignty over the Chincha Islands other than that extended by Peru. The Chilean Government, hinting at the use of military and naval force, promptly dispatched a representative to Europe to buy four additional warships.[206]

In spite of Chile's threatening attitude, Spain ordered five more warships to the area under the command of the more experienced Admiral Pareja to replace Pinzon. In these circumstances, Peru felt obliged to conclude a treaty with Spain in January 1865, and agreed to pay the latter compensation of three million pesos (£600,000 or $US1,080,000) for expenses incurred in the occupation of the Chincha islands, whereupon, the latter were returned to her.[207] However, the treaty's terms were considered by Peruvians to be so humiliating, particularly the acknowledgement that Spain was the aggrieved party, that it sparked a revolution in Arequipa against the Peruvian Government.

War With Spain. Panama Railroad Dispute 1860-1871

Intense anti-Spanish feeling had, by this time, been generated throughout South America, particularly in Bolivia, Ecuador and Chile; the press in the latter republic raising emotions to almost hysterical levels. When the Spanish gunboat *Vencedora* entered port, the Chilean Government, mindful of national animosity toward Spain, denied her coal supplies on the basis that this fuel was classed as a war supply and therefore could not be sold to any belligerent nation. Spain clearly regarded Chile as not being neutral in the Spain-Peru conflict, an attitude, which unsurprisingly, hardened on the discovery of two steamers leaving Valparaíso with arms and Chilean volunteers to fight for Peru.

In September 1865, Admiral Pareja anchored his flagship the *Villa de Madrid* off Valparaíso and demanded that the Spanish flag be acknowledged with a 21-guns salute. Even though planned increases to her Navy had not yet materialized, Chile steadfastly refused and war was thus declared. Her fleet then comprised one 18-cannons corvette and one four-cannons steamship to face Pareja's armada of eight vessels with a combined 207 cannons.

The Spanish Admiral, having insufficient troops to launch meaningful armed landings, was reduced to blockading Chile's main ports. His fleet was soon afterwards reinforced by the iron clad *Numancia*, bearing forty heavy guns; she was then one of the most powerful warships in the world. However, even with this added firepower, blockading all Chilean ports was still highly impractical, given the length of her coastline; Pareja would have needed a fleet several times the size he then commanded to have achieved this. Nevertheless, Chileans and resident neutrals both suffered considerable damage to property from the blockade and bombardment of Valparaíso; the port's facilities were also badly affected.

**Bombardment of Valparaíso by the Spanish squadron.
"El Correo de Ultramar", May 1866 edition**

In December 1865, The Peruvian Government that had yielded to Pareja was replaced in a coup enabling the installation of a National Executive more sympathetic to Chile. An alliance between the two neighbouring nations to fight the

Spanish was soon created, and war was officially declared in January 1866. Peru assigned four ships to the alliance, providing fighting power of 90 cannons and simultaneously closing all her ports to Pareja's vessels. After much persuasion by Peru and Chile, Ecuador finally joined the alliance; although unable to contribute naval forces, she was able to bar Pareja's squadron from entering her ports for re-provisioning, forcing them to make for Atlantic coastal towns for this purpose.

Bolivia had not then joined the union against Spain; in fact, diplomatic relations between Chile and Bolivia had been non-existent following bitter disputes over territory in what is now the Province of Antofagasta. Agreeing to a Chilean proposal that the cause of their quarrel be set-aside until the threat with Spain had been resolved, she then joined her West Coast neighbours. Spain was then faced with an adversary comprising four South American republics. These developments spread concern throughout Europe; the Spanish population became panic-stricken. Before the outbreak of war, Peru had commissioned two powerful state of the art iron-clads from England, the *Huascar* and *Independence*. They were still in England on the outbreak of war but were believed by the Spanish to be heading directly for Cadiz to bombard their then seat of power. Spain had also been concerned that her merchant ships would be threatened in international waters. In fact, the Peruvians did capture three Spanish transports off the coast of Brazil.

Thereafter, the Peruvian Navy underwent a period of modernization and by November 1866, was ready to take the war to Spain by attacking her other colonies, principally the Philippines. With Spain beginning to weaken, so too did the Peruvian-Chilean alliance, and the war petered out following the submission of peace proposals by the United States' Government. Isabella II was forced to abdicate and it was not until June 1883 that peace with Spain was finally achieved following the signing of a treaty in Lima.

The Spanish squadron's hostile actions had generated a great deal of anger throughout the foreign community on the West Coast. The war, it claimed, had severely damaged its commerce and trading premises when, according to internationally recognized war conventions, they should have been regarded as neutral and treated accordingly. At the commencement of hostilities, Spain had a naval force but no army and there was no way she could have transported one to occupy Chile or any other West Coast nation. Chile, for her part, had an army but no navy; she would have been unable to assemble the latter for many months.

An economic blockade of Chile's principal ports was, therefore, the only meaningful weapon that Spain could launch against her opponents, an action that led to vociferous complaints by foreign business houses to their respective Governments. A Scottish brewery, for example, exporting beer to Chile, together with Chambers of Commerce of British cities, such as Aberdeen and Manchester, made strong representations to the British Government demanding its intervention in the war.[208] It is notable that Alsop & Company, which figured prominently in drawing the United States deeper into the subsequent Chile-Bolivia conflict, had clearly and significantly considered itself at this time to be a North American enterprise based and operating in Chile.

These protests and representations to various foreign Governments, including that of Chile, caused the latter and the Spanish naval force to conclude that its blockade could not be sustained for the entire Chilean coast. The Spanish commander, therefore, confined his strategy to closing the principal Chilean ports of Valparaíso, Coquimbo and Talcahuano. The Chilean Government responded by declaring all the nation's other ports as principal areas, thus opening them up to foreign vessels, previously excluded under Chilean cabotage legislation.

When Spanish Admiral Pareja decided to lift the blockade on Caldera to concentrate his forces elsewhere, he ordered the burning of several captured Chilean merchant ships stationed there. Ten Chilean vessels were set on fire and another 24 sunk or captured during the fighting.[209] Chile, by then, had lost most of her merchant fleet, either as direct battle casualties or due to vessels surrendering Chilean registration to seek the protection of neutral foreign flags at the onset of war. Even the floating dock anchored in Valparaíso Bay had been re-registered under the Prussian flag.

Sailing under a neutral nation's ensign, however, did not always secure the envisaged protection. The steamship *Paquete de Maule*, for example, at first acquired Colombian registration but soon transferred to the British flag, under which, and in clear breach of international rules of conduct, she transported Chilean officers and crew to Montevideo to man new warships for their return voyage to Chile. The Spanish squadron captured her as she entered the Bay of Arauco, south of Concepción. [210]

El Matías Cousiño.[211]

The steamship *Matías Cousiño* was the first steam collier belonging to Compañia Explotadora de Lota y Coronel. Built in Newcastle in 1859, she was also captured while flying the British flag but eventually returned to her owners following British Government intervention. A more tragic incident involved the small steamship *Guayacán*, when carrying copper between the minor ports of Tongoy and Guayacán. She had changed to British registration on the outbreak of hostilities, but despite this protection, Spanish warships in October 1865 relentlessly pursued her, forcing this small steamship onto coastal rocks resulting in her sinking with the loss of all hands and cargo. El Mercurio reported the tragic event on November 2, 1865, but commented, perhaps in the hope of stimulating British intervention: "*It looks as though the Spanish wish to cross swords with the British....*" .The Editor had used the more derogatory word "*godos*" in preference to the normally used "*españoles*".

In 1867, Peruvian liberals, led by the dictator Prado, having established control of Congress, imposed their decentralist views on the nation regardless of cost, and sought to curtail the influence of the Catholic Church, especially in education. Importantly, attempts were made to introduce a balanced revenue system or budget that would remove Government reliance on financial advances from guano consignees. Export duty of 3%, and a stamp tax were introduced; an excise tax was applied to the consumption of alcohol and other legislation was introduced to reduce national expenditure.[212] These measures provoked considerable infighting in Congress leading to another revolution that overthrew the Prado administration.

Unfortunately, these prudent economic policies were indiscriminately extinguished to the delight of Peruvian's generally, who had long protested against the economic reforms that Prado had tried to impose upon them. Nevertheless, the Peru of 1867 was no better off than it had been in 1845, a fact attributed to the inability of successive regimes to effect a compromise between liberal and conservative factions.[213] While some contemporary economists thought it prudent for Peru to free herself from dependency on guano consignees, there were others, in 1869, who possessed unbridled optimism about the nation's wealth and resources, particularly guano, copper and nitrates.

These views were based on traditional Catholic and colonial visions of "*miraculous overnight, painless and easy, material development*" rather than the slow accumulations of capital generated by savings, investment and a degree of effort and sacrifice. In August of that year, the regime performed what historians have considered as one of the most controversial actions in the economic history of Peru by entering into an agreement with the French firm Dreyfus. Government dealings with other guano consignees were to cease, and in lieu of these, the French company was assured the supply of two million tons of guano. The price paid for each ton was significantly more than that received from previous contractors, and importantly for the Peruvian Government, the French firm had not only consented to an immediate and substantial financial advance, followed by twelve further but smaller pre-payments, but had also agreed to assume responsibility for servicing Peruvian foreign debt. In this way, the Peruvian Treasury was saved from bankruptcy, but its Government failed to introduce the promised national balanced budgeting system.

Perceiving Dreyfus and Company to be an inexhaustible source of additional capital, the Peruvian Government arranged to draw considerable loans from the French firm, resulting in an unreasonably large debt tied-in with penal interest and commission rates. This disastrous financial policy continued until 1872, by which time Peru's foreign debt had totalled forty-nine million pounds sterling (US 88,200,000 dollars), ten times the liability in place when the Peruvian Government had assumed control.[214]

Profits from the exploitation of Peru's mineral resources, led to the establishment of many utility companies and commercial concerns together with a mushrooming of mercantile banks. These in turn generated new wealth, predominately along the coastal areas populated by the élite landowners and agricultural business houses. It also enabled the introduction of a railway system to criss-cross Peru. This was not only welcomed by the military as a way of quickly moving troops and materiel to quell potential revolutions, but also received the support of those who envisaged that railroads would facilitate the country's exploitation of her mineral resources. The Government's economic advisers had assured that such railroad systems were the main, if not the sole reason, for incredible growth in the United States' economic progress after her disastrous Civil War.[215]

Unfortunately for Peru, precious investment capital had been directed at military and railway initiatives, bypassing essential national infrastructure programmes such as irrigation projects, education, sanitation, mining expansion and industrial development. Tax Collection had been ignored as her Government devoted all its efforts into channelling income from her rapidly depleting guano reserves and borrowed capital into railroad construction, without making provisions for maintenance or enabling measures to ensure its future profitability.[216]

The war with Spain had ended with the famous bombardment of Valparaíso in Mar 31, 1866. Apart from destroying a significant part of the port and its shipping facilities, the blockade had had no major overall impact on Chile's economy, but the total tonnage of her merchant fleet had fallen to almost zero. Long after the war, the rebuilding of her merchant marine was painfully slow. Even by 1878, total available tonnage was just over half of the 1865 figure. It must be appreciated that foreign nationals resident in Chile owned most of her merchant ships, the majority of which had been constructed abroad, mostly in the United States and Great Britain. To compound the problem, nearly all the officers and crews of these ships were of foreign nationality.

The war had begun a year after the introduction of the Ordenenza de La Aduana(Customs law) 1864, confirming the adoption of Chile's free trade policy with those nations who reciprocated with similar practices. This strategy gradually undermined the mass of ineffective legal restraints previously introduced to protect and encourage the Chilean shipping industry. There were other factors contributing to the re-development of Chile's merchant fleet; the discovery of silver at Caracoles and the legal protection afforded to investors by the formation of "*Sociedades Anonimas*" (similar to the status of a British limited and US incorporated companies), encouraged the growth of Chilean shipping firms.

An opposing contribution was the opening of the Suez Canal in 1869. Being more suitable for steamships, it effectively rendered sailing ships uneconomic in that region, compelling many like Balfour Williamson Company to relocate their business interests to South America. Moreover, a European-wide financial and trade crisis following the Franco-Prussian war, together with worldwide reductions in freight costs and the lowering of coal prices, caused a slowdown in the rate of shipping growth on the West Coast. Consequently, the development of the Chilean merchant marine was rapidly infected by the vagaries of world shipping markets.

Technological improvements, stimulated by the Industrial Revolution in Britain and Europe, had clearly contributed to general economic successes. Direct progress in naval and engineering design, and improvements to and the provision of extra port facilities also figured significantly in the expansion of commercial shipping on the WCSA, particularly when combined with the success of the wider and popular free trade policies. Protectionist measures operating in the first half of the 19th Century disappeared from Chile, allowing her to fall in line with the rest of the world's free-market system.

World demand for Chile's copper and nitrate resources, her coal imports stockpiled at important positions on a coastline strategically available to steam shipping, and the conveyance of cereals from the Pacific coast to Northern Europe, swiftly projected Chile into the global trade arena during the second half of the 19th Century. Accordingly, between 1866 and the beginning of the 1870s, a period of recovery emerged, aided by Chilean resources and the positive economic conditions operating in that country.

There was a tendency for Chilean ship owners, still mistrustful of possible surprise attacks by Spanish squadrons, to remain registered under neutral flags. This was one of the main reasons why there was no increase in the total tonnage of Chile's merchant marine after the Spanish bombardment of Valparaíso. Additionally, the Chilean Government had not then produced any incentives to encourage Chilean ship owners to re-register under the national banner. Her Government, for example, could have especially simplified the bureaucratically demanding re-registration process that posed a formidable obstacle for Chilean ship owners. There was also deep concern that if the latter re-registered their foreign-flagged vessels under the Chilean pennant, they would lose potential freight from those shippers wary of further possible outbreaks of hostilities with Spain.[217]

Consequently, the majority of Chilean shipping firms owning one or more vessels in 1865, did not proceed to re-register them for at least another three years after the conflict. Typical of these was the United States' firm, Alsop & Co with five Chilean registered vessels totalling 1,608 tons. The ships actually belonged to a Chilean citizen resident in Europe[218]. Except for two small steamships, the *Antonio Varas* and *Concepción*, all those vessels registered as Chilean during 1867-1869, whether by a foreign firm, or by groups of foreign businessmen, were either financially-backed by individual enterprises or registered corporations.

The question of national and foreign ownership was only of secondary importance to the issue of the composition of crew nationality on Chilean ships. Although Chile's Government must have considered the possibility of requisitioning her registered merchant ships for military duty in times of emergency or war, it appeared apathetic to generating the means to encourage the formation of her own merchant marine. This lack of Government action created a gap quickly filled by Pacific Steam Navigation Company(PSNC) and others. It is not known how badly PSNC was affected during the war with Spain; probably the affects were minimal, given her neutral flag and the impractical Spanish strategy of attempting to initially blockade all ports with such a small naval force, and the Chilean Government's counteraction in opening up minor ports to foreign vessels.

During the war, facilities provided by the Panama Railroad had vastly improved conditions on the Isthmus crossing, the latter then taking a minimum of three and a half hours. Royal Mail Steam Packet Line steamships, operating a monthly service from England, arrived at either Chagres or Colón on the seventh of each month. Once conveyed across the Isthmus, passengers and cargo were then transported southwards on the ninth of each month by PSNC vessels. Since their introduction in 1840, this firm's services on the West Coast, embracing the port of Panama, had improved both in frequency and punctuality, thereby contributing substantially to growth in passenger traffic, the transportation of bullion and general merchandise across the Isthmus.

On completion of its line, the Railroad Company had naturally taken advantage of those increases in passenger and freight volumes generated principally by the two British companies, in partnership, servicing the Europe-WCSA trade. Similar benefits were also obtained from the operations of the US-owned Pacific Mail Steamship Company then serving the West Coast of North America, in conjunction with the United Mail Steamship Company plying the Eastern Seaboard. The continuing colonization of the United States' Pacific Coast contributed to the flow of passengers and freight between New York, the Atlantic and Californian ports, increasing the Railroad Company's traffic to demand levels that could hardly be accommodated at the time. The Railroad Company increased its tariffs, as Ira E. Bennett had reported in his *"History of the Panama Canal"* (1915), to prohibitive rates, but prospective passengers and shippers were still not deterred. However, Royal Mail Steam Packet Line and PSNC, both of whom had an agreement with the Railroad Company, were adversely affected by these excessive charges. Minutes of the two companies' Board Room meetings record conflicting views on the apportionment of freight revenues and costs.[219]

Bennett confirmed that in 1869, on completion of the United States' coast-to-coast Union Pacific Railroad, the PRC lost most of its Californian trade, but retained its custom with South and Central America, *"borne to it almost exclusively by the ships of the PSNC."* However, he commented:

"This haulage too [to and from the WCSA] the railroad subsequently lost when, in consequence of a dispute, the [Pacific Steam] Navigation Company was obliged to give up its shops and dockyards on the Island of Taboga, in the Bay of Panama, and send its ships by way of the straits (sic) of Magellan direct to England".

Bennett never attempted to explain the cause of the dispute, which obliged the Railroad Company Directors to rethink their attitude, but the PRC must have been aware of the implications for its future operations following the commencement of the trans United States' Central Pacific and Union Pacific Railroads in 1862. It must surely have deduced that on completion of these projects, a considerable share of the traffic then conveyed by the Panama Railroad would be lost to it.

The Panama Railroad Company's Superintendent, Colonel A.J.Center, for a long time, was subjected to a barrage of claims and representations from the PSNC. The latter not only cited unsatisfactory sharing of freight revenues brought by its fleet for conveyance across the Isthmus, but also complained that railroad facilities had not kept pace with the needs of the shipping company's own increased growth and development.[220] Colonel Center, bowing to PSNC pressure, travelled in 1865 to Callao to discuss these issues with George Petrie, the shipping company's General Manager on the West Coast. A deal was quickly struck whereby the Railroad revenues derived from freight and passengers jointly sourced by PSNC and Royal Mail Steam Packet Line, were to be shared equally between the three parties. Colonel Center, highly satisfied with this deal, headed for New York to report to the Railroad Company's Board of Directors. To his astonishment, they refused to sanction the Petrie agreement. Center, deeply shocked at this decision to reject the draft contract, warned his Directors of the likely retaliatory and potentially damaging action that would be undertaken by PSNC.

The latter's West Coast Manager had emphatically declared that, unless a permanent and fair settlement was reached on the division of freight and passenger revenues, his company would resort to building bigger steamships to establish a

War With Spain. Panama Railroad Dispute 1860-1871

regular European service via the Strait of Magellan, thus substantially reducing levels of freight and passenger input to the Panama Railroad. Center, when advising his Directors, emphasized the adverse affects on the Railroad Company if such services were introduced; they would, he re-iterated, eliminate the need for the PSNC to voyage to Panama. Center's warnings, however, went unheeded and the Railroad Company's Directors continued to insist on receiving the largest percentage of passenger/freight revenues for transport across the Isthmus, a decision they would, inevitably, come to regret.

For PSNC's West Coast Manager to deliver such a warning to Colonel Center, he must have been confident of two factors. Firstly, PSNC would surely have needed prior assurance from the British Government, that if it elected to build larger vessels to make regular voyages between the WCSA and Great Britain, it would be granted an amendment or supplement to its existing Charter of Incorporation. Secondly, the company must have felt confident, or have even received a prior commitment from the Chilean Government, that it would sanction an additional European service out of Valparaíso. If no such confirmation had been made, then it could reasonably be assumed that PSNC believed that one would eventually be given. This view is re-enforced by the Valparaíso business community's earlier and numerous campaigns supported by the local press, urging the Chilean Government to renew the English Company's privileges, subject to it undertaking the much demanded monthly steamship service to the southern provinces.

The British Government's rivalry with the United States, and its concern at the latter's growing economic power and influence in Central America, might have also prompted an unofficial Government commitment to motivate PSNC to effect this strategy. A revised Royal Charter did emerge in 1865, enabling the English company to operate on the East and West Coasts of South America, including the Falklands as well as North and Central America.

In practical terms, PSNC's new strategy would have enabled Britain's growing exports to be shipped directly to Chile and both coasts of South America. Moreover, it would have facilitated the importation of valuable resources to fuel the insatiable appetite of England's Industrial Revolution. A comparatively minor domestic side-benefit would not only have arisen from the creation of extra employment in Merseyside, but would also have generated profit for those industries associated with PSNC, e.g. stevedoring, provision of engineering spares, warehousing, repairs and the myriads of trades associated with merchant shipping.

Chile had never made any secret of her opposition to an Isthmian transit; she had wanted to cultivate her own strategic position embracing the Strait of Magellan and to make Valparaíso the leading port for world trade with South America. She had, up to that point, not adopted measures to obstruct or curtail PSNC's use of the Panama transit, as to do so might have only antagonized the Great Powers to her own disadvantage. By encouraging PSNC to use the Magellan Strait route to

Europe, Chile might have perceived that the Panama Railroad's future prospects, without the input from PSNC and Royal Mail Steam Packet Company, would be very bleak.

There was a more important and furtive strategy behind Chile's attempts to create a direct shipping service to Europe. Her traditional enemy was Peru; Chile's military analysts would surely have deduced that the PRC was becoming strategically more important to her northern neighbour. This fear was confirmed on the outbreak of the War of the Pacific over the Peruvian alliance with Bolivia and the latter's coastal territories. The railroad began to be viewed by Chile as an important conduit for her opponents to tranship war supplies purchased from the Great Powers of the Atlantic. The PRC route was, consequently, deemed to be strategically more important to Peru; her alternative and traditional line of supply via Cape Horn, being several thousand miles longer, would not only have added many weeks to voyages, thus making the cost of purchasing supplies dearer, but would also have rendered them susceptible to attack by Chilean forces.

This view is supported by Chilean consular action in May 1879; her representatives in Panama City had lodged an official protest with the Colombia Government[221] complaining that arms' shipments across the Isthmus bound for Chile's enemies, not only violated an existing Colombian-Chilean commercial treaty, but also militated against the principles of internationally accepted conduct of neutrality.[222] Colombia's Government remained intransigent but Chile continued to submit protest notes. She had long regarded W.R.Grace & Co., as a favoured "*Peruvian House*";[223] the North American company's support for Peru was confirmed when Charles Flint, a partner with the Callao house of W.R.Grace who had, hitherto, performed the role of Consul for Chile in that port, immediately resigned the latter position on the outbreak of war. The Peruvian Government enlisted the Grace House to acquire and transport munitions to Peru. Neutral Colombia was not enthusiastic about her position, often ignoring Grace Company's consignments of war materiel to Peru transported by the PRC. Former Chilean Consul Charles Flint had wanted to supply ten "*dirigible torpedoes*" and torpedo boats to Peru's war effort via the PRC, without attracting the attention of Colombia, the Chileans or friends of Chile resident in Panama. Lawrence A Clayton wrote:

"The problem was the [torpedo] craft's length. It was fifty feet long and difficult, if not impossible to disguise. He thus shipped it to Panama with no attempt at concealment and billed it to the Compañia Cargadora del Peru, a guano dealer in Callao. The fastest carrier then operating on the West Coast, the Pacific Steam Navigation Company was controlled by English sympathetic to the Chilean cause.[224] They refused passage to the steam launch (i.e. the torpedo boat), quite rightly suspicious of its ultimate function. Yet when the Peruvian Government made a generous offer to purchase two PSNC steamers, the company accepted and the Hershoff (torpedo) boat and five others eventually reached Callao." [225]

It was not until it had captured the Peruvian ironclad *Huáscar* that Chile's Navy was able to take control of the sea-lanes from Panama; Peru, by then, had been relying almost entirely on the PRC for delivery of her war matériel.

The resistance of the Panama Railroad Directors to the Center-Petrie agreement might have arisen from a belief that the very large revenues earned would continue to increase, given the rapid pace of development and North American industrialization. The PRC might have also concluded that any PSNC re-routing of vessels through the Strait of Magellan would have had little impact on their operations. Such thinking may have been based on findings similar to those of F.N.Otis, later revealed in his *"History of the Panama Railroad"*[226]:

"The fact that up to the establishment of the Isthmus Railroad, the trade of South and Central America had been carried on almost exclusively with Europe (that between the United States and those countries being estimated at less than ten per cent of the whole) has prevented its magnitude and importance from being fully appreciated by the American people.
The managers of the Panama Railroad Company, from its earliest existence, were aware of that important circumstance, and looked confidently to the business of those regions already existing, and that which would undoubtedly be developed by the facilities afforded by the railroad, as one of the surest elements in its ultimate and permanent success.
It was not lost sight of that the European trade (as far as the European influence extended) would cling tenaciously to its circuitous track around Cape Horn, fully aware that, when the business was turned into the direct route across the Isthmus, a large portion of the trade would be inevitably directed to the nearer markets of the United States..."

Otis drew attention to the amount of railroad business in 1858 originating from the South and Central American nations, that had exceeded the value of the Californian trade via the Isthmus by nine times. By 1860, less than $1/15^{th}$ of the total railroad freight was attributed to this source, the remaining $14/15^{th}$ resulting from shipments originating in the Eastern United States, British manufactures and other goods shipped directly to South and Central America, and the produce from those regions in return. However, in 1867, Otis reported:

"The California trade over the Panama road has increased since 1860 to such an extent, that now in 1867, about one third of its business is due to that source."

He detailed the eight steam ship lines then utilizing the services of the Panama Railroad viz:

"THE PACIFIC MAIL STEAMSHIP COMPANY, plying tri-monthly between New York, Panama, Mexico, California, Japan and Chime. Their total steamship fleet was twenty-five.

THE GENERAL TRANSATLANTIC COMPANY. (Compagnie Générale Transatlantique) sailing between St.Nazaire France, the West Indies, Mexico, and Aspinwall (otherwise known as Colón) [No quantities are given by Otis, he merely recites "with a large fleet of powerful steam-ships."].

THE WEST INDIA AND PACIFIC STEAMSHIP COMPANY running between Liverpool, England, the West Indies, the western coast of South and Central America, and Aspinwall, with a fleet of nineteen large steamships.

THE ROYAL MAIL STEAM PACKET COMPANY running semi-monthly between Southampton, England, the West Indies, the eastern coast of Mexico, South and Central America, and Aspinwall with a fleet of nineteen large steamships.

THE PANAMA, NEW ZEALAND AND AUSTRALIA ROYAL MAIL COMPANY running between Panama, New Zealand and Australia

THE BRITISH PACIFIC STEAM NAVIGATION COMPANY, running between Panama and the ports of New Granada, Ecuador, Peru, Bolivia and Chili.

THE PANAMA RAILROAD COMPANY'S CENTRAL AMERICA LINE of steamships running between Panama, Nicaragua, Costa Rica, Salvador and Guatemala

THE CALIFORNIA, OREGON AND MEXICO COMPANY. A line of steamships, running between San Francisco, California and Mexico and between San Francisco, Portland, Oregon and the Island of Vancouver."

In addition to the references to steamship lines, Otis listed the following sailing ship services:

"THE BREMEN AND ASPINWALL LINE. Vessels sail monthly
THE BORDEAUX AND ASPINWALL LINE. Vessels sailing quarterly.
THE PANAMA RAILROAD COMPANY LINE. Seven sailing vessels from New York to Aspinwall."

Steamship services through the Strait of Magellan had already been the subject of an approach by British businessman Henry Griffin in October 1853. He had proposed that the Chilean Government provide an annual subsidy of 60,000 pesos (£12,000 or $US21,600) to any company providing a steamship service via the Strait between Caldera in the northern provinces of the country to Liverpool;[227] The Government accepted this proposal in principle, and Griffin, being the only one interested in participating in such an operation, was awarded the concession subject to a company being formed in Great Britain to provide regular propeller driven steamship services between Caldera and Liverpool.

This concession was to last for ten years and benefit from a Government annual subsidy of 60,000 pesos. The steamship services provided under this privilege were, importantly, to be exempted from all port and tonnages dues, and the successful company was to also enjoy the right to search for and mine coal, and assemble fuel and stores depots at any one or more points along the Strait. Griffin, for his part, was to provide and maintain at least six steamships of 1500 tons each, to be certified as A-1 on Lloyds Register.[228]

It is strange that during these discussions between the Chilean Government and Henry Griffin, and despite the matter being extensively reported in the Chilean press, PSNC had shown absolutely no interest in bidding for the direct Caldera-Liverpool service via the Strait. Chilean Historian Claudio Véliz suggested,[229] firstly, that this was attributable to PSNC's shareholding in the Panama Railroad Company (PRC), which in 1853 was nearing completion, and accordingly, it did not wish to compete against its own probably profitable interests. At the same time, Véliz added that the English company might have wished to preserve its European monopoly on the Isthmus crossing. On the other hand, the PSNC's European monopoly could still have been guaranteed for ten years by virtue of the exclusivity offered by the Chilean Government for providing a steamship service to Liverpool via the Strait of Magellan.

If PSNC had anticipated that its profitable interests in PRC could be damaged by competition created by a Chile to Europe service, then its shareholding must have been extensive, leading to a reasonable conclusion that the latter might have been sufficiently large to influence PRC's decision making process. Véliz's second argument[230] was based on technical assumptions, and here one must mostly support his reasoning that by 1853, when Griffin had outlined his proposals, steamship engines were still at a primitive stage of development; good enough for coastal work and generally inland placid waters, but economically unsuitable for ocean crossings.

Coal consumption on early steam engines was extremely high; stocks of fuel taking-up much valuable storage space, and leaving little room for cargo and passenger accommodation, and would have resulted in higher transport charges. Additionally, in order to replenish fuel for these vessels, huge amounts of coal needed stockpiling at strategic ports along the route at considerable expense. This was one of the reasons why sailing ships were able to compete for so long; they were able to carry higher volume cargoes over longer distances without the need to refuel. Accordingly, PSNC might then have considered a transatlantic service uneconomic.

Nevertheless, at the time of Griffin's steamship recommendation to the Chilean Government, PSNC must have been aware of technological progress and developments taking place with high and low pressure engines. In 1855, this new technology was successfully adopted in the engines of the company's steamship

Valparaíso and a succession of other vessels. If PSNC, with all its expertise, contacts and readiness to keep abreast of this and other steam engine technology, had concluded that the advanced and available steamship engines of the period were not suited to ocean crossings, one wonders what type of power units Griffin and his company had considered for the latter's ships at that time. What must have been available to him would surely have been considered by PSNC.

A more plausible explanation is that PSNC could not then afford the capital outlay for the provision of six propeller driven steamships for the European service and its infrastructure, or that it preferred to wait to assess the impact of the Panama Railroad Company's service on its own existing operations before considering use of the Strait of Magellan route. Another possibility that needs to be considered is the matter of PSNC's British arrogance, an attitude with which it seemed to be afflicted throughout the 19th Century, its lack of regard for the competition on the West Coast or else its Admiral Nelson-like perception of its existence.

PSNC had not previously expressed interest in operating a monthly steamship service to Ancud in the southern provinces of Chile when tenders had first been invited. Only after initial failures by small under-capitalized enterprises had been derided by Valparaíso's El Mercurio newspaper when expressing the open support of the Valparaíso business community for PSNC, did the English company submit its bid to the Chilean Government. Its assessment of the situation might have been clouded by the ensuing publicly expressed clamour for its services; it might have believed that serious competition still did not exist or that if it did emerge, it would fail, leaving the way open for PSNC to solicit improved terms over what had already been offered. The English company might, in its arrogance, have failed to appreciate that the support of the Valparaíso press and the business community would probably have been lent to any other enterprise capable and prepared to introduce European services. On the other hand, might it simply have been a case of PSNC miscalculating the situation?

An article appearing in El Mercurio on October 9, 1861, stated that one of the immediate consequences of the breakdown in negotiations with PRC and PSNC was the announcement by the latter that it planned to introduce a steamship line to connect the Atlantic and Pacific Oceans via the Strait of Magellan. Three days later, the same newspaper published an extensive editorial detailing the case for the Chilean Government making available a large subsidy to PSNC to ensure that this proposed service went ahead. The English Company, perhaps to apply further pressure on the Government, announced in the press that for technical and financial reasons, such an operation might not take place before 1864. El Mercurio also revealed that a French sailing ship company had been interested in obtaining state funding from South American nations to establish a rapid sailing clipper line from there to Europe. The newspaper, however, supported the Government's reasoning in rejecting this project; it considered that there already existed sufficient sailing ship services round Cape Horn, and that its subsidy scheme should only be applied to assist steam navigation.[231]

Whether the PSNC announcement was genuine, or whether it had been deliberately concocted to pressure the PRC, or even to constitute a warning shot to Henry Griffin and his supporters that, if they proceeded, it would be at the cost of meeting stiff PSNC competition, can only be speculation. It did not appear to have deterred the Griffin group; three years later in June 1864, El Mercurio published the following information:

"It looks as though there will soon be a steamship line from Lima and Valparaíso to Liverpool via the Strait of Magellan with interim calls at Buenos Aires, Montevideo, Río de Janeiro and Bahía. As a result of this service, the fervent hopes of many of our businessmen are going to be realized. Despite many still believing the service's launching to be impossible, it will provide competition on the European sea routes for the powerful PSNC which for so many years has ruled as Queen of our seas and from which she has derived huge profits.[232]

The newly formed enterprise was the British and South American Steam Navigation Company (BSANC), which had publicly proclaimed that its ships would complete the Liverpool-Valparaíso voyage in 50 days and to Lima in another 10. In the months following its emergence, this company's representatives approached the Chilean Government to seek other concessions, chief among them being an annual subsidy of 100,000 pesos (£20,000 or $US 36,000) for a period of 10 years.

In December 1864, the Chilean Chamber of Deputies considered whether the following motion should be sent to the Government Executive for consideration:

"That the President of the Republic be authorized to grant that shipping line establishing [Valparaiso to Liverpool] services through the Strait of Magellan, an annual subsidy not exceeding 100,000 pesos for a period of not more than ten years". [233]

This motion was subsequently ratified, but it is noteworthy in not containing any specific reference to BASNC, suggesting that there may have been doubts as to the ability of the latter enterprise to execute the scheme, thereby leaving the way open to PSNC or others. It looked as though PSNC had indeed miscalculated, but its future was once again fortunately determined by events beyond its control, rather than its pursuit of any deliberate and meaningful strategy. By the end of 1864, war between the allied nations of the West Coast and Spain was in full swing and caused a two years' suspension of further Chilean Government discussion with BASNC on the provision of a Magellan Strait steamship service.

After the war, the Chilean Government reviewed the issue but by then, the latter Company seemed to have disappeared. The Government, therefore, was obliged to re-launch its offer of an annual 100,000 pesos subsidy, but this time for a period of twelve years. On this occasion, PSNC did not hesitate to submit its bid to the Chilean Government and, in the absence of other approaches, won the contract together with a further subsidy for carrying mails. The other West Coast nations, not wishing to be excluded from any European mail service, promptly awarded their own subsidies:

Chile	five years	£3360	$US	6048
Peru	three	£2860	$US	5148
Ecuador	three	£2400	$US	4320
Bolivia	three	£1000	$US	1800
New Granada	three	£720	$US	1296

PSNC's spat with the Panama Railroad had been real enough, whether politically contrived or not. Had the Railroad company lowered its freight and passenger charges, as initially requested by both PSNC and Royal Mail Steam Packet Company, then the cause of their dispute, presumably, would have been immediately resolved. In such circumstances it is not known whether PSNC would have proceeded to commence a European Steamship service via the Strait of Magellan on its own initiative. The Chilean Government had been keen to expand the country's influence internationally, and a steamship link to Europe would not only have fortified Chile's position on the Strait of Magellan, but would have also created the desirable lines of international communication that she craved.

The suggestion of the Chilean Government's clandestine support for PSNC in its spat with the Panama Railroad Company appears to have some foundation. Chile was, by 1870, becoming increasingly involved with Argentina in a dispute, which had grown throughout the previous decade over the boundary between the two nations. Chile regarded the Strait of Magellan and adjoining land as being under her sovereignty, an area that especially needed her military protection. It was, by 1872, the route for most European commerce to the Pacific. Control of the Strait by Argentina or any other nation, could not only have endangered Chile's trade during peacetime, but would also have constituted a powerful strategic advantage during times of war. Argentina, for her part, had previously focused her claims on Patagonia rather than the Strait. However, towards the end of 1870, she had let it be known that she was prepared to dispute Chilean control of the Magellan territory, and announced that she could not afford to provide Chile with an Atlantic outlet because of her possession of the eastern sector of the Strait of Magellan.[234]

The development and effectiveness of more modern marine engines was beginning to be extensively proven, especially on the North Atlantic routes. Warnings by PSNC to build larger and more efficient vessels must, surely, have been assessed as a plausible proposition, and not easily dismissed as empty threats. It could also be argued that the PRC believed that such was the strategic importance of the Panama Isthmus to the United States, that her Government's assurances would subsequently be quietly and confidentially given, or would, unofficially, provide measures to protect the transit whatever economic difficulties the railroad company might face. It was highly likely that the US Government had shared Otis' conclusions that a large proportion of the WCSA trade would, inevitably, be directed to the nearer markets of the United States should an Isthmian canal transit ever be completed. The PRC, of course, still possessed that valuable concession granted by the New Granada Government for such a *"transit by whatever means"* and the concept of a canal across the Panama Isthmus was, at that time, beginning to be discussed as a realistic proposition.

In 1863, PSNC launched a new paddle steamer, the *Chile (II)*. She grossed 1672 tons and cost nearly £54,000 (US 97,200 dollars) to build. Some innovative features had been introduced to her interior décor, including picture panels in the passenger lounges, a reflection of the substantial passenger trade then existing. Five months later, the same shipyard handed over the iron paddle steamer *Quito (II)* to PSNC. A correspondent from the Illustrated London News commented:

"On a trial voyage in Liverpool, a few days before her grand departure, the ship attained an average speed of 13½ knots with a very low rate of fuel consumption. Using 1372 kilos of Scottish coal per hour, steam pressure was raised to 25 lbs and 24 revolutions [of paddle wheels per minute] were achieved. She will be a valuable addition to the Company's fleet. The latter started with just three[235] small steamships but now operates seventeen first class vessels whose numbers will be increased next July by the addition of the 1800 tons steamship *Payta* now being built in the same shipyard."

The *Quito (II)*, considered to be one of the most beautiful vessels afloat at the time, was sold by PSNC within a year of completion after being found to be too small for the Company's rapidly expanding operations. In 1864, the *Anne* was also sold for not being large enough, but the fleet was later expanded by the acquisition of the *Payta* and her sister ships. These were to have a considerable bearing on PSNC's development. Another addition was the wooden hulled, 837 tons paddle steamship *Favorita*, built in North America specifically for North American river traffic; she was, therefore, considered just as suitable for the calm waters of the West Coast. On January 25, 1865, the small steamship *Cloda* was shipwrecked off Huacho but, fortunately, with no loss of life.

Further problems arose during 1864 when PSNC, once again, experienced coal shortages on the West Coast, resulting in substantial increases in operational costs. It was possible that Chilean coal-mining production had been curtailed during the war with Spain or, in view of it being a *"war commodity"*, its sale to foreign vessels, which would have included all PSNC vessels, would have been prohibited. It was, however, more likely that Chilean coal-mining production could not keep pace with the ever-growing demand for this commodity from her developing copper foundries and the sharp increase in the number of foreign merchant and Chilean naval steamships. Leslie Bethell in his "*Chile. From independence to the War of the Pacific*" explained that wood had, initially, been the main fuel for the foundries but coal became the main alternative:

"This was increasingly mined along the coast to the south of Concepción from the 1840s onwards. Here domestic production was vulnerable to imports of higher-quality coal from Great Britian or occasionally from Australia but held its own in the longer run, in part because a mixture of local and foreign coal was found to be ideal in smelting operations".

The gas networks in the cities were also adding to coal consumption. West Coast General Manager George Petrie resolved the problem by reducing coal delivery costs from the United Kingdom through a commercial arrangement with the Peruvian Government. The latter regularly chartered twenty sailing ships to convey guano to Europe. These vessels, normally returning empty, were then utilized by PSNC on the return voyage to carry coal for the Company's steamships on the West Coast. This agreement remained in force for many years, mutually benefiting the Peruvian Government and PSNC by ensuring that the steamship company received a steady supply of coal at economical prices.

By 1865, PSNC was operating a fleet of 12 steamships providing fortnightly voyages between Valparaíso and Panama. According to one contemporary Latin American correspondent, it was described as one of the best-managed and most prosperous companies in the world. In supporting this claim, attention was drawn to the Company's considerable establishment on the Isle of Taboga near the port of Panama. Given the expanding West Coast trade, PSNC continued with its shipbuilding programme, placing orders at the John Elder shipyards for four new paddle steamships, the *Pacific, Limeña, Santiago* and the *Panama*. All these new vessels were introduced into service before the end of 1866, and were essential in enabling George Petrie, PSNC's resident manager in Lima, to translate threats made to the Panama Railroad Company into action, namely, the establishment of a direct steamship service between Valparaíso and Europe. Plans promoted by former Liberator Bernardo O'Higgins had then become a reality; the Chilean Government must have been heartened with the outcome of the spat, whether contrived or not, between the Panama Railroad Company and the PSNC. Valparaíso, because of the new direct links to Europe, once again became the predominant port on the WCSA.

The new direct service to Europe put paid to an imaginative proposal to encourage sailing ships to use the Strait of Magellan. The idea had first taken hold

War With Spain. Panama Railroad Dispute 1860-1871

two years after the arrival on the West Coast in 1840 of the pioneering steamships, *Peru* and *Chile*. A petition had been submitted to the Chilean Government for a ten years' exclusive privilege to operate a steam tugboat company in the Strait. Because sailing ships could not properly manoeuvre in the narrow channels of the Strait and due to unfavourable winds, they were forced to round Cape Horn, a longer and much more dangerous voyage. The tugboat enterprise had envisaged stationing tugs at strategic locations along the Strait and towing sailing ships along it in both directions, from one ocean to the other.

The proposals had considerable merit but consideration was deferred until the Chilean Government resolved to give the project its earnest consideration. Unfortunately, for this scheme, because of political and internal strife the matter was delayed, and then was set aside because of presidential elections. When the time came to finally decide the issue, PSNC had already initiated its direct steamship service via the Strait of Magellan, thus finally sealing the fate of the tugboat scheme.[236]

At the time of the launch of the Valparaíso-Europe contract with the Chilean Government, PSNC's fleet comprised the following vessels:

Name	Type	Tons
Arica	paddle steamer	740 tons
Bogotá	paddle steamer	1461
Bolivia	paddle steamer	773
Callao	paddle steamer	1062
Colón	propeller steamer	1995
Ecuador	propeller steamer	500
Favorita	paddle steamer	837
Guayaquil	propeller steamer	661
Inca	paddle steamer	200
Limeña	paddle steamer	1622
Morro	paddle steamer	132
Pacific	paddle steamer	1631
Payta	paddle steamer	1344
Panama	paddle steamer	1642
Peru	paddle steamer	1307
Peruano	paddle steamer	639
Quito	paddle steamer	743
San Carlos	propeller steamer	652
Santiago	paddle steamer	1619
Supe	propeller steamer	298
Talca	paddle steamer	708
Valparaíso	paddle steamer	1060

This sizable fleet provided the following coastal services, which at first glance resemble a railroad timetable; its very regularity made it so attractive as a transport medium on the West Coast:

British Mail route. Panama (Taboga) to Valparaíso
A twice-monthly service connecting with the arrival and departures of Royal Mail Steam Packet Line steamships in Colón. Passengers were conveyed to and from Taboga by the Company's steam launch, the *Morro*. Round trip 5724 miles.

French Mail route. Panama (Taboga) to Valparaíso
Monthly service, calling at 22 ports, connection in Colón with steamships owned by Générale Transatlantique Company. Round trip 5796 miles.

Panama to Callao route.
Monthly service. Main ports were Guayaquil, Callao and Panama but voyage included calls at 21 intermediate ports. Round trip 3933 miles.

Callao to Valparaíso route.
Monthly service with 17 ports of call on voyage. Round trip 3,052 miles.

Callao to Guayaquil route
Monthly service calling at 13 ports. Round trip 1,926 miles.

Callao to San José route
Twice per month service calling at 10 ports. Round trip 768 miles.

Callao, Chinchas and Pisco route.
Twice a month service from Callao, calling at Cerro Azul, Tambo de Mora, Islas Chincha and Pisco. Round trip 260 miles.

Chiloé route. Valparaíso to Puerto Montt.
Monthly service calling at new ports during the voyage. Round trip 1318 miles.

Coronel route. Valparaíso to Coronel.
Monthly service calling at Tomé, Talcahuano. Round trip 560 miles.[237]

The new direct Chile to Europe operation was launched from Valparaíso on May 13, 1868, using the paddle steamer *Pacific*, carrying 170 passengers destined mainly for St.Nazaire and Liverpool, and transporting £65,000 (US 117,000 dollars) in bullion plus general cargo. En route to Liverpool, the ship put in at Punta Arenas, Montevideo, Río de Janeiro, San Vicente, Lisbon and St.Nazaire. The voyage "*was completed in magnificent sailing conditions*" and within 43 days, including forced delays caused by wintry conditions in the Strait of Magellan.

Once in Liverpool, the Pacific was quickly turned around for the return voyage. A local newspaper article on July 16, 1868, stated:

"DEPARTURE OF FIRST STEAMSHIP. LIVERPOOL TO VALPARAISO
The *Pacific*, captained by George N.Conlan, is the first steamship to sail on the new Mail route, established by The Pacific Steam Navigation Company, between Liverpool and Valparaíso. She is contracted to the Chilean Government, and left Liverpool at one o'clock on Monday afternoon with 50 passengers, general cargo and space reserved for a considerable quantity of merchandise to be loaded at St.Nazaire, her first port of call. Other destinations will include Lisbon, where she will arrive on July 19, the Cape Verde Islands, Río de Janeiro, Montevideo and the new Chilean colony in the Magellan Straits"[238]

Thus in July 1868, the first direct steamship service between Great Britain and the West Coast of South America commenced, continuing without interruption until 1983, although after 1914, vessels passed through the Panama Canal rather than the Strait of Magellan. The Panama Railroad Company continued to operate on a reduced basis; nearly 40,000 passengers had used the railway in 1868, but after completion of the United States trans-continental railroad in 1869, annual numbers dropped rapidly.

However, the Railroad Company still enjoyed a number of assets in the form of substantial land holdings on the Panama Isthmus. It held a trump card in that any future canal needed its consent, a fact that de Lesseps discovered to his great cost when forced to buy the Railroad Company in order to obtain the concession to start work on the construction of his intended Panama Canal. The latter company's shares in 1879 had been trading at around $US100 (£55.56) each; de Lesseps' Compagnie Universelle du Canal Interocénique was obliged to pay $US250 (£138.89) per share or $US 25 millions (£13,900,000) for a railroad that had only cost $US 8,000,000 (£4,400,000) to build.

While stockholders in the Railroad Company may have had the last laugh, its reluctance to lower passenger and freight charges had only served to propel the PSNC towards becoming the largest shipping company in the world. Perhaps after William Wheelwright's pioneering efforts, the PRC's stubbornness must surely qualify as one of the most important factors contributing to the development of merchant shipping on the WCSA and to the West Coast nations themselves.

Although the first steam navigation service from Liverpool to Valparaíso had been launched in 1868, sailing ships had been making similar voyages round Cape Horn to Chile and beyond for centuries, and continued to do so into the early 1900s. The first steamships were generally too small to carry cargo over long distances at economic rates, especially bulk items such as grain, nitrates, coal, and mineral ore. In the 1840s, it was the widely held view that a steamship's cargo carrying capacity was severely restricted by the space needed to accommodate steam engines and the storage of coal. Cargo carrying capacity was also considered to be limited by the weight carried versus paddle wheel efficiency; the deeper the paddles wheels were forced into the water by the weight of cargo, the less effective their operation. Additionally, the rolling of a vessel in heavy seas often caused one paddle wheel to rise out of the water, whilst the other would be forced to labour at unacceptable angles and depth. As engines became more fuel efficient, space, previously taken up by coal storage, was released for cargo stowage and passenger accommodation.

Sailing ships were ideally suited for carrying guano and other bulk cargoes such as wheat and sugar. The famous North American Grace Shipping Line had been established on the back of exports of Peruvian guano to the United States from the Chincha Islands; two Irish-born brothers William and Michael founded the firm in the 1850s in the port of Callao. Sailing ships were still operating along the West Coast in the 1920s and formed the backbone of the maritime trades in the first half of the 19th Century, the majority being French, North Americans and British.

The President of the Chilean Society of History and Geography revealed to a Symposium on Maritime History in February 2001 at the Center of Central American Historical research,[239] that with the introduction of Chile's free trade policies following independence early in the 19th century, two important businessmen in Valparaíso, Alvarez and Ramos, had created an international network of agencies in major Far Eastern ports. This included areas such as Manila, Gulf of Bengal, Siam, Bali, Shangai, Canton, Hong Kong. Bangkok, Singapore and Macao, as well as other maritime centres in New South Wales, North, Central and South America. Ramos, being both a wheat producer in Chile and a sugar magnate in Peru, launched a shipping line ultimately amounting to about twenty cargo and passenger carrying sailing ships. Shipping agencies were established at Montevideo in 1846, San Francisco (1849), Lima (before 1851), Panama, Río de Janeiro and Hamburg (1857). San Jose de Costa Rica (1861), Guayaquil (1865), and Buenos Aires (1867).

Balfour, Williamson Company, for example, since 1851, had been Liverpool based owners and part owners of several sailing ships. The development of steam navigation combined with the opening of the Suez Canal in 1869, had temporarily put that firm's sailing ships, mostly employed in the Far Eastern waters, out of business. The march of steamships was unstoppable, but they were useful only as long as they could make frequent calls at ports for coal supplies. They also commanded higher rates for conveyance of cargo, passengers and mail than those offered by sailing ships.

The British, mainly on the India routes, had assiduously created these conditions favourable to steamships, and it was not long before the Suez route

War With Spain. Panama Railroad Dispute 1860-1871

according to Balfour Williamson Company, became "*studded with coalbunkers*". Given the large and strategically situated ports where coal supplies were obtained throughout the Mediterranean and the Red Sea, steamships were able to reduce the amount of fuel used in between ports and thus release room to provide extra passenger accommodation and/or cargo space. Superior speed and reliability gave steam a monopoly on the trade runs to India and beyond; sailing ships remained useful only on long routes where bulk cargoes predominated.

The Suez Canal reduced the length of the voyage from Britain to India by half of the distance when using the Cape of Good Hope route. However, it was only suited to steamships, because for the hundred miles of the canal's length, sailing ships had to be towed through at high cost, rendering such voyages uneconomical when compared with those undertaken by steamships. In the face of such competition from steamers, Balfour Williamson's sailing ships were re-assigned to the WCSA, and a business house, dealing initially in general merchandise, was established in Valparaíso.

This latter enterprise considered that steam was then too extravagant for those long voyages to Liverpool, believing that the latter were more suited to the huge American clippers. At that time, there were more British sailing ships at sea than ever before. Although the tonnage under construction in 1870 was 5/6ths steam, sail was to hold its own for many years in the Chilean nitrate and Australian grain trades.

The advantage sailing ships enjoyed over steamships derived from the fact that the former's movements were not restricted by the availability of coal supplies. Sailing ships were more economical; they charged lower freights and were good carriers; they could enter almost any port, and stay there almost any length of time. They often provided good free warehousing on their long voyages while upward turns in the commodity markets were awaited.

However, life on board sailing ships was extremely dangerous, particularly on the dreaded Cape Horn route, frequently negotiated by a variety of international vessels similar to those of Balfour Williamson. Although the latter company's sailing ships were well constructed and maintained in sound condition, they were, like those of contemporary enterprises, not built for comfort and were unheated. The crew's quarters were cramped. In heavy seas, the forecastle either had to be closed, creating a stifling atmosphere or left open allowing water to pour-in.

Lengths of voyages varied greatly, making it difficult to calculate food requirements. In any case, it was impossible to have fresh food on board for more than a few days after leaving port. Sometimes livestock, particularly pigs, would be carried but these would take up valuable space, and might be washed overboard. The ship's freshwater pump might be inoperable for days at a time, for fear of salt water penetrating and contaminating the supply. The galley fire, doused by the seas, could not be lit so that nothing could be cooked.

Ploughing The South Sea

When storms approached, crew were ordered aloft to take in topsails. At that height above the water, movement was tremendous. Footropes were the only footholds and thick spars the only place for their hands when they were not at work on the sails. Both ropes and spars might be coated with ice; one slip meant death. The decks were constantly awash; even with safety lines rigged, men could easily be swept over board as they moved about. The helmsman, waist deep in icy water, was lashed to the wheel throughout his watch; it was one of his duties to keep an eye on the men in the rigging, and to warn against falling spars.

The huge mainsails, wet with rain and spray could become a tremendous weight. Working them was a laborious task; hands would become chafed and raw from the long and hard contact with salt soaked lines. There was little rest for these seamen; repairs to ripped sails, broken lines and tackle had to be carried out between storms and those crew ordered aloft in high wind and spray remained there for two hours and more at a time. Clothing, no matter whether boots and oilskins were worn, would become sodden and cold. There was seldom time or opportunity for it to be dried before the next watch was due. There might be no dry place , whatsoever, in the ship. If a man was washed overboard, it was hard for the Master and crew to respond, due to the difficulties in lowering boats in a storm. If one could have been launched, it might never have been able to return to the mother vessel. Even if heavy seas had not swamped the boat, it might still have to be abandoned in mid-ocean, where there was little hope of it ever reaching land or being rescued by another ship.

Ocean going steamships still carried sails up to the end of the 19th Century because steamship engines were then mostly regarded as auxiliary to sail power. Nevertheless, seamen on these vessels still faced those same dangerous conditions voyaging round Cape Horn. Doctor Robertson, aged 26, of Hamilton, Scotland was, in 1871, the ship's surgeon aboard the Pacific Steam Navigation Company's iron hulled steamship *Araucania*, 2877 tons gross built in 1869, recorded in his diary entry for April 15, 1871,[240] relating to the outward-bound voyage to Valparaíso, the dangers that even the larger steamships encountered:

"Since 11 o'clock the last evening, a strong gale has continued to blow. About 2, I was awoken by it and I rose and dressed and got out on deck. The sailors were taking in the sails as they were in danger of being blown away. A very heavy sea was running and the captain was obliged to slow the engines as the vessel was shipping some very heavy seas indeed which nearly washed away the wheelhouse and at another time, four sailors were nearly washed overboard. The sea continued to increase until it got like mountains rolling past the ship, which actually stopped against these awful waves. This was a dreadful sea and the vessel was almost lost in it, taking in large waves behind at the stern. My cabin and all the officers' [cabins] were floating full of water and the sailors, busy keeping water from the engines to keep the vessel afloat. Everyone was in terror that she would not come through it."

War With Spain. Panama Railroad Dispute 1860-1871

An earlier entry for March 23, 1871 described how Dr.Robinson had been called out at midnight to a sailor who had fallen from one of the yardarms whilst working on at a sail:

"When I arrived the poor fellow was dead, having been killed instantaneously. He fell upon the vertex of his head and the skull was driven-in..."

Balfour Williamson Company was well aware of the extreme dangers and hardships seamen experienced on their vessels. The firm had energetically tried to improve the lot of sailors by constantly lobbying for the introduction of legislation to improve seamen's conditions and was largely responsible for the passage of the Merchant Seamen Payment of Wages and Rating Act 1880. They also generously contributed to seamen's charities in Liverpool and Valparaíso. Alexander Balfour founded the Duke Street Home (Liverpool) for Sailors and regularly subscribed to the training ship *Indefatigable* and the Seamen's Orphans Institution.

In contrast with sailing ships, the decisive factors in the European passenger trade were speed and comfort. Soon after the launch of the direct Liverpool-Valparaíso run, four new ships entered PSNC's service, *Magellan*, *Patagonia*, *Araucania* and *Cordillera*. They were all iron-hulled vessels with propeller propulsion and equipped with the highly reputable high-low pressure Elder engines. Vessels fitted with these 500 horsepower units were able to attain speeds of 13 knots. Each steamship was around 2800 tons gross and accommodated 145 passengers in first class, 75 in second class and 300 in third class. Their individual cargo carrying capacity also increased to 2500 tons.

The *Magellan*, the first to be commissioned, left the Mersey in March 1869, to inaugurate the regular monthly service to Valparaíso. Such was the growing emergence of other steamship companies at this time, that newspapers and the public would try to sharpen the prevailing competitive spirit by identifying situations that would provoke further rivalry between various shipping firms, especially if the prospects for a race might be indicated. The *Magellan's* second voyage became one such unofficial ocean-going contest, earning the following mention in the Liverpool Advertiser on August 26, 1869:

"STEAMSHIP RACE TO BRAZIL AND THE RIVER PLATE.
On Friday 20, of this month, two splendid steamships left the Mersey; the *Magellan* bound for the West Coast of South America and the well-known and popular steamship the *Hipparchus* belonging to Lamport Holt Company. Considerable interest has been generated in learning which of the two will be the first to arrive in Río de Janeiro. The *Magellan* a large and powerful vessel belonging to the Pacific Steam Navigation Company, will call at Bordeaux, Lisbon and San Vicente; the *Hipparchus* will visit the latter port only or more likely will be instructed to proceed directly to Río de Janeiro but her engines

are considerably less powerful than those of her opponent. The *Hipparchus* can only carry a limited number of passengers while the *Magellan* provides a magnificent lounge adorned with the most luxurious and modern fittings. The damage sustained to its engines during the first voyage has been completely repaired and a trial voyage to Belfast was so successfully undertaken that they are expected to perform well during this voyage. Both vessels will carry full cargoes of general merchandise."

The *Magellan* was the first to arrive at Río de Janeiro and the publicity earned for PSNC was undoubtedly very useful in portraying its transformation from a South American coastal shipping line, operating far from its native shores and little known outside South America, to being one of the leading British shipping organizations. PSNC maintained an ocean-crossing service of vital importance to Britain and other WCSA nations. Its new success was assisted by avoiding the inconvenience for thousands of potential passengers having to transfer in Panama from ship to railroad, and thence again, to ship for the southbound voyage down the West Coast.

One of the affects of operating the Liverpool-Valparaíso service was the PSNC's rational decision to relocate almost all of its large workshops, stores and personnel from the Isle of Taboga, in Panama Bay, to a new base at Callao, which quickly evolved into the Company's headquarters on the West Coast. Otis in his "*History of Panama*" simply reported that PSNC had been "*obliged to relocate*" because of its spat with the Panama Railroad Company.

The new direct service from Liverpool did not reduce or restrict existing intra West Coastal services; on the contrary, more new ships were built for this operation. The demand for passage to Panama, however, declined considerably as the direct steamship service to Europe increased both in frequency of voyages and in the size of PSNC's steamships. The loss of such traffic to the Panama Railroad Company was Merseyside's gain. PSNC acquired quayside facilities within the Bramley-Moore Dock complex at Birkenhead, which eventually mushroomed into offices, repair yards and workshops, providing work for hundreds in the local community.

9. West Coast Competition 1869-1878

In 1859, John Elder, the renowned Clyde Engineer and shipbuilder, when speaking at a British Association conference, announced the conclusion of testing of his newly introduced high and low-pressure steam engine. He cited, as proof of its efficiency, results recorded by PSNC steamships, *Valparaiso*, *Callao*, *Lima* and *Bogota*. Highlighting the fact that the latter vessel, with her older engines, had formerly achieved an average speed of only 9.75 knots, with a coal consumption rate of 38 cwts an hour[241], he proudly contrasted that with data produced from her following voyage when fitted with the new type of engines. On that trip, he reported that she had reached an average speed of 10.47 knots with a 50% reduction in the rate of fuel consumption.

The long association between John Elder's engineering firm and PSNC culminated in his appointment to the latter's Board of Directors. Such was its appreciation of this man, that in 1870, the company temporarily departed from its traditional ship-naming policy by christening its latest and most modern vessel, the *John Elder*, a propeller driven steamship of 3832 gross tons. Her overall length was later increased with a commensurate rise in gross tonnage to 4151 and she was able to deliver 2800 horsepower. Described in the Merseyside press as the very model of elegance and good taste, the *John Elder* was the first of six similarly sized steamships to be launched. During 1870, PSNC placed orders for a further eleven vessels totalling 25,019 tons, with a combined value of £630,000 (US1,100,00 dollars approximately). This, claimed Arthur Wardle, was then the largest single shipping contract ever placed by any one company in a single year.

Seven years before the opening of the Suez Canal, the British Government, having introduced policies to encourage investment to modernize industry, allocated approximately £3,700,000 (US 6,660,000 dollars) for merchant shipping construction[242], of which PSNC's eleven ships formed part and whose tonnage and description were:

Chimborazo	Iron hull. Propeller	3847 tons
Garonne	Iron hull. Propeller	3871
Lusitania	Iron hull. Propeller	3825
Aconcagua	Iron hull. Propeller	4105
Coquimbo	Iron hull. Propeller	1821
Santiago	Iron hull. paddles	1451
Truxillo	Iron hull. paddles	1449
Huacho	Iron hull. propeller	329
Iquique	Iron hull. propeller	323
Taboguilla	Iron hull. propeller	154

The Chimborazo class steamships, including the *John Elder*, were each equipped with five steam winches, especially useful for enabling speedier loading and unloading at docksides unequipped with cranes or, more usually, in open bay ports where cargo had to be discharged into large wooden barges or lighters. Once these steamships were operational, PSNC was able to deliver fortnightly services between Liverpool and Valparaíso. Despite the increased frequency of sailings, demand for cargo space continued to intensify, leading to requests for larger capacity ships. Such was the extra work generated, that in 1870, PSNC twice had to relocate to larger offices in Liverpool within twelve months.

Reductions in freight charges also stimulated trade between Liverpool and Valparaíso, while scheduled calls at Bordeaux, Lisbon and other ports created passenger and cargo volumes to levels far in excess of PSNC's expectations. This was especially the case at the French port, where so much cargo had built-up at one stage, that one PSNC ship after another was unable to clear the backlog. This unsatisfied demand for cargo space raised this company's ambitions; new additions to the fleet were ordered, mostly from John Elder & Co. While these steamships were being built, PSNC resorted to chartering others, often-foreign ships, in order to meet contractual obligations, a practice drawing harsh criticism from shareholders. The company's actions seemed reasonable in the circumstances, particularly as powerful competitors were ready to fill any gap that materialized if PSNC had been unable to satisfy the increased clamour for cargo space.

Once the goodwill of shippers had been lost, it would have been extremely difficult for the latter enterprise to recover lost custom. Competition from other shipping lines was never far away, and PSNC's continuing successes only served to draw attention to the increasing volumes of cargo being carried as a result of the valuable trade between Europe and South America. These lucrative trading conditions continued up to 1873, producing returns of approximately 25% for those invested in merchant shipping.

On the West Coast itself, a series of events raised warnings of strong competition; some had already occurred in January 1860. Valparaíso's newspaper El Mercurio reported that two Chilean businessmen in Valparaiso, having purchased the 476 tons United States steamship *Polynesia*, had registered her under the Chilean flag with the name of *Herminia*.[243] Ten days later, the same newspaper announced that the latter steamship was to operate out of Valparaíso, taking-in Talcahuano, Tomé and Corral [244]; this was, of course, in direct competition with PSNC. Some days later, a United States' ship owner launched a service to the very same ports using the 822 tons steamship *Bío-Bío*. Accordingly, at the end of January 1860, there were three steamships operating on the same southern Chile route, the *Herminia*, the *Bío-Bío* and PSNC's 699 tons *Cloda*.

The *Herminia* was the first to be put out of business by PSNC's powerful and relentless pressure; she had only made three voyages on the southern provinces run before quitting to sail to the port of Paposo in northern Chile, where she was eventually consigned to Loring Y Cia of Valparaíso. PSNC's strategy with regard to countering the *Bío-Bío's* threat was to announce in the press across-the-board reductions in passenger fares and freight charges to and from the southern provinces. The *Bio-Bio's* owners, already disadvantaged by not benefiting from the same Chilean Government subsidies and mail contracts granted to PSNC, had little option but to follow the latter's lead.

The *Bío-Bío's* enterprise countered with a surprise announcement of a proposed increase in the frequency of their steamship service, from two voyages per month to three. At the same time, it announced the purchase of the steamship *Peruano*, which was consigned to Alsop and Company, a United States owned company operating in Valparaíso.[245] The *Peruano* remained in port for some days before unexpectedly sailing north from Valparaíso, apparently reluctant to oppose one of the largest and most powerful shipping companies in the world.[246] Three months later, the *Bío-Bío* was actually undertaking four voyages a month on the southern provinces route but, having experienced severe operating difficulties in completing voyages and receiving insufficient cargo to sustain a timetable of four voyages per month, she eventually had to re-schedule her sailings following longer and more frequent stays in port. In due course, she not only had to revert to the same timetables as the competing PSNC, but also had to adopt the same freight and passenger tariffs.

These changes in the pattern of the *Bío-Bío's* operation caused angry reactions from users of her service in Concepción, and provoked the following article in El Mercurio's sister newspaper, La Crónica Nacional, circulating in that port:

"We now have two ships operating a service to Valparaíso, the *Cloda* and the *Bío-Bío*. The two vessels jointly provide us with four voyages per month, but the truth is that we hardly benefit from them at all. For some months, it has been noted that the regularity of these voyages has now degenerated into competition between the two, and we now have both companies trying to outfox the other resulting in them arriving and departing together while ten or twelve days elapse before these steamships re-appear...."[247]

Undoubtedly suffering from the struggle against their powerful competitor, the *Bío-Bío's* owners announced, in October 1861,[248] an extension to their southern provinces service, revealing that their steamship was, thenceforth, to operate along the entire Chilean coast. These changes only took place after the small company had been sold to a Henry Watson who decided to continue the struggle against PSNC. The ship sailed from Valparaíso for Chiloé with a cargo of wood and assorted merchandise. Two weeks later, it was announced in the local press'

Ploughing The South Sea

shipping pages that the newly amended service to be provided in 1862 by the *Bío-Bío* would include calls to Tomé, Talcahuano, Coronel, Corral, Ancud and Puerto Montt. In February of that year, the new owner, Henry Watson, took the bold step of announcing a 25% reduction in freight and passenger tariffs.

Two months later, the following stark announcement appeared in the shipping movements' section of El Mercurio newspaper for June 10, 1862:

"Ship movements-departures: American steamship 832 tons *Bío-Bío*, Captain Rodgers. [Bound for] Tomé, Talcahuano, Coronel and thence in ballast to Río de Janeiro"

PSNC was free of competition, at least for the time being. On December 31, 1863, a letter appeared in El Mercurio revealing that the owner of the *Bío-Bío* had been facing financial ruin due to competition from the English Company who had offered him 20,000 pesos (approximately £4,000 or $US7,200) as an inducement to abandon the southern provinces' route. The letter was apparently written just as the formation of a Chilean shipping company based in Concepción[249] was in the planning stages.

The *Bío-Bío's* withdrawl from the southern service provoked the publication of an open letter in El Mercurio on June 1862, expressing the feelings of some of the Concepción business community:

"To the English [i.e. PSNC] Company:
We have just learned that the *Bío-Bío*, which is expected in Talcahuano at any moment, is not to continue sailing between Valparaíso and the south but rather is in transit for the United States. The consequences of the *Bío-Bío's* absence are not difficult to imagine. Henceforth, there will be only two steamship voyages per month instead of the previous four. Moreover, it will be seen that a monopoly will be created by virtue of only one shipping line operating, and will surely lead to a rise in the cost of shipping tariffs.... to avoid.... these consequences, it is imperative that the English [PSNC] company be advised that, in its own interests, it should not take advantage of, nor even abuse the situation to seek more profit...we, therefore, request you, on behalf of our business community, not to make any alterations to your [existing passenger and cargo] rates which are already high enough...."[250].

Although PSNC did enjoy a monopoly on the service between Valparaíso and Puerto Montt, two independent steamships continued to operate, probably safe in the knowledge that because of their very small size and restricted operations, the English Company would regard them as having an insignificant or negligible affect on its business. The larger of the two vessels was the 159 tons *Emilia* making regular trips between Los Vilos and Valparaíso and eventually becoming the principal asset of the registered company Sociedad del Vapor Paquete de Los Vilos (Steamship Packet Society of Los Vilos). The other steamship was the

West Coast Competition 1869-1878

40 tons *Rapel*, sailing between Valparaíso and San Antonio. Both these small steamers continued to operate for some years without suffering any reprisals from PSNC.

A more serious and lasting threat to the English Company was to emerge. The central regions of Chile had long been huge producers of wheat. The growth of accompanying flourmills had led to an increased export trade, principally through the ports of Talcahuano, and Constitución on the River Maule. This sector of commerce, conducted principally with Peru, received an enormous boost when demand for flour reached very high levels because of the 1849 Californian Gold Rush and increased commercial links with Australia. The difficulty with the use of Constitución as a port to export grain was the presence of a submerged sand bar across the mouth of its river, only surmountable by vessels drawing a low draught. The River Maule, thereafter, was navigable as far as Loncomilla where the huge complex of flourmills was located.

The presence of the sand bar across the entrance to the River Maule was the main reason why Simpson Y Cia's *Arauco* had failed to conform to her contractual obligations to enter the port of Constitución. It was why PSNC had specified in its own subsequent agreement with the Chilean Government that its vessels would anchor in the small cove near the river entrance rather than actually enter the port. Shippers of wheat and other cereals from the River Maule district, therefore, were obliged to hire lighters at their own expense to ferry cargo to and from the cove where PSNC ships would anchor.

It was clear that if a vessel was able to safely surmount the sand bar, tremendous savings could be achieved and she could, in effect, enjoy a near monopoly of the River Maule's trade. The Chilean Government had previously licensed a group of German engineers to provide such an operation, but the project had failed to emerge, leaving the way clear for a group of Valparaíso ship owners and businessmen to form a company, in February 1861, called the Sociedad del Vapor Paquete del Maule (SVPM). The latter firm had ordered a specially designed sea-going vessel from a United States' shipyard capable of sailing over the sand bar. The 407 tons *Paquete de Maule* was delivered on October 6, 1861; it drew only nine feet of water.

PSNC, having decided to compete with this steamship, brought the 290 tons iron hulled paddle steamer *Inca* into the Maule service until a larger vessel could substitute her. The operation, however, turned out to be a financial disaster for the English company; the *Inca*, when loaded, had been unable to surmount the sand bar. It is surprising that PSNC, with all its technological expertise, had not calculated the likely draft drawn by the vessel when laden. Moreover, this debacle coincided with the approaching expiry of the Chilean Government's subsidies to PSNC for carrying the mails and operating the southern provinces service. These two events had, by then, alerted a group of businessmen in Concepción to the possibility of introducing a profitable and competing operation, which they announced would be launched under the name of Compañia Chilena de Vapores (CCV).

The proposal was well received by El Mercurio newspaper, particularly as it involved a national enterprise rather than a foreign establishment. It attracted a series of editorials criticizing the Chilean Government's policy of granting subsidies to shipping firms, whether foreign or nationally owned, on the grounds that a far stronger case could be made for the Chilean State to more usefully apply the subsidies it dispensed to acquiring its own vessels for coastal and mail shipping services. Typical of these newspaper articles was the following:

"We have and never will support the concept of granting subsidies to maintaining steamship lines in Chile. It is in the Republic's interest not to subsidise these but rather to undertake her own [merchant] shipping operations by purchasing steamships with Government resources. This can be achieved by utilizing the present annual total 50,000 pesos (approximate;y £10,000 or $US18,000) subsidies to purchase three steamships, and assign them to a company specifically formed for their operation or alternatively [the delegation of] a State administered office to be made responsible for administering maritime mail operations."[251]

El Mercurio's editor strengthened his case by citing the example of the SVPM. This company's stockholders mostly comprised foreigners resident in Chile, and the *Paquete de Maule* had actually sailed under the flag of the United States for the first three months of her operation. Nevertheless, the Editor emphasized that this company, despite not receiving any State financial assistance, would still be able to reap huge profits from the operation of its steamship service on the southern provinces route.

Shortly after the appearance of this editorial, one of the CCV's founders was recorded in El Mercurio as announcing his company's intention to service the entire Chilean coast, from Caldera in the north to Puerto Montt in the south. Confirming his company's support for the continuation of Government subsidies to help establish Chilean steamship enterprises, he supplied data to show that the monthly cost of operating a twice-monthly service to Puerto Montt would cost 6,800 pesos, (£1,360 or $US 2448) and suggested that the Government could purchase and operate at least three steamships with the amount it was currently expending on subsidies. Dismissing El Mercurio's rationale for the success of the *Paquete del Maule's* service, he submitted that the absence of competition from PSNC on the latter service had only emerged due to the English Company's inability to provide a vessel capable of sailing over the Maule sand bank.[252]

PSNC had already started its attack campaign by making an initial generous offer to buy-out the owners of the *Paquete Maule*, but after having been repudiated, surprisingly took no further action at that time, possibly believing that the SVPM's operations would never amount to a serious threat. This was to be one of the

English Company's gravest errors. As wheat production increased in the Maule area, the American-Chilean group purchased an additional vessel, the 336 tons *Huanay*, of similar design to the *Paquete del Maule* and in 1868, re-formed as the Compañia Nacional de Vapores (CNV).[253] J.N.Orrego, shipping agent and ship owner managed the ship on behalf of CNV, but shortly before the outbreak of war with Spain, this small company was in financial difficulty.

In their March 1862 annual report to the Chilean Government, ship owners, ships' captains and other maritime interests expressed their views on the services provided on the shipping route between Constitución and Valparaíso:

"PSNC has created a shipping monopoly along the Chilean coast, resulting in the deployment of its steamships to call at every port and cove, no matter how small. Its purpose is to reduce freight charges [to unsustainable levels] from Constitución to Valparaíso, such that they are now asking only fifteen centavos per quintal when the previous corresponding charge was fifty centavos. This premeditated action was designed to kill-off the nationally registered firm Vapor Paquete del Maule (VPM) in its infancy, and thus retain her position as Queen of the Chilean seacoast. This is the sad reality, which has obliged those investors not able to sustain continued losses to withdraw their capital from the (VPM) enterprise." [254]

The outbreak of the war with Spain interrupted CNV's operations, causing the *Huanay* to restrict her voyages between Valparaíso and Constitución. Owing to the Spanish blockade, she was obliged to change her national flag as well as her normal sea routes in order to claim neutrality. Moreover, in 1870, trade difficulties arising from the war resulted in a shortage of capital for CNV, and its registered office was transferred to Valparaíso. To generate additional investment funding, more company shares were issued. These were mostly purchased by foreign-owned but Chilean registered enterprises, or directly by foreigners resident in Chile, and led to the removal of the company's original founders.

Another steamship line was formed following new silver discoveries at Caracoles in 1870, which provided a huge boost to the Chilean economy. Those who had invested on the emergence of these silver mining enterprises amassed surplus funds to invest in the launch of new businesses, which in the shipping sector included ten or more new merchant shipping companies. A considerable amount of financial capital was committed to the newly formed Compañia Chilena de Vapores (CCV), established on August 19, 1870. This concern launched its operations with the purchase of three well-used but sound condition ships, given the names of *Bío-Bío*, *Maipú* and the *Limari*, and manned by English officers and crew. Such was the potential envisaged for this new shipping line, that it immediately set about purchasing a new vessel, the *Copiapó*, followed by orders for a further three freighters. The CCV had intended to operate principally along the Chilean coast, but soon decided to provide services to foreign ports with their three-second hand steamships.[255]

PSNC, caught unawares by the sudden appearance of these smaller shipping lines, was now faced with new rivals plying their trade in what it perceived as its own area of operations. The English Company again employed the well-tried and tested strategy of drastically reducing freight charges in an attempt to render the young Chilean companies uncompetitive. Apart from the CCV and CNV, the smaller companies soon disappeared under a mountain of debt and liquidation. The two surviving firms were also nearly bankrupted in the commercial battle that ensued, and CCV, in order to continue operating, had to cancel orders for its new vessels.

During this fiercely competitive assault, the Liverpool firm had actually made overtures to the CCV to establish a joint merger, which up until then had emerged as its strongest competitor. When these approaches were rebuffed, PSNC attempted a share takeover. However, a significant portion of CCV's shareholders, also holding stock in the CNV, expressed a preference for a merger of the two Chilean shipping companies. The stockholders of both firms were, undoubtedly, influenced by the Chilean Government, which approved the merger by decree on October 9, 1872. The newly authorized enterprise was launched under the name of Compañia Sud Americana de Vapores (CSAV). Claudio Véliz in his "*Historia de La Marina Mercante de Chile*", indicated that there had been some reluctance on the part of Chilean investors to invest additional capital to fund this new merchant shipping company, in view of the direct competition the new company would have to face with the much more powerful PSNC.

The English Company had already applied its mighty muscle to demonstrate its power in putting many smaller steam ship lines out of business, and into which, many investors had sunk their newfound wealth. Accordingly, the newly created CSAV was obliged to reserve one third of its stock in an attempt to attract Peruvian investors, and to facilitate the latter, it decided to drop any reference to "*Chile*" in its title. By October 1872, the CSAV fleet had increased to seven steamships; the *Paquete de Maule* and *Huanay* continued to transport their grain cargoes from the River Maule to Valparaíso and the remainder of its vessels operated on Chilean coastal trade. When delivery was taken from British shipyards of five new vessels, the CSAV, in August 1873, in a highly significant action, introduced its first steamship service to Callao. This operation was at first unprofitable, but the following year, CSAV secured a ten years contract with the Chilean Government along with regular subsidies to aid its profitability.

CSAV, however, wisely eschewing short-term profits, used these grants to fund an extension of its operations to take-in Panama. Consequently, in a short space of time, the CSAV had encroached into areas that, hitherto, had remained the dominion of PSNC. The latter had been slow to realize that CSAV had become a serious competitor, but like a lumbering giant, it then gathered all its considerable might, adopting ruthless techniques which, years later, were adopted by self-interested Ocean Conferences, some of which PSNC was an active member.

One of the practices embraced by PSNC was to advertise substantial reductions in shipping rates and, at that same time, position one or more of its vessels next to or very near to a CSAV ship that was due to depart. PSNC, on one occasion, targeted a CSAV vessel by setting its freight rates at levels 70 per cent lower than those set by its competitor. The practice sometimes varied; the English company's competing vessel would leave either a day earlier or simultaneously with the CSAV ship. To employ such strategies, PSNC brought into play the full force of its very large steamship fleet in direct opposition to CSAV. Whenever the latter tried to match the reduced rates, it would react by again reducing its freight charges and passenger tariffs, sometimes to incredible and unsustainable low levels in order to sink this new competitor.

PSNC was not alone in adopting this practice; competition on North Atlantic and North Pacific routes to the Panama Isthmus, for example, had been considerably more intense. John H.Kemble remarked:

"Competition, bitter and ruthless which was to be the chief characteristic of steamship operation on the Panama route,[256] was not welcomed by the mail lines which had pioneered this service. They generally met competitors either by reducing fares, with the idea of making the business unprofitable for the newcomer, or by purchasing the opposing ships and adding them to their own fleets." [257]

Despite PSNC's cutthroat reductions in freight rates, the Chilean company attracted considerable national support, especially from those Chilean shippers not wishing to be restricted to the formerly monopolistic Liverpool firm. In November 1875, in a bid to raise finance, CSAV released a second stock issue, which was fully subscribed. Fortunately for CSAV, Pacific Steam Navigation Company's actions in pushing the young company to the verge of bankruptcy, had not gone unnoticed by the Chilean Executive.

The Chilean Government was well aware of the important wartime role provided by a responsive and effective national mercantile marine. Consequently, it contracted to support CSAV, making finance immediately available, and at the same time, guaranteeing the protection of its coastwise trading rights. However, in granting these assurances, the Government reserved the right to requisition CSAV's vessels in times of military conflict. Wheelwright's earlier warnings to PSNC concerning Chilean Government intervention in developing national enterprises, had obviously not been heeded by his successors. Nevertheless, CSAV's debts and losses continued to mount; the Chilean Government, already subsidizing it at twice the level it was paying to PSNC on a ten years' contract, was unable to provide any further assistance

Apart from those enterprises operating in direct competition against the Liverpool based company, there were a number of small one-ship concerns continuing to sail undisturbed on non-scheduled voyages to ports within easy reach of Valparaíso. For example, agricultural landowner N.Ovalle had acquired the small steamship *Catalpico* to ship his farm produce from Norte Chico to Valparaíso. This vessel was shipwrecked off Pichidangui in January 1858. Alsop and Company's 780 tons steamship *Antonio Varas* made irregular coastal voyages between northern Chilean ports and Valparaíso before being similarly lost.

The year 1873 witnessed a worldwide depression following the Franco-Prussian war; the considerable downturn in trade caused corresponding reductions in freight charges, partly due to excess tonnage capacity accumulated during the post Suez Canal prosperous years. During the period 1873-1875, the index of British import freight charges had dropped from 226 to 194 and the export freight charges index had fallen from 117 to 94.[258] Europe seemed to bear the brunt of the economic decline; during the same period, numbers employed in the Germany Iron and Steel industry tumbled by 40%. By 1876, of the 435 original iron and steel enterprises, only 225 were operating. In Britain, as well as throughout Europe, coal production had been high, leading to this fuel being stockpiled and then later sold at cheaper prices in an attempt to clear the over-production; this in turn contributing to reduced freight charges.[259]

Many British ship owners, linked at this time to mining and steel producers, and perceiving no signs of a recovery on the horizon, decided to expand into a very important sector of the maritime trade with Chile. Taking advantage of low prices, they began to ship coal to the latter nation, in the process, enjoying the additional advantage of being able to use it for ballast, thus further reducing operational costs. Ships leaving Swansea with coal earmarked for Chilean northern copper foundries would return to Britain laden with Chilean copper.[260] Many ship owners involved in this coal-out copper-return trade soon discovered that market freight charges were insufficient to meet voyage costs and, accordingly, many such firms loaded their vessels with coal and on arrival in Chile, attempted to sell their ships there. While only a minority were successful, this action, taken together with Chilean orders already placed with British shipyards, was sufficient to increase the percentage of Chile's merchant tonnage built in Great Britain.

Not only had stockpiles of imported cheap coal created a favourable trading climate for Chilean steamship companies during the period 1870 to 1875, but trading conditions were also enhanced by discoveries of silver in Caracoles in the Bolivian Atacama region,[261] and by the stock market upswing that followed. The discovery of silver in this area was likened to the Californian Gold Rush; many miners and speculators were attracted to Antofagasta at the height of the finds.

Chile was the main beneficiary of the discoveries rather than Bolivia, and some of the surplus wealth accumulated by mining interests and speculators was applied as capital to purchasing and forming some of Chile's shipping enterprises, although the major part was invested in banks and other financial institutions. Chilean Government regulations, however, had made it almost impossible for a single individual or small groups of investors to build even one ship; such enterprises became the prerogative of larger capitalized concerns. One such smaller firm was Franco-Sudamericana de Vapores, owned by Germain Hermanos y Cia of Paris, which had tried to introduce a steamship service between Le Havre and the South American Pacific coast, but its available capital was deemed insufficient to launch the venture.[262]

By 1876, Chile's merchant marine comprised 22 steamships, 17 of which belonged to larger limited corporations and only 5 to the smaller sole owner firms.[263] After the War with Spain, growing shipping interests caused a rapid development of marine insurance. Lloyds Maritime Company had actually started trading in Valparaíso before the conflict and the growth in more complex shipping transactions together with the increasing national and foreign traffic in the port, led to the emergence of specialist shipping and insurance brokers.

One such name was the famous Gibbs y Cia, which before 1860, had registered ships under its own name, but after the conflict with Spain, it ceased to register or acquire new vessels, restricting its trading activities to acting as shipping agents and negotiating freight charges on behalf of its clients. Chilean legislation, by allowing the establishment of a progressive maritime insurance infrastructure, had created in the process, healthy competition within the widening shipping sector. This in turn led to further increases in marine traffic within Chilean ports, particularly from foreign shipping companies deciding to extend their areas of activity. But by 1873, worldwide depression affected shipping movements in Chile. This can be seen from the following totals passing through Chilean ports:[264]

1873	8,078,785 tons
1874	7,68 4,482
1875	7,485,619
1876	7,060,587
1877	7,504,339

The trade slump in Chile in 1876, aggravated by a collapse in copper and nitrate production, affected both CSAV and PSNC as they continued their bitter rivalry in a declining market. The Chilean Company, obliged to suspend its Panama service, was on the verge of bankruptcy. PSNC incurred substantial losses as a result of not only chartering additional vessels to compete against CSAV, but also from its strategy of lowering freight rates to unrealistic levels to try to eliminate the Chilean line. Apart from these setbacks, the South American trade bonanza continued throughout the 1870s, enabling PSNC to increase its scheduled departures from Liverpool to three ships per month, and continue its expansion policy by chartering other companies' vessels in addition to the placing of new ship orders.

New vessels delivered to PSNC were quickly pressed into service. During 1871, it had placed further orders with both Clyde and Mersey shipyards for 13 additional vessels with a total tonnage of 39,780 and a combined value then of £1,174,401 (US. 2,114,000 dollars). The largest of these steamships was the *Britannic* at 4129 tons, two funnelled, three masts, and with propeller propulsion. She was equipped with high and low pressure inverted engines enabling her to attain a speed of 12.75 knots.

The acquisition of further steamships in that year culminated in the purchase of the *Iberia* (4671 gross tons) and *Liguria* (4666 tons) from the Clyde shipyards of John Elder. The former vessel was, at that time, with the exception of the supreme *Great Eastern*, the largest ship afloat in the world. She could maintain an operational speed of 13 knots and served the Company well for thirty years on the Pacific and Australian routes. PSNC, by then the largest shipping undertaking in the world, introduced a weekly service between Liverpool, Valparaíso, and Callao. The Merseyside community was reported to have become so familiar with the Company's black coloured funnels with their green trimming band, that PSNC's fleet was dubbed the "*Birkenhead Navy*". Quite often, three or four of the Company's vessels were seen together on the River Mersey.

In 1873, the Company's West Coast fleet comprised the following ships with their respective tonnages:

Ship	Tons	Ship	Tons
Eten	1853	Valdivia	1861
Colombia	1823	Atacama	1821
Coquimbo	1821	Santa Rosa*	1817
Lima	1803	Ilo	1794
Chile	1672	Panama	1642
Pacific	1631	Limeña	1622
Islay	1577	Oroya	1577
Santiago	1451	Truxillo	1449
Payta	1344	Peru	1307
Arequipa	1065	Callao	1062
Talca	708	Quito	743
Guayaquil	661	San Carlos	652
Peruano	639	Tacna	612
Huacho	329	Iquique	323
Supe	298	Inca	290
Taboguila	154		

*See endnote 265

By 1872, four large European shipping firms had begun to infiltrate the South Pacific coastal market, presenting stiff competition not only for PSNC but also for CSAV. These were the British Imrie and Company, the French line Compagnie Générale Transatlantique, the German Kosmos steamship company and the Belgian Compagnie de Navigation. The following table details the size of competing merchant fleets operating on the West Coast of South America with respective total steamships, sailing vessels, fleet tonnages and total crews employed:[266]

P.S.N.C	56	0	118695	4870
Cia Sudamerican de Vapores	10	0	12400	572
Kosmos	6	0	12750	210
Cie Navigation Belgique	4	0	10300	151
White Star	4	0	6603	262
Cie General Transatlantique	3	0	6000	300
Cia Buques y Maderas	0	14	12180	195
Cia Marítima	0	17	13450	240
Cia de Buques	0	29	22421	364
Cia Explotadora de Lota/Coronel	4	2	3980	100
Total	87	62	218779	7264

In 1872, Messrs Imrie and Company, shortly afterwards to become the White Star Line, announced the planned departure of the *Republic*, one of its newer steamships from Liverpool, on October 5, for Valparaíso and Callao. The announcement in the local press was seen as an open challenge being issued, given that it was widely accepted that the Liverpool-Valparaíso-Callao steamship service was firmly in PSNC's uncontested sphere of operations. The latter did not hesitate to rise to the invitation to compete; indeed, given the press publicity, it could hardly have done otherwise. It immediately announced that the 3525 tons steamship *Tacora*, its most recent fleet addition, would leave Liverpool on October 4. The British public immediately perceived the event to be a straightforward contest between the two rival companies. The Nautical Magazine remarked at the time that the situation had all the ingredients of a race to Callao, a distance of 11,000 miles:

"This is, undoubtedly, the greatest event of its kind to take place in Liverpool and we can all too easily pass ourselves off as experts in this contest by speculating on each rival vessel's performance. The *Republic* was built by Harland and Wolff in Belfast, the *Tacora* by John Elder and Co. Both ships are equipped with modern high and low pressure engines and should be able to make a race of it, both being able to make the non-stop crossing from Lisbon to Río de Janeiro, a distance of around 4300 miles. Both vessels will call at the same ports on the West Coast until completing the voyage at Callao."

Unfortunately, for Pacific Steam Navigation Company, the race ended in disaster; the *Tacora* was wrecked on the approaches to Cape Santa María, near Montevideo. The White Star Line was unable to take advantage of the result of this unfortunate challenge by establishing an extensive and permanent service to replace PSNC's existing European-West Coast operations. Even if the *Republic* had gained an outright victory, suggesting that the White Star Line should lay claim to or compete for part of this service, the latter enterprise would have had to rapidly establish an extensive infrastructure to support a West Coast programme, similar to that which PSNC had carefully assembled over thirty years or more. Without that type of logistical support, the White Star Line would probably have succumbed to either direct competition with PSNC or else to a combined assault from the latter and CSAV.

What White Star Line lacked was a West Coast service similar to the one which acted as a feeder to PSNC's direct Liverpool-Valparaíso route, and which was still the subject of its contract with the Chilean Government, the latter making generous subsidies to PSNC, as did other West Coast republics. Chile would most likely have declined to award a similar contract to White Star Line, given that to do so might have created further unnecessary competition for her struggling national carrier CSAV, and would have angered those in her Government opposed to the concept of subsidies. Moreover, White Star Line might have had to secure UK Government Mail contracts to make regular sailings to the West Coast worthwhile. In short, there would probably have been too much ground for White Star Line to recover to pose a serious and enduring threat to PSNC, although by 1873, the former company had managed to operate four ships between the West Coast and Europe, a minimal operation when compared with PSNC's frequent and regular schedules.

The first foreign shipping firm to succumb to the intense competition was the French company, having, until 1874, undertaken regular voyages between Chile and Europe. Announcing the suspension of this service in June, 1873, it diverted its South Atlantic voyages to the Isthmus of Panama, where after rail transit of the latter, passengers and cargo would link with PSNC coastal vessels to the West Coast of South America. This event coincided with CSAV's momentous decision to launch its own Valparaíso-Panama service and one, which was welcomed both in the Chilean and Peruvian press. The newspaper Opinión Nacional de Lima wrote just before the arrival at Callao of CSAV's steamship *Loa*:

"First reactions to the CSAV's new steamship service to Panama have been quite splendid. The *Loa* on her maiden voyage has discharged 4350 items of cargo in Guayaquil, though only loading 106 pieces there for Panama, a lot more cargo would probably have been available had her arrival received more publicity". [267]

CSAV was only able to compete with PSNC on this service, and on other international routes, because of a Chilean Government subsidy of 100,000 pesos (£20,000 approximately or $US36,000) paid annually for a period of ten years, and granted on condition that the CSAV would manage and operate certain routes, including Valparaíso-Panama. Importantly, it was required to make its ships available to the Chilean Government in cases of emergencies or in times of war. Subsidies were generally granted by other national Governments to their leading shipping lines. Kosmos, for example, received generous allowances from the German Government calculated on the number of miles sailed, enabling this company to successfully resist CSAV and PSNC competition on the West Coast until the end of the 19th Century. The White Star and Belgian lines appeared not to have received any such benefits from their respective Governments, and were partly displaced in the same way as the French Line. The Compañia de Buques and Cia Marítima were wound-up in 1876 and 1878 respectively; none of these two enterprises could sustain operations in the face of strong foreign competition (See endnote 268). By the mid 1870s, CSAV represented almost the entire Chilean registered merchant marine.

In 1874, PSNC's fleet amounted to 57 vessels with a combined tonnage of 127,000 tons, then equivalent to that of the United States Navy. The activity of this great merchant fleet and the rapid development of the company in England, as well as abroad, were cited as contributing significantly to the economic and commercial advancement of many towns on the West Coast. An independent observer, Thomas J. Hutchinson, author of "*Two years in Peru*", who travelled in the *Cordillera* in 1871, commented:

"When one sees the large expanse of ship repair yards, engine workshops, the residence of the Callao Manager of the Pacific Steam Navigation Company, the quantity of cargo, as well as the large number of Company ships in the Bay, it is easy to understand why this Company has come to be the greatest British power on the West Coast of South America."

The Callao workshops extended over 50160 square metres, more than the area covered by six soccer pitches, in a suburb of the old port called Chucuito. They comprised warehouses near the Customs House, and a wharf equipped with locomotives and steam cranes for loading and unloading freight, overlooked by the West Coast Manager's residence. The repair centre housed an extensive iron and bronze foundry unit, joiners' workshops and a forge. There were, in addition, a Chinese manned steam laundry which could daily handle 1000 pieces of ship's linen, a bakery equipped with Perkins ovens capable of baking 120 4-lbs loaves simultaneously, living quarters for the workers, nicknamed "*Glasgow Terrace*" and which, amongst other things, were provided with a theatre.[269] An abattoir with cattle stalls operated to supply vessels with fresh meat. Such was the level of this

Ploughing The South Sea

company's activities in Callao that not counting ships' crews, around 500 workers were continually employed there.

To serve this community a hospital had been opened in 1865. Dr Robert Robertson, the young surgeon on the *Arauncania*, recorded in his diary of Monday May 1, 1871, that he had been offered the position of surgeon to the Company's hospital at a salary of £1000 per annum[270]. He had accepted the appointment for approximately three months but during his brief stay, he became concerned with the overall sanitary conditions in Callao, and felt compelled to publish the following letter in the Lima and Callao Gazette on June 13; it gives a rare insight into contemporary conditions in that port:

"The Sanitary Condition of Callao.
From the number and character of the letters, which have recently been published in your columns from the pen of our esteemed British Consul, I think that there is no lack of evidence to prove that we want very much indeed, a new system of Hygiene in Callao. In such a serious matter as the present, the issue of which will be of vital importance, we want plain speaking to expose fallacies and dispel phantoms—we want two things 1. A proper system of sewage, 2. An abundance of pure and wholesome water.When we get these things we shall necessarily get pure air and better health—when we trust we shall not have the dreadful account laid before us, average life term 20 years. Let us take warning from the dreadful epidemic which has been raging in Buenos Ayres[271].Such that an epidemic had not been heard of in history before—that may happen to Callao some time soon, the day will come, perhaps too soon for us. Therefore, let us be up and doing. There is an old story but a true one. It's no use locking the stable after the horse is stolen. Callao is becoming every day more and more important in shipping and we must expect it will increase in the number of inhabitants and in a year or two it will become very serious indeed if there is no proper sanitary means for the preservation of the health of the town. Trusting that instead of correspondence we shall hear of something being done soon and thanks for your space."

The following further information was supplied by the doctor:

"Further Rough Notes In Connection With The Above:
We are erecting new docks, bringing in new railway connections, proving distinctly that the exportation and importation of goods and produce in the port is daily and rapidly increasing and that Callao is one of, if not the most important ports on the coast of Peru. Let the municipality at once make a move towards establishing a proper Sanitary Commission with a properly qualified Sanitary Inspector at the head of the affair and make Callao what it ought to be, one of the healthiest towns on the coast of Peru."

Wharf and Docks in Callao at end of 19th Century

A protestant church to administer to the Callao district was built in 1863, partly financed from funds raised by George Petrie the Company's Manager on the West Coast and William Wheelwright. The latter donated some of the required building materials for the church. Both became church trustees and consuls in the port for Great Britain and the United States respectively. Petrie was also responsible for the introduction of a floating dock in Callao. The Callao Dock Company was formed in 1863, in which the Pacific Steam Navigation Company purchased a considerable number of shares. The unassembled units had been fabricated in Glasgow at a cost of £42,000 (approximately US 76,000 dollars) and taken out on PSNC ships to the Peruvian port. An unknown contemporary correspondent in Callao provided the following description of the unit:[272]

"This magnificent construction is 300 feet in length, 100 feet wide and 76 feet internal width, 38 feet high and containing approximately 3000 tons of iron including 1 million rivets. It is capable of raising a 6000 tons steamship, with 21 feet draught, out of the water and was successfully launched on 24th April 1866 and then towed out to its anchorage. The undertaking was a Pacific Steam Navigation Company initiative and the contract was awarded to Randolph Elder and Co of Glasgow from where different sections of the dock were brought out to Callao by steamship.
The project was successfully completed under the supervision of George Petrie, the Company's General Manager on the West Coast of South America. Owing to the lack of a similar facility anywhere between Panama and Valparaíso, it is reasonable to assume that the enterprise will turn out to be profitable.

Ploughing The South Sea

The different stages of construction, without exception, have been accompanied by good luck and the project's success has been the result of the tremendous enthusiasm for it in Callao. The Dock was christened St. George. Gathering speed as it slipped down the launch way at the first attempt, it ploughed into the sea amidst applause from the crowds of spectators and was then immediately towed to a safe anchorage point."

For many years, thereafter, this floating dock was extremely well used by warships and other companies' merchant vessels including ships from the Pacific Mail Steamship Company sailing down from Panama.[273]

The description of Callao hardly seemed to have changed over the next fifty years. James Bryce in his "*South America. Observations and Impression*" gives the following commentary of his visit in 1910:

"The town of Callao, consisting of steamship office and warehouses and shops dealing in things that ships need, offers nothing of interest, except the remains of the fort of St. Philip, the last building where the flag of Spain floated on the mainland of the New World. So the traveler hurries by the steam railroad or the electric line up to Lima".

The steamship *Sorata* inaugurated the PSNC's weekly service from Liverpool to Callao, calling at Bordeaux, a number of Spanish ports, Lisbon, Montevideo, and Punta Arenas. Over a 12 months period, this firm's steamships operating the Liverpool-Valparaíso route covered more than a million miles in 45 round voyages. The considerable ship movements had, by 1873, again alerted competitors to the continuingly valuable South American cargo and passenger trade. PSNC's vessels providing the direct West Coast of South America to Liverpool Service via the Magellan Strait were, with respective tonnages, as follows:

John Elder	4151	Aconcagua	4105
Britannia	4129	Illimani	4022
Cotopaxi	4022	Potosi	4218
Sorata	4014	Garonne	3871
Chimborazo	3847	Cuzco	3845
Galicia	3829	Lusitania	3825
Corcovado	3805	Puno	3805
Valparaiso	3575	Araucania	2877
Patagonia	2866	Cordillera	2860
Magellan	2856		

Various foreign companies had tried to secure a portion of the trade for themselves and, although the threat from French competition had already faded, the new Chilean steamship line (CSAV), which the Pacific Steam Navigation had tried to strangle at birth, was beginning to make an impact with the support of the Chilean Government. The year 1873 was the apex of PSNC's progress, but it was also the year in which its founder, William Wheelwright died. In the history of the South American republics, his name and reputation are permanently writ large, whether fully justified or not. He had devoted at least 15 years of his life to the promotion of steamship navigation on the West Coast of South America.

Besides being credited by his biographer, Juan Bautista Albérdi, with the discovery of coal deposits and related mining, he was noted for introducing brick building manufacture, finding deposits of borax and saltpetre, otherwise known as sodium nitrate, and installing equipment in the Atacama Desert to convert salt-water to freshwater. In some of his earlier projects, he undoubtedly received appreciable and effective support from his colleague, Captain George Peacock, but his greatest achievement on the West Coast occurred much later following Peacock's return to England.

In 1851, he built Chile's first railroad connecting the port of Caldera to Copiapó in the nitrate belt. In recognition of his valuable and extensive contribution to maritime and land communications, the Chilean President Manuel Bulnes decreed the striking of a special gold medal depicting, on the obverse, the national emblem together with the following inscription: *"From the Government of Chile to Don William Wheelwright, September 18, 1850."* On the reverse of the medal was an image of one of the early steamships together with an additional inscription: *"In testimony of our gratitude for having introduced steamship navigation and promoting railway networks in Chile."*

During 1872, Wheelwright also initiated the first telegraph service in Chile; actually the first in South America. He subsequently built the railroad from Valparaíso to Quillota. Henry Meiggs, another pioneering and illustrious North American, later extended this line to Santiago. In association with the American engineering partnership of Brassey and Wythes, Wheelwright laid the Argentine railroad from Córdoba to Buenos Aires, widely regarded as a huge construction feat at the time.

A measure of Wheelwright's skills and foresight was amply demonstrated in 1871, when he presented the President of the London Chamber of Commerce with a detailed map outlining steamship navigational routes for eastern and western bound North Atlantic crossings. It was claimed that if these proposals had been made mandatory, they would have reduced the incidence of sea collisions and, at the same time, obliged steamships to avoid the troublesome fishing areas off Newfoundland. Similar ideas had already been aired in 1846, but it is likely that Wheelwright was the first person to have actually compiled them into detailed and viable proposals. Other nations, as well as individual shipping companies, later adopted his scheme.

Wheelwright finally left the West Coast in 1873 to settle in London where he died in September of that year, his wife and daughter surviving him. His remains were carried across the Atlantic and interred in Newburyport, his place of birth. This energetic man with his reputed winning and kind ways made many lasting friendships. At Wheelwright's memorial service, it was stated that he was respected for his honesty, patience and, reportedly, for his frequent support for deserving causes; he successfully earned the trust of many South American statesmen and other men of high stature such as Lord Abinger, Peter Campbell Scarlett and of many other respectable associates who had backed his earlier schemes and projects.

Such was the esteem in which he was held, that in 1877, the Republic of Chile paid him her highest honour by commemorating his achievements through the erection of a memorial statue in Valparaiso. Many considered that this tribute paid to Wheelwright was as much merited as that of Chile's other national hero, Admiral Cochrane, for conducting her famous maritime campaigns in the struggle for Independence. One Chilean statesman commented:

"If Cochrane has contributed, as well as by the sword, to the nation's well being, by opening up her ports to trade, breathing life into them with the prosperity that was eventually attracted to this city, then appreciate what Wheelwright has given this nation by his introduction of direct and speedy communications with the great European and American countries, thereby propelling our country forward by means of those great projects, which in only a few short years, have changed our way of life."

This reference to Cochrane appears to have arisen from his non-military benefits to the Chilean economy, by his influential lobbying in England. It was perhaps little known, or else the fact was deliberately suppressed, that Cochrane, prior to becoming involved in his Chilean battle campaigns, had originally advocated that Napoleon Bonaparte be invited to South American and made President of the entire sub-continent. Cochrane had wanted to travel in his own ship to the Isle of St. Helena to collect the exiled Bonaparte and transport him to South America[274].

Such indiscretions appear to have been overlooked given his subsequent glorious and renowned association with Chile. He was thus able, on his return to England, to convince London businessmen that the Chilean Government had created conditions entirely favourable for commerce and a pleasurable way of life. In due course, London bankers were persuaded to make loans available to the latter Government totalling a million pounds sterling ($US1,800,000), a huge amount at that time.

A major part of this financial credit was applied to bankrolling the War of Independence. Further large amounts were authorized by Great Britain, which had the affect of not only bringing about the introduction in Chile of that class of new technology that had driven the UK Industrial Revolution, but also fostered an enduring relationship between the two nations. The London banks' early financing of the Chilean Government was specifically for military purposes and not for stimulating her economy. Importantly, it did have the affect of creating considerable business confidence in the future economic prospects of that country.

Following the Chilean Government's exhortations to achieve national progress, i.e. modernization, based on the European model, hundreds of British entrepreneurs emigrated to Chile to realize their commercial ambitions. Many, earning fortunes in the process, made Chile their permanent home. Prominent families to this day, to name a few, bear such famous names as Edwards, Bunster, Walker, Lynch, Ross, Budge, McIver, McKay, Hudson, Cox, Eastman and Campbell.

Wheelwright's memorial statue was unveiled on February 27, 1876 in La Plaza de La Aduana by Chilean President Don Aníbal Pinto, accompanied by Ministers from the Departments of Foreign Affairs, Finance, and Justice. Also present at the unveiling ceremony were members of the Diplomatic Corps, Municipal executives, Army and Navy Chiefs and heads of all the major business houses in Valparaíso. The crowd during the ceremony was reported to have been at least 5000 persons, and because there was so little available space, it overflowed into the side roads. The Square was described as being completely bedecked with garlands of myrtle and pennants; tricolour flags hung from the surrounding buildings.

Some time in the early part of the 20th Century, it was relocated to the corner of the Avenida Brasil and Calle Las Heras, having been displaced by a monument to Francisco Bilbao[275]. It remained there until 1999 and the following year was restored to its original position.

These memorial events speak for themselves. Wheelwright's contribution to the Chilean nation is permanently engraved in her history. His native United States, somewhat belatedly, found his achievements sufficient to warrant naming one of the World War 2 Liberty ships after him, and it was not until 1960 that the PSNC honoured him by launching their first oil tanker in his name. When the company relocated from its Liverpool James Street offices to premises nearer to Canada Dock, the new offices were re-named *"Wheelwright House"*.

mv *William Wheelwright* **31,320 tons gross.**

10. Preludes To Protectionism. 1873-1889

In 1873, poor commodity prices, credit restrictions and economic uncertainty caused many commercial failures in Chile, when not only the viability of the prestigious Banco Nacional had become suspect, but even the most respectable business houses had begun to experience financial difficulties. The Pacific Steam Navigation Company (PSNC), during this financially fragile period still dominated shipping on the West Coast, a position that could not have been attained without considerable investment. An 1872 supplementary Royal Charter had initially restricted PSNCs capital base to £2,000,000 (US 3,600,000 dollars), but was later increased to £3,000,000 ($US 5,400,000). In view of the additional finance required to meet increased demand for freight transportation, a situation exacerbated by its already established weekly Liverpool-South America services, PSNC was allowed to further augment its capital base to £4,000,000 (US 7,200,000 dollars).

The affects of a downturn in world trade had also extended to Chile, and were soon felt by PSNC and its competitors. Expansion plans, consequently, were deferred and PSNC's newly permitted capital limit was never breached. Balfour Williamson Company's Valparaíso business house reported that the mid 1870s had been bad for business everywhere; a widespread economic crisis persisting for five years had already hit the United States in 1873: [276]

"The deterioration of trading conditions in Chile in the 1870s was a much more gradual affair than the 1873 disaster four thousand miles away to the north [United States]. Because the collapse in Chile was less explicable, it was perhaps more ominous. Too much money, it is true, had gone too rapidly into mining ventures."

The depression persisted prompting Balfour Williamson to report to its Liverpool head office:

"In the case of many of the mines, the outlay has been entirely unremunerative and has given no better result to the proprietors than had they engaged to dig holes in the Playa Ancha [277]. Crops have been affected by a grain glut in the States.[278] Unfortunately, Chile is in a lamentable state financially and has been obliged to suspend specie payments. There has been a complete stoppage of our business and as many failures are occurring, it is difficult to know what the end may be. Our sales of late have not been a third of what they once were so that our outstandings are light but nevertheless, loss and anxiety are inevitable. I see no hope for nitrate nor do I see any daylight through copper."

PSNC's freight revenue levels were maintained for the first half of 1873 but its intra West Coast trade suffered serious setbacks; general earnings fell considerably producing a £70,000 (US 126,000 dollars) loss and causing a boardroom crisis leading to the resignation of its Company President and other leading figures. The real reason for the latter appeared to be PSNC management's inability to deal with the rising threat from the Chilean steamship company and its continued adherence to a policy of chartering ships. These were sometimes used not purely for normal business transactions, but rather employed in negative fashion to deliberately create market shortages of available cargo space, and/or to prevent the emergence of new competition.

PSNC executives had pleaded in response to criticism of this policy, especially from its shareholders, that for many years, British and European competitors had coveted its operations and if given the opportunity, would have tried to snatch hard-won business. Accordingly, appropriate pre-emptive measures had been introduced to try to thwart such actions. The Board of Directors continued to harangue competitors for falsely accusing it of monopolizing West Coast South American trade, claiming that they had conveniently overlooked the fact that the company had only acquired its predominant trading position at substantial cost, tremendous effort and in 1840, not without some degree of risk and danger.

Of course, one would not have expected the company to add to its defence commentary that, not only had it been the beneficiary of abundant good fortune brought about by the necessities of West Coast Governments, but also by their generous subsidies. Furthermore, PSNC submitted that conditions attached to British and South American Government postal contracts were not only onerous but also not very profitable. The British Government contract obliged PSNC, in return for an annual payment of £10,000 (US 18000 dollars), to provide weekly services at operational speeds in excess of those required by other steamship lines also receiving large subsidies. PSNC, not unreasonably, insisted that costs of higher coal consumption required to sustain these obligatory speeds rendered its mail contracts even more expensive to perform.

In order to meet the competing Royal Mail Steam Packet Company and other European companies head-on, PSNC decided to expand its fleet with high-speed vessels. Unfortunately, one of the disadvantages of then operating a fast steamship fleet was very high and expensive coal consumption. This decision had been taken during a period of recession on the West Coast, forcing PSNC to adopt strict cost cutting measures including an agreement with the British Post Office to allow weekly services from Liverpool to be downgraded to fortnightly events. Installation of more-efficient engines and enforced small reductions in vessels' speeds enabled considerable fuel savings.

Despite introducing new schedules with fewer sailings, eleven large vessels were laid-up, each at an annual cost of £6000 ($US 10800). At the same time, various other economic measures were introduced to cut operating costs in Callao, Valparaíso and Liverpool. These drastic measures arose from *"recommendations"* contained in an 1874 shareholders' report, resulting in the resignation of PSNC's President, Charles Turner, and other Board Members.

A few weeks after the election of a replacement President, news was received that the new steamship *Tacna* (612 tons gross) had capsized. She had left Valparaíso on March 7, 1874, bound for Pan de Azucar and intermediate ports. Her first port of call had been Los Vilos. Other steamship companies operating on the West Coast and elsewhere had also suffered occasional unfortunate losses, but the conditions prevailing just before the *Tacna's* tragic sinking are noteworthy, given that they allow an insight into the often deceptive sea conditions on the West Coast.

On the *Tacna's* main deck, 14 head of cattle had been corralled; some boxes of vegetables and 250 bales of hay were also stacked. The weather had been reported fine and as the vessel neared port, the Captain assumed the watch from the second officer. Hardly had he given the command for the vessel to turn towards land when a gust of wind caught her starboard stern, causing her to list sharply. As this became more pronounced, the Captain gave orders to try and right the vessel; the crew frantically jettisoned cargo, but before this could have any affect, she sank with the loss of 19 lives. The unexpected gust of wind was characteristic of the "*northers*", sudden and treacherous winds that could whip up the sea into a vicious frenzy.

Between 1873 and 1877, PSNC and its main competitor, Cia Sudamericana (CSAV), were continually involved in bitter trade battles in which the English company's principal weapon was the systematic reduction in freight charges. This had a beneficial knock-on affect for other West Coast trading concerns, given the widespread economic crisis during this period. CSAV, consequently, found itself in dire financial straits, and in 1873, had to reduce insurance cover on its vessels to reduce costs. It did, however, continue to operate until the following year without state assistance, but the Chilean Government was eventually compelled to alleviate the Chilean company's precarious financial position with generous annual subsidies of 1,000,000 pesos,[279] paid every six months over a ten years' period.

These were granted subject to a certain amount of Government administrative oversight, but without day-to-day operational involvement, and on condition that CSAV continued to operate regular services along the coast of Chile and extend its steamship operations from Callao to Panama. It was also required to carry Government dispatches, civil servants and Government employees, sometimes free of charge. The most important requirement obliged CSAV to allow Government requisitioning of its vessels in times of emergencies and war. Unfortunately, the service from Callao to Panama consumed much of the Chilean company's state funding, and after representations to the Government, CSAV was allowed to operate a reduced service to Callao every fifteen days [280]

Preludes To Protectionism. 1873-1889

Although CSAV had warmly welcomed state assistance, subsidies did little to actually aid the development and growth of the Chilean shipping industry. Chilean Government grants fell far short of the considerably more generous assistance schemes allowed by Germany and Japan, whereby financial aid was dispensed and calculated on the amount of cargo tonnage shipped by high-powered nationally-registered vessels, and on the distance they travelled on international trade. In fact, Chilean subsidies were confined to aiding the CSAV, and this very selectivity risked creating a monopoly out of the latter within the Chilean shipping industry. No provision was made for assisting smaller shipping companies or encouraging related investors to finance their expansion to a size sufficient to attract similar Government grants.

By 1877, the economic situation had not improved, and CSAV, on the point of bankruptcy, had to suspend its Panama service. In order to guarantee that CSAV did not re-introduce the latter line, PSNC, having already conducted an unrelenting onslaught against the Chilean company, obliged it to virtually surrender unconditionally to the English company's demands by entering into a five years "*pooling*" agreement under terms dictated by PSNC. The main contractual requirement reduced CSAV's voyages to Callao to one third of its normal schedule, and halved the Chilean company's timetable of all voyages north of the Peruvian port.

Because the number of its sailings had been considerably reduced, CSAV was financially compelled to sell to PSNC two of its ships which had become surplus to requirements; the English Company promptly incorporated them into its own West Coast fleet. The agreement established common freight rates and delegated PSNC with the responsibility for loading, staffing and servicing both company's vessels. This was a relatively easy arrangement because the crews of both establishments were generally English. To add further embarrassment to the Chilean firm, PSNC retained the right to inspect the latter's accounts. Perhaps these incidents created the myth that many Chileans were said to espouse, that the English had destroyed the Chilean merchant fleet. Indeed, the CSAV has often been accused of total surrender but, in effect, it did nothing more than tread water to survive to fight another day; this it did until the outbreak of war in February 1879.[281]

The war ended in 1883 and during the intervening years, CSAV's ships were requisitioned by the Chilean Government for conveying troops and supplies, mostly at favourable terms, enabling the company to become not only profitable, but also to generate fervent support from the military and the Government. This new found strength prompted "*La Sudamericana*" to give the required one year's notice to PSNC that it would not renew the contract favouring the latter, but offering to renegotiate a new one in an attempt to raise the level of sailings to Panama from one third, and from one half of the scheduled voyages between Valparaíso and

Callao. It also insisted on loading, handling and crewing its own vessels without the oversight of PSNC's Valparaíso office.

The former contract did have certain advantages vis-à-vis the uniform application of rates. To make the terms of the new accord more appealing to PSNC, the Chilean company proposed that one person from each company should serve in either firm's Valparaíso office as a liaison agent.[282] When these Chilean proposals were submitted to PSNC's Liverpool Head office, its directors were reported to be thunderstruck. The Board assured La Sudamericana that they had *"given long and careful consideration to the subject and being quite sympathetic with the opinion that it is desirable, in the interests of both companies that competition should be avoided if possible"* but largely accepted the Chilean company's proposals. However, the English firm stipulated that if CSAV returned to operate the Panamá service, then the latter company's half share of the Callao-Valparaíso scheduled voyages would revert to one third. It did, additionally, confirm that each establishment would maintain its own staffing and ship handling through its respective Valparaíso offices.

PSNC, however, drew the line at accepting the proposals for liaison officers, commenting indignantly that it *"would never consent to a system of espionage but would rather trust to the good feeling and good faith of the respective staffs in Valparaíso to obviate any cause for suspicion or other dissatisfaction on either side"*.[283] The English company never, officially at least, recognized the ill will and resentment that the former contract generated within CSAV. To add further insult, the English firm's directors stated:

"That in accepting the principal conditions suggested by your (CSAV) Board, they (PSNC) have been guided by a desire to continue those friendly relations which have existed during the present contract and which must be the best safeguard to mutual protection and support".[284]

Despite a lengthy reply from CSAV, PSNC was inflexible and although giving the impression that it had made voluntary concessions to the Chilean company, it would have been surprising if the English Company's Board had failed to recognize the changed fortunes of La Sudamericana concerning its re-enforced relationship with the Chilean Government and military.

Distrustful of English crews during the Pacific War, due to a perception that they were inclined towards the Peruvians, CSAV sought to hire North Americans for its officers and crew, and by 1880, all CSAV vessels were commanded by US nationals. PSNC sensing changing circumstances, also used an increasing number of Chileans and Peruvians within its crew complements; in 1891, it gave command of two of its vessels on the West Coast to Chileans. In 1883, the Chilean Government renewed CSAV's subsidy for a further ten years allowing the company to extensively modernize its fleet. Subsequent Government financial protection afforded to the latter only served, on the one hand, to strengthen the alliance between it and PSNC to the detriment of other smaller Chilean steamship lines, but on the other, CSAV failed to use the situation to expand its operations until the end of the century.

The Chilean company might have argued that its State subsidies were offset by Chilean Government grants to PSNC for continuing to operate its steamship services to the south of Chile, and which amounted to 50% of financial aid to CSAV. Accordingly, it could have submitted that it was in no position to expand its already fragile operation. Moreover, it could have argued that to have done so would surely have had to be at the expense of PSNC's market share, or else it would have had to establish services in areas then devoid of a PSNC presence or interest.

In the late 1880s, PSNC again encountered stiff competition on the West Coast, partly from CSAV's fleet, almost causing the breakdown of an existing agreement between the two shipping lines. In 1888, the Chilean Government granted an additional subsidy to CSAV to allow the resumption of the Callao-Panama run. Because no agreement had then been enacted with regard to the application of freight and passenger rates on this service, the latter charges declined considerably, on some occasions by as much as 80%. The Chilean Line had been able to achieve these low prices, not so much because of the generous subsidies it received, but because of the effective performance of its modernized fleet.[285]

In a petition of May 3, 1887 to the Chilean Government for an additional grant to enable the launch of a new steamship line between Callao and Panama, CSAV described its predicament:

"Throughout the seventeen years of its existence, CSAV has struggled unceasingly, and for the last seven years has virtually existed in a state of war with its most powerful rival, the English Pacific Steam Navigation Company...the end of that bitter competitive period, notwithstanding the [Government] grant, was only ended when the [Chilean] company was obliged to accept humiliating and onerous conditions...this truce permitted the company to undertake only specific voyages and to subject all its passenger and cargo transactions to the unbearable oversight of the English company"[286]

Following the success of its service to Panama, CSAV decided to extend its operations outside Latin America, which was still under the strong economic influence of the Great Powers, and proposed to implement a service to Chile and Europe, the latter then providing the bulk of West Coast trade and immigrants to Chile. The Chilean Government, in order to encourage the introduction of such an operation, repeatedly promised large subsidies for this purpose together with guarantees of a 6.7% dividend to local investors. Clearly PSNC, as far as the Chilean Government was concerned, would no longer be needed.

CSAV enthusiastically accepted the Government's offers but, surprisingly, then invited the English company to form a joint service to Liverpool. PSNC, preoccupied with devising strategies to prevent the German Kosmos line from establishing connections to Chilean ports, initially assessed the Chilean proposals as more competition for its own Liverpool-Chile line but sensibly did not reject the CSAV invitation to participate; it forecast that to do so would risk the outbreak of an all-out war on cargo and passenger rates. The English firm promised to assist CSAV in its operations, but according to maritime historian Rena De La Pedraja, intentionally complicated the issue in order to gain time, and deliberately detailed high start-up costs to ensure that CSAV would demand much larger subsidies than the Chilean Government had anticipated.[287] PSNC, of course, also received Chilean subsidies but at 50% of those granted to CSAV. In 1891, the Government administration that had been sympathetic to CSAV was overthrown and lack of interest by the new regime sidelined the Chilean company's proposed Chile-Europe service.

During the period 1884 to 1892, there had been a rapid fall in Chilean coastal trading figures, partly accounted for by the number of ships previously engaged in coastal work, but having later transferred to foreign-going voyages for conveying exports of nitrates. Improved steamship technology gradually displaced sailing ships from the bulk export cargo trade such as nitrates and copper, as shippers demanded faster services. In 1892, a spectacular fall in freight rates caused such vessels to abandon that activity and revert once more to coastal trading.

The owners of smaller Chilean shipping companies were wont to attribute the failure to develop the Chilean merchant marine on the difference in tax rates paid by Chilean and foreign owners. They claimed that Chilean ships should have been treated in the same way as foreign-owned vessels then exempted such taxes, conveniently forgetting that non-Chilean ships importing cargo had been subjected to the same level of Chilean taxes in their ports of origin. El Mercurio, the Valparaíso newspaper, tried to provoke Government discussion on the matter but completely ignored the country of origin tax:

"Navigation law, which actually applies to our Merchant Marine, emerged in 1836. Much of its requirements and those of other related legislation impose considerable restrictions and obstacles on Chilean ships which were only tolerable when, to compensate [for tax payments], Customs Directives reserved to national carriers the privilege of cabotage; but while [the nation's] current maritime trade is freely open to all foreign registered ships, those restrictions [on Chilean vessels] are simply obstacles to the development and prosperity of our national [Merchant] Marine." [288]

Despite the removal of restrictions on ownership and operation of Chilean ships, growth in the Chilean merchant fleet was modest, and there was still a lack of legislation to progress further development until well into the 20th Century.

Like its Chilean competitor, PSNC continued to experience financial problems; in 1875, it was forced to sell to Royal Mail Steam Packet Company, its newest and largest vessels, *Puno* and *Corcovado*, which were re-named *Para* and *Don*. The years 1875 and 1876 had been very difficult for PSNC, especially as it had been undergoing a complete re-organization. One of the latter consequences was the laying-up of eleven of its transatlantic vessels in Merseyside's Birkenhead docks.

Neither did United States' merchant shipping escape the prevailing poor trading conditions. Its situation was exacerbated in the early 1870s by North American ship design. United States' vessels were generally built of wood and fitting then with propeller propulsion had caused excessive vibration when compared with similarly propelled European iron-hulled craft. Consequently, the North Americans were reluctant to depart from their traditional policy of constructing high-sided paddle wheel steamships.

In the latter vessels, a large amount of space was taken-up by coal. Because of their wooden construction they had no tanks, which could be filled with seawater to act as ballast as coal supplies were consumed. As a result, the North American type of vessels rose higher in the water as the weight of the remaining coal diminished. The Chief Engineer of Pacific Mail Steamship Company's *Oregon*, in July 1849, recorded in his log that as the ship's supply of coal was consumed, the vessel became very light and rolled considerably:

"[Paddle] wheels out of the water half the time...burning wood and small coal mixed. Ship rolling, paddles six feet out of water". [289]

Continued American adherence to its traditional ship building methods allowed the more efficient British propeller driven ships to rapidly displace United States' vessels on many routes, prompting the latter's Government, after acknowledging that its nation's shipping was in dire straits, to appoint a special commission to investigate and report on the state of her merchant marine.

As the largest merchant fleet then existing, it was only natural that the Pacific Steam Navigation Company would be closely scrutinized. US Rear Admiral Preble submitted the following report to his Government in 1877:

"I submit this summary indicating the names and respective tonnages of the 48 ships, now comprising the fleet of the British Pacific Steam Navigation Company. Some of these vessels are propelled by paddle wheels but the majority are iron-hulled craft with propellers, high-powered, fast and of modern design. Removing their open passenger decks and installing artillery would, in times of war, convert them into effective and formidable support vessels for British Naval forces in these waters, such as [battle] cruisers and destroyers.

An average speed of about 10 knots within the Company's operational area along the Pacific coastline is considered the most economic.

The 18 steamships on the service route through the Strait of Magellan appear to be only about half the tonnage of our squadron's five main ships. However, they surpass ours in speed and are capable of being fitted with heavy armament. Apart from having useful cargo carrying capacity, they can carry enough coal supplies for a 40 days run at a speed of 11 knots, operating under adverse wind and tide conditions. This last factor is of considerable importance for a country like the United States which has no colonies and whose ships depend exclusively on their own national ports for coal supplies, a resource now classified as prohibited during war.

With the permission of the Commander of [PSNC'S] *Aconcagua*, I prepared the following notes on that vessel's operation culled from her logbook. She is one of those sailing on the Strait of Magellan route. She left Liverpool on June 13, 1877 at 8 pm, arriving at Callao, Perú, on August 9, 1877 at 7 am. During her outward voyage, she called at Pauillac (Bordeaux), Lisbon, San Vicente, Río de Janeiro, Montevideo, Punta Arenas, Valparaíso, Arica, and Mollendo. The entire voyage took 56 days, 5 hours and 50 minutes but of these, 40 days 11 hours and 35 minutes comprised actual sailing time. The distance traveled was 11,033 nautical miles; coal consumption was 1900 tons. She also consumed 656 gallons of oil and 132 pounds of tallow. She took on board at Liverpool 1746 tons of coal and in San Vicente a further 750 tons. The daily fuel consumption was 4.691 tons. The *Aconcagua* has one funnel while PSNC's other vessels have two. The Strait of Magellan ships each have two steam launches and all of PSNC's fleet is equipped with steam capstans. The PSNC fleet's total tonnage is 120,000 tons while the total of the United States Navy fleet is 143,338 tons. The Company owns an island in the Bay of Panamá where a dry dock is provided to clean vessels' hulls."

In additional notes accompanying his submissions, the US Rear-Admiral drew attention to PSNC's huge repair complex at Callao and the experienced personnel required to staff it. He mentioned that this company had provided support for schools and the clergy in Callao, Valparaíso and Panamá and noted that it was the principal stockholder of the Callao Dock Company's floating repair dock in that port.

By the end of 1871, facilities for undertaking emergency main repairs to steamships appeared not to have been installed in Valparaíso. The *Lusitania*, a few hours after sailing from Valparaíso for Liverpool on December 14, 1871, lost three of her propeller blades. There was no dry dock in the Chilean port capable of accommodating her, nor for that matter was there a site anywhere within hundreds of miles where she could safely be beached to effect repairs. This was surprising given that Chile's Navy had grown considerably, and must have experienced similar problems. One would have thought that in these circumstances, suitable facilities would have been provided.

Faced with this situation, PSNC's Marine Superintendent in Valparaíso put repairs in motion by constructing a large enclosed wooden caisson, and suspended

Preludes To Protectionism. 1873-1889

it over the vessel's stern by cables. This "*workshop*", having had the new propeller placed inside it, was lowered over the stern and then secured in position to enable the fitting of the new unit. In order to expose the damaged propeller, the vessel would have had to be lightened in the stern by relocating cargo towards the bow and forward sections. Nowadays, this feat is not so extraordinary, but one needs to appreciate the difficult conditions faced at that time, the differences in modern equipment and the lack of adequate repair facilities in Valparaíso. The question of upgrading and modernizing ports to keep pace with advances in ship technology did not figure in West Coast Governments' strategies until well into the 20th Century.

There are similarities in this instance with those experienced by Peacock when repairing the *Chile* of 1840, and the same type of operation was performed on the *Colombia* when she lost her propeller and its huge holding nut, together with various iron plates from her hull. In Callao, a similar repair platform was constructed and hung over the vessel's stern whilst she was safely moored; a new propeller was fitted followed by repairs and replacements to damaged and missing hull plates.

PSNC, like CSAV, had been receiving important subsidies from the West Coast republics as well as from Great Britain. CSAV, for its part, had done remarkably well to remain in operation, threatened as it was, by the sheer size and power of the PSNC fleet. By 1876, "*La Sudamericana*" had a fleet of 17 steamships, mostly built in the first half of the 1870s, and noticeably only one of which, the *Huarnay*, had been constructed in Great Britain in 1864. By 1877, PSNC had disposed of a large quantity of old tonnage, but following the punitive agreement with CSAV it acquired the latter's two surplus vessels the *Lontué*, and *Amazonas* for the Valparaíso to Panama route. That year also saw the loss of the steamships *Atacama*, *Iquique* and *Eten*; the latter foundered in the seas off Punta Ventura in Chile with 120 persons drowned. This tragedy was attributed to a change in the direction of currents caused by the 1877 earthquake. Over the next few years, the paddle steamers *Chile* and *Payta* were sold to the Chilean Government. *Bogota, Callao, Pacific, Panama* and *Peru* were hulked and converted to storage pontoons. The remaining older hulks were towed out to sea and sunk. The *Guayaquil*, one of the first propeller driven vessels, was scrapped.

A.Gallengo, in his "*Sud America*" (1881), gave an account of PSNC's organization on the West Coast in 1880:

"I boarded the small auxiliary steamer *Ayacucho* at the quay in Panama. This steamship, although constructed in England, was based on designs for passenger steamers operating on the Mississippi and other great North American rivers. This steamship has her interior accommodation facing outwards; the top deck gives the impression of being suspended in the air. The lounges, staterooms and first class cabins are all situated on this deck, overlooked by large skylights and cabin doors, thus affording them as much fresh air they may require throughout the day or night.

I also visited the Company's Callao headquarters. I saw there a veritable beehive of operations of every kind, engineers, carpenters, coal workers and so forth, along with a host of writers, cashiers and clerks of all types; a complete maritime establishment. It was almost a small city; an English Community on its own soil, independent, autonomous and displaying all that marvel of cleanliness and order, of calm but industrious and incessant activity, which when I saw it, reminded me of all that was admirable in the docks and wharfs in Portsmouth [England]. I was rowed out to a floating dock in the bay; a gigantic iron construction transported [290] from Glasgow in 1866. It was 300 feet long, 76 feet wide internally, and displacing 5000 tons. It has held more than 1000 vessels in its cradle, some of them between 2799 and 4350 tons, all of which give an idea of the power and energy of this British enterprise, hardly surpassed by the national Naval dockyards which administer to the war fleets of the English Channel or the Mediterranean."

In 1881, PSNC, owning 41 vessels with a combined tonnage of 91,217 tons, was awarded a supplementary British Government Charter extending its rights and privileges for another twenty-one years. It was said of this company's ships that they were the best equipped of all the merchant vessels of any nation.[291] Nevertheless, in order to attract new business in 1884, PSNC lowered freight charges on the Panama route to 39 shillings (approximately 195 new pence or $US 3.51) per ton and, at the same time, to stimulate passenger trade to Punta Arenas in the southern-most reaches of Chile, where immigrants were eligible to apply for low-cost land, cabin fares were reduced by 25%.

During the 1870s, Chile's southern longitudinal railway had been extended as far as Talcahuano and in 1884, the year in which levels of coastal maritime cargo tonnage had begun to decline, the railroad was extended to Renaico linking the agricultural areas of the south with the more heavily populated areas of the central regions of the country. These railways had obvious advantages over coastal shipping; railway stations were located within easy reach of agricultural producing areas and required little handling and loading when compared with ships and the outdated port support facilities.

Moreover, there was less risk of loss using rail compared with sea transport; importantly, conveyance of freight by railroad was faster and simpler. Eventually, the advantages of railways serving the Chilean coast began to tell and Chilean ship owners in the northern ports began to withdraw their vessels as a result of railway competition. This was at a time when foreign-registered ships were becoming more involved in transporting nitrates, and when the Chilean economy was beginning to grow leading to increases in the amount of cargo transported from the agricultural south to the central areas of Valparaiso and Santiago.

The Chilean Government failed to provide sufficient incentives for national ship owners to take advantage of this situation, and the opportunity and prospects for an expansion of the Chilean merchant fleet disappeared once more. Even if Government support for the nation's shipping industry had been available, it would have faced a difficult period due to the adverse worldwide economic conditions. The prolonged shipping crisis affected PSNC as well as the Chilean merchant fleet, even though the English company, operating as a near monopoly, enjoyed sufficiently strong conditions to weather the storm.

Many other nations, e.g. Norway, and Japan, had adopted subsidy systems to aid individual companies. Germany used a very successful method of direct grants to shipping companies in conjunction with a structure of railway freight charges favouring goods carried on German ships. Consequently, foreign fleets operating such subsidy and grant schemes rose from very low levels of tonnage to a point where they were able to challenge the British merchant fleet's supremacy. Other nations soon adopted the practice of State intervention, which led to a considerable growth in world wide shipping tonnage. Not only had the latter increased, but commensurate with technological improvements, ever-larger vessels were being launched with greater cargo carrying capacity.

While merchant ships themselves had become more efficient, their operation had been improved by the development of the telegraph, enabling ships to be directed to selected ports to load new cargo without the need to go in search of it. As the 19th Century progressed, world freight rates tended to become uniform, partly due to the consolidation process brought about by the setting of high freight rates by the large monopolistic shipping concerns, and partly by the ever growing fleet of "*tramp steamers*" searching for cargo in whichever port they could. Before the advent of the telegraph, steamship owners often wasted weeks or months sailing their vessels in ballast to ports across the world. By use of the telegraph, a ship's captain, once in port, could remain in permanent contact with his firm's head office and receive precise instructions for picking-up cargo. This factor alone considerably increased worldwide cargo-carrying capacity and eliminated wasteful voyages in ballast.

Sailing ships were more disadvantaged when compared with steamships, not due to bad weather, but rather because very fine conditions usually meant being becalmed. Unlike steamships, which could sail directly between two points in fair or adverse weather, sailing ships were obliged to follow favourable winds. Failure to locate them meant that "*sailers*" were prone to being carried of-course for weeks by ocean currents. Before 1830, masters of sailing ships had tended to navigate their vessels by habit, tradition and superstition, rather than approaching navigation scientifically. A Major James Rennell in the 1830s published charts showing directions of prevailing winds and ocean currents.[292] This accomplishment was later perfected by M.F Maury of the United States Navy in a work published in 1850 entitled "*Explanations on Sailing Directions to Accompany Wind and Current Charts.*" This quickly bred success; for example, crossings from Great Britain to

Australia, previously taking 125 days, were shortened to 92. With the unstoppable advance of the Industrial Revolution and the emergence of new technologies, international trade changed and developed rapidly obliging major ports to update facilities in order to keep abreast of these advances and to avoid bottlenecks in the discharge or loading of cargo.

Port of Pisagua around 1890 showing the nitrate clippers awaiting cargo Reproduced from Basil Lubbock's "Nitrate Clippers")

Most major ports in industrialized countries created purpose made dockside facilities to deal with specialized cargo, e.g. the port of London provided special quayside storage and wharfs for loading and unloading of coal; others were integrated with refrigerated stores for handling dairy produce and meat. In the minor West Coast South American ports where absence of proper wharfs for steamships or "*sailers*" often meant that wooden lighters had to be towed or rowed out into the bay to be moored alongside a waiting ship to supply or receive her cargo. Their loading/unloading process was very slow amd later arriving vessels had to queue for weeks before being able to either enter the operational area or even to enter port if the vessel was able to do so.

Loading nitrate in the port of Pisagua 1890. From "A Visit to Chile and the Nitrate Fields of Tarapacá" by W. Howard Russell. London 1890. Published by J.S.Virtue & Co. Ltd.

The above image shows the typical method of loading nitrates and demonstrates the lack of proper facilities along the WCSA at that time. The average layover of a sailing ship at the Chincha Islands, for example, waiting to take guano on board was three months.[293] Even into the late 1970s, there were still many West Coast ports where cargo was loaded and unloaded into large lighters towed backwards and forwards by small motor launches. The introduction of cranes and winches together with wharfs equipped with railway and rolling stock, onto and from which cargo could quickly be loaded or discharged, considerably reduced waiting times in ports; quick turn-rounds across the world consequently contributed to extra cargo carrying capacity.

The demand for imports of raw materials made by the advanced nations of Europe, their need for foodstuffs, cotton, wool, nitrates, copper and so forth, and the corresponding need to export manufactured goods to the source countries together with advances in communications, made sailing in ballast virtually unnecessary. This was especially the case with the export of much-in-demand coal and increases in passenger trade because of emigration to Australia and South America; ship owners were usually assured of available cargo for both outward and inward voyages.

Coal shipments were better suited to the bulk cargo-carrying sailing ships. Welsh coal, much in demand in South America, would be loaded at Swansea and sailed out to northern Chilean ports of the copper producing regions. Export of copper ore eventually gave way to shipment of copper bars produced by foundries at Caldera, Copiapó, Coquimbo, Guayacán, Tongoy and many other smaller ports along the northern coastline of Chile. Such was the extent of British interests in this resource that British shipyards constructed specially designed sailing ships for carrying these cargoes. This metal's enormous weight posed the danger of vessels capsizing if this commodity shifted even slightly. Specially re-enforced compartments were, therefore, built into ships' holds, and hulls were suitably strengthened for this purpose. In spite of such safeguards, sailing these copper-laden vessels around Cape Horn was one most dreaded by sailors who were apt to view these voyages as among the most dangerous and hardest in the world.[294]

The copper trade, despite all its attendant difficulties, offered excellent investment opportunities for British capitalists to provide shipping enterprises to import this commodity. Shipping companies such as Beynon & Co., and Bath & Co., constructed dozens of specialized ships, which operated successfully on the Chile-Cape Horn-Britain route for many years. The names of "*sailers*" like the 313 tons *Pathfinder*, the 730 tons *Valparaíso*, the 591 tons *Niphon* and the 352 tons *Lima* were regularly included in the arrivals and departures notices on the Chilean coast. Due to the low volume of copper ore that could be economically carried, sailing ships on this route were specifically built to smaller sizes. Contemporary vessels, rarely exceeded 800 registered tons.[295] During the last decade of the 19th Century, the copper ore trade began to decline, partly attributed to the increase in numbers of Chilean copper foundries.

It was during this period that Chilean exports of nitrates to Europe reached its ascendancy. Nitrate cargoes did not pose the low volume to high weight factor of copper; the larger non-copper carrying vessels could be filled to capacity. These larger sailing ships, especially British, French and German vessels, were used to advantage bringing out capacity cargoes of coal to Chile and returning to Europe with maximum loads of nitrates. British ships were, in the 19th Century, the most frequent callers at Chilean ports, but there were also a number of other European firms making their mark on the history of navigation in South America; their presence certainly highlighted the opportunities that were initially available to Chilean ships. Perhaps the most famous of the nitrate clipper firms was the German ship owner F.Laeisz whose first sailing ship, the 985 tons *Polynesia* was constructed in Hamburg in 1874 for transporting guano and nitrate between the Chilean coast and the latter port. Soon afterwards, Laeisz added two more ships, the 537 tons *Professor* and the wooden 647 tons *Henriette* to his fleet. The latter was the only vessel whose name did not begin with *"P"*; the firm soon became widely known as the *"P"* line.

Despite prosperous business conditions, Laeisz was unable to finance the construction of new vessels and the company was restricted to buying four cheap British sailing ships, which were re-christened: *Pluto, Poncho, Paquita,* and *Puck.*

The first *sailer* actually constructed to Laeisz's specifications was the German built 1230 tons iron-hulled clipper *Plus*. Later the steel hulled 1273 tons *Potrimpos* and the 1445 tons *Prompt* were launched. At the same time, three further vessels were acquired all of 1000 tons, the *Pirat, Pestalozzi* and the *Paposao*. With trade in exports of coal and the import of nitrates from Chile growing tremendously, the German firm was able to keep its fleet operational on the routes between Europe and Chile; the only problems were those connected with time lost due to the inefficient loading and unloading procedures on the Chilean coast. To resolve these difficulties, Laeisz's crews were trained to speed-up operations; state of the art winches and derricks were fitted to their vessels. Such efforts were eventually rewarded with record unloading and loading times being noted, halving the time achieved using previous procedures. One of the main reasons for the continuing success of using sailing ships on nitrate and coal routes emanated from these transported commodities not being considered as *"urgent delivery cargo"*. Three or four months spent on the high seas was not as an important consideration as the price of the cargo prevailing at its destination port, usually determined by other economic considerations. Nevertheless, Laeisz realized that although voyages between Europe and Chile could be completed more rapidly, the more trips undertaken within a fixed time period, the more profitable the overall outcome.

The *Preussen*. From Basil Lubbock's "The Nitrate Clippers".

On this account, the "P" line became famous for the high speed and quality that the firm demanded from its shipbuilders when adding to its fleet. Compared with the conventional slow and heavy sailing ships of other lines, the German *"clipper"* not only achieved average speeds of 12 knots on the Atlantic crossings, but was also especially re-enforced to support the more efficient equipment for assisting those loading and unloading practices instigated by Laeisz. Between 1889 and 1891, the German firm constructed more new ships, the first of which later became known as the *"nitrate clippers"*, and led to even larger vessels being built for the nitrate routes; they would become the largest of their class in the world. All these German built vessels were steel constructed and registered as 1700 tons each: *Palmyra* (built 1889), *Parchim* (1889), *Pera* (1890), *Pampa* (1891) and *Preussen* (1891). In 1892, the Pampa took 67 days for the run from Dungeness to Iquique and 69 days from Iquique to Cuxhaven.

Two additional and even larger clippers were launched from German shipyards in 1892, the 2895 tons *Placilla* and the 2906 tons *Pisagua*. Despite their large size and, even when fully loaded, they achieved incredible speeds; the *Placilla*, for example, covered the distance between England and Valparaíso in only 58 days. However, Laeisz did not enjoy a monopoly of the nitrate transportation trade; a French company operated almost in parallel with the *"P"* line, and at the beginning of the 1890s had an even larger fleet. The shipping company Antonio Dominique Bordes, was founded in 1847 when M. Bordes teamed-up with a businessman by the name of Le Quellec to establish the firm of Bordes & Le Quellec. This company acquired four wooden ships: *Antonio, L'Anita, Eugenie* and *St. Vincent de Paul* to operate between Peruvian and Chilean coasts and French ports.

For twenty years, the growth in their business was steady rather than spectacular. In 1868, Le Quellec died leaving Bordes as sole owner of the enterprise. The latter launched into expansion and renovation programmes; between 1868 and 1870, Bordes ordered thirteen vessels from British shipbuilders, one wooden hull and 12 of iron ranging from 581 tons to 735 tons. These were specifically designed for the Chilean coast and carried between 1000 and 1200 tons of copper, guano and nitrates to British ports. In 1870, he extended his trade to France; business prospered so rapidly that between 1870 and 1879 he had another 27 ships constructed, most of then being given Chilean place names and varying in size from 630 tons to 1217. In 1880, he constructed the *Union* 2139 tons. This clipper proved so successful on the nitrate run that another three were quickly built in Glasgow, the 2230 tons *A.D.Bordes*, the 2511 tons *Perseverance* and the 2408 tons *Tarapacá*.

The Bordes Line's most famous vessel was the *France*, at the time, the largest sailing ship afloat and built by Scottish shipbuilders S.W. Henderson. The masts and the ship were constructed of steel and she was designed specifically for the nitrate route; at 3800 registered tons, she was able to carry 5500 tons of nitrate cargo. However, five years after her launch, the competing firm of Laeisz, the *"P"* line launched an even larger clipper, the 4026 tons *Potosi*, built in Germany with a cargo carrying capacity of 6400 tons, and able to travel at an average 16.5 knots.

In 1923, she was sold to the Chilean firm of Gonzalez, Soffia and Cía and renamed *Luisa*.

Unfortunate to be in Valparaíso at the outbreak of World War 1, she was interned for the duration of the conflict. In 1918, the Laeisz company sold her to another German firm, Vinnen, but before the latter could take possession of her, she was handed over to the French Government as part compensation agreed in Versailles following the end of this war. However, during her spell of internment, her German crew had systematically sabotaged all mechanical devices on board to thwart their use by enemy forces. On being given control of the vessel in 1923, the French Government did nothing with her and she remained at anchor in Valparaíso Bay until sold to the Chilean firm. On her last voyage, she delivered nitrates to Britain and after loading coal at Cardiff, headed back for Mejillones in Chile. On the return voyage, her cargo caught fire and despite seeking refuge in the Gulf of San Jorge, Argentina, fire tenders at the nearby port were unable to extinguish the blaze. Having failed to beach the vessel, her captain ordered her to be abandoned.[296]

The *"P"* line, in 1902, decided to construct an even larger clipper, the 5081 tons *Preussen II*, more famously known as the *"Pride of Prussia"*, with nitrate cargo carrying capacity of 8000 tons. Her speed, on one occasion along the Chilean coast, was recorded at an average 17 knots and distance covered in 24 hours as 658 miles. She met an unfortunate end on November 6, 1910, after colliding in thick fog with the passenger steamship *Brighton* in the English Channel, and had to be abandoned.

These sailing ships had the advantages of not only being free of time pressure but also, during the period of nitrate-import-coal-export trading, they functioned in a worldwide atmosphere of very low rates of freight. Accordingly, the costs of servicing these imports/exports were extremely cheap when compared with the operational needs of steamships whose loading/unloading facilities tended to be inefficient by comparison. Furthermore, advances in ship design allowed clippers to accommodate sufficient extra cargo carrying capacity to rival larger contemporary steamships; it was these characteristics, which made them into very sound commercial investments.

Sailing ships also received their fair share of State subsidies. France, for example, executed a system of grants during the 1890s that was extremely favourable to the construction of large capacity sailing ships for importing nitrates. Bordes Line, during the first 50 months of its operations, received more than 40% of the 10.5 millions of francs paid to the whole of the French shipping industry. This firm, responding to national criticism at the time, revealed that the subsidies it received only amounted to one sixth of its entire operating costs. Whether this was true or not, its receipt of State assistance was an important factor in the firm's growth.[297] Germany also awarded financial grants to her shipping industry; these were not as favourable to the sailing clippers as those of the French nation, but did not seem to hinder progress of the *"P"* line.

Over the latter half of the 19th Century, there had been differences of opinion in Chile between those politicians and economists who espoused such *"protectionist"* policies, and others who advocated *"free trade"* strategies. Evident problems in Chilean merchant shipping circles had already begun to fan the flames of protectionism. In 1860, France and Great Britain had established mutual free policies but few nations copied their actions.

In 1866, the USA, followed by Germany and most of Europe, began to introduce trade protection measures entailing high customs barriers. The southern cotton producing States of the USA had supported unrestricted trade measures, given that cotton constituted their major exports to France and Great Britain, and also their ability to import manufactured goods from Europe at prices substantially cheaper than those obtained from their northern neighbours. The northern States were diametrically opposed to such policies. After the American civil war, the victorious northern Government extended its protectionist strategies to the whole nation incorporating high customs tariffs to protect their nascent trades against European competition. The American southern States viewed the imposition of protective barriers as a means of subsidizing the less efficient industries of the north.

A similar situation was then occurring in Chile, especially in the exporting mining regions of the north, the exporting agricultural provinces of the south, and the importing commercial centres of Valparaíso and Santiago whose many foreign business houses were operating in all three of these sectors. All interested parties were, naturally, inclined to keeping taxes and freight costs as low as possible. Political factions, lobbying for the abolition of customs taxes to assist the nation's economy, also lent them support. Such thinking was additionally identified with those who proposed that Latin American nations should be united as one entity. The opposing school of thought called for protectionist measures comprising special privileges, subsidies and semi-monopolistic concessions comparable to those of the Spanish colonial period, rather than those of the more practical German and USA models.[298]

The Chilean method of Protectionism was considered by historian Claudio Véliz to be highly inefficient, leading inevitably to the creation of monopolies in all commercial sectors subjected to such measures. He remarked that these protectionist rules were not statutorily created, but often emerged as *"gentlemen's agreements"* between opposing liberal and nationalist factions. This situation arose because both sides were sufficiently represented in the elected assemblies to ensure that neither party's particular policy was adopted as legislation, or so severely diluted as to be ineffective; stalemates invariably led to State intervention with the continuation of a system based on the award of privileges, subsidies and concessions.[299]

Such methods enabled favoured enterprises to establish quasi-monopolies benefiting from Government financial assistance while still free to distribute generous dividends to their stockholders, but not obliged to improve or expand their fleets. The shipping company, to which this description clearly applied, was the CSAV, otherwise known as "*La Sudamericana*". In May 1887, CSAV petitioned the Chilean Government for further subsidies, which would have brought the total of Government financial assistance to 250,000 pesos, approximately £50,000 (US 90,000 dollars). La Sudamericana claimed that this subsidy was essential for constructung a new 1500 tons steamship, and to carry out technical improvements to its other vessels in order to achieve operating speeds of 16 knots. It had also dangled before the Government the bait of its preparedness to operate regular services between Valparaíso and Panama. This petition for a subsidy review was submitted six years before the expiry of its contemporary grant.[300]

The Chilean Government's decision to provide financial support to CSAV in 1874 was logical and reasonable, given the Chilean company's dire financial position in the face of fierce competition from the more powerful PSNC. That logic, however, no longer appeared tenable to many, and provoked strong criticism, especially from those who recalled that the Chilean Government had been obliged to pay CSAV unacceptably high freight charges when it requisitioned its vessel during the War of the Pacific, in the process, enabling the company to create a very healthy financial position. Féliz Vicuña writing in "*Revista Economica*" in June 1887 commented:

"At the outbreak of the War of the Pacific, we unexpectedly found ourselves without ships to convey our troops and having to make enormous sacrifices to provide money to not only purchase freighters but also for the hire of those steamships belonging to La Cía Sudamericana and the resulting payment of compensation. In less than two years of service, the company received a total figure that was higher than the purchase cost of these vessels. Afterwards, this company, already powerfully rich thanks to State finance, is once again using its influence to obtain a further unjustified subsidy of 1,000,000 pesos. It is not difficult to realize that because of this strong [Governmental] protection, the company may have gained even greater influence and any further subsidies paid to it will only lead to demands for more."[301]

In order to allay criticism of its petitions for additional subsidies, CSAV tried to elicit public support by announcing its intention to sever links with PSNC on the 1877 agreement for the setting of freight rates. Apart from appealing to nationalistic sentiment, it was unlikely that such a divorce would have achieved much. It was clear, at that time, that foreign competition had grown considerably, and while its component shipping firms received generous financial assistance from their respective Governments, the basis of calculation used to assess those subsidies was entirely different from those used by the Chilean Executive to provide for its merchant marine. Financial grants paid to the latter involved a straightforward payment unrelated to miles travelled or tonnages carried, as in the case of foreign Governments' subsidies.

The Chilean system did not actually assist the development of her mercantile fleet, but rather served, in practice, to protect the creation of a monopoly. This mode of grant-making lasted until the end of the 19th century, and did not generally assist the formation of other Chilean limited-status shipping firms; some enterprises were formed, but they were too small to compete against a collective of foreign shipping companies, which still having free access to trade along Chile's coast, constituted too strong a force. Such small shipping companies would have been too weak to compete against the CSAV, virtually a national body financed and supported by the Chilean Government. The foreign shipping companies undertaking Chilean coastal trade after the War of the Pacific were PSNC, Gulf Line, Compagnie Maritime Transatlantique, Compagnie Maritime du Pacifique, Kosmos Line and Hamburg-Pacific Line.[302]

Féliz Vicuña, having stated his opposition to the simple direct payments system of subsidies to CSAV, recommended the Chilean Government to adopt the European system of providing financial assistance based, for example, on vessels' mileage, the type of ships operating, their age, and engine horsepower. He believed that such a method would encourage the construction in Chile of more modern ships, if the Government provided sufficient and attractive inducements. These arguments and opposition proved useless; CSAV's application for further subsidies was granted, but not entirely in the form requested. In 1892, the Chilean Government dispensed an additional award of 100,000 pesos (approximately £20,000 or $US 36,000), paid annually for two years; it also handed over to CSAV ownership of the completely refurbished steamship freighter *Amazonas*. These concessions were granted on condition that La Sudamericana engaged Chilean nationals for at least 75% of its vessels' crew complement, one of which was to be of officer rank.

It came as no surprise to critics of CSAV to learn that these stipulations were never met; nor was it unexpected when the same procedure and degree of awarding payments to CSAV were renewed at various times until the end of the 19th Century. In fact in 1895, the financial grant had been increased from 100,000 to 146,000 pesos (£29,200 or $US 52,560). The Chilean Government, clearly, had no problem of continually making subsidies available to CSAV, prompting many to believe that it had abandoned any attempt to place the Chilean merchant fleet on a sound footing. Véliz suggested that the reason for continuing with direct financial help to CSAV was the low freight levels prevailing at a time when Chile was predominantly an exporting nation. Political and economic groups of the period, accordingly, were interested in ensuring that low freight costs were sustained. These levels of transport charges continued to apply until the end of the 19th Century, a situation that could not have been more favourable to Chile. Consequently, any Government initiative threatening the status quo, either directly or indirectly, was vigorously opposed.[303]

Political and economic groups supportive of Government policy were generally associates of those influential commercial interests in the export of copper and nitrates from Chile's northern ports, the agricultural producing concerns in the southern regions, and the railway companies allied to both sectors. Various alternatives submitted to Congress during the 1890s were passed backwards and forwards between various Government ministries before being pigeonholed. In January 1898, after twenty years under consideration, draft legislation was finally approved by the Chamber of Deputies which, inter alia, stipulated that within five years, coastal trading would be restricted to Chilean vessels to the exclusion of all foreign ships.[304]

As soon as this draft law was approved, agents and consignees of foreign-owned shipping companies emphatically voiced their opposition to the Senate on the grounds that, although the legislation had been designed to encourage the development of a viable Chilean merchant marine, its short sighted actions in this respect would seriously damage the nation's commerce. They asserted that not only would it be practically impossible to create a strong national mercantile fleet within the period stipulated, but that additional foreign investment would be needed to progress such an initiative. More importantly, in a petition detailing their representations, they warned that the subject legislation was preparing to displace foreign shipping companies at a time when much needed foreign investment, far from being attracted to the country, would actually be deterred.[305]

Santiago newspaper El Ferrocarril published an editorial on September 3, 1898, commenting on the Chamber of Deputies' decision to approve the new Cabotage law:

"What is the main requirement accepted by everybody in business? Undoubtedly, it is the capacity to have at their disposal the means of easy, effective and above all, cheap transportation. In order to secure this basic need, it is clear that competition between mercantile shipping companies must be encouraged, but at the same time ensuring that no advantage is given to some [firms] while denying others the ability to compete "[306]

Clearly, critics of the proposed legislation agreed that if implemented, it would tend to create unacceptable increases in freight costs compared with then prevailing low charges in the rest of the world. It has to be noted, however, that the overall picture on the West Coast was complicated by a small group of foreign shipping companies effectively controlling a large part of maritime trade, especially from Chilean ports. Their dominance was attributed to the uncontested but illegal agreements between them on the setting of uniformly high freight rates on principal shipping routes.

In May 1899, La Sociedad Nacional de Agricultura submitted a petition on the question of foreign shipping and freight charges in Chile. Various other publications had emerged at around the same time on similar themes, one in particular entitled *"La Marina Mercante Nacional. Estudios y Proyectos para su Organización."* (The National Merchant Marine. Studies and Proposals for its Organisation). The latter contained a series of articles reproduced from the correspondence columns of the newspaper El Ferrocarril. Some letters related to a Chilean Government subsidy awarded to a Spanish shipping firm for the introduction of a steamship line between Valparaíso, South American Atlantic ports and Europe. Others supported the formation of a Committee, representative of Chilean economic affairs, to try and resolve the problem of inflated freight charges levied by PSNC for the transportation of merchandise and other products from Chilean ports.

Such a Committee was formed from representatives of La Sociedad Nacional de Agricultura, La Sociedad de Fomento Fabril (The Society for Promotion of Manufacturing), La Sociedad de Viticulturas, La Sociedad de Minería and el Centro Industrial.[307] It debated the situation at length, but concluded that until political action had been taken to bring the merchant marine up to the standards of the larger and more powerful nations, there was no ready solution to resolve the issue. The Committee, however, did specifically refer to proposals submitted to the Chilean Executive in 1894, and unanimously approved by the Chamber of Deputies in 1898. It commented:

"These proposals, should they become law, will directly benefit the nation by creating new trade opportunities for industry and agriculture. These issues have been taken into consideration by the membership...and by unanimous agreement, the Committee will make representations to the National Legislative Council requesting that preference be given as far as possible to those proposals seeking to protect the Chilean Merchant Marine."

In this way, those interested groups traditionally exerting the greatest opposition to protectionist legislation for Chile's merchant fleet, had now performed an about-turn, precisely because of the higher freight charges applied by the cartel of foreign-shipping lines on the West Coast. When the Senate finally examined proposals dealing with the reservation of coastal trading for Chilean registered vessels, but which allowed foreign operators a period of five years' grace before their final exclusion, a Senator from Chiloé, Fernando Concha remarked:

"I fear that approving this law, will create a situation where sufficient Chilean investment capital will not be available to provide the very shipping which the country needs. The logical result of implementing these proposals will be that once foreign ships, which represent foreign capital, are forced from our waters, there will be no ships left to assist the development of our industries. It is most likely that Chilean ship owners will be inclined to increase their freight charges, seriously prejudicing national production. Before driving out foreign capital, we must strive to enrich our nation; that will not happen while there is a lack of investment loans enabling capital returns not exceeding 6%". [308]

Many politicians supported the Chiloé senator; his solution required the State to launch a large limited company funded by private and Government capital, and supported by the Executive when necessary. He reminded the Senate that the Government had already achieved success with railroads' construction and other land transportation systems, and saw no reason why a similar national initiative could not be directed towards Chilean mercantile marine operations. Opponents of Concha's recommendations had little difficulty in exposing the flaws in his argument, claiming that by creating a large shipping company on the lines suggested, would form a Chilean registered monopoly from the outset. Moreover, they declared that because such an enterprise would benefit from State subsidies, it would become considerably more powerful than CSAV; the establishment of a new State enterprise would, therefore, deter the emergence and development of other shipping firms to provide appropriate competition for La Sudamaericana. Unsurprisingly Concha's proposals were disregarded.[309]

While it is true that the Chilean Government had failed to avail itself of promising opportunities for its merchant marine after the end of the War of the Pacific, there had, shortly afterwards, been an increase in the total tonnage in the Chilean fleet. However, the quality of these vessels was either very suspect, having been purchased from European firms, or was in the worst possible condition for sailing. Féliz Vicuña remarked in 1887:

"Chile has no first rate sailing ships; the majority of these vessels were condemned [by the Europeans] and have reached our shores in such a damaged condition that they have had to undergo extensive repairs before undertaking coastal trade or the timber run to California" [310].

It was the very unacceptable state of these Chilean "*sailers*" that led to their replacement by steamships, even though technical advances had been made in sailing ship construction; steel hulls effectively ending the working lives of the old wooden vessels. Great Britain effected the fastest change from sail to steamship with the United States and Canada following this rapid trend. It was the displacement of sail by steam that had led to a large surplus of mostly poor quality sailing ships, mainly acquired by Chilean companies with little, if any, financial assistance from the Government to halt their decline. Like the progress of the proposed protective legislation, development of the Chilean merchant marine continued to stagnate.

11. War Of The Pacific.
   Causes and Affects.   1879-1898.

Students embarking on research for South American history are usually cautioned as to the reliability of opinions and claims of some South American historians, especially on the Chile-Bolivia question and the war with Peru. Some commentators from these countries, perhaps understandably, are inclined to submit versions of historical facts, as they are wont to interpret them, often slanting events to defend or promote particular views.Bolivia's sovereignty, following her hard-won independence from Spain, extended over 61,000 square miles; it included the Littoral, an extensive Pacific coastal strip incorporating the nitrate and copper rich resources of that part of the Atacama Desert which now forms the present day Chilean Province of Antofagasta. Her territory then comprised 250 miles of coastline embracing the main ports of Antofagasta, Mejillones, Cobija and Tocopilla. Chile, for her part, still vigorously defends her seizure and continued occupation of this territory and, in any case, regards its annexation as being finally settled by internationally recognized treaty in 1904.

Map of modern Bolivia. Courtesy: Texas University Library

War Of The Pacific. Causes and Affects. 1879-1898.

Bolivia, on the other hand, having adopted a policy of seeking to recover her lost lands by soliciting international support and co-operation, has already obtained the official backing of Brazil who, in the event of Bolivian success, it has to be said, would benefit from railroad rights across Bolivia to a Pacific port. Bolivia continues to actively make such representations for the return of her lost territories and in September 1977, ex-US President and 2002 Nobel Peace prize-winner, Jimmy Carter announced:

"It is our hope that Bolivia, Chile and Peru can arrive at an agreement over the establishment of a corridor to allow Bolivia to have direct access to the sea over her own property."

Evidence to support Bolivia's claims to sovereignty over the disputed coastal region before Chilean annexed them in 1873 is indisputable. Indeed, Juan Bautista Alberdí, William Wheelwright's biographer recorded that the latter established a sailing packet service in 1829 between Valparaíso and Cobija, *"the main port of Bolivia"*.

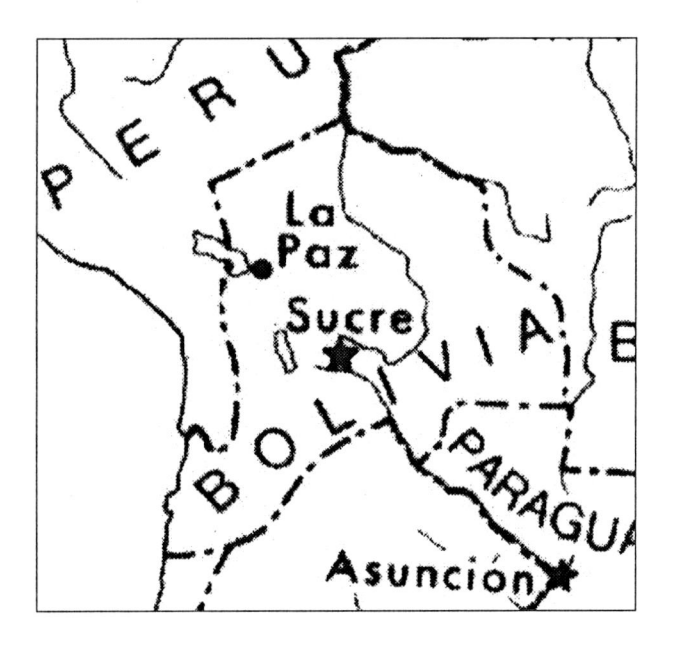

The above 1826 map of Bolivia clearly shows her to be in possession of part of the Littoral, the coastal strip between the southern region of Peru and the then northern frontier of Chile. The map was extracted from one depicting the Latin American States in 1826, in *"People and Politics of South America"* by Mary Wilhelmine Williams 1930. National frontiers were, up to the early part of the 19th Century, somewhat indistinct. To the Spanish, they represented mere administrative detail when most of their colonies were governed as separate Vice-Royalties. The lesser status of Captaincy-General had been granted to Chile and Venezuela; these two units not being considered as important to Spain as Peru due to the latter's greater gold and silver producing capacity. Accordingly, Spain regarded Peru as the jewel in her crown.

Clear demarcation of common frontiers between Vice-Royalties and Captaincy-Generals was largely irrelevant to Spanish administrators; the crucial factor centred on the combined colonial areas remaining under the complete jurisdiction of Spain. When measuring techniques had developed sufficiently to allow detailed surveys and economic conditions had improved, and when circumstances demanded, further exploration and more extensive mapping of the colonial regions did produce more accurate boundaries. Chile won her independence in 1817, but even in 1833, her own Constitution could still only vaguely define the northern extremity of her national territory. Describing this as extending from the Atacama Desert to Cape Horn, it identified her most northerly town as Copiapó. This approximate description of Chile's northern boundary with Bolivia was sufficient for identification purposes at that time.

In order to launch his Pacific Steam Navigation Company, Wheelwright first had to obtain the appropriate concessions from the Pacific Coast nations in South America. Having obtained one from the Republic of Chile on August 25, 1835, and having consented to the terms of a Decree from the Peruvian Government on September 13, 1836, Wheelwright, according to Juan Bautista Alberdí, then crossed the mountains to Potosí,[311] the then Bolivian seat of Government[312]. There he petitioned that young republic for the right to use her ports for his proposed enterprise. The following concession was quickly granted:

"This Supreme Government Decree hereby extends all those privileges granted by Northern and Southern Peru to include all Bolivian ports. All those privileges granted to William Wheelwright on September 12, 1836, [i.e. the Peruvian Decree] to undertake steamship navigation in the Pacific are hereby extended to include all ports of the Republic of Bolivia. I hereby order my Secretary General to execute this Decree, print, publish, and circulate it. Granted in Lima, November 6, 1836 Andres Santa Cruz[313]. By Order of His Excellency Pío de Tristán."

The former component of this voluntary union was called *"Peru-Bajo"* (lower Peru) and *"Peru Alto"* (higher Peru) was the name often applied to Bolivia. Chile immediately perceived the Confederation as a substantial threat to her existence and in 1836, supported by Argentina, invaded Peru. Considerable dissent had already erupted amongst those Peruvian and Bolivian élites not prepared to accept the rule of then Bolivian President Santa Cruz.[314] Northern Peruvians, mostly the land owning and influential ruling classes, joined with the invading Chilean army

War Of The Pacific. Causes and Affects. 1879-1898.

Map showing Bolivia's principal ports prior to the War in the Pacific. Based on data from "Strategy in the Southern Oceans" by Virgina Gamba-Stonehouse

in Peru and the short lived Confederation was dissolved.

As early as 1836, the issue of national boundaries between Bolivia and Chile had begun to take hold.[315] Discussions between the two countries on the matter lapsed, but were re-opened in 1858 by Chilean president Manuel Montt, declaring that it was his country's intention not to seek "*any increase in territory but to preserve what we hold and what we have always possessed*".[316]

It was the Chilean perception of Peru accumulating wealth from resources in the latter's own region, similar to that found in the disputed territory, especially from guano, that prompted the Chilean Government to claim jurisdiction of that region north of the 23rd parallel, a claim not hitherto supported by military force. Considerable new deposits of guano discovered in the disputed region only increased tensions. Chile dispatched a warship to the port of Mejillones, and having expelled Bolivian authorities, replaced them with her own appointed officials.

To underpin her *de facto* sovereignty, licences for the exploitation of guano had, thereafter, to be obtained from the Chilean Government. Further incidents arose over the following decade to foment tension and in 1863, the Bolivian National Assembly, having been summoned to consider the "*illegitimate possession that Chile has taken of Bolivian territory*", authorized President Acha to declare war on Chile if an honourable solution to the occupation could not be obtained.[317]

Chile and Bolivia were on the verge of war when Spanish attacks on Peru in 1865 diverted attention from boundary disputes and ushered Chile and Bolivia into hostilities but, this time, as allies against Spain. This alliance produced a long friendship leading to an agreement on August 10, 1866, establishing a definite frontier between the two nations along the 24th parallel of latitude, just south of the port of Antofagasta. It virtually drew Chile into a joint leadership over territory between the 23rd and 24th parallels, that is, the Atacama region possessing the most valuable known resources.

Under the terms of the agreement, Chilean business interests in the area enjoyed equal rights with those of Bolivia; the Chilean Government was guaranteed half of any tax revenues generated from the exploitation of mineral resources. The more efficient and aggressive Chilean enterprises rapidly began to develop the region, applying large amounts of capital, technical, managerial and labour resources. The Bolivians could hardly compete with this commercial onslaught.[318] Chile argued throughout the 1860s for her official borders to be moved further north, both in recognition of her huge commercial interests there, and of those areas which had become heavily populated by her own nationals. Discussions continued for the next two years, producing the odd agreement, but these were insufficient to prevent Chile from tightening her practical hold on those territories in which her mining interests lay.

The terms of the 1866 accord required that both countries, notwithstanding the agreed boundary, would equally divide revenue produced from the extraction of guano deposits in Mejillones, and other subsequent finds of this fertilizer anywhere in the territory between the 23-degrees and 25-degrees parallels. Both countries were also obliged to equally share taxes received on mineral exports originating in the latter territory. The agreement, additionally, obliged Bolivia to open the port of Mejillones and establish a Customs House there, to which Chile had a right to appoint one or more Treasury employees. Reciprocal rights were reserved to Bolivia to make similar appointments to any similar unit established by Chile in the subject territory. Moreover, mineral ore, nitrates and guano exported through the port of Mejillones were to be tax-free, and Chilean naturally-produced goods imported through the same port were exempted from duties.

Both nations agreed that a system be established for the future exploitation of guano, the levying of mineral export duties, and that no transfer be arranged of their rights acquired by the treaty to any other nation, corporation or private

War Of The Pacific. Causes and Affects. 1879-1898.

individual, except to each other.[319] What Bolivia had not then realized when concluding this pact with Chile, was that she had given the latter a legal foothold in the rich revenue producing territory as far north as the 23-degrees parallel, one that later enabled Chile to pursue her claim to sovereignty over it.

The existence of nitrates on Bolivian territory near to Antofagasta attracted further immigration to the port. Although still under Bolivian sovereignty, the composition of that city's population, drawn by earlier discoveries of copper, and then by world demand for nitrates to make explosives and fertilizers, was about 90% Chilean. President Morales of Bolivia in April 1872 had granted permission to the Chilean Compañia de Salitres y Ferrocarril (Nitrates and Railway) de Antofagasta to extract these deposits, acknowledging at the time, that the Chileans were better equipped than the Bolivians to undertake these operations. The Chileans built *"ofiicinas"*,[320] as well as making improvements to and developing Antofagasta as a major port. Rapidly becoming a large and important city within recognized Bolivian territory, in practical terms, it quickly evolved into an established Chilean settlement.

Chile also had ambitions in the Peruvian nitrate field of Tarapacá where private enterprises, mostly British and Chilean interests, operated. Peru, clearly alarmed at these developments, had signed a *"secret"* defence treaty in 1873 with Bolivia. She had tried to involve Argentina but the latter, having peacefully settled her own border disputes with Chile, decided to remain neutral. It was Chile's desire to acquire the Peruvian province of Tarapacá that was the main cause of the Pacific War.

Professor Lawrence A. Clayton, Director of the Latin American Studies Program of the University of Alabama contending that the treaty was neither *"secret"* nor *"a defensive alliance"* aimed at Chile, commented:

"Chile rapidly learned of its provisions and it simply provided for consultation between Peru and Bolivia before any boundary change might be made".[321]

Argentine national, Virginia Gamba-Stonehouse, Visiting Professor at the Maryland and American Universities in the United States and the Department of War Studies, Kings College London, took a different view. She claimed that because Chile had proceeded to increase naval forces by ordering the construction of two naval ships in 1871, Bolivian President Ballivian and Peruvian President Manuel Pardo had signed a *"secret"* alliance in 1873 to protect *"their sovereignty, independence and territorial integrity from external threats"*.[322]

Revenue from sales of guano in the early 1870s dwindled rapidly, causing Peruvian Government debt to escalate. This combined with a general economic downturn in both countries, obliged Peru and Bolivia to try to steer their economies away from Chilean influences. In 1875, the Peruvian Government nationalized the

Tarapacá nitrate fields and in 1878, Bolivia imposed a further but not excessive ten cents tax on each quintal (100 pounds) of exported nitrates from her sovereign areas.[323] Fredrick Pike, in his *"Modern History of Peru"*, remarked that Chilean investors were justified in refusing to pay the tax on a resource that they were exploiting by agreement; Bolivia like Peru, had been unable to do so properly due to constant internal disorders.[324] Given that the non-renewable *"fruits of her earth"* were being exported, a ten cents tax was reasonable but certainly did not justify Chile waging war.

This was the start of a series of disastrous events for Bolivia; Chile considered this action to be in breach of an earlier agreement between the two countries. Moreover, it affected most of the British and Chilean mine-owners in the Tarapacá and Antofagasta regions. Understandably, the Chilean Government protested to Peru and Bolivia but to no avail. In January 1879, after a minor dispute with the Chilean-British owned Antofagasta Nitrate Company, which, having refused to pay the tax, appealed to Chile for support. The Bolivian authorities arrested the English manager of the latter enterprise and expropriated the company, its oficina and stores. This action inflamed Chilean passions and the following month, just before a public auction of the stores confiscated by the Bolivian authorities, a Chilean naval squadron suddenly appeared off the port of Antofagasta. Six hundred troops were sent ashore to successfully occupy the town.[325] At this stage, Chile had only declared war on Bolivia but then, having discovered her 1873 *"secret"* treaty with Peru, asked the latter to nullify the accord.

There was a strong pacifist element in Peru, at this time, which wanted its Government to ignore the treaty with Bolivia and avoid war at all costs because of the nation's military unpreparedness. Peace envoys dispatched to Santiago to negotiate a settlement became convinced that Bolivia would settle her dispute with Chile, and ally herself with the latter to seize the nitrate rich Peruvian province of Tarapacá.[326] Consequently, Peru refused to withdraw from the treaty and Chile inevitably declared war on her and blockaded the Peruvian port of Iquique. By mid 1879, the entire Bolivian coast then lay under the control and occupation of Chile.

Sea power, as former Chilean President Bernado O'Higgins had claimed, was the key to overcoming conflict in South America. The Peruvian monitor *Huascar* successfully launched a series of raids along the coast. In the ensuing battles, Peru seemed to have acquired the upper hand. However, when the Chilean fleet captured her off Punta Angamos in September 1879, the war began to turn in Chile's favour.

Following her victory over the Peruvian fleet, Chile moved rapidly; the ports of Iquique and Pisagua fell to her in November; the occupation of Tarapacá, her primary objective, was secured. In 1880, the Chileans took control of Ilo, Mollendo, and Moquegua; Tacna was taken only after a bitter struggle with the Bolivians who were so severely beaten here that they withdrew from the fighting altogether. Meanwhile, the Chilean fleet continued to blockade Callao and after six months, landed troops to march on Lima. By 1881, the Chilean army in Callao had become a formidable force, easily pushing aside local defence units in Lima. Peruvian resentment at the Chilean occupation of her capital was to endure for decades.

In November 1880, the United States tried unsuccessfully to mediate in the conflict. Some historians claim that jealously between the latter nation and the European powers prevented an adequate mediation process. No commission or other international body had emerged to intercede in the dispute, and in the absence of any intervening official executive, the status quo favouring Chile was maintained. The apparent inability of Britain and the United States to become directly involved suggests reluctance on both sides to prejudice the interests of their many respective nationals in Chile and the disputed areas. The United States claimed that she had tried her hardest to persuade Chile to accept compensation and withdraw claims for a permanent transfer of territory, but negotiations lost their momentum and Chile, not only continued to occupy Lima for almost three years, but also remained in possession of those valuable lands she wrested from Bolivia.

Bolivian conviction carries more than a grain of truth that American and British self-interests sacrificed justice for their nation. The November 14, 1891 edition of Harper's Weekly re-asserted Chile's claim that James G. Blaine, the United States Secretary of State in 1881, had supported Peru against Chile in the War of the Pacific and accused Great Britain of encouraging Chile's military aggression:

"Hoping to enhance American trade in Latin America, Blaine criticized British economic interests in Chile. Chilean nationalists shared Blaine's anti-British sentiment but distrusted the American Secretary's motives. Chile and the United States were also on a collision course because influential elements on each side hoped to make their respective country the dominant power in South America". [327]

Chile withdrew her troops from Peru following the signing of the Treaty of Ancon in 1884, which ceded the province of Tarapacá to Chile forever. She was also to remain in occupation of the provinces of Tacna and Arica for ten years, at the end of which, an international plebiscite would determine their future. This agreement was so vaguely worded that Chile was able to postpone the process; a solution was not reached for many years. Chile continued her effective occupation of the two provinces, reaping the huge revenues they produced, but the truce left Bolivia without an outlet to the sea following the transfer of the Peruvian province of Arica to Chile. The agreed surrender of this territory was finally ratified in 1904.

Ploughing The South Sea

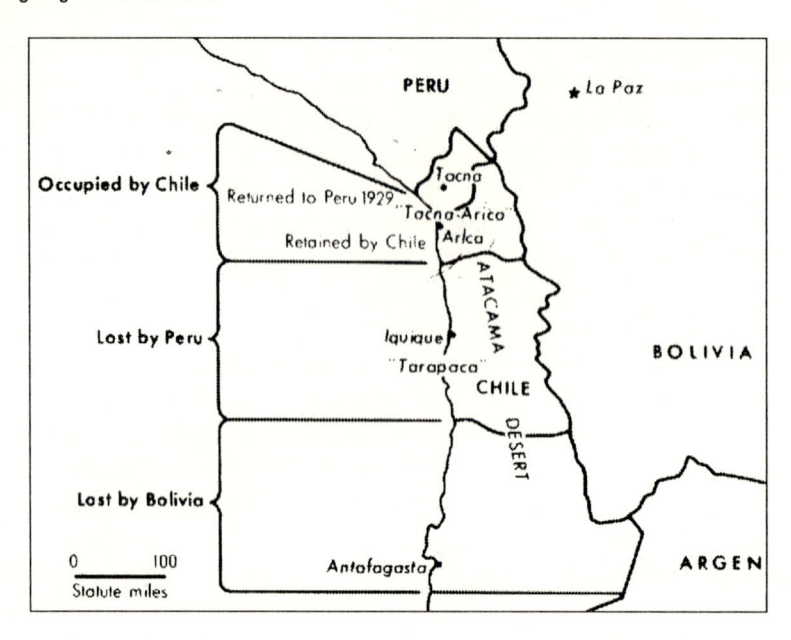

Plan showing the territories lost and occupied after the war. Based on detail in *"Strategy in the Southern Oceans"* by Victoria Gamba-Stonehouse and Gordon Ireland's *"Boundaries and Conflicts of South America."*

The Tacna and Arica issue, subsequently known as the *"Pacific Question"*, was still not settled at this time but was finally concluded through the later efforts of the United States, whereby Chile retained sovereignty over Arica while Peru re-acquired Tacna and received six million dollars in compensation. Chile also undertook to build a railroad from Arica to La Paz and to provide Bolivia with Custom's authority over this route. However, the affects of the Pacific War, having almost destroyed Peru's economy, caused her to suffer a seven-months civil war.

When the Peruvian Government initially nationalized the Tacna mining complexes, it did not then possess sufficient reserves to finance their acquisition, but resorted to issuing compensation certificates to former owners, intending to honour them later. These legal documents, consequently, retained transferable and negotiable values, but became almost worthless on the outbreak of war as panicking owners disposed of them as best they could.

One person benefiting from this widespread panic-selling was John Thomas North, a Yorkshire man working in that region for over ten years. Not having openly aligned himself with any of the warring factions, North was able to pass freely within Peru, cheaply buying up large numbers of title certificates to the mines and their oficinas during that frenzied selling period.[328] He correctly forecast that at the war's end, the Chilean Government would remain in control, eventually re-privatise the mines and return them to their respective owners, that is, to the holders of the Peruvian certificates.

Although there is no conclusive evidence, some historians still claim that North, together with many other mining entrepreneurs and speculators contrived this action. Certainly North and others involved in the nitrates sector wielded considerable influence within the Chilean Government. Having provided secret aid to the Chileans during the early stages of the war by loaning them a small steamship for transporting wounded soldiers, and a further eight small boats for their military operations, he was then in a position, like many other business interests, to call-in favours. As holder of a considerable number of Peruvian certificates, he was thus able to provide proof of ownership to a large number of mines and oficinas. The Chilean Government was obliged to privatise the nitrate complexes, given its inability to provide the necessary capital to develop these resources. North subsequently acquired many secondary businesses associated with the production of nitrates, where operating conditions were akin to slavery. Moreover, workers, being almost completely dependent on the oficina's store, had to purchase their goods, often at highly marked-up prices; everything they bought was deducted from their wages. The formidable presence of British banks in Chile, at the time, was much influenced by their compatriot owners of the nitrate oficinas.

Since the beginning of 19th Century, there had been a strong and growing British community in Chile, especially in Valparaiso, where an efficient and powerful banking network had become entrenched. Like many other British entrepreneurs, North was able to fund his nitrate operations, not only through British bankers in Chile, but also by inducing investors in England to speculate in his proposed enterprises. Some of the issued stock schemes turned out to be extremely dubious investments, but his overall operations soon expanded to such huge levels that he was dubbed the *"Nitrate King"*.

North eventually formed his own bank in Iquique, acquired the Iquique Water Company and a majority holding in the Nitrate Railways company. By administering the railways, North was able virtually to control the Nitrate region. His freight charges were assessed on a mileage basis but based on the railway's longest, indirect and looping routes. According to Andy Beckett, author of *Pinochet in Piccadilly,* the success of his near monopoly awakened North to the broader possibilities. Beckett quotes a letter from the London Office of Anthony Gibbs, one of North's bankers to the managers of its branches in Valparaíso and Iquique explaining North's intentions:

"A grand scheme is being hatched of bringing out the whole Nitrate business as a company, his [Norths's] idea being to use his power in the Railway as a lever to make all the producers, especially the small ones, to come into the company. He would virtually say:

My interest in the railway is so great that I will never permit another combination to be formed to restrict production; you small people cannot live with open competition, therefore, you will be ruined. As, however, I am a benevolent man, I will suggest to you a way of escape, and that is to try to have a general company formed that will take your oficinas over.
If, however, they refuse, Mr, North proposes to arrange with the banks to sell the oficinas to him as they foreclose on them."

North and his actions were symptomatic of the problems then facing Peru and Bolivia; Peruvian historians highlight the fact that Chilean expansionism was supported by British interests in the nitrate sector, and cite British involvement as one of the most important advantages Chile enjoyed over its opponents. One of the largest affected concerns was the Chilean-British owned Antofagasta Nitrates Company.

Many Peruvian historians portray Bolivia's act in imposing a tax on British-Chilean nitrate companies as naïve, providing Chile with the very pretext she needed to justify waging war, and thus carry out her real motive of seizing the nitrate rich Peruvian province of Tarapacá. Given the alternative view that Peru pressured Bolivia into imposing a tax increase to prevent Chile from underselling nitrate suggests a certain Peruvian innocence in believing that such a strategy would be effective in deterring Chile. Bolivia displayed her inexperience in unquestionably accepting Peruvian thinking on this matter. Chilean historians, on the other hand, blame Bolivia's political anarchy and naiveté, and her mishandling of diplomatic and international obligations, especially with regard to Chile. The latter exploited Bolivian weaknesses in these areas to advantage; there is more than a grain of truth in all these assertions.

Chile, more politically astute in international matters, and assuming the mantle of a nation wronged, widely broadcast her complaints against Bolivia throughout diplomatic circles. She complemented this strategy by vigorously promoting her justification in actions to annul frontier treaties, and extend her sovereignty over the Bolivian Littoral, as being in accordance with international law. Many Bolivian historians have since been highly critical of their own country's then ruling class, describing their leaders as inept and unable to progress their country, especially in the development of relations with other nations. Bolivia, particularly untutored in the ways of international diplomacy at the time, was therefore, unable to secure meaningful support from the influential and industrialized countries to deter Chile's territorial ambitions.

Brian Fawcett, in his *"Railways of the Andes"*, provides an example of the deterioration in Bolivian behaviour within diplomatic circles. Bolivia, he said, had until 1864 made some progress as a State until the megalomaniac Melgarejo overthrew the more economically aware President Achá:

"Melgarejo's presidency from that year until 1871 was marked by unceasing civil strife and acts of crazy savagery. It was this lunatic Melgarejo who at a state banquet ordered all the ambassadors present to kiss the naked posterior of his favourite prostitute, an honour that Queen Victoria's representative declined with some heat. In reprisal, Melgarejo had this grave diplomat tied face to tail on a donkey and paraded thus through La Paz streets before a jeering multitude. On hearing of this insult, Queen Victoria called for an atlas and a blue pencil and struck Bolivia off the map, an act that was quickly communicated to Melgarejo, who then mobilized his troops and ordered them to march to England and conquer it."

Such indiscretions and abuse of a superpower's foreign ambassador would only have exacerbated international ill feeling towards Bolivia. Certainly, they would have inclined Great Britain and allied European nations, given their already strong commercial interests in Chile, to tacitly support the latter's seizure of Bolivian soil. Although recognizing a United States' contribution to the mediation process, Bolivians still consider that Chile's bellicose actions prevailed because of her stronger connections and influence with Britain and the United States.

Harper's Weekly of November 1891 is illuminating on this point, indicating that the United States could, if she had been sufficiently motivated, have taken stronger diplomatic or even direct intervention to restore Bolivia's interests, but was more disposed to stealing a march on her British rival:

"In March 1889, US President Benjamin Harrison (1889-1893) named James G. Blaine as Secretary of State. Blaine was pleased to find that the new Chilean president, José Manuel Balmaceda, was seeking to undermine British influence through a nationalistic campaign of *Chile for Chileans*. To further twist the [British] Lion's tail, the US Secretary of State named Patrick Egan as the US Minister to Chile. Egan had fled Ireland in 1882 when the British Government had issued an arrest warrant against him for alleged crimes committed in the service of Irish independence. In the United States, Egan obtained American citizenship and backed the political aspirations of Blaine (who was the Republican presidential nominee in 1884)."

On the outbreak of civil war in Chile, early in 1891, the United States had declared its support for the Balmaceda Government while Great Britain supported the rebel Chilean Congressionalists. In May of that year, in response to a Balmaceda request, the US Government arrested the rebel Chilean ship, the *Itata*, while she was loading a shipment of arms in San Diego, California. Following the Congressionalists' victory in the civil war, the United States released the rebel vessel and by August, had granted the new Chilean Government full recognition.

Relations between the United States and Chile, however, continued to remain tense and the US Navy Department prepared contingency plans for war. In fact, relations between the two countries deteriorated because of Egan. The US Minister for Chile had granted asylum in the American mission to approximately 80 refugees from the defeated Balmaceda faction. By October, only 15 of these remained at the mission and Egan refused an order from the Chilean Government to surrender them. In response, the Chilean secret police surrounded the building to prevent the refugees escaping. A then unrelated event on October 16 exacerbated the situation even further. Harper's Weekly reported:

"The Captain of the *U.S.S. Baltimore* gave shore leave to 117 American soldiers in Valparaiso, Chile's second most populous city and an important port. Later that day, an altercation between an American sailor and a Chilean escalated into a riot involving numerous sailors, boatmen, longshoremen, and townspeople. Both side blamed the other for initiating the violence, but American sources suspected a planned assault on American sailors."

The United States Government, already angered by the refugee issue, was even more furious at the "*Baltimore incident*", but demands for *"prompt and full reparation"* elicited no response from the Chilean Foreign Minister. The dispute cooled for several weeks until early December when US President Harrison, in his annual address to the US Congress, laid the blame squarely on Chile.

Having been sharply criticized for his *"offensive tone"* to the United States, Chilean Foreign Minister Matta again replied in kind. Communications with the Chilean Government were cut and the Chileans responded with a more intensive surveillance of the American mission. The United States resisted going to war and in January 1892, after the Chilean Government replaced its Foreign Minister with the more conciliatory Luis Pereira, communications between the two countries were restored; the Chilean secret police were removed from the American mission and the refugees were allowed to leave the country.

It seemed as though normal diplomatic relations would have resumed at this point, but the atmosphere soured when the Chilean Government called for Egan, the US Minister for Chile, to be replaced. Moreover, a Chilean court had already arrested and charged three Chileans and one American for their involvement in the *Baltimore* incident. In a strongly worded letter, the US Government rejected the court's findings, describing the affair as a deliberate attack on uniformed American servicemen. Refusing to discuss the question of replacing their Minister for Chile, the United States demanded a suitable apology and adequate compensation for the injury inflicted on the US Government. On January 25, 1892, having been warned by European ministers that the United States was on the verge of war, the Chilean Government conceded on all issues. In February, the Chilean court sentenced the three indicted Chilean rioters only, and later in that year, offered to pay the United States $75,000 in reparation. The offer was accepted and Egan remained in office.

During the Pacific War, there were many firms owned by or associated with British and US nationals, making it difficult for both nations to remain strictly neutral in their approaches to mediation and diplomatic settlement. Despite this, Bolivia's complaints have largely centred on the tenets of the *"Monroe Doctrine"* when US President Monroe proclaimed in 1823:

"The occasion has been judged proper for asserting, as a principle in which the rights and interests of the United States are involved, that the American continents, by the free and independent condition which they have assumed and maintain, are henceforth not to be considered as subjects for future colonization by any European powers."

Importantly President Monroe had pledged US assistance to any American country whose sovereignty was threatened by nations from outside the hemisphere. Of course, at the time of this declaration, the US was in no position to translate her words into action, given the weakness of her economy and military position. Nevertheless, it did signal that collective security and co-operation between American states against external threats was a desirable objective for the United States to attain.

The declaration had emerged because of US perceived fears of interference by European nations, Great Britain in particular; their growing economic power and influence permeated South America and, importantly, was perceived by the United States as posing a growing threat to the Isthmus of Panama. Although, the Monroe Doctrine specifically related to *"European powers"*, the very idea of US intervention when any hostile country threatened any Latin American nation was implicit. It was not only self-evident that those Latin American nations should stand together against any aggressor, but it was also fundamental that Latin American nations should respect the sovereignty of their neighbours. In October 1875, Balfour Williamson Company's records confirmed that Chile had actually gone to the aid of Peru in the war against Spain *"in defence of the Monroe Doctrine"*.

Edwin Wilkinson in his *"History of Latin America"* emphasized the increasing perception by Latin American nations of the dangers of US interpretations of the Monroe Doctrine:

"In the course of the 19th Century, as the USA grew in strength and extended its borders at the expense of Spanish America or began to exercise economic influence abroad, the Latin American republics were able to appreciate how easily the Monroe Doctrine could be used to justify US meddling in the internal affairs of other weaker countries in order to advance its own interests. The self-serving notion of manifest destiny which had underwritten the settlement of Great Plains and the opening of the "Wild West", would be used to justify the military conquest of half of Mexico's territory in the war of 1845."

Ploughing The South Sea

Current Bolivian cynicism is perhaps understandable and embittered by the subsequent intervention of US troops in several Central American and Caribbean countries, the overthrow of Governments deemed hostile to US interests, and the installation of puppet dictators friendly to US investors. This self-serving behaviour enabled US President Theodore Roosevelt in 1904, to strengthen his political popularity by commencing construction of the Panama Canal; it had, for a very long time, been merely a talking point. Hugh Brogan, in his *"History of the United States of America"*, describes this latter venture as being:

"...a squalid intrigue, from the disgraceful details of which most Americans were happy to avert their eyes, engineering a revolt in Colombia which gave birth to a new country Panama; which then agreed that the United States might build the canal through its territory on spectacularly favourable terms; the USA was allowed to create a colony from sea to sea, the Canal Zone, through the middle of the new republic."

So effective had been the political spin Roosevelt placed upon the Canal Zone project, that nobody in the US seemed to care that in bringing about an independent Panama republic, he had in 1904, created the *"Roosevelt Corollary"* to the Monroe Doctrine. This openly declared that the United States had, thenceforth, a right to do what she liked, with or within Latin American nations, as long as she could plead and demonstrate that it was in her own security interests to do so, or that she could justify the implementation of an ill-defined duty to police the western hemisphere on behalf of the civilized world.

From the Bolivians' perspective, such a policy was never applied with equanimity in the Pacific question. One specific Bolivian complaint concerning lack of direct US action in the territorial dispute with Chile focused on Alsop & Company whose registered address at the outbreak of war was in Valparaíso. This firm had been operating along the coasts of the three war participant countries well before the commencement of hostilities; its most important activities were focused on mining in the Bolivian Littoral and the construction of a railroad from the coast to the country's interior. Alsop & Company had always considered itself, its managers, and administrators as North American.[329] The company's owners, almost ruined by the War, had asked the American Government to intercede on their behalf and demand compensation from Chile, arguing that the latter had, in effect, extinguished its mining rights. Accordingly, US diplomats raised the matter with the Chilean Government during the course of the War.

Some Bolivian historians argue that this awareness of the Alsop situation should have given the United States sufficient cause to take direct action against Chile in support of this claim. They highlight the latter nation's use of Bolivia's interference with the Antofagasta Nitrate Company as an excuse to occupy both Antofagasta and the territory to its north; the two events, they claim, were very similar. The United States Government was certainly aware of the complications of this issue. To take action against Chile for damaging the interests of Alsop & Company would have meant conceding that the Chilean case for invading and occupying Bolivian territory was internationally unacceptable and illegal. On this basis, direct international pressure and/or action would have had to be taken against Chile, with the United States certainly conducting a dominant role; British and American private interests in the disputed territories would then probably have suffered permanent damage in this event.

It was not until November 1909 that the North American Government delivered an ultimatum that Chile meet Alsop & Company's claims. The United States Government let it be understood that if the latter demands were not accommodated, her legation would be withdrawn from Santiago, the Chilean capital, shortly before a scheduled Pan-American Conference in Buenos Aires; an act which could have proved acutely embarrassing to Chile. The Chilean Government responded that it never imagined that such a small pecuniary claim by Alsop & Company could be deemed so important as to bring about the suspension of diplomatic relations. Disproportionate reaction or not, Chile, faced with unrelenting United States pressure, felt obliged to accept a proposal to lay the matter before a Court of Arbitration headed by King George V of England.

The fact that the British Monarch was involved might have persuaded Chile that, given the extent of British business interests already in her country, the outcome would be favourable to her; she had, after all, been formerly successful at pressuring British firms in Chile to make representations to the British Government when she was threatened by Spain. Such thinking has some foundation in the following extract from the Chilean plea to King George V, who was responsible for declaring the Arbitration Court's award, following its decision in July 1911. Chile, although admitting her annexation of Bolivian territory, continued to proclaim her justification for doing so. In this situation, the following Chilean response to the Arbitration Court appears both petulant and arrogant:

"[Chile] did not undertake to pay the claim, [of Alsop & Company] because she considered it a just one. She had agreed to it as part of the price she was willing to pay for securing the recognition and acceptance by Bolivia of Chilean title to the territory, wrested from that republic by force of arms. And, even if [Chile] may consider the sum your Majesty may be pleased to award as being large, having regard to all the circumstances, it is certainly small compared with the advantages of a strong title to a valuable territory."

It is interesting to note that a British-administered international panel was also involved in a 1978 dispute between Chile and Argentina, relating to claims on the islands of Nueva, Picton and Lennox, located south of an already agreed boundary line in the Beagle Channel. The British-led panel decided in favour of Chile; Argentina's refusal to accept the decision nearly led to war but for the intervention of a Vatican delegation in 1978. When it appeared to Argentina that the latter was also likely to find for Chile, she diverted domestic attention by attacking the Falklands.[330] The co-operation that Britain received from Chile during the Falklands war is well documented.

The United States and Great Britain, although accepting that Chilean action against Bolivia in the Pacific War had been contrary to international law, decided not to interfere any further on the basis that any additional action would be impractical. The greater commercial interests of both countries were clearly more influential in Chile than in Bolivia. One cannot help feeling that if Bolivia had developed firmer international and diplomatic ties after winning independence, she could have effectively used these to rescue her lost lands. As it was, Chile had a head start having implemented her progressive and Europeanization policies, which had enticed large numbers of British and American interests to settle there to implement and secure her objectives. William Wheelwright and the Pacific Steam Navigation Company fall into this category.

Chile, comparatively free of the internal and often bloody disputes that wracked both Peru and Bolivia, used this war and mostly revolutionary-free period to establish a stronger economy and a more powerful military base. One of those British companies benefiting was Balfour Williamson in Valparaíso. Nitrate and copper prices soared and general goods sold well, prompting the Company's Liverpool Head office to write to its Valparaíso House in 1881:

"We are very much gratified at the splendid results of last year's business and must congratulate you on the energy and ability, which have been brought to bear on our concerns. The gains shown are larger than for any former year. This, during a time of war and disturbance, makes our congratulations and thankfulness all the more emphatic."

It was during the war years, that the re-named Williamson Balfour first embarked on investments in the nitrate area. Early in 1882, only two years after its capture from the Peruvians, they opened their first branch office in the port of Iquique. Their trade mainly comprised the provision of bags, hardware, and coal for the nitrate oficinas. Exports of this commodity started modestly but soon expanded. Williamson Balfour also purchased some nitrate fields but before the completion of development plans, overproduction caused a fall in nitrate prices.[331]

The War not only adversely affected Pacific Steam Navigation Company's operations but also its reputation. In his "*Crónicas de La Marina Chilena*", (Chronicles of the Chilean Merchant marine), published in Santiago 1909, Chilean Admiral Alberto Silva, revealed that PSNC had not emerged very gracefully from the war; its behaviour prompting Chilean criticism and ridicule during hostilities. The letters "*P.S.N.C.*" he remarked, were said to denote the surname initials of four British captains in the English company openly hostile to the Chilean cause namely, *P*etrie, *S*teadman, *N*aoden and *C*ross. Other critics during the War commented that the letters stood for the phrase "*P*oca *S*erá *N*uestra *C*omida" [Our food (supplies) will be small]; a phrase that passengers travelling on PSNC ships were reported to have experienced and to which some pragmatic crewmembers responded with "*P*eor *S*erá *N*o *C*omer" [Far worse not to eat].[332]

Although the English Company had always stressed that its strict rules on neutrality must be followed, this was almost impossible for those of its employees and agents based at local ports throughout the respective warring countries. Problems were compounded for PSNC by trying to operate control centres based in countries at war with each other; loyalties must have been divided, especially as some personnel had married nationals in the country in which they were based. René De La Pedraja claimed that the PSNC had been blatantly pro-Peruvian during the war, and although accepting that its Liverpool-based Directorate had been at pains to publicize the company's required observance of strict neutrality, he alleged that company's employees at Callao, because of their strong connections with Peruvian society, stretched the limits of that neutrality.[333]

This is a Chilean view; undoubtedly, similar Peruvian accusations were levelled at PSNC's personnel in Valparaíso. PSNC publicly, at least, strove to maintain its supposed rigid neutrality throughout this dispute, but incidents involving the captains of the *Lima II* (1804 tons) and *Islay* (1588 tons) did not assist; both these vessels provided coastal services. The English company was obliged, in 1880, to dismiss the *Lima*'s captain for towing a ship full of contraband goods to Peru. In the case of the *Islay*, the captain had arranged for the conveyance of rifles from Panama to Peru during the conflict. Chilean warships captured the vessel and although she was later released, PSNC was obliged to dispense with her Captain's services.

The Chilean company (CSAV), on the other hand, was handed a slice of good fortune when the War in the Pacific commenced in 1879. Up to that event, La Sudamericana had experienced a difficult operating climate despite generous annual subsidies from the Chilean Government. The conditions attached to the latter required that in the event of war, CSAV's steamships were to be requisitioned, but that compensation to be paid to the CSAV would be calculated on its normal shipping revenue prior to the ships' handing-over to the Chilean War Ministry. Given the weak levels of shipping activity before the War, the fact that these vessels were taken-off CSAV's hands, just as it was experiencing severe financial difficulties, was fortuitous for the Chilean company. The Chilean Government's requisitioning of CSAV's steamships was not, however, just a device for justifying further subsidies; eleven steamships and one sailing ship together conveyed 11,178 officers and troops and 135,017 deck passengers during the period of hostilities.[334]

During a Chilean Senate debate in 1911 on proposals to promote the development of Chile's merchant marine, a Santiago Senator had commented on the use of CSAV's vessels during the War of the Pacific:[335]

"I do not believe in supporting a law favouring CSAV; one should recall its past [war] service, because this firm did very well out of it. All my colleagues know full well that for every 500 pesos share initially issued by that company, they eventually traded at 50 pesos each in the Valparaíso Exchange. Once War was declared, these shares rose to over a thousand pesos when the Government requisitioned them for its own use."

Apart from CSAV's vessels, the Chilean Expeditionary Force had used the services of three ships of Compañia Explotadora de Lota y Coronel to transport approximately 15,000 officers and troops. Combined with the CSAV troop figures, a total of 161195 uniformed troops were conveyed.

The war created economic and distribution problems for the Chilean nation and her merchant fleet. The latter, having being used to convey troops to the north, had left the populated and agricultural central and southern regions of the country with very few vessels capable of serving their supply needs as well as exports of their produce. Additionally, Chile's increased coastline at the end of the war exacerbated the scarcity of vessels. Tarapacá and Antofagasta had been under the sovereignty of Peru and Bolivia respectively before hostilities, but because of Chilean occupation and control, these territories considerably increased her coastal and maritime responsibilities.

Chile's merchant ships, called upon to supply her troops stationed in these inhospitable regions, added to the overall shortage of cargo space for the remainder of her coastal trade; inevitably freight rates increased. These, because of the military situation, were indirectly subsidized, making large profits for ship owners. Indeed, because of this, Chilean shipping lines and business houses tried to purchase whatever vessels were available. Consequently, after the outbreak of war, levels of shipped tonnages began to rise rapidly. Between 1880, the second year of war, and 1883 at the end of the conflict, the tonnage of Chile's merchant fleet had risen from 10,618 to 53,071 tons.[336] However, account must be taken of the low starting base attributed to the transfer of the Chilean flag to foreign registration at the war's outbreak. The amount of tonnage in the Chilean fleet fell drastically after 1885, and by 1898, it had fallen to its lowest point of 20,000 tons.

The lost Peruvian and Bolivian regions, having been occupied by Chilean enterprises and supported by British bankers and other interests, developed at an even faster pace. Ports along the disputed coast were, by 1894, operating normally. Bitterness between the three warring countries, however, continues to smoulder even today; Bolivia continues to press for an outlet to the sea, a cause, if the result of a small random poll on a Chilean Web site is any measure, is a hopeless one. The question *"should Chile accept Bolivian demands to be granted an outlet to the sea?"* was opposed by 80% of voters.[337] Nevertheless, discussions with Chile continue; Bolivia has recently commenced negotiations with Peru over use of her southern ports for the export of Bolivian natural gas.

Because of the War in the Pacific, the Peruvian merchant marine, which, in 1877, amounted to 139 sailing ships and 7 steamships, completely disappeared; the majority simply switched flags at the onset of the war and the remainder was captured.[338] For approximately the first two years after the war's end, the Peruvian nation was still in shock and generally resentful at her politicians for the way in which they had handled events. A period of further turmoil ensued until the popular election of Cáceres as President in 1886. Although uniting the Civilistas and the Constitutionalist parties, the Democratic faction was unwilling to join them. One of the pressing problems encountered by Cáceres was Peru's seemingly unmanageable international debt. Most of the latter comprised bonds issued during the late 1860s and throughout the 1870s. They had a face value of between 40 and 50 million pounds (between US 72 and 90 million dollars), a debt that Peru was then unable to meet; the servicing of this debt was suspended.

To complicate matters, a group of London bondholders had formed an association to apply strong pressure for the debt servicing to resume. In 1886, the London group appointed Michael A. Grace, cousin of W.R.Grace ship owner, to represent their interests and travel to Lima to conduct lengthy discussions with Cáceres lasting until 1887. The outcome was that:

(a) Peru would meet its obligations for repayment of the debt to the London group by granting that body control of her national railways for a period of 68 years.

(b) She would deliver to the London group up to 3 million tons of guano annually that was surplus to her domestic requirements

(c) The Peruvian Government would pay £80,000 per annum for 33 years to the members of the London group.

In this way, Peru was able to cancel most of her foreign debt. The London bondholders, having agreed to invest in the Peruvian Railroad system to effect repairs and undertake the extension of various lines, also advanced new loans to her Government up to the value of six million pounds (US 10,800,000 dollars).

This arrangement, known as the Grace Contract, not only improved Peru's international credit rating, but also enabled the revitalization of her railroads; they had either fallen into serious disrepair or were destroyed by Chilean invaders. The Peruvian Government ultimately decided that it required all the nation's guano for domestic use and the London bondholders obtained relatively little of this fertilizer. Despite the contract being a very favourable arrangement for the nation, bitter infighting within Congress ensured that it did not come into effect until 1889. On being approved, the London bondholders groups re-formed as the

Peruvian Corporation Ltd to fulfil their contractual obligations. It controlled not only the Peruvian railroad system, but was both heavily involved and influential in the Government's entire financial administration. Inevitably, the Peruvian Corporation became widely criticized and accused of the *"chicanery of foreign capitalism"*. Nevertheless, this body generally managed to meet its obligations and extended Peru's railroads into her main mining areas. For example, in 1893 the Central Railroad from the port of Callao was laid up to La Oroya, the core of a region containing abundant and rich ores.

The Grace Contract boosted the Peruvian economy enabling the development of her silver industry. Between 1886 and 1895, production of this resource amounted to nearly 33 million US dollars (£18,300,000 approximately) providing a welcome launch platform for growth of the national economy.[339] To counter severe economic problems and rampant inflation, Cáceres introduced taxes on tobacco and alcohol. He also attempted to curtail the ravages to her paper currency that the Peruvian landowning élites were abusing. The latter would sell their agricultural produce abroad in return for stable currencies such as pounds, dollars or francs, which when repatriated to Peru, earned steadily increasing amounts of the depreciating Peruvian currency. Cáceres was obliged to call-in the old Peruvian paper money in exchange for a new circulation medium backed by treasury reserves. Some regarded the level of exchange as so unfavourable that they lit bonfires of the old paper money in the streets of Lima. Unfortunately, the cancer of internal political feuding that had emerged in 1880 continued to fester, leading in 1890 to a military power seizure. This bitter internal hostility, often degenerating into bloodshed, especially in the provinces were 8000 men perished and a further 3000 killed in a final battle in Lima, persisted until 1895 when the military Government was deposed and replaced by an Executive comprising well educated and patriotic civilians who were more economically astute than previous incumbents.

Peru in 1870, like Chile, had witnessed an emergence of new social thought in élite circles, embracing the principles of Positivism and Social Darwinism. Apostles of such philosophies frequently preached the need for ruthless and unregulated economic struggles that only the fit, i.e. the élite, would survive; the unfit, the majority non-élite masses, would be eliminated by natural process; they were obsessed with material progress and rejected the traditional teachings and values of the Catholic Church.

The latter body, however, had offered little help for the masses to extricate themselves from their lowly situation; it continued to emphasize that the poor should resign themselves to their lot on earth, no matter how cruel and difficult it might seem. Indeed, the Catholic Church had even patronised a philanthropic approach for the lower orders following ithe issue of the papal encyclical in 1891 of *De Rerum Novarum,* the first *ex cathedra* prouncement to relate seriously to social and economic questions according to Leslie Bethell in his *"Chile since*

Independence". The majority of the élite also took the view that the Indian, because he represented the *"unfit"* element that restrained the nation's development, was, therefore, vastly inferior to them, and would eventually die-out.

Between 1880 and 1890, there emerged a body of opinion styled *"neo-positivism"*, which being in immediate conflict with Positivism and Social Darwinism, was concerned more with benefiting and uplifting the Indian rather than suppressing and eliminating him. This more charitable mode of thought emanated from a belief that the Government should generally regulate and oversee the affluent members of society, so that some wealth generated by private Peruvian capitalism could be re-directed towards state-planned projects. These would be designed to benefit a wide cross-section of society. Such thinking and influences introduced into education were continually inculcated into future Peruvian leaders until the end of World War 1. Education became the keyword and its wide and popular embrace ensured that élite thinking rather than élite landowners led the masses instead of ruling them. By the late 19th Century, new political, economical and social values had provoked the widespread introduction of practical education.[340]

Piérola, on assuming the Presidency in 1895, channelled these ideas through to his Government. The Administration, holding fast to the belief that it should intervene in economic and social matters, created the Ministry of Development and the Sociedad Nacional de Industrias to assist the development of private industry. The Peruvian currency became more stable as a result of his decision to return to the gold standard; industrial enterprises rapidly advanced and a new industrial bourgeoisie emerged to challenge the land-owning élites in national politics. More efficient tax collecting regimes, the imposition of duties on exports and imports, together with strict adherence to budgets set by the Government soon achieved economic and fiscal stability. This was exemplified by Government revenue amounting to seven million pounds (US 12.6 million dollars) in 1895, rising to twelve million pounds (US 21.6 million dollars) in 1899. Increases in Government revenue enabled the resumption of foreign debt servicing in 1896, after its suspension a year earlier, thus enhancing the nation's international credit standing.

Under Piérola's leadership, the Peruvian economy rapidly accelerated, an achievement highlighted by the combined value of exports and imports increasing from 2.46 million pounds (US 4.43 million dollars) in 1895, to 4.9 millions (US 8.82 million dollars) by 1899; Peru had been clearly catapulted into the modern world of capitalism. [341] Such economic progress clearly had a beneficial effect on maritime trade, but it would mainly have served the foreign steamship lines including the Chilean company. In 1888, Chile's maritime fleet operating on the West Coast of South America amounted to 159 sailing ships and 30 steamships, which due to the absence of any Peruvian competition, assumed control of Peru's merchant shipping. It was not until 1906, that the Peruvian Government tried to recover this situation when it established the Compañia Peruana de Vapores (The Peruvian Line) along with a floating dock in Callao. The initial routes planned for this shipping company were to link Callao with Panama and Valparaiso in addition to serving Peru's smaller ports.[342] By the end of the 19th Century, foreign-going shipping remained principally in the hands of the British, North American, French and German merchant fleets

Piérola frequently demonstrated his careful reading of national sentiment; the loss of Arica and Tarapacá had caused national trauma and he sought to obtain their return to Peruvian sovereignty. Envisaging that his country would have to pay heavy damages or compensation for their return, he introduced a tax on salt, the revenue being expressly applied to a fund for this purpose. The War of the Pacific had ended with the signing of a treaty at Ancon, stipulating that an international Plebiscite would convene to discuss the future of the two provinces. Due to Chile's skilful political manoeuvring, this Commission was continually postponed. Piérola hoped that the re-emergence of Chile's dispute with Argentina over the southern boundaries in the Strait of Magellan and Patagonia might cause Chile to return the two provinces, to ensure that Peru did not support Argentina, or otherwise take advantage of the situation. His hopes were dashed when the Chile and Argentina signed a settlement in 1898.[343]

12. Sailing Towards Protectionism. 1890-1915

The nitrate fields that Chile acquired in the Pacific War quickly dominated her economy but eventually contributed to civil war. Chile's President Balmaceda, elected in 1886 for the usual term of five years, although autocratic in Government, was a committed social reformer. He failed, however, to check the rapid depreciation in the country's paper currency, causing severe hardships for the working classes. The élite ruling sectors of society, too, were unable to cope with fast growing economic changes and increasing political and constitutional crises. The role of the Catholic Church in its relationship with the State had also begun to be questioned, as well as the increasing involvement of foreign investment in nitrate production and exports.

The unacceptable economic situation, and the increasing employment of large numbers of foreign labourers, stoked bitter resentment among ordinary Chileans. A new presidential election had been scheduled for 1891, and Balmaceda had followed tradition by nominating a friend to succeed him, but both Congress and the Senate frustrated his plans. When Balmaceda retaliated by arranging for the collection of taxes based on the previous year's budget, Congress openly revolted. Deserting members commandeered the ironclad *Encalada,* anchored in Valparaíso harbour, and sailed her up the coast to Iquique to form their own Government. Workers in the nitrate fields, who, like other sectors of the working class, had become more articulate in their demands, lent them their support. These labourers provided the backbone of the new Democratic Party, whose aims attracted many Congressional sympathizers.

Nine months of skirmishing and guerrilla warfare caused severe handicaps for business houses in Valparaíso and surrounding areas. Outbreaks of violence led to heavy fighting on August 28, reportedly lasting only two hours, but ending in Balmaceda's troops being routed, many deserting to the Congresionalistas. Balfour Williamson and Company in Valparaíso recorded:

"During the fortnight [of fighting], there has been an entire cessation of business owing to the interruption of railway traffic. Some kinds of provisions have become rather scarce in the city. The foreigners have behaved very judiciously during these troublous times and have done good service in acting as police on the hills and in ambulance work among the wounded. The hospitals here are full of these poor people. It is hard to say what the losses would be in both battles but they are probably rather over than under six thousand men killed and wounded."

Despite the bloody battles, the cause of the civil war had been largely political rather than economic. Most Chileans and foreign residents welcomed the election of new president Admiral Jorge Montt, described as both prudent and conciliatory. The firm Balfour Williamson was well aware of the underlying strength of the country's economy and of the fact that the causes and affects of the revolution were not as deeply rooted as they had first appeared to be:

"Chile is now too much in the swim of material improvement to have time for revolutions. You may have a few riots and then all will go on again as before...only a cool head is wanted."

By 1893, new patterns in South American trade were beginning to emerge. Cargo shipments relative to passenger traffic increased both from the Americas to Europe. South American countries were becoming wealthier overall and their growing purchases were reflected in increased exports out of Liverpool. Similar trends were appearing worldwide and inevitably, cargo shipments overtook passenger volumes except on the North Atlantic crossings. To cater for increases in its cargo trade, the Pacific Steam Navigation Company (PSNC) launched four new standard ships, the *Magellan [II]* (3090 tons), *Inca [II]* (3593 tons), *Sarmiento* (3603 tons) and *Antisana* (3584 tons), together with two even larger mail vessels for the Australian service, *Orellana* (4821 tons) and *Orcana* (4803 tons). For the period 1894 to 1904, it joined forces with its main competitor CSAV to operate regular steamship services from Valparaíso to Panama, which were then subsidized by the Chilean Government.

The two companies, in association, decided to approach the five Central American republics to gauge their willingness to financially assist an extension of the route from Panama to ports within their respective countries. This proposed service extension had been suggested at an International Exhibition in Panama when the Chilean Government undertook to encourage increases in the exports of Chilean produce to the Caribbean. It granted the steamship partnership a 10,000 pesos (£2000 or $US 3600) subsidy for the extended service from Panama and a total, of 45,000 pesos,(£9000 or $US16200) was received from the five republics to provide a weekly operation between Panama and Ocós in Guatemala, conditional on the two companies conveying certain public officials free of charge between Panama and San Francisco, California.[344]

In the early days of the "*Chilean steamships*", as the partnership commonly became known in Central America, difficulties were experienced with the Panama Railroad Company, then exclusively contracted to the United States registered Pacific Mail Steamship Company. The latter already provided steamship services between Panama and the West Coast of the United States. For this reason, cargo sent from Central American Pacific ports to the Caribbean had to be carried round

Cape Horn or transhipped at Valparaíso or Callao. Pacific Mail Company, on the other hand, had the advantage of having its cargo transported across the Isthmus by the Panama Railroad. Competition between the North American steamship line and the Chilean partnership, inevitably, resulted in considerable freight charge reductions, leading to an unprofitable operation for the PSNC-CSAV Central American service.

Why such an obvious fact that Pacific Mail Steamship Company enjoyed an exclusive contract with the Panama Railroad had not been discovered before the launch of the operation is surprising. It is reminiscent of the 1863 debacle at the Rio Maule when PSNC, having loaded its vessel with wheat at the inland port, found that the ship could not sail over the submerged sandbank at the river mouth, unlike the competing shallow-draught steamship *Paquete del Maule*.

Accordingly, this unprofitable situation with the Central American service lasted another three years until PSNC applied its own form of pressure on the Railroad Company's shareholders, the majority of which were then British, to rescind the contract with Pacific Mail Steamship Company and to substitute it with one awarding the PSNC-CSAV partnership the exclusive right to the Isthmus railroad for a period of five years. It might have been arrogance on the part of the all-powerful PSNC, but logic should surely have demanded that a tripartite arrangement be diplomatically explored between the parties concerned. The situation, of course, changed dramatically; the *"Chilean steamships"* partnership became extremely profitable, but the tables were overturned at the end of the contracted five years in 1902. The Railroad Company's extensive property interests in the Isthmus of Panama, later to form the Canal Zone, were transferred to another United States company.

The latter was pressured to break its contract with PSNC and CSAV and restore its exclusive arrangement with the Pacific Mail Steamship Company. This time there was no remedy; the two partner firms, realizing the pointlessness of continuing operations abandoned the field to the North American enterprise.[345] Four years later, the Chilean Government, after reviewing the experiences of the short-lived partnership, and after acknowledging the United States Government's control of the Panama Railroad, decided that a diplomatic approach would be more feasible in obtaining a less exclusive access to the Railroad.

This setback was said to have traumatized CSAV; for many years, it feared to venture beyond the familiar territory along the WCSA[346], but soon discovered what PSNC had known for years, that calling at smaller ports, although lengthening the voyage by up to 30 days, earned larger profits than the direct service between Valparaíso and Panama. There was still strong public demand for CSAV to provide a faster service between these two ports, but before considering its introduction, the Chilean Company first insisted on further subsidies for the acquisition of additional vessels. As a result of its policy review, it decided to employ that strategy operated for some years by PSNC, by assigning its vessels into one of two divisions, a faster Europe-Valparaíso-Callao line for one and a slower contingent of older vessels plying the WCSA in the other.[347]

At the end of the 19th Century, all the Liverpool Company's shipping services had been managed within a theatre of intense competition, resulting in some of the older vessels being sold and others dismantled. Eleven new replacements were acquired including the twin propellers steel ships, *Orissa* (5317 tons), *Oropesa* (5303 tons), *Oravia* (5321 tons) and *Ortona* (7945 tons). The latter vessel provided accommodation for 130 first-class passengers, 162 second-class and 300 persons in third-class. These additions to PSNC's fleet coincided with continued drought in Australia, resulting in an economic depression. In this situation, the Orient Line, struggling to maintain its operations, became more closely tied to PSNC, and led to a name change to the Orient Pacific Line. This re-formed company opened an office in Manchester the following year, and the Liverpool Company transferred its star liners to the new enterprise.

The size of vessels providing PSNC's West Coast service continued to increase; in 1899, *Colombia [II]* (3335 tons) and *Guatemala* (3227 tons) sailed out to the Pacific coast to operate the Valparaíso service.

ss Peru(III)

Typical of the PSNC's vessels confined to the West Coast of South America was the *Peru*, 3225 gross tons, the third vessel to be given that name. Built in 1896, for the Valparaíso-Callao route, she was powered by two three-cylinders engines developing 324 horsepower to drive two propellers. Able to achieve a service speed of 12.5 knots, she was of steel construction, had two decks and a "*shade deck*"; she carried 100 first class, 50 second-class, and 300 deck passengers.

Sailing Towards Protectionism. 1890-1915

In 1921, she was transferred to the Valparaíso–Cristobal service along with her sister ship *Chile*. Both vessels were sold in 1923, the latter to Sociedad Marítima y Comercial R.W.James y Cia. Valparaíso and renamed the *Flora*. The *Peru* was sold to Sociedad Marítima Chilena who retained her name.

At the end of the 19th Century, there had been an enormous demand for cargo carrying capacity due to the very high prices the British Government had been prepared to pay for freighters and transports to carry materiel and troops for the Boer War (1899-1902). This Government not only chartered ships, but also purchased them from foreign countries; many Chilean ship owners, taking advantage of this policy, sold their vessels. [348] At the beginning of the 20th century, shipping business declined, forcing PSNC into an immediate sale of one of two ships then on the stocks; the *Potosí* (5300 tons) was a straightforward disposal, but the *Galicia* (5896 tons) underwent extensive structural alterations for conversion to a cargo transport before her disposal.

The North American firm of W.R.Grace did not pose any direct threats to PSNC or CSAV until the 1890s. Grace Line since 1869, had operated a line of sailing ships mostly in the nitrate trade, but had been reluctant to invest completely in steamships. In order to reduce the risk of losing capital, this shipping company sought a partner to share operations on a New York to Peru route. Given the virtual monopoly practised by PSNC, the only suitable alternative was CSAV. The latter, however, remaining wedded to stronger links with the English company, rejected Grace's overtures, a decision that would cost the Chilean company dearly in the coming decades. Grace persevered with its steamship operation on the New York-Peru service, and although incurring losses in 1893, the line became more profitable, inevitably attracting competitors.[349]

Continuing debates throughout 1902 within the Chilean Government on the crisis within its merchant fleet, prompted W.R.Grace and Co., to petition for a Chilean State subsidy of £25,000 (US 45,000 dollars) to establish a steamship line between Valparaíso, Punta Arenas and Brazil. In support of its petition, this steamship company, then more commonly known as the "*Merchants Line*", owned and operated the following six vessels: *Cumbal* (4259 tons), *Cuzco* (4302 tons), *Cóndor* (3058 tons), *Cacique* (3052 tons), *Coya* (3039 tons) and the *Capac* (3052 tons). It reminded the Chilean Government that since 1893, it had established a valuable steamship service connecting Chilean ports with New York. Earlier in December 1902, it had even expressed its willingness to re-register all its vessels under the Chilean flag and provide regular sailings between Valparaíso, Punta Arenas, Brazil and the United States. Moreover, it confirmed its preparedness to employ two Chilean deck officers and two engineers on each of its ships and reduce passenger fares by 50% for Chilean public employees.[350]

Shortly after W.R. Grace Company had submitted its application for a subsidy, a rival agency, Beeche, Duval y Compañía, protested angrily to the

Chilean Government, declaring that in association with Hemenway y Cía it had been operating a similar service to that proposed by Grace for many years, firstly with sailing ships, but since 1887 with steamships. Beeche, Duval y Cía asserted that its reputation was sufficiently well known and strong enough to withstand any competition from Grace and Co., and conveniently reminded the Government that it had never requested subsidies nor intended to do so. Nonetheless, it submitted that if grants were afforded to the North American firm, the fine competitive balance maintained in competition between the two firms would incline towards W.R.Grace & Co. Stressing its Chilean credentials, Beeche, Duval y Cía submitted that if either of the two companies was to be favoured, then it should be the one.[351]

W.R. Grace and Co., without waiting for the Chilean Government's response, sent a strongly worded protest at the facts submitted by Beeche, Duval y Cía. It drew attention to its own readiness to adopt Chilean registration, subject to receipt of the requested subsidies, while revealing that Beeche, Duval y Cía was not, in fact, the owner of any West Coast Line nor a shipping company in its own right, merely a consignee agent not owning any vessels whatsoever. In support of this accusation, the Grace firm produced a list of ships' calling at Chilean ports over the previous twelve months, together with details of their actual owners who had consigned their vessels to Beeche, Duval y Cía. Of the ten ships listed, British companies owned nine vessels and one was registered to a Danish concern. The Chilean Government, belatedly, decided that the best course of action was to reject both companies' applications, but this only served to highlight its own lack of resolve in dealing with issues that might have nurtured the Chilean merchant fleet.[352]

By 1903, suitable legislation to reserve coastwise trading to Chilean vessels only, had still not materialized despite a range of suggestions being tossed backwards and forwards by various Chileans ministries. Frustrated by lack of progress, the Chilean Navy's Director General submitted his own scheme entitled "*Definite Proposals for Overcoming the Problems of Developing the Chilean Merchant Marine*". Although concentrating Government thinking on this long outstanding matter, the document contained no radical changes on previous submissions, in fact they were those approved by the Chamber of Deputies in 1898. Significantly, the document referred to "*Article 17*" concerning the reservation of coastal trade to Chilean vessels, but only after the expiry of ten years from the promulgation of the envisaged statute.

Arguments raged over the period of grace to be granted to foreign shipping firms, but agreement having been reached on reducing the interval from ten to five years, the proposal was then withdrawn. For the next six years the debate continued, but the proposal was ultimately pigeonholed. Thereafter, interest in the matter waned, even in the press whose earlier recommendations and strong editorials had provoked prolonged and emotional comments in its correspondence

Sailing Towards Protectionism. 1890-1915

columns. Draft legislation that did reach the statute books was one requiring special contributions from all ships to cover construction and maintenance costs of lighthouse and buoys along the Chilean coastline. The proposed draft also formed the basis of a revised ordinance in 1917, seeking the imposition of shipping taxes calculated on a vessel's tonnage, whether foreign or Chilean registered, to be collected at the first Chilean port of call.

When PSNC accepted CSAV as a rival on the Europe-Chile line, the Kosmos line soon targeted La Sudamericana. The German company had already sparked bitter clashes with PSNC by a relentless rate war, which only ended in 1904 when Kosmos joined the freight rate-setting Europe/South Pacific and Magellan Conference.[353] While the latter body enabled the maintenance of an uneasy truce between the two European firms, it did not abate the rivalry. Kosmos concluded that the best way to force PSNC's withdrawal from its still dominant position was to absorb the Chilean company and, in this respect, it introduced in 1908, its most efficient and modern steamships to the WCSA; the earnings of both CSAV and PSNC were, as a result, sharply reduced.

To counter the German threat, CSAV re-assigned some of its better ships to coastwise trade, but in doing so, was unable to benefit from the more profitable services to Peru and Panama. The Chilean Government had still not been able to introduce a protectionist policy for her merchant marine, and lacked the financial resources to subsidize all her mercantile fleet. The introduction of the tonnage tax added a measure of assistance; it did not in itself discriminate against foreign shippers, but because it was calculated on a vessels' gross tonnage, it impacted more on the larger German vessels than the smaller ships engaged on coastal operations. Kosmos was soon forced to suspend its plans for displacing CSAV.[354] While PSNC must have derived satisfaction at the Kosmos withdrawal, it would, at the same time, have envisaged that CSAV's growth potential was likely to remain strong, but other European and Japanese competitors were emerging.

Prior to the latter events, a bitter strike of stevedores, lighter-men and Chilean merchant marine crewmembers erupted in Valparaiso in 1903. Tragic deaths and injuries suffered by the strikers had powerful and profound effects on a later Chilean Government's decision to intervene in the 1921 strike, when legislation relating to the merchant fleet was once again under consideration. Three trade unions were involved in the 1903 conflict; the port's lighter men had asked for 25 centavos (approximately 5p) wages increase for each ordinary cargo conveyed by lighter and 50 centavos for each special cargo together with the setting-up of an official inspection body to oversee correct payment of their wages. In addition to these increases, the stevedores demanded that their working hours be regulated and incorporate a 12 hours maximum working period from 5.30 am to 6 pm with a half-hour midday break.

The unions also alleged that the CSAV had been employing non-union labour from the south of the country, which was prepared to work for much less than the strikers received, and that the company was housing and feeding them on one of their vessels, the *Lontué,* anchored in the bay of Valparaiso. The stevedores also insisted on the Government establishing a control centre in the port to supervise the loading and unloading of cargo. The union, representing crewmembers of merchant ships working the Chilean coast, additionally stipulated that their members should only work fixed hours with overtime paid for any in excess of this; it requested that medical care facilities be provided on board ships to which they were assigned.[355] The shipping companies concerned, not only steadfastly refused to meet the three unions' demands, but also chose to malign them.

Cía Transportes Marítimos and W.R.Grace Cía asserted that wages paid were, at that time, already too high and, condescendingly, remarked that had the strikers got into the habit of saving, they would then have been in a better position financially, adding that the lighter men's claims were "*exaggerated*". PSNC sharpened the criticism by commenting that seafarers' duties had always been considerably more extensive than those working ashore, and that accordingly, the seafarers' complaints were unfounded. The English company also attempted to muddy the waters by adding:

"To fix hours of work on board a ship is not only contrary to maritime law but would pose serious dangers for navigation".

CSAV, on the other hand, was more realistic stating that it was prepared to offer a 10% across the board increase provided the strikers dropped their additional demands, which the company found impossible to accept.

The strike had started on April 15th and lasted three weeks. During this event, considerable concern and fear had emerged at the Port Authorities' open support for the strike-breakers who had been afforded army and police protection. This anxiety had been sufficient to prompt the Chamber's Deputy for Valparaiso to telegram the Government on May 10, requesting it to end the conflict before it boiled over into violence. On the day the telegram was sent, the strikers had already agreed to refer their dispute to arbitration and returned to work pending investigation by the Arbitration Commission; the shipping companies involved, however, resolutely refused to recognize this body.

Two days later, a dockside fight between strikers and strike-breakers soon overflowed into much of the city. One group of protesters ransacked and burnt the CSAV's offices while another assailed the offices of El Mercurio newspaper; the latter's staff, armed with pistols and rifles, and entrenched on the upper floors of the building, managed to repel the invaders. Following the arrival of troops from

Santiago and the south of the country, peace and calm were restored and the subject shipping companies finally agreed to the arbitration process.

Chile had never experienced such social unrest and violence; this tragic event, both deeply shocking and disturbing to the nation, prompted the newspaper El Mercurio of Santiago to publish a highly critical editorial analysing the reasons for the fatal dispute; it highlighted three main causes:

(1) The steamship companies' obstinacy in first refusing to refer to arbitration. (2) The culpable unpreparedness of Valparaíso's public authorities to head-off the violence. (3) Malevolent and self-serving agitators working in the background to foment unrest amongst the workers. [356]

El Mercurio of Valparaíso, whose offices had been singled-out for attack by the strikers, would surely have appreciated the significance that its sister newspaper's criticism of the shipping companies would have on public opinion. Another factor having a powerful influence on the public was the report delivered by the Intendent of Valparaíso to his Government, claiming that Naval troops had repeatedly refused to fire on the strikers and had joined-in the ransacking of properties.[357]

Despite the unions' struggles, the very bad conditions under which seafarers and associate workers laboured; no fixed hours, low wages, no union recognitions and without State protection of any kind, did not change for twenty years. In 1923, a new strike paralysing Chile's entire coastline again made newspaper headlines; rapid intervention by Government authorities avoided bloodshed, but prompted legislation for social improvements as well as measures to develop and improve the Chilean merchant marine.

Amidst all the concern at emerging competition, PSNC identified another profitable opportunity. Since the middle of the 19th century, the Peruvian Government had tried to create its own merchant fleet, but despite offers of generous subsidies and other investor benefits, this desired objective remained elusive. It was not until 1906, that the Peruvian Government, once again, having offered generous subsidies and advantageous terms for investors, managed to bring about the creation of a shipping line and a floating dry-dock company in Callao. Local business interests accepted the Peruvian Government's terms and contracted in July 1906 to form the Compañia Peruana de Vapores y Dique del Callao (Peruvian Shipping and Dry-dock Company) otherwise known as the "*Peruvian Line*".

The business concerns involved committed little of their own capital to the venture; they acted merely as brokers to attract unwary investors into the scheme. A total of 300,000 low nominal value shares were issued; these were further subdivided into fractions to enable small businessmen and the working class to participate in what was labelled a "*patriotic endeavour*". The smaller purchasers eagerly acquired these shares but defaulted on payment causing the stock price to fall. The Peruvian Government was, consequently, obliged to acquire 10% of the stock issue in an attempt to rescue the venture. Peruvian Banks had generally avoided any involvement in the launch of the Peruvian Line, having considered it too risky. The latter shipping company, therefore, attempted to float its bonds on the London market in an attempt to raise sufficient investment capital to progress its proposed services.

Two steamships were ordered from British yards in 1908, as was the floating dry-dock, brought into use in April 1909. The company became operational the following December with the introduction of its two new vessels the *Ucayali* and the *Huallaga* to provide an express service between Callao and Panama. The two steamers were oil-fired, given the shortage of coal on the West Coast, and both capable of maintaining a service speed of 19 knots; they were, at the time, the fastest ships in that region. The Chilean Line believed from the outset, that the Peruvian Company's two vessels had only been purchased as part of Peru's military build-up and would soon be seen as white elephants.[358]

At the time of the launch of the Peruvian Line, the Chilean Government had withdrawn its subsidy from CSAV's express service to Panama, forcing La Sudamericana to rethink its plans in the light of the new Peruvian competitor. CSAV, once again, turned to PSNC, but unknown to it, the English company had secretly been co-operating with the Peruvian Line in breach of its agreement with the Chilean company.

Between 1908 and 1910, the group of foreign shipping companies which included PSNC, South Mail Packet Co., Lamport & Holt,[359] Kosmos, Gulf Line and Roland Line, had effectively established high uniform levels of cargo rates when prevailing world freight charges were much lower. Importantly, these lower costs were not available to Chilean shippers. This cartel-fixing arrangement only served to alienate the very commercial interests that had previously opposed legislation requiring Chilean coastal trade to be reserved to her nationally registered vessels and to totally exclude foreign shipping.

One such group comprised the agricultural producers of southern Chile who had consistently rejected legislation favouring the development of a Chilean merchant marine. This group's opposition, based on reasoning that such development would, inevitably, lead to higher freight charges, was quickly dissipated on the discovery that the foreign cartel's WCSA rates were actually higher than those prevailing world-wide. Unsurprisingly, support for the foreign shipping lines was redirected towards legislative initiatives that would render Chilean national shipping more competitive.

By the second half of 1909, CSAV's profits dwindled considerably and remained at low levels over the next few years. Indeed, the situation became so bad that management and shareholders had even considered liquidating the company to re-invest remaining assets into land based holdings. Moreover, the Chilean Government was finding it difficult to regularly dispense subsidies but when it did, even more stringent and costly conditions were attached to the grants. So onerous and costly were they that CSAV concluded that further Government grants would actually damage its long term future, a view sharply illustrated when the Chilean Executive offered financial inducements for the acquisition of new vessels, subject to their being purchased from United States' ship yards, then the most expensive in the world. Accordingly, CSAV declined the offer.[360]

In 1910, the Chilean Government introduced further draft legislation for the protection of its merchant fleet. The only difference between this and previously submitted formats was the omission of specific proposals to re-introduce provisions to reserve coastal trade to nationally registered vessels. Debate on this matter continued well into the second half of 1911, with long standing arguments repeatedly highlighting the defects and virtues of open trade versus protectionism. The main concern at any policy reserving coastal trade to Chilean merchant vessels, or cabotage, was based on the notion that then existing excessively high freight charges might rise even further following the unavoidable creation of a monopoly in the process. This had been the main plank of resistance to previous attempts to launch this piece of legislation.

On November 9, 1912, the Peruvian line introduced an additional service to Valparaíso. For the Chilean company this was bad news, exacerbated by the discovery that PSNC had secretly signed an agreement, earlier in June, with the Peruvian Line in breach of contract with the CSAV. The problem, to some extent, was overtaken by events. After six months operation, the Peruvian company's steamship *Huallanga* was burnt-out at sea to become a complete loss. Moreover, her sister ship, the *Umcayali*, due to her fuel-thirsty engines, suffered high operating costs compared with the slower but more economical triple expansion engines of the Chilean company. The chronically under-funded Peruvian Line was obliged to float another bond issue in Paris to secure the acquisition of four French-built ships for the Chilean route, but heavy losses forced the Peruvian company to suspend the service in 1913.

Despite the Peruvian Government continuing to throw money at its national shipping firm, the latter was managed incompetently, becoming increasingly dependent upon State assistance. It even failed to fulfil generous contractual terms with PSNC, forcing the latter to cancel its agreement with that company. Finally, in April 1913, the Peruvian Government removed the shipping company's Directors from office. Although the Peruvian Line technically remained a private enterprise, the State, controlling it through an appointed officer, had the final say in the care and disposal of the company's assets. The threat of Peruvian competition against the Chilean company was in due course removed. CSAV eventually returned to profit in 1912 when it placed orders for new vessels in early 1914, buoyed by optimism at the imminent opening of the Panama Canal.

In 1913, PSNC announced the cancellation of the contract with the Chilean firm, the one that the English company had frequently breached when pursuing separate arrangements with the ill-fated Peruvian Line. The English company was still the largest fleet in the Pacific, and had arrogantly believed that CSAV would forget its past transgressions and negotiate a new contract. The Chilean company had already entered into discussions with United Fruit Company for securing transhipment arrangements on the Caribbean side of the Panama Canal.[361]

In the period leading up to World War 1, freight rates were, generally, set at very low levels, an important exception being the much higher charges demanded by CSAV and that cartel of five foreign shipping companies including PSNC. There was a widespread, and a not unreasonably held view in Chile, that by introducing legal measures to prohibit coastal trading by foreign shipping companies, La Sudamaericana, whose charges were already high, would suffer no serious competition and be virtually free to impose even higher charges. Consequently, actual support for such legislation was weak; it was only when worldwide rates were driven higher because of global conflict that the clamour for the introduction of legislation to protect coastal trading reached a crescendo.

In the debates that followed in the Chilean Congress, criticism continued to be levelled at the Government's system of subsidies paid to CSAV, still in direct competition at that time with PSNC and other foreign shipping companies. The Chilean Government found itself in a difficult situation; if it did not continue the practice, it was likely that CSAV would eventually cease operating. The question of subsidies to CSAV, therefore, continued to dominate never-ending discussions about proposed legislation; the issue was again pigeonholed without any action being taken.

PSNC's fleet, at this time, had been increased by the construction of four twin propellers-driven steamships, the *Panama* (5891 tons), *Mexico* (5549 tons), *Victoria* (5967 tons) and *California* (5547 tons). The *Panama* had been provided with side hatches to allow typical loading and unloading from lighters; her bridge was positioned nearer the bow than was normally the case on Pacific coastal vessels to facilitate sailing into ports that were difficult to access, or into ports where no tugs were available. Her main deck, used for the transportation of live cattle, stretched the whole length of the ship. There was included a recreational deck and a "*roundhouse*" section of cabins with direct access to this deck. She was engaged on active service in Europe during World War I from 1914 to 1918. At the time of her addition to the PSNC fleet, the latter comprised 47 ships with a combined tonnage of 162,813.

The Valparaiso earthquake of August 16, 1906 caused substantial setbacks and hardships; trading conditions in the aftermath were extremely difficult, but a year later they did not prevent PSNC from adding the following Glasgow-built ships to its fleet: *Huanchaco* (4524 tons), *Junin* (4536 tons), *Kenuta* (5025 tons),

Lima (4946 tons) *Quillota* (3674 tons) and the *Quilpué* (3674 tons). All had twin propellers systems.

In that year evidence submitted by PSNC to a Royal Commission appointed to investigate "*Shipping trusts*", gives some idea of the difficulties facing this company in the development of its services. PSNC reported to the Commission that it was then operating in almost impossibly bad conditions on the West Coast of South America, mainly because of earthquake damage. This, it claimed, had caused congestion at various ports and a severe shortage of cargo-handling facilities. These long delays on the West Coast persuaded some shipping lines, not regular visitors to that region, to seek custom elsewhere. Arthur C. Wardle commented:

"[PSNC] having long been established in this area and accepted as almost a permanent fixture, felt obliged to maintain its normal mail and cargo services, and made 16 powerful ships available to satisfy the needs of commerce. It was a courageous but risky decision of the Company to dispatch ships at regular intervals knowing that they might be delayed on the West Coast and incur considerable financial loss in the process. It had also become impossible for the Company to maintain fixed and reliable itineraries without chartering ships from third parties at high rates." [362]

The Commission was informed that PSNC's shareholders had collectively suffered losses of between £40,000 (US 72,000 dollars) to £50,000 (US 90,000 dollars) due to having to charter vessels and another £20,000 (US 36,000 dollars) because its steamships had often to wait weeks before being able to discharge their cargoes. Throughout this uncertain period, a more efficient direct mail service was extended northwards from Callao following the establishment of an express steamship service between Valparaíso and Panama. Added to this was the launch in Glasgow of the *Orcoma* (11546 tons) described as "*the electric boat*". She left Liverpool on her inaugural voyage on August 27, 1908.

Steamship Orcoma 1908

Fitted with all the latest equipment and gadgetry, newspapers described her as "*a floating hotel*" whose décor, design and furnishings made her one of the most luxurious liners then afloat. Powered by two quadruple expansion engines delivering 7100 horsepower, the *Orcoma*, overall length 511.6 feet, provided accommodation for 246 passengers in first class, 202 in second class, and 556 passengers in third class. Her crew complement was 247. This ship was also the first to cater for a conducted tourist group especially organized by Thomas Cook for "*distinguished persons*" at a reduced fare of £300 (US 540 dollars) per person. The package tour included travel over thousands of miles by steamship, railroad and other vehicles. The Thomas Cook contingent included a party travelling down from the United States to board the *Orcoma* at Río de Janeiro.

Over the previous five years, PSNC had had to take measures to counter more intense competition. Rapid and notable economic development in other European countries had caused their respective merchant ships to infiltrate those shipping routes normally the preserve of the Company. Although the extension of the direct Valparaíso-Callao route to embrace Panama had been successful, the venture was short-lived following the Chilean Government's decision to withdraw the Company's licence to operate this service from Valparaíso.

Chile, in the early half of the 19th Century, had consistently believed that the Panama Canal would never be a practical proposition. During that period, she had envisaged her power and maritime influence being sustained by a continuation of services from Valparaíso via the Strait of Magellan. In accordance with this policy, she had encouraged the direct service from Valparaíso to Liverpool following PSNC's threats to the Panama Railroad over the distribution of freight revenues. The withdrawal of the permit to operate the Valparaíso-Panama service was a clear warning signal to PSNC, which it could hardly have ignored, given the Chilean Government's willingness to continue to subsidize CSAV and its voyages to Callao and Panama.

The spat with the Panama Railroad Company over the division of revenue generated by freight transported over the Isthmus had certainly propelled PSNC to new heights. The same railroad, by providing its strategically important land holdings, enabled the construction of the Panama Canal, which by the time of the withdrawal of the Chile-Panama service, had already commenced. It was evident that its completion would mean the total or partial loss of PSNC's lucrative first class passenger and emigrant trade, attracted by its direct service vessels to South America via the Strait of Magellan. These services had operated from the Mersey since 1868 and had taken-in ports of call at France, Spain, Brazil and the River Plate. PSNC Directors and stockholders alike were thus obliged to carefully consider likely outcomes for that company's trading position once the Canal was operational. Accordingly, a delegation was dispatched to the Isthmus, with the task of assessing and reporting on the situation.

Just as threatening to PSNC's future prospects were those competing shipping lines casting covetous eyes on the vast extent of its operational areas. Royal Mail Steam Packet Company was one such competitor. This London Company had been a former associate of the Liverpool firm during the era when cargo and passengers negotiated the infamous Isthmus crossing, firstly by mule and then by railroad to connect with each others ships; the Royal Mail Steam Packet Company at Chagres and later Colón, and the Pacific Steam Navigation Company at the port of Panama. This partnership had ended following PSNC's break with the Panama Railroad Company and its decision to operate a direct Liverpool-Valparaíso service via the Strait of Magellan. In 1910, the London Company seized an opportune moment to submit proposals, which were carefully studied by the PSNC Board before being referred to an Extraordinary Shareholders meeting.

Within a few weeks, Royal Mail Steam Packet Company had taken control of the Pacific Steam Navigation Company, although the latter continued to operate under its own name and Directorate with representation from Royal Mail. It was surprising that in so relatively short a period, such an important shipping firm, owned and directed by Liverpool ship owners and local businessmen for 70 years would so readily cede control to a London competitor. The arrangement, it would appear, was too good for PSNC shareholders to refuse. By then, the Chile-Argentina railroad had been completed and the East Coast of South America had become more prosperous than the West Coast. Royal Mail Steam Packet Company, therefore, was especially well placed to operate services to Argentina and Brazil, and had already consolidated its strong shipping presence throughout the Caribbean.

Passenger trade to South America in the first two decades of the 20th Century had been increasing and PSNC was especially suited to take advantage of these opportunities. In 1913, its first steamship with triple propellers and built by Harland and Wolff was launched in Belfast; the *Andes* (16620 tons) was the last word in sea travel according to standards set before World War I. The same builders constructed, in 1915, two powerful steamships, *Orduña* (15507 tons), and *Orbita* (15495 tons); a third vessel, the *Orca* (15120 tons) was built in 1918.

Ploughing The South Sea

ss Orduña **1915**.

13. Affects of Protectionism. Return to a Free Market. 1915-1994

World War 1(WW1) enabled the Compañia Peruana de Vapores (the Peruvian Steamship Line), to redeem all its debts. Unlike its Chilean counterpart, it took the opportunity to acquire three German ships interned during the hostilities. Their purchase price, however, was high, leaving the Peruvian Line with insufficient finance to fund replacement vessels after the War; this and the operation of three pre-war freighters hampered the Peruvian company's development.

The immediate post-war boom turned to a slump in 1921. The Peruvian Line's profits decreased, and losses accumulated. The Peruvian Government, its majority shareholder, concluded that only new management could reverse the loss. In 1924, it tried unsuccessfully to hand over the company's operation to the Wiese syndicate, a private Peruvian concern; the following year, the Government tried to persuade United Fruit Company to manage it.[363] These plans foundered, according to René De La Pedraja, because:

"Grasping officials had already learned to exploit the Peruvian Line for their own benefit. These well connected officials operated the company as part of a larger web of patron-client relationships where loyalty and friendship rather than efficiency and quality were the key components" [364]

This was a view shared by the United States' Authorities:

"It is even claimed that its existence for some time has been solely due to the [Peruvian] Government's support, which is reported to have taken the form of paying the deficit and concealing the losses of the company in order that a national shipping company might continue. This situation seems due to gross mismanagement and graft on the part of certain of its directors...The balance sheets of the company do not show this condition, because, I am informed, many of the expenses listed were only paid on paper."[365]

The Peruvian Line's service, naturally, deteriorated due to poor management. Prospective passengers and shippers preferred to use foreign shipping lines for overseas voyages and the Chilean Line for trips along the West Coast. PSNC and Grace Line did attract some coastal traffic but it was not very profitable for them. Peruvian coastal shipping trade, however, became a remunerative operation for the Peruvian Line's corrupt officials, and was the subject of an attempt by them to rally national support in favour of a protectionist bill. The Chilean company did not attempt to lobby against the proposals, given that Peru and Chile were then discussing the disputed provinces of Tacna and Arica; the possibility of another War in the Pacific still loomed large.

The Bill passed into law on May 14, 1928 and reserved coastal trade for Peruvian vessels only. Although foreign shipping companies had found the proposals unacceptable, only Japan had vigorously opposed them. The cabotage law failed to protect the Peruvian Steamship Company from a progressively worsening financial situation; crew wages were not paid on time; its ships were in poor condition and rapidly deteriorating. Inevitably, the last Peruvian Line vessel was withdrawn from service in 1930, leaving the dependent coastal communities stranded. On settlement of the Tacna-Arica issues, and with the threat of war averted, the Chilean Line's management conducted secret negotiations with the cash-strapped Peruvian Government; CSAV emerged with a two years contract to undertake Peruvian coastal trade, an arrangement that actually lasted until the 1940s.[366]

Peru's conflict with Colombia over disputed territory in the Amazon region prompted her Government to renovate the Peruvian Line's ships to assist possible military operations. This followed upon the loss of Callao's floating dock, leaving Peruvian ships highly vulnerable because of a United States' policy requiring her shipyards to deny Peruvian vessels even routine maintenance while the war with Colombia continued. A new dry-dock and ships were, therefore, indispensable to the Peruvian Government, but the latter, lacking the necessary capital, had even considered handing over control of its merchant steamship company to Japanese firms in exchange for the construction of a new dry-dock in Callao.[367] The 1932-34 war with Colombia caused the resurrection of the Peruvian Line.

In Mar 1935, the Government made large subsidies available under a system that lasted 20 years. The Peruvian Executive had intended to attract private investment, but being unsuccessful, continued to manage the company like an unwieldy bureaucratic Government institution. Progress was, accordingly, painfully slow, but two second-hand ships were acquired in 1937 and 1938 for coastal trade. The Peruvian Government had wanted to place orders for new ships with German yards in 1939, but was prevented from doing so by the outbreak of WW2. Peru, having failed to take opportunities at the end of WW1 to develop its merchant fleet, had, at the onset of WW2, found her merchant marine in an even worse situation.

In 1916, the US Congress had passed a Federal Shipping Act to launch the United States Shipping Board whose remit was to create an adequate and efficient national merchant marine. The Board, armed with wide ranging powers, was launched with $US50,000,000 (£27,800,000 approximately) funding to implement its shipbuilding and acquisition programme. It soon realised that its national ship building yards had insufficient capacity to meet national needs, and in order to satisfy scheduled requirements, the Board, in addition to placing orders with

Affects of Protectionism. Return to a Free Market. 1915-1994

Japanese and Chinese concerns, signed contracts with US private companies to form *"Agency Yards"*. These concentrated on building ships by assembling prefabricated sections rather than employing traditional construction methods.

One such private concern was the American International Corporation, which had bought-out the New York Shipbuilding Company of Camden, New Jersey. Plans for extensions of the latter's shipyard were thwarted by the availability of limited land. Fortunately, across the Delaware near Philadelphia, there existed a little known swampy and barren isle called Hog Island; its redeeming feature comprised a shoreline extending to over two miles and fronted by sufficiently deep water to allow ship launches. The island was soon converted into a busy shipyard, and the first freighter was completed in August 1918.

The US Shipping Board's plans had been drafted with a view to providing badly needed cargo and troop carriers during World War 1. The contract with the Hog Island shipyard required the construction of 180 vessels, but at the war's end, only 122 of these had been built. It was not until January 1921[368] that all the completed diesel-powered vessels were vested in the ownership of the US Shipping Board, which then came under intense pressure from private ship operators to sell these surplus but modern vessels. After the war, a trade boom developed, resulting in shortages of cargo-carrying capacity. Many ship owners, desperately needing to acquire some of the Board's surplus vessels, had no option but to pay the inflated prices it demanded.

Despite the slump in world trade, the US Shipping Board had still insisted on applying selling prices for the *"Hog Islanders"*, as the vessels were commonly called, which were then triple the market rate. Due to financial difficulties experienced by vessel-purchasing enterprises, most of the ships sold in the early part of the Board's construction programme did, in fact, revert to US Government ownership. The latter, whose primary objective had been the development of its own merchant marine, promptly introduced a subsidy scheme whereby ship owners could not only bid to operate on established routes and be assisted by Federal funds, but importantly, were also able to acquire Hog Islanders at very reasonable prices. This resulted in the emergence of many revitalised shipping companies previously operating on uneconomic routes, which together with the more established shipping firms also benefitting from state subsidies, targetted the WCSA market.

Throughout World War 1, Pacific Steam Navigation Company (PSNC), and other European ship operators, had been compelled to commit their respective fleets to the demands of active Government service. For the Chilean company, WW1 provided record-high profits; withdrawal of European fleets from the WCSA had, inevitably, caused a huge demand for cargo space, which could not be satisfied initially by the fleets of the West Coast nations, the Hog Islanders not being available until late in WW1. At the War's end, PSNC's losses due to enemy action amounted to eight steamships totalling 42,427 tons and 71 persons.

In the post war period, it found itself in a dilemma as to whether to continue provision of services via the Magellan Strait or make use of the Panama Canal, opened in 1914. PSNC's traffic through the Isthmus during the War had been insufficient to assess which of the two routes to the West Coast was the more effective. Certain misgivings had been expressed about abandoning the remunerative Strait's service and those voyages undertaken on the Panama Canal route had not then produced profit, despite the reduction in the Liverpool-Valparaíso round trip by about 3000 miles.[369]

Faced with these uncertainties, PSNC reasonably chose to assign half of its fleet to the West Coast service via the Strait of Magellan while the other half was deployed to develop the Canal route. Unfortunately, this policy coincided with the General Depression and it soon became clear to European shipping lines that larger passenger liners could no longer operate on the West Coast direct service without incurring heavy financial losses. The Royal Mail Steam Packet Company, having reviewed its own organisation, decided to lease three liners, *Orduña*, *Orbita* and *Oropesa* from PSNC to try to stimulate trade with the introduction of a North Atlantic service.

The Chilean Line's (CSAV) decision not to establish a joint venture with Grace Line in 1889 must be considered a major blunder, which subsequently returned to haunt it. The opening of the Panama Canal in 1914 had enabled the United States to become Chile's most important trading partner. The North American Grace Line, having displaced PSNC as the dominant shipping company on the WCSA, posed the biggest competitive threat to CSAV. The latter's priority was to establish itself on the New York-Chile service, the one on which she had been formerly invited to partner with Grace Line in 1889. For this objective, she lacked suitable vessels and there was little prospect of the Chilean Company obtaining them quickly due to the huge unsatisfied backlog of orders already placed with foreign shipbuilding yards, in addition to the exorbitant prices being charged and the delays in delivery of new vessels.

Nevertheless, pressures on CSAV were so great that, in 1920, she was obliged to gamble on purchasing a twenty-two years old Japanese freighter, which was renamed *Renaico*. The Chilean company saw no alternative to this acquisition, believing that the post war boom would continue. The old cargo carrier generated heavy losses on the New York run, but when re-assigned to the European service, and being unable to obtain cargo due to opposition from the Ocean Conferences, she had to make the return trip loaded with coal to supply other CSAV ships. The *Renaico* fared no better on the Chilean coastal service and was eventually laid-up in December 1922.

Affects of Protectionism. Return to a Free Market. 1915-1994

Public demand and Government subsidies ensured that the New York-Chile service continued to exist, but obliged CSAV to acquire two cargo-passenger liners in 1920 when shipyard prices were at their highest. Moreover, public and Government insistence on greater speed had led to turbine engines being ordered rather than the slower but more economical triple expansion engines. The Chilean company had obviously forgotten its former criticism of the Peruvian Line's purchase of the high fuel consuming turbine-powered *Umcayali* and *Huallanga*.

CSAV's *Aconcagua* inaugurated the New York run in October 1922; her sister ship *Teno* joined the operation in 1923. Both vessels were deemed adequate for passenger services but high operating costs devoured profits generated from cargo operations. Despite being subsidized by freight revenue, overall earnings were insufficient to offset high operational costs and loans' repayments forcing the company to declare losses in 1922 and 1923.[370]

The bulk of West Coast South American trade was generated by Chile when political events were beginning to emerge that would not only have huge and long lasting impacts on merchant shipping, initially along the WCSA, but would subsequently extend worldwide. Several important economic and political changes had taken place in Chile at the end of the 19th Century, and the greater part of her copper resources was almost exhausted. The War of the Pacific, however, had provided substitute national revenue from the newly acquired nitrate fields and mines. Agriculture, although its share of the national economy had declined, continued to assume an important economic role. Land distribution, still highly unequal, caused an increasing migration of rural workers to the cities where living conditions for the Chilean working class continued to remain harsh and insecure.

By 1910, significant progress had been made in education leading to the more efficient organisation of urban labour; the middle classes had thus become capable of significantly influencing national life. Such educational and organisational advances enabled the emergence of a Liberal Alliance, which promised the urban classes more say in Chile's political system. This political party had, by 1918, drawn enough votes from the cities to sustain a majority in the Chamber of Deputies. In 1920, their candidate Arturo Alessandri, on election to the Presidency, sought to expand the Chilean State's economic role by redistributing national income through labour and educational reforms, social welfare, low cost housing and nationalization of banks and insurance companies..

It was against this background that the Pacific Steam Navigation Company (PSNC) and other foreign shipping lines, having managed to recover somewhat from the severe affects of World War 1, were dealt another crippling blow in February 1922, following the emergence in Valparaíso of a new law. This legislation, the possibilities of which Wheelwright had warned in the 1850s, had a huge and adverse impact on all foreign shipping operating between Chilean ports. Entitled "*Cabotage*", the statute reserved to Chilean national steamships, the sole right to transport cargo of Chilean origin along the Chilean coast. Passengers, however, were still allowed to travel on foreign registered vessels between these ports; connections to other countries on the WCSA were also unaffected.

The "*Cabotage*" proclamation, originally approved by the Chilean Congress in 1918, was to have become effective by July 1928, thereby allowing the Chilean Government ten years in which to consolidate a nationally registered merchant marine and, which, in practice, would have given PSNC and its non-Chilean competitors time to re-organize their shipping interests. This date was brought forward, firstly to January 1928 and then to January 1923, but due to a resurgence of national feeling, the decree was again amended in February 1922 to allow it to take effect the following August.[371]

Such was the public support for this law, that its promulgation was cause for huge celebration. Almost the entire population turned out in Valparaíso and in the evening an enormous torchlight procession threaded its way through the central streets, no doubt passing the commemorative statue of Wheelwright where similar scenes were enacted when it was ceremonially unveiled in 1876 in La Plaza de la Aduana. Banquets were also held; speeches delivered and fiestas organised:

"Indelibly imprinting on the minds of the port's inhabitants that the new law marked the beginning of what they perceived as a new era of prosperity in the shipping industry". [372]

The 1922 celebrations were also reminiscent of those held in Valparaíso when the two PSNC pioneering steamships entered the port in 1840. The wonder is that it should have taken successive Chilean Governments so long to reserve Chilean coastal trade for its own merchant shipping.

The emergence of this Cabotage law should not have surprised PSNC or other foreign shipping firms such as the German Kosmos Line. Britain, other leading European nations, and the United States had practised it for many years; the earliest occurrence being the 1650 English Navigation Act, requiring that all commerce conducted between England and the colonies had to be carried only on British vessels or under the British flag. Wheelwright, some sixty years before the appearance of this new legislation, had warned his company about the affects of Chilean citizens and their Government voicing nationalistic sentiments in this respect. Since those warnings, regular editorials and numerous correspondence had been published in the local and national press, leading to prolonged debates in the Chamber of Deputies and the Senate on ways to improve Chile's mercantile fleet.

The question of introducing reliable and effective legislation to achieve this objective had focussed on the introduction of protective measures. For over thirty years, the many proposals submitted to the Chilean Chamber had never passed into law because polarised interests, either supporting protectionist measures or open trade policies, had contributed to the political and administrative chaos within

Chile's parliamentary system, resulting in the subject propositions being shelved. Those opposing protectionist measures, not unreasonably, considered that they would mainly assist Compañia Sudamericana de Vapores (CSAV) to operate in a near monopolistic environment and thus be free to levy whatever rates of freight it wished. Supporters of protectionist legislation, on the other hand, drew the nation's attention to the enormous difficulties facing the national economy due to foreign-owned business houses such as PSNC, repatriating profits generated by conveying Chilean goods and materials, not only as valued exports, but also from coastal trade earnings, particularly from supply lines between the northern, central and southern ports.

The 1922 Chilean cabotage statute had been drafted on the premise that it would be linked and supported by three other basic items of draft legislation. These had been expected to pass into law and had been compiled for the protection of the Chilean merchant fleet in 1917 by the Commission for Trade and Shipping. The first of these proposals was "*La Ley de Primas*" (Subsidy Law), but due to the polarised views of different factions in both Chambers, it was never approved and remained filed away within the Commission.[373]

The second proposal actually passed into law; entitled "*La Ley de Contribución de Tonelaje*" (Tonnage Levy Law), it required all ships, whether Chilean or foreign to pay a levy to the Chilean Government calculated on each vessel's tonnage at the first Chilean port of entry. Those vessels undertaking coastal trade would only have been required to pay if they left territorial waters and returned. Accordingly, foreign ships, typically the German Kosmos Line, contributed mostly under this particular statute. Its objective had been to create a revenue source to finance initiatives encouraging the development of Chile's merchant marine, as required by La Ley de Primas. Because the latter had never passed into law, the proceeds collected from the Tonnage Levy during the period 1918 to 1929 inclusive, amounting to 5,355,042 pesos[374], approximately £1,071,008 (US 1,927,814 dollars), were never applied to achieving the intended objectives.

The third proposal, "*La Ley del Crédito Naval*", (Law to provide credit for commercial shipping interests), was also entered in the statute books. The Chilean Government intended to set up a Commission providing mortgages and financial credit to ship owners and shipbuilders in a determined attempt to encourage the expansion of the Chilean merchant marine with better and larger ships. Because of an initial lack of finance to kick-start the Commission's operations, the law was considered ineffective and repealed. The most logical solution would have been to utilise the revenue earned from the Tonnage Levy law but the administrative chaos within the Chilean Chambers brought about by prolonged debates and posturing by the different factions, probably signalled the hopelessness of achieving a solution with this proposed legislation.

The 1922 cabotage law was similar to statutes of 1811 and 1836, but according to Claudio Véliz, was only passed by a majority of two votes:

"[It] could be considered as a last minute concession by a Parliament exhausted by debate which for sheer tedium, duration and lack of intelligibility had no parallel." [375]

Its implementation had primarily assisted Chilean small coastal shipping firms, operating under constant threats from PSNC and other foreign shipping concerns. Although it helped to generate a small improvement in this sector, it was not until 1923 that CSAV itself moved into slight profit; it remained so for the rest of the decade, assisted by Chilean Government subsidies for the still unremunerative New York service. The Chilean company, in fact, blamed the Government for the many mistakes that had been committed in the launch and operation of the New York service:

"The experience has been disastrous for its [the company's) interests due to it having to suffer all the consequences of excessive [Government] official oversight which in some cases had condemned highly efficient ships to be sold or broken-up or on other occasions had authorised the construction of new vessels bereft of all practical considerations". [376]

Competition with W.R.Grace Line had exhausted both the company's finances and the will of its Directors, resulting in the latter's reluctance to embark on providing additional services outside of Chilean coastal areas. However, Government regulation and fears of accusations of being a monopoly restrained CSAV from expanding its coastal services. Even after WW2, the Chilean Line could only claim between one quarter and one half of the total Chilean coastwise home trade.[377]

Chilean Cabotage did provide opportunities for two small but progressive shipping companies, the Chilean firm of Braun & Blanchard and Argentine company, Menéndez Beherty. Both were business houses providing shipping services to the southernmost regions of South America, particularly from Valparaíso to Punta Arena and from Buenos Aires to Patagonia. An accord between the two required that the Chilean firm concentrate on the Chilean coast and the Argentine company on its own coastline. This arrangement worked well and the combined tonnage from both operations was soon approaching that of CSAV, which by 1929, was still operating larger vessels mainly on foreign trade routes.

In that year, the Chilean Government offered subsidies to encourage a steamship service to Argentina, Uruguay and Brazil. The Braun & Blanchard-Menéndez Beherty association (BBMB) gained extensive public support to provide this route, and was duly awarded financial grants enabling it to place orders for vessels for the new foreign line. The BBMB partnership, not wishing to risk all its ships on this joint venture, decided in December 1929 to form a subsidiary

Affects of Protectionism. Return to a Free Market. 1915-1994

company, Compañia Chilena de Navegación Interoceánica.[378] The Argentine firm of Menéndez-Beherty acted as the latter company's agents in Argentina, Uruguay and Brazil. This well-managed enterprise soon began to earn good profits.

Unfortunately, the Great Depression, following upon the Wall Street Stock Market crash in 1929, caused worldwide falls in cargo trade. In Chile, specifically, nitrate exports ceased and copper shipments sharply declined. The loss from these traded commodities caused the country's exchange reserves to evaporate and they were soon insufficient to meet the costs of the nation's imports. Cargo shortages by the middle of 1930 had caused CSAV to tumble from small profits to huge losses, forcing the company to take drastic action by laying-off personnel, a situation lasting for several years. The *Aconcagua* and the *Teno*, operating on the New York service, had caused most of the Chilean company's losses, but the Chilean Government refused to provide higher subsidies to compensate.

In June 1931, despite La Sudamericana terminating the New York line, its losses continued to mount[379]. Both the latter and Interoceánica demanded Government financial assistance and drew attention to the country's harbours filled with laid-up ships because of the desperate economic conditions. The Chilean Government's response, without addressing the real issues behind the crisis, was to propose a merger of all Chilean shipping companies in the belief that one larger company could achieve considerable savings through economies of scale. The proposal was thwarted by rivalry between the existing firms for control of the proposed new shipping concern. Nevertheless, it prompted CSAV and Interoceánica to devise their own survival strategies.[380]

The Chilean Line continued to reduce its crew complements and returned the *Aconcagua*, the *Teno* and the *Tollen* to the English shipyards in August 1932. The first two vessels had been losing money and their disposal partly helped to redeem accumulated debts. By 1932, CSAV's capital had been reduced by 20% but during that year, although further large losses were suffered, it was able to declare a small profit from improved conditions in coastal trading and also from the growth of banana imports from Ecuador.[381]

Despite this hopeful sign, improvements were still insufficient to prevent an attempt to either directly dispose of its three under-used ships to Colombia or to offer them as its contribution to a proposed Colombian-Chilean shipping venture. The Chilean Government, still alert to possible war with Peru, considered that it was still strategically short of ships in that event and blocked the transfer.

The financial climate slowly improved and by June 1936, CSAV saw a steady rise in profits, enabling the company to place orders with a Danish shipyard for three new diesel engine vessels, the *Imperial, Aconcagua* and *Copiapó*. These new vessels satisfied the huge demand for passenger services; each providing 32 berths in first class and 132 in tourist class. The new ships had also been fitted with refrigerated cargo compartments to carry fruit. This became a valuable source of freight, and according to René De La Pedraja, it was used as a strategic lever in attempts by the Chilean Company to gain admission to the Magellan Shipping Conference.

Notwithstanding these potential profit earners, minutes of CSAV Directors' meetings reveal that the company concentrated on providing a more profitable European service, in view of Grace Line competition making a return to the New York Service a very risky venture.[382] Interoceánica, meanwhile, had found that occasional "*tramp*" voyages to New York were encouraging and, in June 1934, announced a monthly service to the North American port.

By 1935, Interoceánica and CSAV, in common with smaller Chilean coastal shipping companies, had again experienced financial difficulties. An initiative by a group of these smaller shipping companies devised a strategy to obtain financial assistance; the two principal shipping concerns would completely relinquish coastal operations to the smaller Chilean shipping companies, receiving in return huge subsidies for their foreign going activities. CSAV, while not being opposed to regulation of merchant shipping, but still hostile to the award of subsidies, attempted to prevent the proposals being implemented. It identified Interoceánica's participation as a serious and unwelcome rival, perceiving this stratagem as a repeat tactic previously and successfully employed to obtain subsidies for the New York service, but this time, with the aim of securing financial assistance for the Strait of Magellan operation. The Chilean Government quickly rejected the plan.

Competition from Grace Line remained fierce and Interoceánica increasingly suffered harassment with frequent and repeated US customs' inspections and searches; in summer 1937, it suspended its New York service.[383] CSAV, declining the opportunity to introduce its own service in the light of Interoceánica's experiences, decided to concentrate on progressing its European operation, particularly as Chile's trade with Germany had substantially increased to the point where that nation was then second only to the United States in terms of commercial interchange.

CSAV launched the first voyage to Europe in March 1938 with the *Copiapó*, and by the following October, had assigned two other vessels to enable monthly departures on this service. Initially, freight volumes from Chile to Europe remained high, but cargo was scarce for the return trip. The reverse was true of passenger traffic, but the Chilean Line, although facing strong public pressure to provide better accommodation and facilities, was not then confident that European passengers to South America could be lured away from the luxurious transatlantic liners, especially those calling at New York, particularly where speed was an essential consideration.

CSAV voyages were essentially cargo trips of two months duration or more, thus making it virtually impossible to find passenger traffic to Europe. Passenger trade for the return voyage was a different story; German Jews, desperate to

Affects of Protectionism. Return to a Free Market. 1915-1994

emigrate to Chile, would book every available berth months ahead. CSAV remained unenthusiastic; its assessment that this passenger trade would be fleeting was reasonable given the war clouds looming on the horizon.

The Chilean company's homeward bound ships started putting-in at New York from October 1938, causing consternation at Grace Line, who had thought it had seen the last of Chilean competition on the New York to Valparaíso route. Despite threats and doubtful joint participation offers by the American company, CSAV declined to withdraw from New York. It had planned the service to the east coast port merely as a temporary arrangement to complement low levels of cargo on return voyages from Europe.

Trade conditions at the time were favourable, but the Magellan Conference retained the means to obstruct CSAV's ability to obtain meaningful levels of freight in European ports. Membership of this Conference was essential; European shippers faced reprisals if they engaged non-Conference shipping companies. La Sudamericana had applied for membership in March 1938 but, even with strong support and diplomatic pressures from the Chilean Government, was refused admission; its members, including PSNC, not wishing to lose any business. However, by 1939, the company was reluctantly admitted as an affiliate member without equal rights; it retained a right to voice an opinion and vote on matters affecting the Chilean coast, but it was excluded from issues relating to the rest of South America.

René De La Pedraja, referring to minutes of CSAV Directors' meetings,[384] indicated that retaining the European service had not been a foregone conclusion:

"After analysing the results of the first eight voyages, two of the Directors concluded that the company was earning twice as much on each voyage with full loads to Ecuador as on each voyage with partially empty holds to Europe. Should not the company then transfer ships from the European service to the Ecuador run? The President explained that the sole objective was to earn the maximum amount of revenue; therefore, the answer was obvious. The agent in Ecuador reported that the cargo loadings had reached their maximum and might even decline; instead the European agents promised considerable bookings once the company entered the Magellan Conference, and in any case the trade had every prospect of increasing considerably. Also, the banana trade was proving less lucrative than originally expected, and although the company would try to maintain its existing services in both places, if a choice had to be made it would transfer ships from the Ecuador run to the European service." [385]

Even membership of the Magellan Conference for European shipping lines, including the PSNC, became meaningless with the outbreak of World War 2 and CSAV had no option but to suspend its European service and reassign its three diesel ships to the New York-Valparaíso run. WW2, however, did provide CSAV and other South American lines with a lifeline, but the future of European shipping companies such as PSNC, having already suffered the loss of Chilean and Peruvian coastal trade, became very bleak indeed.

It is worth briefly recalling events leading to the position of PSNC and other European shipping lines on the WCSA. When the 1835 Chilean decree had declared that PSNC was then the sole non-Chilean registered shipping company permitted to undertake Chilean coastwise trade using steamships, it had not excluded sailing ship enterprises. By 1840, Chilean merchant sailing ships were, of course, already operating along her coast, especially between the agricultural ports of the south and the mining regions of northern Chile.

Simpson y Cia, a nationally registered Chilean enterprise, had been awarded the right in 1851 to operate the Valparaíso-Ancud service with the 200 tons steamship *Arauco*, supported by an annual subsidy of 35,000 pesos, approximately £1500 (US 2700 dollars). In 1864, the Chilean steamship line Compañia Nacional de Vapores (CNV) was founded followed in 1870 by another steamship enterprise, the Compañia Chilena de Vapores (CCV).

Shortly afterwards, to the dismay of the Chilean Government, PSNC had tried to eliminate the competing Compañia Sud Americana de Vapores (CSAV) following its creation from the merger of the former two smaller Chilean companies[386]. Wallace Carter, a Purser on the *ss Chile* recorded that in the years leading up to the Cabotage law of 1922, he had witnessed the growth and intensity of CSAV operations with their fast clipper steamships navigated by many British deck and engine room officers.

Before preparing to cease Chilean coastal operations, PSNC's Directors had carefully assessed whether to continue with a more limited service along the Peruvian, Colombian and Ecuadorian coasts but soon abandoned this proposal, undoubtedly influenced by probable copycat action by the Peruvian Government. Indeed, in 1928, the latter did follow Chile's action by implementing its own cabotage law, ostensibly to protect the nascent and weak Peruvian Steamship Company but in reality, to preserve the lucrative position of its corrupt Directors.

The Chilean and Peruvian Cabotage laws provided difficult but not insurmountable hurdles for PSNC and European associates. The European service was still profitable, but CSAV and later competitors recognised years afterwards that, as Chile's road and rail transport infrastructure improved, profits from coastwise services began to wane. PSNC might have continued with its successful operation of the direct Liverpool-WCSA services via the Strait of Magellan, had it not been for the existence of the Panama Canal. Its opening in August 1914, slowly but surely, hastened this shipping company's decline.

President Roosevelt's "*Big Ditch*" had become another major turning point for PSNC. While, on the one hand, it created significant reductions in voyage times, on the other, and unlike the advantages reaped from the spat with the Panama Railroad in the 1860s, it created an immediate and adverse affect on the English

Affects of Protectionism. Return to a Free Market. 1915-1994

company's operations. The new waterway reduced the distance from Valparaíso to the United States' east coast by one half, but the reduction between the Chilean port and England by only one quarter. Liverpool, which before the opening of the Canal, had only been 1500 kms further than New York was, thereafter, 4500 kms more distant.

Importantly, the United States' Eastern seaboard was now nearer to Chile than Europe, and even nearer for Peru and Colombia; the potentially adverse affects were clear even before the opening of the canal. PSNC's Directors had been sufficiently aware of likely impacts on company revenue once the Canal was fully functional; their recommendation to PSNC shareholders to accept union with Royal Mail Steam Packet Company, albeit sudden, had been based on sound reasoning.

Although the opening of the Panama Canal was hailed as a benefit to the world, apart from US military considerations, its construction mainly served to provide even better prospects and opportunities for North American shipping concerns, particularly as they became eligible shortly afterwards for US Government's generous financial assistance. After World War 1, Britain had been in no financial position to compete with similar subsidies and provide special purchase arrangements for surplus Government vessels on the North American scale; she had lost some 40% of her merchant shipping.

It was this state of affairs that signalled the start of a general decline in British and European shipping firms, although it would take many years before the repercussions finally told. Nevertheless, transit of the Panama Canal still provided the best route for PSNC and its other British and European competitors shortening, for example, the Liverpool-Valparaíso round voyage by some 3000 miles when compared with voyages through the Strait of Magellan. It may be difficult, therefore, to accept that the canal's opening sounded their death knell, given the huge cost reductions and timesaving it provided.

When California became part of the United States, the US Government had begun to review the possibility of a canal across the Isthmus of Panama or through Nicaragua. In 1846, the United States had already been making diplomatic approaches to the New Granada Government[387] for permission to provide some form of transit arrangements across the Isthmus of Panama. The latter country was then part of the Republic of New Granada. In that year, the United States had been accorded the right of transit across the Isthmus by any means then existing, or which might come into being. Importantly, the Republic of New Granada received a United States' guarantee that the Isthmus' neutrality and New Granada's sovereignty over it would be respected.[388]

The US Navy had conducted surveys between 1870 and 1875 of all possible overland routes, and a high-powered Naval Commission had been appointed to examine their feasibility. In 1876, the Commission reported in favour of a

Nicaraguan route; a Nicaraguan Association was, in fact, formed in New York in 1886, but went bankrupt shortly afterwards. An overland route across this Central American republic, connecting Atlantic and Pacific ports, was actually effected in 1851 to provide a New York-Nicaragua-San Francisco service, but the time taken on this voyage was not much faster than that achieved on the established route across the Isthmus of Panama and it soon lost its attraction.

The Panama Canal was foremost a United States' enterprise, one that was very much the personal project of then President Theodore Roosevelt. It was built and financed by Americans and, as Roosevelt had gambled politically, the American nation was justly proud of it. Whilst it was certainly true that the Canal's construction has been for the benefit of all nations, its primary function was military; it enabled US naval forces to pass to and from the Atlantic and Pacific areas of operation more easily and swiftly. The Spanish American War of 1898 had highlighted the need for speedy redeployment of US naval vessels. The US battleship *Oregon* dispatched from the Pacific Ocean to join the fighting off Cuba, had taken 90 days to round Cape Horn; such a long delay thus focused the military's attention on the importance of a canal connecting the Pacific and Atlantic oceans. The link that the US Government then envisaged was to have transited Nicaragua.

The French Company, owning the rights for a Canal across the Isthmus of Panama, had been anxious to dispose of an asset whose value would disappear if a Nicaraguan waterway emerged. It was eventually obliged to reduce its original asking price of 100,000,000 US dollars (£55,500,000 approximately) and to accept a United States Commission's valuation of 40 millions US dollars (£22,220,000 approximately) for the acquisition of the canal rights including the Panama Railroad. Given the considerable reduction in the asking price, the Commission appointed to investigate the two possible canal routes subsequently reported in favour of Panama.

President Roosevelt, having been authorised to acquire the rights and property of the French company for not more than 40 millions US dollars, sanctioned the negotiation of the Hay-Herran[389] Treaty between the US and the Republic of Colombia. The terms of this accord enabled the French Company to dispose of its rights to the United States. Colombia granted the latter administrative control for a period of one hundred years over land that was to form the Canal Zone, although the South American republic retained sovereignty. For such executive oversight of this territory, the United States was to pay $US10 million (£5,550,000 approximately) in gold plus a further 250,000 dollars (£139,000) annually for nine years after the signing of the treaty. The US Senate approved the treaty without difficulty but the Colombian Senate refused to endorse it.

A considerable body of opinion within the Colombian Executive logically concluded that, if their Government stalled long enough, the French concession would eventually expire and the 40 million dollars earmarked by the US to pay the French firm would have to be paid directly to the Colombian Government. The latter's delaying tactics, however, infuriated the United States Government prompting President Roosevelt to send it an extraordinary series of threatening telegrams.[390]

Panama, at that time a State within the Republic of Colombia, was isolated from the capital Bogotá; journeys between the two taking two or three weeks. It also felt neglected by the Colombian Government and had previously tried to declare independence. When rumours of a new attempt at separation began to circulate, US Secretary John Hay advised President Roosevelt that he would either have to wait *"for the result of the impending revolution or take a hand in rescuing the Isthmus from anarchy."* [391]

Although Roosevelt supported Panamanian moves to declare independence, he had always insisted that he had not lifted a finger to incite the revolutionaries. Many American historians still believe that Roosevelt, having attempted to bully the Colombian Government, must have given the Panamanians some assurances of his support, otherwise they would not have risked life and property. Even if a revolution had not taken place, he had been prepared to seize the Isthmus and construct the canal despite any Colombian representations or actions.

A week before the commencement of the revolution, Roosevelt drafted a message to the US Congress:

"Either we should drop the Panama Canal project and immediately begin work on the Nicaraguan canal, or else we should purchase all the rights of the French company and, without any further parley with Colombia, enter upon the completion of the canal which the French company has begun. I feel that the latter course is the one demanded by the interests of this nation".[392]

The event, which for many underlined Roosevelt's implication in the 1903 Panamanian Revolution, was the ordering of the *USS Nashville* to the Isthmus to arrive precisely when Colombian troops were expected. Whether Roosevelt was unjustly accused or not, within a few days of the revolution, his official recognition of the new Government sent an explicit warning to Colombia not to interfere. In 1911 Roosevelt's rash remark in a speech: "*I took the Canal Zone and let Congress debate*" convinced many of his complicity in the uprising.

The Panamanian revolutionaries who had been propelled into Government were vastly inexperienced and extremely naïve about international affairs and negotiations. They had been misled and persuaded by French national, Bunau-Varilla, who for his own personal glory and for that of his country, wanted to see the Canal completed. He had persuaded the provisional Panamanian Government to appoint him as their official representative to renegotiate the terms of the Hey-Herran Treaty with the United Sates Government.

Following the 1903 Revolution, the latter accord's official document had been modified to officially recognise Panama, but the space on the page where the figure of ten millions US dollars had once been inscribed, had been left blank. Bunau-Varilla was well aware that there was a body of opinion within the American Senate, which wanted to divide the 10 millions dollars equally between Panama and Colombia. Given the strong criticism of the behaviour of President Roosevelt in the Panama affair and impending elections in the United States, Bunau-Villa, without consulting the Panamanian Government, amended the terms of the Hay-Herran Treaty to render it more favourable to the North Americans and thus ensure its safe passage through the Senate.

The treaty had originally granted the United States administrative control of the Isthmus land required for the canal but Bunau-Villa had changed the wording to read:

"The Republic of Panama grants to the United States all the rights, power and authority within the zone...which the United States would possess if it were the sovereign of the territory...to the entire exclusion of the exercise by the Republic of Panama of any such sovereign rights, power or authority". [393]

It was reported that Secretary Hey clearly believed that Bunau-Villa was acting on instructions from Panama but from his following remarks he must have realised that something was wrong:

"As soon as the Senate votes we shall have a treaty in the main very satisfactory, mostly advantageous to the United States, and we must confess with what face we can muster, not so much advantageous to Panama...You and I know too well how many points there are in this treaty to which a Panamanian patriot could object. If it is submitted to their consideration they will attempt to amend it in many places...they will feel that the treaty was safe, that their independence was achieved, and that now it was time for them to look out for a better bargain than they were able to make at first". [394]

The five innocent and naïve members of the Panamanian Government who had only been in the job for a fortnight, knew little about diplomacy and international law; they were local tradesmen and landowners, probably unaware of the difference between "*sovereign rights*" and "*administrative control*". What they did know was that their new country was already heavily in debt and quickly needed ten millions dollars if their newly gained independence was to endure. Few Americans today probably realise how they came to possess such rights in the Canal. Had they been so aware, they might have been less possessive of them for so long when faced with protests from the Republic of Panama. Could North American conscience have contributed to the motto of the Panama Canal Company "*The Land Divided-The World United*"?

Affects of Protectionism. Return to a Free Market. 1915-1994

Unfortunately for British and European ship operators, the Panama Canal also provided opportunities for United States merchant shipping concerns, heavily subsidised with their modern "*Hog Islander*" vessels, to reduce their own voyage times, rendering them more economical and bringing the industrial and financial centres of the Atlantic shoreline of North America closer to the WCSA. The United States' Pacific ports thus had easier access to Europe and the East Coast of South America. The Panama Canal profoundly affected world economies; it changed the patterns of South American and Atlantic trade. PSNC's long and carefully cultivated investment of the services to Peru and Chile via the Strait of Magellan had rapidly become obsolete; Valparaíso became the terminus of the Company's maritime shuttle service rather than the hub of its South American business.

The Chilean Compañia Sudamericana de Vapores (CSAV), subsidised by the Chilean State, together with the US Grace Line, filled any vacuum left by the British Company. Moreover, the latter's finances, like other British and European shipping concerns, mostly drained because of the First World War, were insufficient to allow it to compete with the more adventurous policies of the State-supported American shipping companies, then expanding into areas hitherto the preserve of PSNC, and other British and European steamship lines.

American interests, like the British, had been widespread and steadily developing in Peru and Chile since the early part of the 19th Century. The list of famous names associated with important early enterprises from both nations is long and impressive. It includes the following to name but a few: Anglo Lautaro Nitrate Corporation, Compañia Salitrera Anglo Chilena, American Bridge Company, American Locomotive Company, Antofagasta (Chile) and Bolivia Railway Company Ltd., Bank of London, Mexico and South America, Baldwin Locomotives, Beyers-Peacock Locomotives, Guardian Insurance Co., Braden Copper Company, Cerro de Pasco Corporation, J.H.Schroeder, N.M.Rothschild, Duncan Fox, Anglo South American Bank, S.Pierson & Sons, Gibbs Y Cia. W.R.Grace Co., and the Chile Exploration Company. The Guggenheim Family of New York financed the latter firm, which eventually sold out to the vast Anaconda Copper Company. English entrepreneurs founded Valparaiso's daily newspaper, El Mercurio, to serve the huge English speaking population there. Inevitably maritime traffic between the US and South America steadily increased on the back of these commercial enterprises.

One British firm, in 1864, with a high profile in Chile was the seemingly invulnerable Balfour Williamson & Company. Unable to expand its trade in that country due to market saturation, the firm decided to open an additional "*Business House*" in San Francisco. It was a very bold initiative at that time. The Pacific Coast was then largely virgin territory and a raging Civil war had severely disrupted the young United States nation. It took four years for Balfour Williamson to make the move; the firm had initially been reluctant to take the final decision given the need for long and perilous voyages from the North American Pacific coast round Cape Horn. They were also aware of the tendency of American Governments to pass measures restraining foreign trade for the protection of its own manufacturing industries.[395] However, visionaries within that firm were aware of inventions in the field of transport and communications, which were primarily responsible for the rapid development of the 19th Century United States.

The introduction of the steamboat, especially on North American Rivers and the railroads, had enabled the US population to extend outwards into the mid-west. Before this, it had expanded ribbon-like along the eastern coast but the advent of new technologies facilitated access to the Pacific Coastal regions. Balfour Williamson took that brave decision in 1868, knowing that a canal through the Panama Isthmus was a real possibility. As early as 1850, the United States had become seriously involved in a project to construct such a canal, being well aware that freight from the Eastern seaboard of the United States had to be carried by sailing ship round Cape Horn; journeys taking from three to six months. From Britain, it took somewhat longer and voyages of a year were not uncommon.

Wallis Hunt described Balfour Williamson Company's thinking in "*Heirs of Great Adventure*":

"As for transport across the States, it was unthinkable that anything substantial should be carried far over terrible roads. Even the railway was at first too light to fulfil all needs. Obviously, if the hopes of anyone who anticipated an isthmian canal were ever to be realized, the potentialities of San Francisco and the whole of the Far West would be greatly increased. Britain had forbidden manufacturing in the American colonies, and the almost limitless resources by the United States had still scarcely been touched by the middle of the nineteenth century. Agricultural development took pride of place, but the methods used were prodigal and short-sighted. Money and men were scarce. The land was vast. When a cultivated area declined in fertility, the farmer simply abandoned it to break virgin ground farther west. His ingenuity was challenged, however, by the need for making the best use of the men he had. His wants were purely satisfied by the invention of McCormick's reaping machine (1834) and other devices, which hardly became known to the world at large until the Crystal Palace Exhibition in 1835. Wheat, corn cotton and other crops more than doubled in size between 1830 and 1860."

The remit of the US branch of Balfour Williamson Company, set-up in 1869 in San Francisco under the title of Balfour Guthrie and Company, had been to receive and execute orders for the purchase of grain and other Californian produce, and to accept for sale consignments of merchandise suited to the needs of the local market. Their first dealings were in "*rough goods*" such as chemicals imported from England and coal from Australia. Their most important export was wheat, then California's principal crop, such cargoes often being dispatched to

Affects of Protectionism. Return to a Free Market. 1915-1994

Falmouth in England. In 1878, Balfour Guthrie opened a branch in Portland to take advantage of the growing lumber and grain trades. It later formed the Pacific Loan and Investment Company Ltd and the Pacific Trust Association Ltd., to help finance local farmers, thus linking the produce they produced with Balfour Williamson's shipping interests. The volume of trade prompted the firm to purchase a new grain warehouse and loading wharf in Portland from where the firm also exported lumber to Chile. Balfour Guthrie's business was aided considerably by more-efficient contact with its partnerships in Liverpool and Valparaíso, as well as its clients, by new developments in 1881 of mail and cable communications. In Chile in 1873, Balfour Williamson Company was financing the Anaconda copper mine and had become its agents in the United States and England.

The Balfour Guthrie business was only one commercial entity amongst many involved in the South American trade. Shipping enterprises to service these businesses mushroomed; one such company was Grace Line. In the mid 19th Century, two Irish brothers, William and Michael Grace had established their own business in Peru at the same time as many other British and American entrepreneurs. Developed as a commercial and shipping enterprise in Callao, it thrived initially and especially on provisioning ships waiting for long periods to load guano from the Chincha islands to the United States. In 1865, William departed to New York and founded the firm of W.R.Grace & Co. This enterprise converted part of its sailing ship fleet to steamships, operating a line of freighters, initially under the British flag,[396] between New York and the West Coast of South America via the Strait of Magellan. As Grace Line developed, more ships were constructed in the United States, causing the company to switch to American registration.[397]

In 1913, it introduced a service from the Pacific Coast of the United States to the WCSA. Typical of its fleet was the *Colusa* (5873 tons) built by Hamilton of Glasgow. She was able to carry fully assembled steam locomotives for the South American ports and, like her sister ships, was able to transport large deck loads of lumber from the Pacific Coast ports to Chile with intermittent ports calls along the West Coast. A major threat to PSNC and European passenger traffic emerged in 1916, when Grace Line introduced similar services from New York via the Panama Canal to West Coast South American ports, as far as Valparaíso. Four Grace passenger ships were eventually operating on this route. In 1913, the American concern took a controlling interest in the Pacific Mail Steamship Company, then the leading North American West Coast and trans-Pacific shipping enterprise.

In an attempt to counter the Grace Line threat in 1920, PSNC commenced direct services from New York to Valparaíso, shortly followed by a New York-Cartagena-Callao service. The English company also launched the *Oropesa II* in 1920 for the Liverpool-Rio de Janeiro-Buenos Aires route, but the following year, she was chartered to its sister company Royal Mail Lines to operate the Hamburg-Southampton-New York service. Two Royal Mail Lines ships, the

Ebro and *Essequibo*, complemented by PSNC's *Quilpué* and the *Quillota*, were commissioned to compete against Grace Line, but the American shipping company, then the beneficiary of US Government grants and subsidies, was too strong to succumb.

In 1923, Grace Line formed a new enterprise, the Panama Mail Company, to operate in the Central American regions. In 1926, it initiated a new secondary service from New York to Antofagasta and assigned two additional ships to this operation, extending it in 1929 to take-in Valparaíso. However, in 1932, the Great Depression caused its suspension although it resumed the year after. In 1934, competing North American shipping companies made representations to the US Government in an attempt to bar Grace Line from operating on North American coastal trade. The complaint derived from US Government subsidies paid to Grace Line for operating foreign trade routes and which, according to the plaintiffs, was indirectly and unfairly assisting that firm in its coastwise operations.

Royal Mail Lines, faced with US subsidised competition, was obliged to terminate its unprofitable New York services in that year, disposing of the *Ebro* to Yugoslavia, the *Essequibo* to Russia and the *Champerico* to Chilean owners. The slump forced PSNC to lay-up some of its ships and reduce its fleet, but in 1931, that company took a risky but farsighted decision to build the passenger liner ss *Reina del Pacifico*.

ss *Reina del Pacifico*. 17,702 tons gross. Built 1931 by Harland & Wolff at Belfast. The fore funnel was a dummy. Powered by four propellers, she had five cargo holds, accommodation for 280 First Class passengers, 162 Second class and 446 in Third Class.

PSNC's Directors had correctly forecast that the end of the General Depression would leave their company well placed to take advantage of increased passenger traffic, which they felt would surely arise. One immediate and clear advantage of this new passenger liner was her speed, enabling her to reduce the Liverpool-

Affects of Protectionism. Return to a Free Market. 1915-1994

Valparaíso round voyage from 78 to 60 days. Unfortunately, this popular liner was beset by problems and events beyond the company's control. She started her career well enough and, in 1932, resumed the annual "*Trip Round South America*" service. A large proportion of the *Reina del Pacifico's* passenger traffic originated in Spain and was bound for Cuba, but the Spanish Civil War of 1936 removed this valuable source of revenue. Before the vessel could make a real contribution to PSNC's finances, World War 2 intervened. After the introduction of the *Reina del Pacífico,* the liner *Oropesa (II)* was overhauled to allow an increase in her speed. She was to have acted as consort to the new liner, but she spent much of her time laid-up between 1931-34.

During this period Royal Mail Lines, then part of the Lord Kylsant's shipping empire, began to fail. In an attempt to raise finance, he had issued false statements in his company's financial prospectus, was found guilty and imprisoned. Pacific Steam Navigation Company, owned by Royal Mail Lines, was afforded Parliamentary protection and allowed to continue operations, but only under the control of its creditors, principally Martins Bank, which was represented on the Board of Directors. This situation continued until Royal Mail Company was placed on a firm financial footing. PSNC suffered another blow in 1937 when the Falkland Island Company cancelled its contract with the Company and commenced its own service. By 1939, PSNC's ships had been reduced to just 14 vessels. A further re-organization of its fleet was undertaken but before construction of new ships could start work, World War 2 broke out.

In economic terms, this war proved beneficial to most of Latin America, producing strong demand for its raw materials and foodstuffs by the United States and her allies' war effort. Exports from South American nations led to an accumulation of large surpluses in their balances of payments, thus enabling the clearing of national debts and the creation of strong capital reserves to allow domestic investment in industrial projects. Furthermore, the United States decisively assisted development by making loans available and providing technical expertise and equipment to enable those countries initialise their own industrialization process.

In the early years of the war, US delegations had been despatched to Latin America to secure trade agreements; those South American republics signing-up were obliged to declare war on the Axis powers and provide the United States and her allies with essential minerals and commodities. The sole major republic not benefiting from this economic alliance was Argentina; her Military Junta then harboured sympathies for Germany and Italy, resulting in the maintenance of an uneasy neutral position. Such political inclination caused Argentina to forfeit that technical and financial assistance provided to her neighbours by the United States. Bolivia's military Government was, initially, sympathetic to the Axis cause, but a change in Government administration caused her to ally herself with US

Ploughing The South Sea

thinking. Not only did these economic and industrialization benefits continue after the war, but those shipping enterprises created or strengthened as a result of the considerable movement of goods between the United States and Latin America, also consolidated their positions and continued to prosper in the post war period until their situation was virtually unassailable.

As in World War 1, European shipping companies were obliged to place their vessels at the disposal of their respective Governments. The resulting gap in cargo carrying capacity had to be filled to enable the conveyance of essential resources for the United States' and Allies' war effort. Chile, as a member of the latter alliance, was thus able to provide strategic resources such as nitrates and copper. To transport these cargoes to the United States, the Chilean CSAV had three fast diesel ships, but each with accommodation for over 200 passengers. The latter space could not be used effectively for cargo storage and the United States War Shipping Board was, therefore, obliged to purchase the three Chilean vessels and replace them on charter with four old but adequate *Hog Islander* vessels to convey the urgently required mineral ore. Importantly, the United States Government promised the Chilean Company that it would sell it new replacement vessels at the termination of the War.

La Sudamericana's management, at that time, has to be admired; the expense of chartering the four *Hog Islanders* was insignificant when compared with the minimal cost it was guaranteed for the renewal of what was then considered the core of its fleet, and which would have been ten years old in 1947. The United States' Grace Line thought that this contract was too favourable to the Chilean shipping company, and tried to persuade the US State Department not to honour the agreement to sell the three Liberty C-2s cargo carriers to CSAV. Actually four C-2s were needed to replace the total cargo capacity of the three vessels the State Department had purchased from the Chileans. Grace Line's complaint did have some merit because C-2s were then in very short supply. Nevertheless, the US Government, believing that non-fulfilment of the terms of its guarantee to Chile would be internationally damaging, supplied CSAV with the four C-2s between September 1946 and January 1947.

The terms of the US Ship Sales Act were considered by the Chilean company to be so favourable that it acquired another surplus US Liberty C1-MA-VIs vessel.[398] Indeed, these ship purchases turned out to be extremely profitable to the CSAV; it had sold its three diesel vessels to a US Government Agency in 1943 at four times what it paid for them in 1938 and had, moreover, acquired the surplus vessels as replacements after the war at rock-bottom prices. The profits accumulated by CSAV were wisely re-invested, not in shipping, but channelled into diverse investments such as steel mills, property and banks. Generally, in the post war years throughout South America, capital production and industrialisation had increased, but many capital investors had chased short-term profit rather than seeking to reinvest over the longer periods of development that accompanied industrialisation processes. Foreign investment, in which the United States was predominant, was targeted at petroleum, manufacturing, mining and public utilities. Indeed, most investments in Chile were foreign-based. While offering that nation short-term advantages, difficulties emerged when profits needed to be repatriated by foreign-owned firms. This seriously added to the drain on foreign exchange reserves.

CSAV's management, dissatisfied with the revenues raised by its diversified investments, and having conducted a review of its shipping business in 1949, petitioned the Chilean Government, once more, for special protectionist measures termed *"Cargo Preference"*. These had already been requested in 1944 when representations had been made to have 50 per cent of all foreign trade with Chile conveyed by Chilean registered vessels. Understandably, the petition generated vigorous opposition from nitrates' exporters who had tended to transport their bulk cargoes in Greek tramp ships. CSAV, accordingly, sidelined its proposals but renewed its lobbying for Cargo-Preference in 1949, following the European/South Pacific and Magellan Conference.

This was one of a number of ocean conferences whose members collectively set rates and frequency of voyages to their areas of interest, and which had, initially, refused to admit CSAV, even though the latter had achieved, not without difficulty, *affiliated* membership in 1939. CSAV had felt slighted by not being allowed *full* membership status, especially after having failed to gain re-entry into the supposedly *"open"* Conferences in the United States. René De La Pedraja[399] highlighted a deliberate and collective attempt to undermine the company's trading position:

"The Grace Line, in the hope of prying concessions, delayed the re-entry of the Chilean Line into the Atlantic and West Coast of South America Conference; not until February 1950 did the Chilean Line become a full member. More insulting was the attitude of the Magellan Conference whose members arrogantly believed that Latin Americans should not, and in any case, could not operate a reliable service to Europe." [400]

The attitude of the shipping Conferences to CSAV only hardened the latter's determination to seek some form of result. La Sudamericana was further motivated by potential competition from another Chilean shipping line, the 1929-launched company *"Interoceánica"* (La Compañia Chilena de Navegación Interoceánica or CCNI) The latter concern, operating principally through the Strait of Magellan on South American coastal trade, had proposed a merger with CSAV in 1939; talks continued until 1947 but ended unsuccessfully. CSAV recognised the possibilities of competition to its foreign trade services when CCNI acquired two Liberty C1-MA-VI ships in 1947, and shortly afterwards, an additional three similar vessels under the generous terms allowed by the US Ship Sales Act. Although CCNI had not then commenced operations on foreign trade routes, it had, with these ship purchases, acquired the potential to do so.

CSAV, having deduced that earnings from coastal shipping trade were waning due to competition from road and railroad operators, calculated that foreign trading ships could earn twice as much as could be obtained from coastal trade. CCNI, not then having identified the declining trend in Chilean home-trade shipping, increased her coastal fleet tonnage. When this realisation finally dawned, the latter company promptly tried to convert its operations to foreign trade and, in doing so, wholeheartedly espoused the call for a Cargo Preference policy for Chilean shipping companies. Indeed, one of its executives became the chairman of the Chilean National Association of Shipowners, which directed the campaign, and which naturally, was fully supported by CSAV.

Although the Chilean Government had refused to endorse representations for Cargo Preference in 1944, it had, in 1959, experienced a severe and deteriorating shortage of foreign exchange, a situation mostly produced by the repatriation of profits of the large multi-national concerns and the import of foreign manufactured goods. Shipping importers were the first to suffer; they needed US dollars to purchase goods from abroad but due to scarce foreign exchange, the Chilean Government rationed this currency. As importers began to experience difficulties, so their long-standing opposition to Cargo Preference dissipated. The Chilean Congress recognised that the one area of Chilean commerce virtually able to guarantee the provision of much needed foreign exchange was the Chilean merchant fleet. Accordingly, the Chilean Government finally surrendered to the Chilean Shipping Association's pressure and passed legislation introducing a Cargo Preference policy.

In April 1950, CSAV, having reviewed its operations, introduced regular monthly services to Europe via New York, provoking the Magellan Conference to retaliate with a price-slashing war on freight rates. This, in turn, was countered by the Chilean Government the following August, when it decreed that fifty per cent of all Chilean imports be conveyed by Chilean flagged vessels. This policy was easily administered through the issue of import licences, the Government making a point of giving priority consideration to applications from importers specifying Chilean ships to carry their cargoes. Those not nominating national shipping lines had to suffer long delays while their documentation was processed. The lesson was soon learned; importers began to employ Chilean vessels resulting in a backlog of cargo waiting to be transported. CSAV, reportedly swamped by demands for cargo space, was forced to charter vessels to clear the build-up and, accordingly, along with other Chilean shipping lines, made enormous profits. Importantly for the Government, the Chilean shipping companies not only generated considerable foreign exchange, but also helped to improve the nation's balance of payments.

Affects of Protectionism. Return to a Free Market. 1915-1994

Most of Grace Line ships, sailing empty into Chile, succumbed to her protectionist policies in October 1950 when signing an agreement for a *"revenue pool"*. This required Grace Line to surrender most of the profits earned whenever its share exceeded fifty percent of cargo imported. René de La Pedraja noted:[401]

"For the Chilean Line [CSAV], the results were almost magical; since its share of southbound cargo had been under 35 per cent, while the share of the Grace Line normally exceeded 50 percent, automatically at the end of the each quarter, the Grace Line paid a hefty sum to the Chilean Line. Just by signing a piece of paper the Chilean Line received the funds needed to begin a new wave of fleet expansion while the Government gained sorely needed foreign exchange. Cargo Preference had demonstrated its power."

Having brought the mighty Grace Line to heel, CSAV then employed the same tactics on members of the Magellan Conference, which included the Pacific Steam Navigation Company. The Conference's members could do little to prevent European exports to Chile being directed to Chilean registered vessels. They countered in vain with lowering freight rates but:

"The haughty Magellan Conference...refused to believe that its moment of absolute power had passed. Continued resistance only heightened nationalistic feelings in Chile, and by the time the Magellan Conference at last agreed to accept the Chilean Line as a full member in December 1953, it was too late to put away the genie of Cargo Preference." [402]

The Association of Chilean Shipowners successfully petitioned the Chilean Congress to add a requirement to the August 1950 law, obliging foreign registered shipping companies to create a revenue pool with a Chilean shipping company whenever the formers' share of cargo to or from Chile exceeded 50%. Extensive and relentless lobbying of the Chilean Congress by foreign ship owners, especially the US registered Grace Line, tried to have the 50% Cargo Preference law repealed. This, unfortunately for the objectors, partly coincided with the passing of the United States Congress Cargo Preference Act of 1954, thus weakening the case of foreign shipping companies against the introduction of similar legislation in Chile. By June 1956, the protectionist measures passed into law, but with the amendment that Chilean export cargoes were excluded, thus allowing foreign shipping companies to bid for low value bulk cargoes that formed the majority of shipments to the northern hemisphere.

Cargo Preference policies, in 1956, arose from Chile's urgent need to earn foreign exchange and, undoubtedly, considerable foreign currency did accumulate. By the late 1960s, the economic situation had worsened. The Chilean Government, having failed to remove the cause of the problem, began to exchange foreign currency earned by the shipping companies at lower than market rates. Consequently, the latter's operating costs in Chile became higher than those of the industrialised countries. To avoid bankruptcy, these shipping firms relocated some of their operations abroad. Although it was possible for them to transfer their vessel's registration to a flag of convenience such as Panama, they would have lost the advantages of Cargo Preference, which compensated for the heavy losses incurred under the detrimental exchange rate. The latter caused delays in the ordering of new ships and often only second-hand vessels could be acquired.

Chilean ship-owners increasingly relied on chartered vessels which were still eligible for Cargo Preference benefits, provided their chartering did not exceed the overall tonnage of the company's fleet. Such protectionism not only considerably softened the worst affects of the foreign-currency crisis, but also allowed Chilean shipping companies to expand their fleets and operations. European shipping establishments reluctantly joined the revenue pools, in the process generating further large profits for CSAV, CCNI, and other small Chilean Shipowners. CSAV, having decided to expand its European service, dropped New York from its schedules and thereafter sailed directly to Europe.

Despite Cargo Preference providing an impetus to the development of Chilean shipping companies in foreign trade, the latter further reduced their coastal trade operations, causing the state-owned railways to extend shipping services, introduced in 1938, through its subsidiary FERRONAVE. This operation thereafter provided the essential transport link to ports in the southern region such as Punta Arenas, previously unreachable by land, but which relied on frequent cargo and passenger services. These successful coastal operations were gradually extended to all Chilean coastal ports. To assist these voyages and to provide non-profitable connections to the more remote communities such as Easter Island, the Chilean Government established the heavily subsidised EMPREMAR, a separate organisation to FERRONAVE, having its headquarters in Valparaíso.

In practice, EMPREMAR's trade mostly comprised general cargo, but in 1964, it began to attract bulk cargoes to the northern and southern coastal ports, giving rise to bitter competition with privately owned coastal shipping companies. The Chilean Line (CSAV), having considerably reduced its coastal activities, was not affected by this move, but was naturally taken aback when EMPREMAR began chartering vessels to compete on foreign bulk trade. The latter organisation's success led to the acquisition of specialist combination ore and oil carriers for this sector. Prior to that event, tankers had conveyed imported oil while tramp vessels transported exported mineral ore cargoes; a single combination vessel performed both roles. EMPREMAR achieved considerable savings with this successful arrangement. CCNI, hitherto, the nation's oil importer was clearly affected and joined with the Chilean Line in placing an order for a partnership-operated combination ore/oil carrier.

By July 1971, the Allende Government had nationalised the copper mines, a widely popular measure, but when nationalisation was extended to other areas, national support waned dramatically. In October 1971, the Chilean Government announced its intention to acquire 51% of the Chilean Line's shares, but company shareholders resisted the move. Similar action was applied to CCNI, whose principal owner having sold his 61% holding in the company to the Government caused more shareholders to follow that action and the Government succeeded in obtaining 91% of the total stock.[403]

It was not until May 1972, that the Government succeeded in gaining majority control of the Chilean Line, but a shareholders' group continued to resist, arguing that both the state-owned CCNI and EMPREMAR constituted a monopoly contrary to Chile's anti-monopoly laws. Two Trade Union appointments were allowed onto the Board of Directors and the company continued to be administered by private shareholders. When the Government again tried to assume control, the Trade Unions called a short strike in support of the private company.

The Chilean economy at this time was rapidly deteriorating as United States' sanctions began to bite; the Chilean Government, desperately short of foreign exchange, appropriated every US dollar earned by the shipping companies, but provided no alternative for them to pay for local expenses; the Chilean Line needed dollars to continue paying foreign ship yards.[404] By September 1973, support for Allende in Valparaíso had weakened to such an extent, that on September 11 the Chilean Navy took just one hour to gain control of the port and nearby Viña del Mar. Allende was killed in the Presidential Palace, and the resulting military dictatorship, thereafter, proceeded to return the nationalised companies to private ownerships, all except for the copper mines. The fall of Allende did not improve the economy; the military dictatorship continued to expropriate foreign currency from the shipping companies. Significantly, it ended subsidies to EMPREMAR and repealed the 1960 law requiring all Government financed cargoes, principally sugar and wheat, to use the latter's vessels.

The currency crisis continued until 1978,[405] but in 1976, the Government started to dismantle all forms of protectionism, an action that most shippers supported. Fruit exporters, for example, claimed that the 50% Cargo preference levels had deterred foreign ship owners from entering the fruit shipping trade because the 50% limit deprived them of enough volume to justify regular services. The Chilean Line, on the other hand, had cornered about 80% of the fruit export trade at this time.

In June 1979, the Chilean Government decreed that 50% of the total tonnage of a shipping company's fleet was the maximum amount that they could charter to continue benefiting from Cargo Preference. This legislation emerged when the transition to containerisation made most Chilean shipping companies highly vulnerable financially.[406] Cargo Preference was weakening as an effective policy and Chile's military Government, fearing a war with Argentina over the sovereignty of the Beagle Islands, began to view its merchant fleet as an essential defensive tool.

The Chilean Line considered that the move to containerisation without the lifeboat of Cargo Preference was a risky policy, but it was more so for its Chilean competitors. A 1979 Government study concluded that CSAV was the only Chilean shipping Line with sufficient resources to finance a replacement of its fleet. Cargo Preference, introduced in 1956, was scrapped; by February 1980, most of Chile's coast was re-opened to foreign ships.[407] Chilean ship-owners were allowed considerable tax shelters and benefits, once again rendering Chilean shipping an attractive investment; the re-opening of Chile to world markets created a prosperity that had eluded previous Governments.

La Sudamericana had already taken precautionary steps to register its new vessels under a flag of convenience, intending to use the profits from these to offset the higher costs of its older Chilean registered ships. Other Chilean shipping lines, having suffered from the loss of Cargo Preference, also adopted this tactic and began to charter foreign-owned hulls. This action was unable to prevent massive lay-offs of crew and office personnel. Chilean registered tonnage declined. It would have dropped further had not the registry-controlling Chilean Navy prohibited the movement to flags of convenience. Chilean shipping companies were, by then, in a much weakened position as foreign nations now received the income, employment and contracts that the shipping sector had previously generated in Chile.[408]

Indeed, the abolition of Cargo Preference threw the whole Chilean maritime industry into crisis; Valparaíso was particularly affected economically, especially with the destruction of its stevedoring and associate unions. The economic climate in 1981/82 was the worst since the Great Depression as the Chilean economy actually registered negative growth. Foreign debt problems re-appeared; re-payments had to be staggered, unemployment mounted and the nation's banking system was near collapse. A new approach was therefore required to re-invigorate Chilean shipping.

14. Grancolombiana Line, Peruvian Line, Ecuadorian Transnave and Flopec Lines. 1946-1973

Present day Republic of Colombia.
Map Courtesy Texas University Library

Colombia did not grant Wheelwright his desired concession for steam navigation in her West Coast waters until 1845. Her initial lukewarm response to his 1840 initiative arose from her advantageous geographical and strategic position. In addition to a Pacific coast, she not only benefited from a Caribbean shoreline providing an Atlantic gateway, but more importantly, she possessed a valuable waterway in the form of the Río Magdalena, reaching into her very heartland to provide the nation's main transport artery.

**The mouth of the River Magdalena near the port of Barranquilla.
Photo: courtesy Fredy Cuello.**

    The port of Baranquilla is situated at the mouth of the Rio Magadalena; 1,536 kilometres in length. This river has a number of important tributaries, the Cauca, San Jorge and César. The Cauca, 1,350 kilometres long, flows into the Magadalena some 320 kilometres below Baranquilla. The last 22 kilometres of the Magdalena are maintained to a minimum depth of 30 feet. The connecting River Patía flows through the Andes and into the Pacific. In the early part of the 19th Century goods were conveyed along these rivers by champanes, long narrow and partly canopied lighters, to four fluvial ports where they were transferred to riverboats for onward shipment to Barranquilla. The first steamers based on the American riverboat models were prone to breakdowns and were insufficiently powered to compete against the often fast-flowing current.

    Given Barranquilla's strategic location on the Caribbean coastline and Colombia's 19th Century cultural sympathies with European enlightenment and technology, entrepreneurs from the latter continent were more successfully attracted to that region; trade and industry increased dramatically. Shipping growth on the Magdalena and through the port of Barranquilla, however, did not translate into a sizeable national mercantile fleet. Even by 1946, the Colombian Government, although aware that cargo volumes passing through Colombian ports were too small to warrant the formation of a national merchant marine, calculated that by combining the cargoes from neighbouring countries, a joint fleet was a viable proposition. The idea was floated in Venezuela, Ecuador and Panama, but

A typical Champán on the Río Magdalena. An illustration from "Barranquilla Gráfica". Reproduced from Antonio Montaña's "A Todo Vapor".

the latter country declined to participate. Ecuador was eager to become involved for security reasons; she was still uncertain about the military aims of her southern neighbour Peru, and saw membership of the three nations' shipping partnership, not only as a means of strengthening links with friendly neighbouring countries, but also as an opportunity to benefit from resources she lacked to establish her own merchant fleet.

A treaty, signed in April 1946 by the three participating nations, led to the launching two months later of "*La Flota Mercante Grancolombiana*" (The Merchant Fleet of Gran Colombia).[409] Colombia and Venezuela each contributed 45% of the capital leaving Ecuador to find the remaining 10%. The latter nation was so impoverished that her two partners had to loan her this amount otherwise she would have been unable to participate.[410] The National Federation of Coffee Growers acquired Colombia's 45% share; the Venezuelan Government acquired a further 45% and the Ecuadorian State's Banco de Fomento purchased the remaining 10%. In effect, "*La Grancolombiana*" had become a state-controlled enterprise with a tax-exempt status, allowing the firm to subsidise its shippers and protect them from those higher rates charged by monopolistic foreign shipping companies.[411]

The new company was located in the Colombian capital Bogotá, and a Colombian manager was appointed to ensure the proper functioning of the organisation. The three national Governments were enthusiastic with the project, but dark clouds on the horizon began to appear in the form of vigorous opposition from a body of officials in the Venezuelan Government's bureaucracy; it was only through the personal intervention of Venezuelan President Betancourt that the project continued to survive. He believed that his compatriots were then incapable of successfully operating a major shipping enterprise and regarded the Colombian management as essential in delivering the desperately needed service.[412]

Significantly, La Grancolombiana encountered the same dilemma as the Pacific Steam Navigation Company some six years later when it planned the introduction of its passenger liner *Reina Del Mar*, just as long haul air travel was beginning to develop, spreading rapidly from North America.[413] It decided to concentrate on cargo transport and not, as it claimed, to waste time and money on passenger services. It successfully obtained a bargain purchase from the United States of eight C1-MA-VI freighters, two of which were registered under the Ecuadorian flag and three each under the respective ensigns of Venezuela and Colombia. British personnel were hired to train local employees in the vessels' technical operations but officers and deckhands, mostly unobtainable in partner countries, were recruited from Spain, a practice that lasted until the late 1950s.

Although the company's launch had drawn considerable and favourable publicity, the North American Grace Line ridiculed Grancolombiana (hereinafter "*GC Line*") as a totally ill conceived venture:

"As soon as they feel the salt-water, they will head back to land and tie-up their ships to keep from going totally bankrupt"[414]

Grace Line, however, appeared to shoot itself in the foot when, in May 1947, it announced a 25% increase in its shipping rates, thus presenting the fledgling shipping company with considerable manoeuvrability. Impatient Venezuela representatives insisted that GC Line's ships operate from the onset under the old freight charges to compete aggressively with the US shipping line. The Colombian management, deciding against outright competition, recommended that the firm seek admission to the ocean conference routes from Ecuador and the northern coast of South America, to the United States. Venezuela had for decades been opposed to ocean conferences and refused to approve the proposal. The Company's management contended that membership would allow it to offer lower charges to those shippers exclusively patronising the conference's member shipping companies.

René De La Pedraja,[415] having undertaken extensive studies of the GC Line's development, by conducting wide-ranging interviews with its Executive and poring over its archives commented:

"Membership in the ocean conferences helped break the grip of the Grace Line over US exports to Colombia, but never over coffee exports to the United States. W.R. Grace, the parent company of the Grace Line, used its control over most coffee cargoes to keep Grancolombiana's ships sailing north practically empty. The pessimistic fears about the new company seemed to be coming true and Grace Line could not resist gloating over the impending collapse of the upstart rival whose survival depended on a parallel struggle taking place in the coffee fields of Colombia." [416]

Normally, only between 2 to 3% of Colombia's coffee were available for export via GC Line at that time. Coffee purchases mostly remained under the control of Grace Line in conjunction with an association of foreign buyers. A tightly linked network of purchasing and shipping services was operated to keep coffee prices low in comparison with those on world markets. René De La Pedraja reported that in 1930, attempts by the Federation of Coffee Growers to bypass the foreign-purchasing network failed due to lack of alternative shipping services. It was, therefore, clearly in the Federation's interests to assist GC Line to break the foreign purchasers' monopoly.

In the post WW2 period, the Federation steadily amassed secret reserves of coffee, which were eventually shipped to New York via GC Line. When Grace shipping company became aware of a large amount of coffee, suddenly appearing as if out of nowhere, it began to apply pressure on the US Embassy in Bogotá to lodge formal protests with the Colombian Government, on the grounds that the actions of GC Line' and the Coffee Growers Federation amounted to discrimination against Grace Line vessels. If ever there was a case of the kettle calling the pot black this must be it, given the deliberate and concerted monopoly that Grace Line and associates had been enjoying for years with the transportation of coffee from Colombia to the United States.

To compound the situation for Grace Line, it inexplicably released a copy of its protest to the New York press; news of its objections was soon circulating in Bogotá. Had Grace Line not publicised its complaint, then it was probable that diplomatic protocols would have allowed the note to be formally submitted, gracefully acknowledged but tacitly and diplomatically disregarded by both sides without it being released into the public domain. When news reached Bogotá, local newspapers voiced resounding support for GC Line in its struggle against the American Grace Lines, sufficient to provoke crowds of protestors to attack the US Embassy and ransack Grace Line's offices. Importantly, those trade unions previously opposed to GC Line, thenceforth declared their unconditional support for it. The Oil Workers Union, then regarded as the most powerful and extremist labour organization, announced its intention to strike if the Colombian Government deferred to United States' pressure. Brazil and Argentina also lent their support, and the Venezuelan President reacted by ordering all official Venezuelan cargo to be conveyed on GC Line's ships.[417]

The US Government was, at this time, probably at Grace Line's request, considering the introduction of a boycott of Colombian shipping. This would have caused a great deal of difficulty for the Colombian firm, especially when it needed to have its vessels repaired in US yards. Fortunately for La Grancolombiana, a series of foreign exchange crises forced the Colombian Government to ration already scarce US dollars used in the shipping of imports. Consequently, GC Line allowed shipping companies to pay their freight costs in Colombian pesos, which could not be converted to dollars, and used the local currency to meet debts and expenses incurred in Colombia. Grace Line did not enjoy this currency flexibility and GC Line was soon carrying most of the Colombia bound cargo from the United States. The American shipping company, though, still maintained its near monopoly on coffee exports and most of the northbound freight to the United States.[418]

In April 1948, Grace Line urged the US Government to introduce a Bill prohibiting entry into the US of any foreign shipping line discriminating against US shipping firms. The proposed legislation was intended to subdue GC Line only, but it also penalised other international companies causing US shippers to contest this action. Grace Line continued its anti-Colombia lobbying and, in July 1948, tried to dissuade the US Government from making loans available to the South American nation until GC Line desisted from its intensely competitive practices. The US Government denied Grace Line's petition on the basis that all loan applications were considered on their economic merits.[419] Grace Line was, therefore, unable to prevent La Gran Colombiana from operating a near monopoly on the US to Colombia route.

The Colombian Line withdrew from the ocean conference in June 1950 to deflect accusations of it violating conference rules prohibiting freight payments in pesos. The Colombian firm advised that it would re-join the organisation once the latter was prepared to sanction payments for US to Colombia shipments in the latter's currency. Fears of a rate war caused Grace Line to pause before considering further action. The New York Times remarked on June 3, 1950:

"In New York, shipping conference sources said that the number of ships owned or chartered by Grancolombiana had increased so much that their withdrawal from the conference could prove very harmful to other lines. Colombian bottoms will be favoured not only by Colombian exporters but by American exporters having balances in Colombian pesos".[420]

In order to avoid the inevitable rate war, the ocean conference had no option but to concede GC Line's demands that US southbound freight be paid-for in either dollars or pesos, thus obliging the Colombian Government in August 1950 to declare it legal to convert dollars into pesos to pay shipping charges. The next logical move would have been for GC Line to accept pesos from Colombian coffee exporters for freight payments to the US but the ocean conference anticipating such a step offered to divert 35% of Colombian cargo exports to the GC Line for three years with probable renewal.[421]

Due to the unexpected amounts of cargo GC Line had contracted to transport, the company was obliged in 1948 to charter 9 ships. By 1951, the number of vessels chartered leapt to 23. The USA's massive shipbuilding programme during WW2 had generated a glut of available shipping tonnage, which freight companies tended to lease rather than operate. GC Line found that an ownership and chartering mix suited its needs and achieved considerable savings that were passed-on to shippers as lower freight rates. Even applying half of its savings in this way, the company remained profitable, declaring substantial dividends and redirecting finance towards modernising its vessels.[422] In order to reduce dependency on chartering, the company, in 1948, ordered three new ships from Canadian Vickers, two vessels from Scottish shipyards in 1951 and four from Germany in 1953.

Ocean conferences on European routes maintained artificially high rates, often charging whatever the market could bear, especially on Colombian/Venezuelan routes. In response to demands from shippers in both these countries, GC Line announced its intention, in 1949, to commence a European service, but existing European shipping companies were anxious to block entry of a new competitor to their "*closed*" conference; admission to the latter only being granted by the unanimous vote of existing members. The situation was different in the USA where conferences were required to be *"open"* by law, i.e. all shipping companies operating on a specific conference route had to be admitted to that association. As in the situation that faced the Chilean Line, European shipping conferences were still powerful organisations in the mid 1950s, and those into which PSNC was admitted, conspired to set rates and force non-conference members from European-South American routes to protect its members' interests.[423]

GC Line discovered that different commercial attitudes prevailed in Europe and the US at that time; the North Americans exercising a less rigid class system that encouraged its business community to trade with anyone interested. For the Europeans, a system of business links and suitable contacts were necessary for a shipping company such as GC Line to establish a network of agencies to provide cargo and support operations. Fortunately, the Colombian concern found a suitable associate in the form of the Royal Netherlands Steamship Company (KNSM), founded in 1856. The Dutch company, then overshadowed by the larger European lines, was searching for ways to improve its precarious position in the Caribbean-European trade. Both shipping firms soon realised the advantages of a joint operation; GC Line had connections with shippers in the ports of Colombia, Ecuador and Venezuela, while KNSM could provide reciprocal European facilities.

In September 1950, a joint venture was agreed for a shipping service between Europe and South America, whereby a pool to divide cargo on an equal basis was established with an agreed itinerary; one ship was scheduled to sail to and from

Europe every two weeks and vice-versa, each party contributing one vessel. The arrangement commenced in January 1951, and was so successful that except for some minor amendments, it lasted until January 1980. Moreover, it enabled GC Line to establish and familiarise itself with the European way of conducting business.[424]

Venezuelan shippers, although readily patronising the new European service, were not completely satisfied with the KNSM agreement, requiring the Dutch company to secure Grancolombiana's entry to the European/South Pacific, Magellan and the West Indian Trans-Atlantic Lines conferences. The Venezuelans consistently blamed the shipping conference system for all their country's ills. The first mentioned association extended to the Pacific ports including Colombia and Ecuador; Venezuela was unaffected by this organisation but the second conference covered Colombia's and Venezuela' Caribbean coastal ports. The latter nation's Directors of the GC Line were consequently outraged at what they perceived as a management *"sell-out"*.

Their concern, based on the fears of Venezuelan shippers at being burdened with higher freight rates, caused business houses to insist on the Venezuelan members of GC Line opposing the joint venture with KNSM, despite being presented with irrefutable company data to the contrary.[425] The Venezuelan contingent, having long been dissatisfied, particularly when Ecuadorian members mostly voted with their Colombian colleagues to sideline it, pressed their Government to take reprisals against GC Line. The Venezuelan ruling military junta, with a considerable cash injection renovated the Venezuela-state owned company's ships. This firm founded in 1917 was, by 1950, barely operating, but was granted a new lease of life to lure shippers away from GC Line, especially on routes to the United States. Because of the Venezuela Line's revitalised operation, La Grancolombiana increasingly suffered losses throughout 1950 and 1951 on its Venezuelan services, but due to its overall profitability, especially on routes from the United States, it did not complain to the Venezuelan Government.[426]

Despite a flurry of diplomatic activity and counter-proposals by the other two partners of Grancolombiana, Venezuela issued a Decree requiring her withdrawal from the tri-nations' company in July 1953. Consequently, six Venezuelan-registered ships and later two vessels under construction were transferred to the Venezuela Line as re-imbursement for that country's 45% share holding in GC Line. To offset the reduction of capital caused by Venezuela's withdrawal, Ecuador through the assistance of the state-owned Banco de Fomento, acquired another 10% of the equity to bring her holding to 20%, while Colombia acquired the remainder, principally through the National Federation of Coffee Growers, an arrangement lasting until 1996.

Following Chile's adoption of Cargo Preference in 1956, this protectionist measure soon spread throughout Latin America, and when considered by

Grancolombiana Line, it had already become a standard economic tool for those Governments wanting to expand their merchant fleets in the 1960s and 1970s. From its formation, Grancolombiana had continued to operate, mostly profitably, without Government support and, particularly, without such measures as Cargo Preference enjoyed by the Peruvian and Chilean Lines. Such protectionist instruments were sought by the Colombian Shipboard Union, which in 1960 presented a Bill to Congress.

The latter was not specifically aimed at benefiting the nation's merchant shipping, but rather at applying this strategy to preserve and strengthen labour relations. The Bill, opposed by GC Line's management, did not progress, but having become aware that the unions were preparing to renew their efforts, GC Line, in June 1962, pre-empted such action by presenting its own proposed statute.[427] The company had been experiencing declining profits and anticipated losses in 1962. Capital shortages had always been a problem in maintaining its self-financing mode of operation; Cargo Preference, it believed, was an easy route to raising additional investment finance, especially when *"containerisation"* was seen as the essential way forward.

GC Line knew that the United States had introduced her own protectionist legislation requiring all US Government-financed cargo to be transported in US-registered vessels. Such US-financed cargo was an important element in the North American assistance programme entitled *"Alliance for Progress"*, specifically directed at the Republic of Colombia as a countermeasure to halt the Cuban Communism from spreading throughout Latin America.[428] Accordingly, the Export-Import Bank, the Agency for International Development and other official US bodies, frequently financed cargoes for Colombian destinations. The US Government, having contributed such aid would, reasonably, have wished to use its own merchant shipping and, therefore, none of this cargo could statutorily be conveyed aboard Grancolombiana's vessels.The US agencies were empowered to grant *"waivers"* according to a particular case's merits, but because of constant vigilance and pressure from US shipping lines, these occurrences were rare. Although Colombian ships were often ready to transport cargo when US ships were unavailable, US agencies delayed shipments until national vessels could be found, creating losses and unacceptable delays for Colombian importers.

Inevitable diplomatic pressures failed to bring about changes in policy despite US shipping rates to Colombia being higher than those offered by Grancolombiana. The latter, therefore, sponsored a Cargo Preference Bill in September 1962, backed by Colombian shippers and shipyard unions, but it met with stiff opposition; European and US Governments had been determined to stop the Colombian Government from applying Cargo Preference. Surprisingly, such opposition received the support of dockworkers' unions and commercial concerns from the ports of Barranquilla and Caribbean coastal regions of Colombia, because if Cargo

Preference had been approved, then GC Line, the opponents submitted, would have become a monopoly with insufficient ships to carry all envisaged foreign trade, consequently affecting employment opportunities for tens of thousands of stevedores. The issue caused deep divisions in the labour movement; shipboards unions and workers from the country's interior supported Cargo Preference, but dockyard workers and those employed on the Caribbean coast opposed it. Elites along the Caribbean coastal regions accepted Cargo Preference as a means of obtaining greater benefits, not out of concern for GC Line, but as the price the Colombian Government would have to pay for their ensuring the Bill's safe passage.[429] However, lobbying and pressure applied by the US and foreign embassies caused the Bill to be rejected in 1963.

Under normal circumstances that would have been the end of Cargo Preference, but foreign intervention in Colombia's parliamentary affairs had so angered the nation that when GC Line refused to bury the matter, the Bill began to generate national and emotional sentiment leading to demands for its approval as a sign of the country's strong independence.[430] The population's passionately expressed feelings forced the Colombian Government, in 1965, to adopt emergency powers to quell disturbances. Before these measures were withdrawn, GC Line had persuaded the nation's Executive to issue a Decree authorising the introduction of Cargo Preference and enabling the enactment of later legislation to specify the exact percentage or adjustment to be used according to changing circumstances.

The Decree emerged under the guise of a national defence measure designating the merchant marine as part of the country's national reserve. It was ratified in December 1965, but the Government was reluctant to take further action to obtain the appropriate power to set the exact percentage of Cargo Preference. It had faced considerable diplomatic pressure from the United States, Britain and France, and the recognition that of the 106,000 metric tons of freight imported into Colombia in 1967, only 20% had been conveyed by Grancolombiana's ships.[431] The Colombian Government was also concerned that Peruvian and Chilean Cargo Preference laws would debar GC Line from commercial interchange with those two countries. The statute was enacted in July 1969, whereby Colombian-registered vessels were to convey a minimum 50% of general cargo; when bulk, liquid and refrigerated cargo were transported, the percentage was not to exceed that level.

To prevent any retaliation from other Latin American nations, shipping companies belonging to the Association of Latin American Shipowners were eligible to benefit from the protected cargo percentage if their own nations entered into reciprocal arrangements with Colombian shipping lines.[432] Grancolombiana Line had, after ten years of lobbying, finally secured the benefit of Cargo Preference but, unlike her Chilean counterpart, it did not use this policy to secure admission to the ocean conferences, but rather employed it to justify and ensure it received equal consideration in the transport of US Government-financed cargoes.

By the time Cargo Preference was implemented, levels of the latter freight to Latin America had begun to decline as the US Government's attention was diverted to Vietnam. Those arguments used to oppose Cargo Preference never materialised; no dockers lost their jobs and non-Colombian registered shipping companies continued to carry overseas cargoes of at least 50% capacity. GC Line continued to aggressively entice shippers to it until, on some US routes, it exceeded the 50% threshold required by Cargo Preference rules. By 1980, the latter had actually become a hindrance; the company's own success leading to accusations of it being a monopoly

La Grancolombiana tried to persuade Ecuador to adopt Cargo Preference; it believed that such a measure would protect the 70% of all Ecuadorian cargo it transported. The company was relying on the support of its junior partner, the Ecuadorian state-owned Banco de Fomento with 20% of the shareholding, to achieve this objective, but :

"Grancolombiana officials in the Guayaquil office had failed to detect the emergence of a very radical group of officers inside the Ecuadorian Navy. These officers, the local counterparts of the statist military in Peru, designed Cargo Preference to foster a state-owned fleet. From the start the naval officers considered Grancolombiana as a rival, if not the enemy, and did everything in their power to impede the operations of the company in Ecuador. Whatever, the exact merits of either state or private ownership, any merchant shipping venture has to be first firmly grounded on the cargo volumes, but this was the calculation that the naval officers sometimes forgot to make when they ignored the lessons from the failures of the state-owned Flota Bananera, or banana fleet, in existence since 1965" [433]

This naval officers' group was hampered by a shortage of capital from the start but, in early 1971, it decided to create a new company using two refrigerated ships, the *Río Amazonas* and the *Islas Galápagos* from the near-bankrupt Flota Bananera, together with the four Ecuadorian registered vessels from Grancolombiana. The Flota Bananera blocked the merger and the Ecuadorian President, wishing to continue maintaining close links with Colombia in case of possible conflict with her traditional rival Peru, refused to acquire the four ships from Grancolombiana. On the other hand, not wishing to be seen to oppose the radical naval officers, the Ecuadorian President sanctioned the formation of a new company on September 1971 called "TRANSNAVE". Shortly afterwards, a military junta overthrew the Government and ruled until 1980, the naval officers having failed to gain control. The Ecuadorian Navy, enjoying the military's support for their proposals for the nation's merchant shipping, provided a large percentage of TRANSNAVE's personnel. These comprised active naval officers and crew paid from the military budget. In effect, this form of crewing constituted a virtual subsidy for the company, but there was still insufficient capital to acquire extra vessels to form a fleet.[434]

By August 1972, oil had replaced bananas as Ecuador's principal export, and although providing additional capital for her merchant fleet, revenues were not as large as had been anticipated. Nevertheless, the Ecuadorian Navy directed the bulk of its oil income towards acquisition of a new tanker fleet for Flota Petrolera del Ecuador (FLOPEC), established in September 1972. When Texaco and Gulf tried to export Ecuadorian oil, the Navy blocked the loading of their tankers by enforcing the Cargo Preference ruling that 50% of oil exports be conveyed by national tankers, which it did not then have. It was obliged, therefore, to acquire two oil tankers from Gulf for FLOPEC; these were named *Napo* and *Pastaza*. The former vessel sailed to the United States on June 4, 1973, but her voyage took 25 days instead of the normal 13.

Clearly Ecuador lacked sufficient expertise in this field and in order to learn how to navigate and manage a tanker fleet, she accepted the offer of Kawasaki Kisen Kaisha (KKK) for a ten years' partnership, loan availability of up to 55% of FLOPEC's capital value and an offer to purchase 45% of the latter's share capital. By accepting these proposals, René De La Pedraja calculated that the Ecuadorian Navy was receiving FLOPEC for practically nothing, while KKK anticipated that Japanese shipyards would be favoured with future tanker orders.[435]

FLOPEC, subsequently, acquired two new tankers from Japan in 1975, the *Santiago* and the *Zamora*, but needed to charter additional vessels to export Ecuador's expanding oil production. By 1978, her naval personnel's efficiency had improved sufficiently to prompt the Navy to prematurely cancel its 10 years' contract with KKK, and thus become the sole owner of FLOPEC. The two tankers *Napo* and *Pastaza* were sold that same year. FLOPEC's fleet continued to expand and, in 1980, it ordered five new tankers from Korean shipyards. Four entered service in 1981 and the last arrived in 1982, by which time the oil boom had collapsed and plans for further fleet expansion were placed on hold.

The Ecuadorian Navy, hoping to repeat FLOPEC's success with TRANSNAVE, decided to commence an Ecuador-European operation to avoid the over-provided regular service between Ecuador and the United States. Unsurprisingly, it came into direct competition with Grancolombiana's European service. Cargo volumes, generally, between Europe and Ecuador had been insufficient to support regular sailings, and GC Line had only managed to include Ecuador within its regular European service because Guayaquil was just a very short sailing distance from Buenaventura, the major coffee-exporting port of Colombia.

Accordingly, the Ecuadorian-flagged ships of Grancolombiana, usually arriving in Ecuador with mostly empty holds, left Guayaquil with light loads. This element of the voyage only remained profitable because before proceeding to Europe, the ship loaded valuable coffee exports at Buenaventura and on the return trip; cargo would be discharged on the Caribbean coast before sailing on to that port. The European route, in effect, was subsidizing the trips to Guayaquil simply to acquire small cargoes. TRANSNAVE refused to admit this reasoning, and blamed GC Line for every setback it suffered.

La Grancolombiana had, since 1973, often wished to terminate its Guayaquil service, but national politics and popular opinion rather than economic considerations were more potent forces in both countries; maintaining unity between Colombia and Ecuador was of paramount importance despite TRANSNAVE's animosity to La Grancolombiana. Nevertheless, the newly formed Ecuadorian company, having commenced operations with chartered vessels, purchased its first ship in 1974, the *Isla de Puná* from the German Hapag-Lloyd line, to inaugurate its European service. It found, just as GC Line had discovered, that it needed to gain admission to the *"closed"* European South Pacific and Magellan conference, and in order to do so, it had to join the revenue pool EUROPAC II. The only other pool member on that service was GC Line to which TRANSNAVE had already directed considerable animosity.

It must have given sweet satisfaction in 1974 to Grancolombiana's executives to witness the Ecuadorian company concede their terms for the latter's entry into the Magellan cartel.[436] EUROPAC II, however, proved unsuitable for TRANSNAVE which withdrew in 1979. The oil boom continued to finance the latter firm's trade and expansion; four ships were ordered from Polish yards and new routes were operated with chartered vessels. The oil boom, however, ended in 1981, stifling any further expansion; the Ecuadorian firm soon experienced problems in obtaining cargo for its ships. It responded with plans:

"To participate actively in carrying Colombian coffee exports to Japan and instead will leave aside the fish meal exports from Ecuador because of bad experiences [437] it has had with this product." [438]

Grancolombiana re-routed its vessels to thwart TRANSNAVE's plans to obtain coffee cargoes; the Ecuadorian shipping line countering with secret discounts on freight rates, inaugurated a direct service to the East Coast of the United States to try to increase its coffee-carrying potential from Buenaventura. The service failed, but was revived in 1984 before finally being withdrawn in 1992. Grancolombiana had declined to engage in a cargo rate war, conscious of the need to avoid diplomatic pressure and of national political considerations; it relied on the Colombian Republic's own Cargo Preference law to curtail TRANSAVE.

The situation with Peru's merchant marine had been no less traumatic. Profits made during WW2, having saved the Peruvian Lines from liquidation, had been applied to the purchase of six US-built freighters in 1947. Unfortunately, its management was ineffective and the company, while not suffering any trading losses, could only provide irregular services. Importantly, it failed to make financial provision for vessels' replacements. By 1962, the availability of cargo space became so critical, that the Peruvian Line had to raise loans in England to purchase five used cargo ships as a temporary measure. Its ineffective management, though, paid twice the going rate for them. Shortly afterwards, this company could not even meet the loan repayments. The Peruvian Government, still harbouring a centuries-old ambition to make the country into the main shipping and shipbuilding centre on the WCSA, once again bailed-out the Peruvian Line. It also expanded the naval shipyard Servicio Industrial de La Marina.[439]

Peruvian shippers since 1950, had mostly relied on Grace and Grancolombiana Lines, regarding them as more reliable than the irregular service provided by the Peruvian company. In 1961, a Peruvian Decree imposed a 2% duty on imports to finance the expansion of naval dockyards, and to authorise the fixing of appropriate Cargo Preference percentages. Introduction of the latter was delayed by intensive lobbying from shippers and foreign companies. It was January 1966 before Cargo Preference legislation decreed that 20% of cargo entering or leaving Peru had to be conveyed by Peruvian vessels. However, due to poor supervision by Government authorities, only 2% of the country's shipments were actually conveyed by Peruvian ships between 1967 and 1968.[440]

Surprisingly, in view of the latter data, Peruvian President Belaúnde Terry authorised the Peruvian Line to acquire 18 ships from an assortment of Finnish, Spanish and Italian yards. Unsurprisingly, the Peruvian Navy supported this action, and one of its admirals was appointed as President of the Peruvian Lines' Board of Directors. By the time of his appointment, orders for six of the ships placed with Italian yards were cancelled. The remaining twelve general-cargo ships, constructed to a standard design in the hope of achieving lower maintenance costs, were found to be unsuitable for shipment of bulk products, which formed the major part of Peru's foreign trade.

The Admiral-President, accordingly, wanted to dispose of some vessels, but the military junta, still fostering ambitions to make Peru a world power, overruled him, and instead ordered the naval yard to build whatever bulk carriers the country needed. The yard continued to be subsidised from the 2% import levy. To keep the twelve new cargo vessels actively employed, the Peruvian Government decided in July 1969 that the 20% Cargo Preference regime introduced in 1966 be more strictly enforced.

The United States, as Peru's main trading partner, had been expected to oppose any attempt to curtail Grace Line's share of the Peruvian shipping trade. Grancolombiana Line's ships had also, since the mid 1950s and 1969, carried a major share of the US-Peru cargo shipments from the time the Chilean Line had vacated the Peruvian shipping trade. The Peruvian Government, in December

1969, decreed that only Peruvian vessels could carry customs-exempt cargo; eighty percent of Peru's foreign trade enjoyed customs exemption and foreign shipping companies carried approximately 80% of such cargo. Consequently, this legislation threatened to exclude those foreign shipping companies who had not formed revenue pools with Peruvian ship owners.

Grace Line had already done so in July 1967 and was thus unaffected, but those shippers patronising Grancolombiana were, thenceforth, sidelined. GC Line's trade between Peru and Colombia continued undisturbed, but Peruvian generated cargo, previously conveyed by the Colombian shipping company to the United States, thereafter had to be transported in Peruvian-registered vessels. Peruvian shippers protested furiously and proposals concerning customs-exempt cargo were withdrawn. The Cargo Preference percentage, on the other hand, was increased from 20% to 50%, still substantially less than the 80% required under the Customs exemption cargo rule. With this kind of protection, the Peruvian Line in 1971 became profitable against a background of real economic progress cultivated by the military junta.

By January 1973, the Peruvian economy was beginning to disintegrate; the Peruvian Line's unions began strike action for pay demands to counter rising inflation. The Military Government seized the installation occupied by the strikers and placed union leaders under arrest. The unions agreed to withdraw strike action subject to the Peruvian Line appointing a Commission to re-organise the shipping company, and secured union representation on the Board of Directors; wage increases were promised out of the shipping company's increasing profits.[441]

In 1974, the Peruvian Line took delivery of two bulk carriers built by the state-funded Navy yard, just as world-shipping rates began to rise as a result of the worldwide energy crisis. These high rates caused the Peruvian Line to make the highest profits in its history during 1974/75, but the pace of change set by the military junta could not be sustained, and the downturn in the world economy adversely affected much of the nation's exports. The Peruvian Government was faced with runaway inflation causing a deficit in the nations' balance of payments. Widespread national discontent precipitated a power change; the new regime restrained the unions and re-privatised state enterprises as a prelude to a return to civilian rule in 1980.

The Peruvian Line, shielded by Cargo Preference, expanded during the 1970s and reaped large profits, but by 1980, it had sunk into its old ways of administrative and operational chaos. The lack of an efficient shipping service left the door open for the Chilean Line, then operating the United States-Peru route from which the American Grace Line had been removed in the early 1970s. Given the lack of services provided by the Peruvian Line, the latter increasingly came to depend for most of its income on revenue pools with foreign companies, and resorted to selling a percentage of its own Cargo Preference capacity to foreign companies for a commission. Despite an injection of Government cash in 1982, the company continued its downward spiral, ignoring a golden opportunity to introduce containerisation.

In 1986, the Peruvian Government also swayed by the need to sell spare tonnage capacity to foreign lines, raised the 50% level required to be conveyed by Peruvian Line vessels to 100%, in effect demanding a commission on all cargo carried to and from Peru. This of course benefited the Peruvian Steamship Line. Its initial objective in using Cargo Preference had been to deter the Chilean Line from the United States-Peru route whose 7% share of this service in 1982 had risen to 33% by 1986. Hoping to capture a greater percentage of the service for itself, the Peruvian Line resorted to those tactics successfully employed against Grancolombiana Line in 1970. United States ships, whose share of this trade route had dropped to 24%, paid the required commission to Peruvian Lines in order to maintain its portion of cargo revenue.

The three Chilean companies, CSAV, CCNI and EMPREMAR, having unsuccessfully tried to negotiate with the Peruvian Line, filed complaints with the United States' Federal Marine Commission, actions that were supported by the Chemical Manufacturers' Association, which had been trying to oppose Peruvian legislation. US companies shipping to Peru were well aware that only they and the Chilean shipping lines could provide fast and dependable two-weekly services, while the Peruvian Line could only operate that route once every five weeks. The Chilean Line normally took 20 days to complete the trip, but the Peruvian company needed 30 days. Moreover, the latter could only accommodate 150 container slots per month while the Chilean Line provided 900. Accordingly, US shippers pressured the Federal Marine Commission to impose biting sanctions on the Peruvian vessels.[442]

By July 1986, the Chilean Line had suspended voyages to Peru leaving the Peruvians with almost exclusive use. This only angered Peruvian shippers, who because of the poor service offered by the Peruvian Line, saw their US markets threatened. No Peruvian ship ever arrived on time; the average delay was 12 days and often as high as 35. By February 1987, the Peruvian company was facing bankruptcy, giving rise to rumours that several of her ships would be seized to pay-off debts.[443] To compound its problems, the US Federal Marine Commission announced that with effect March 7, 1988, Peruvian ships were prohibited from entering the United States. Moreover, three of the Peruvian Line's vessel had been detained in foreign ports for non-payment of debts, forcing the Peruvian Government to invite Chilean ships back into its ports.

The Chilean Line resumed services to Peru followed shortly after by other Chilean companies and Grancolombiana Line. The Peruvian company was discredited; four of its small coastal tankers were sold in 1993 to the Chilean firm Ultragas and the Peruvian Government was obliged to repeal Cargo Preference laws as part of a general return to the free market. Accordingly, all shippers, whether Peruvian or foreign, were free to choose whatever shipping line it preferred.

The Peruvian Government, though, was reluctant to liquidate the Peruvian Line on the grounds that the nation needed a merchant fleet in times of war when foreign shipping could be expected to quickly vacate the scene. Repeated clashes with Ecuador had made war a real possibility; conflicts with Colombia or Chile could never be ruled out. The Peruvian Lines' services were gradually suspended while those ships it still possessed, and which were considered unsuitable for wartime duty, were laid-up. By the end of 1995, Peruvian Lines had ceased to exist.

15. Modernise Or Wither. 1946-2000

Following the restructuring of Japan after World War 2, and later South Korea, the Pacific Basin economies developed rapidly. The West Coast republics were particularly well suited geographically to take advantage of trade routes to the "*tiger economies*" on the Pacific Rim. It was noticeable that during the late 1950s and early 1960s, Japanese "*Maru*" ships were as common in WCSA ports as the ubiquitous Grace Line boats.

Aviation was also beginning to establish itself as a passenger medium; air flight was particularly suited to the South American sub-continent and in 1943, PSNC diversified its interests by purchasing a stake in British South American Airways. After World War 2, growth in air traffic developed faster than this company had perhaps anticipated. Its share in the South American airline was forcibly acquired as part of the British Government's nationalization policy, and which contributed to the formation of British Overseas Airways Corporation. Pacific Steam Navigation Company (PSNC), like other European shipping enterprises, would then have undoubtedly assessed the impact of long-haul flight airlines, but at the time of acquiring the liner *Reina del Mar*, a replacement for the *Reina del Pacifico,* the situation was still uncertain.

The North American firm of Moore-McCormack (MM) experienced similar uncertainty when taking delivery of two new combination vessels in 1958, the *Argentina* and the *Brasil,* for its New York to the Atlantic coast of South America service. These cargo-carrying ships each provided luxury accommodation for 550 passengers. MM, realising that the container age was starting to impose itself on the shipping world, and that international airlines were making inroads into passenger services, was unable to dispose of its obsolete passenger liners.

Harland & Wolff of Belfast built the *Reina del Mar* in 1956, at a cost of five million pounds sterling. She grossed 20,750 tons, was fitted with stabilizers and could develop a speed of 18 knots. After disembarking passengers and cargo in Valparaíso, she would sail south to San Antonio, four or five hours away, load-up with copper, and return to the former port to embark passengers for the voyage home. In the early 1960s, her passenger accommodation was rarely full, and there were constant rumours of her disposal. A considerable amount of lucrative European passenger traffic to and from Cuba had disappeared following the seizing of power by Fidel Castro from Batista in 1960. In March 1964, the ship sailed to Belfast, the last time under the PSNC flag. There she was converted to a cruise liner and, thenceforth, managed by Union Castle Line, who eventually purchased her in September 1973.

Reina del Mar. **20,750 tons.**
Passenger accommodation for 207 first class, 216 cabin class and 343 tourist class. Shown here at Princes Landing stage. Liverpool

Should PSNC and other British companies have realised that the future of shipping lay in containerisation? It was probably in the early 1950s that PSNC planned the introduction of the *Reina del Mar*, and in all probability, like other shipping companies, it would not have then envisaged the rapid shift towards that new development. The US Grace Line had only decided to employ containers in 1950 in an attempt to lure cargo away from competitors on the WCSA. At no additional charge, Grace Line offered shippers the option of carrying merchandise within small select containers measuring 8 feet x 7 feet x 7 feet, and capable of holding six tons of cargo.[444] US Shippers were enthusiastic for this new concept; soon more cargo was being diverted from other shipping firms to Grace Line's ships.

In order to meet this competition, Grancolombiana Line began providing cargo containers, and by 1962, owned 450 units; these were loaded at dock terminals and emptied on arrival at port. Some, importantly, remained loaded until they arrived at their final destination in the interior of Colombia. Grace Line then introduced larger and more efficient units holding 18 tons of cargo, and in 1962

Ploughing The South Sea

converted two freighters into the world's first specific container vessels, each able to carry 476 units.

One of the container ships, the *Santa Eliana,* arrived in La Guaira Venezuela in February 1960, only to discover that the dockworkers union refused to unload her until Grace Line signed a manning agreement. It took a further 18 days of discussion before her cargo was finally discharged, but only after the American company had agreed that no further containers would be directed to that port. The *Santa Eliana* was laid up after this incident, and it was not until October 1962 when Grace Line secured a further agreement permitting container handling, that the *Santa Eliana* was allowed into port, followed a week later by the *Santa Leonor,* the second container ship.

Thereafter, container cargo bookings proved disappointing in Venezuela and by 1963, Grace Line was forced to lay-up its two container vessels which were later sold to American Sea-Land, another pioneering container shipping company, for its US coastal trade. Grace Line's unsuccessful experiences in Venezuela did not deter it from pursuing this novel mode of cargo transport. It acquired four new vessels with one third of their cargo capacity given over to containers for servicing the shipping routes to Colombia, Ecuador and Peru. The American company had earlier launched a massive publicity campaign directed at South American shippers with the slogan "*Everything in Containers*".

Grancolombiana was, by 1963, beginning to be affected by the demand for containers and reacted by installing slots for 80 standard size units, or TEUs (twenty feet equivalent units i.e. 20 feet x 8 feet x 8 feet), in six ships already under construction. It had reasoned that although Grace Line had introduced 180 containers' capacity in its vessels, it rarely transported more than 80 units, suggesting to the Colombian Line that this level would be the norm for some years to come.[445] Grace Line then began to carry dry chemical cargoes in containers and refrigerated units were introduced, which were ideal for transporting shrimp from Buenaventura and Guayaquil, thus demonstrating that their use had endless possibilities. Lack of capital caused Grancolombiana Line to delay the introduction of these TEUs, and it inevitably fell behind Grace Line in the container conversion race; huge capital requirements and the advanced technology needed to implement and support these new developments were the two essential ingredients mostly lacking in South America.

National Railroad of Colombia refused to transport containers on its network, an attitude that not only demonstrated its lack of managerial foresight, but which also affected all those involved in containers' usage, whether shippers or transporters. Grancolombiana adhered to its policy of using a maximum of 80 containers on its ships, a strategy subsequently highlighted by the fact that Grace Line was frequently left with too many empty slots on its vessels.

Container ships were technology's answer to long stays in port, as break-bulk cargo, often comprising a mixture of bales, barrels, crates, boxes and other loose merchandise, was slowly loaded and unloaded in lower holds and tweendecks, using gangs of dozens of workers. A study in 2000 by the Australian firm Armadillo Marine Consultants entitled "*Container ships- Just in time logistic liners*" reported that:

"It was not uncommon for a typical 15,000 tons liner to spend 170 days each year in port and a ship in the Australian trades could spend two months on the coast after a month's voyage from Europe. This was inefficiency, which encouraged innovation. The container revolution effectively abolished all the expensive and time-consuming handling that was done to goods, in and out of lorries, trains and warehouses. Loaded into a 20 feet or 40 feet container at the point of origin and sealed; the goods will not be seen again until they are delivered to their final destination. To handle containers and speed them on their way, a whole logistic system has been developed from specialist road and rail transport, ground handling equipment, like straddle carriers and huge gantry cranes in the port terminals"

The largest deep-sea ships available today are able to carry nearly 7,000 twenty-feet equivalent units (TEUs), slotting into racks in ships' holds and stacked on deck up to five high. A single shore gantry crane handling up to 30 lifts per hour ensures that port stays are measured in hours rather than days.

Grace Line was a firm believer in new technology and had tried to implement a strategy termed LIGHTER ABOARD SHIP (LASH). These vessels carried 60 feet lighters rather than containers and were fitted with a special crane to lift the "*barges*" out of the ship into the sea and vice versa. This technology, first appearing in the United Sates in 1969, was found useful in taking military cargo to the Mekong River in Vietnam. Initial indications suggested that faster performance could be achieved without the expensive capital infrastructure required for containerisation. It was discovered, surprisingly, in actual operations that this method was slower and more expensive than containerisation. One would have thought that extensive "*field trials*" would have been conducted before Grace Line had committed to this new development.

Despite this setback, Prudential Lines, having taken-over Grace Line, decided to employ LASH technology on the River Magdalena flowing past the Colombian port of Barranquilla into the Caribbean. Prudential Line's intention was to unload the lighters and bypass the port by sending them up-river to inland unloading points nearest the capital Bogotá. The river network appeared well suited to this technology and the Grancolombiana company became alarmed at its proposed introduction; it could not afford a similar vessel, having already committed itself to containerisation. The Barranquilla port authorities were understandably concerned at this LASH development. Massive civic protests, over which the Colombian

Ploughing The South Sea

Government claimed it had no control, forced Prudential Lines to abandon the idea.

Grancolombiana, while continuing to containerise its services to the United States, lacked the freedom to act on its European routes due to its earlier entry into a very successful revenue pool with Corporación Anónima Venezolana de Navegación (CAVN) and the Royal Netherlands Steamship Company (KNSM) in June 1966. In 1973, the two South American companies created a pool with four Japanese shipping companies for trade routes between the Far East and the Pacific Coast of South and Central America. The Venezuelan Line throughout the 1970s, still exhibiting animosity to Grancolombiana, decided against following the latter's profitable example and expertise, and refused to install container slots on its vessels.

Strong competition inevitably began to emerge and in 1978, the German company Hapag-Lloyd, Harrison Lines and the Dutch KNSM agreed a joint venture for a container service between Europe and the Caribbean and Central American ports, A later development extended this to Colombia and Venezuela. To counter this competition, Grancolombiana Line introduced a container service on its European routes, but the Venezuelan Line refused to follow this lead; in 1981, the more realistic Venezuelan Government overruled it, and the state shipping line was obliged, belatedly, to containerise.

Following upon its 1963 publicity campaign directed at South American shippers, Grace Line introduced containerisation into Chile. By 1969, Valparaíso was already handling 3,827 containers rising to 5,445 the following year.[446] In 1965, the Chilean Line, having undertaken trial runs, concluded that containerisation was the most economical way to move cargo and rapidly introduced them into the company's operations. In 1969, it supported the important principle of "*through billing*". This procedure comprised a single payment and completion of relevant documentation to secure a container's direct and express through-delivery from an inland loading origin, its transportation by road or rail to its departure port, its shipment on a container vessel, its unloading at the destination port and then its conveyance by road or rail to its ultimate inland destination.

Did the Pacific Steam Navigation Company miss the container boat? The English company would surely have been alerted to Grace Line's and Grancolombiana's successes on the United States-Colombia route, and must certainly have had its attention drawn to Grace Line's 1962 publicity campaign "*Everything in Containers*". The author recalls that the Purser's department of the passenger liner *Reina del Mar* received letters in Valparaíso from Grace Line concerning their proposals, which correspondence was dismissively binned on the advice of the PSNC's local officials. As this was directed at South American business houses, one would have thought that at least one of PSNC's managers in Lima, Callao, Antofagasta, Santiago, Valparaiso or Panama would have been alerted to this development. Ten years passed before the 8396 gross tons *Orbita* was built for PSNC with slots for 300 TEUs. It was sold in 1980 to the Chilean Line.

The number of containers passing though Valparaíso in 1976 was 5,621 units, compared with 5445 in 1970; the slow growth in this shipping development being attributed to the intervening political period that convulsed Chile.[447] It is probable that this political climate also weighed against European shipping companies investing in containerisation for shipments to Chile. By 1975, however, European shipping promoted a revival of interest in container transport, which had by then become the preferred model for South American shipping. By mid 1970s, break-bulk cargo facilities in Europe were being quickly phased-out and converted to containerisation, thus obliging trading partner countries to do likewise; capital for such schemes in South America was again scarce. Fortunately, the Inter American Development and World Banks provided financial loans to enable port modernization and construction of new terminals.

In 1975, members of the European/South Pacific and Magellan Conference proposed to their counterpart shipping companies throughout Latin America, the formation of a joint project called the *"Andes Study"* to determine the ideal type of vessel for that trade. Each constituent company was expected to place an order for one ship of a standard design so that construction prices would be comparatively lower. This was a significant opportunity for the Chilean Line, not only to buy time to recover from years of political upheaval, but also to profit from the collective expertise of its competitors. Not until 1978, did the Andes Study complete its task, producing a short list of three types of vessel, a full container ship, a Ro-Ro (Roll-on Roll-off) where vehicles are driven on and off the vessel, and a multi-purpose ship for both containers and break-bulk cargoes.

By 1978, Chile had fully converted to containerisation, the delay being partly attributable to a shortage of capital. The main reason, however, was the easing of foreign pressure; Grace Line activity had compelled Grancolombiana to respond in kind, but W.R.Grace, the parent company, eventually sold Grace Line, which had suffered very heavy costs in converting to container shipping; its successor Prudential-Delta Line was able to containerise all its services to South America in 1983.[448] This delay enabled the Chilean company to progress its own development of this transport technology, but traumatic political upheaval prevented it from completing the transition.

The European members of the European/South Pacific Magellan Conference proposed in April 1979, to proceed to full operation of container vessels. Latin American members, however, concerned that they would fall behind the European firms if this measure was adopted, rejected the proposal; the Chilean Line supported it. Finding the Andes Study's conclusions so compelling, it decided in 1980 to containerise its vessels on the US service, acquiring, in May 1981, two

Ploughing The South Sea

further ships for this purpose. The Andes Study evolved into the *"Project Andes"* and served as the launch platform for a new revenue pool in the European-South American trade. In order to participate, La Sudamericana ordered a new container ship in December 1981, for a price of 53 millions US dollars (£29,450,000 approximately).[449]

Despite the economic depression at the time, Chilean ports were re-vitalised; ship owners were permitted to provide and operate their own dockside and port facilities in attempts to lure back those Chilean shipping lines that had registered under foreign flags of convenience. Chilean shippers were enthusiastic about the return of such shipping companies and, in 1985, persuaded their Government to re-instate tax benefits to those firms undertaking not to register any further vessels outside of Chile. New laws were introduced, once again limiting the entry of foreign ships to coastal trade. Chilean-owned ships began to re-flag in Chile; normal operations began to assume levels where local crews were engaged, and the maritime sector was able to generate a valuable source of income and foreign exchange for the nation.[450]

Interoceánica (CCNI), nationalised, in 1972, by the Allende Government, entered into a partnership, in 1973, with Kawasaki Kishen Kaisha Ltd (KKK), to provide a new liner service between the WCSA and Japan. This was extended, in 1976, to include calls at South Korea, Hong Kong, Taiwan and the Philippines. This link with the Japanese seemed to have given CCNI a new lease of life; in 1977, it introduced a Car Carrier service from Japan to Chile and in 1980, a regular route between Chile and South Africa became operational. As a result of the Japanese partnership, Chile's first container service from Chile to the Far East was introduced in 1980, under the banner *"Andes Express Service"*. CCNI's official history claims that, in 1982, it commenced the first full container service between the WCSA and the Atlantic coast of the United States, as well as starting the first full container service from Europe to Chile, in conjunction with Sea Land Service Inc.

The Pinochet Military Government had intended to return CCNI to the private sector, but in 1973 no company or person other than the CSAV (Chilean Line), had offered a fair price for it. In 1983, the company was partly privatised after the Government accepted a substantially lower offer than that submitted by CSAV; the privatisation process was not finally completed until 1985. CCNI, however, had been left with insufficient resources to replace its ageing vessels and no longer had the benefit of the Cargo Preference safety net. By 1993, its share of the Chilean merchant fleet had declined to just 6%, compared with the CSAV's 22%.

In 1984, the *Andes Express Service* introduced in 1981, was extended to embrace Peru and Ecuador, following a widening of CCNI's partnership with KKK to include Nippon Yusen Kaisha and Mitsui OSK Lines Ltd. The Great Andes Service, a multipurpose operation involving containers and break/bulk cargo transport between Northern Europe, the Mediterranean and WCSA, replaced this in 1986 and a year later, the first car specific carrier service was introduced between the Far East and Chile. CSAV's only serious Chilean competitor had been EMPREMAR, which, since 1973, had also found commercial life much more difficult. In that year, the Government abolished subsidies along with the requirement that Government-financed cargoes be conveyed on EMPREMAR's vessels. Thereafter, it had to compete on equal terms with other firms. Competition was fierce and this company, barely breaking even in 1978, suffered losses in 1979. By 1980, it was in serious financial trouble. Despite putting several of its oil tankers and bulk carriers up for sale, it was on the verge of bankruptcy. These problems, however, did not stem from the poor economic situation, but rather from internal abuses committed by *"favourites of the Pinochet military Government"*. Funds were quietly provided by the national Executive to bail out the company.[451] Despite this cash injection, EMPREMAR continued to accumulate losses until 1984, not becoming profitable until 1986, albeit only on a small scale even after offering substantial brokerage fees to attract shippers. One of its bulk ore carriers, the *Valparaíso,* was wrecked in May 1986, but the insurance money was not used for the vessel's replacement.

After more financial scandals in 1992, and further losses, EMPREMAR halted its service to the United States in 1994; this had been its main source of revenue. At that point, its fleet had been reduced to just one vessel. On the return of democratic Government in 1994, its privatisation was authorised. Only one serious bid was accepted, that submitted by the firm of Salina P. Lobos, a salt producer and EMPREMAR'S largest customer. The latter's disappearance from the main shipping arena signalled the end of realistic competition among Chilean shipping lines. Thirty small shipping companies continued to survive, but the high capital requirements of containerisation and supertankers obliged them to continue to provide services with used freighters. The only Chilean shipping companies large enough to compete with foreign shipping lines were the CSAV and CCNI (Interoceánica).

Although PSNC's disposal of its flagship liner *Reina del Mar* in 1964 undoubtedly lightened the English company's operating costs, its future looked bleak. Alarm bells began to sound for many employees when Royal Mails Lines acquired the remaining interest in PSNC in June 1965, rendering the latter an integral part of the former. A reappraisal of the company, within a policy of inter group switching of vessels, led to the planned disposal of older and less economic vessels. PSNC was targeted for this purge mainly because of the intense competition on the West Coast, and the uncertain political and commercial outlook in South America. The following table gives an idea of the drastic vessel changes that took place within PSNC.

BUILT	VESSEL	TONNAGE	DISPOSAL	
1943	Talca	7219	1953	SOLD
1943	Samanco	6413	1956	SOLD
1945	Sarmiento	6393	1969	SOLD
1946	Santander	6648	1967	SOLD
1946	Salaverry	6647	1967	SOLD
1947	Salinas	6705	1968	SOLD
1948	Salamanca	6704	1967	SOLD
1950	Flamenco	8491	1966	SOLD
1950	Kenuta	8494	1971	Broken-up
1951	Cuzco	8038	1965	SOLD
1954	Cotopaxi	8559	1973	SOLD
1955	Potosi	8564	1972	SOLD
1959	Somers Isle	5684	1970	Laid-up
1959	Eleuthera	5407	1972	Laid-up
1959	Cienfuegos	5224	1968	To Royal Mail

By 1981, the transition to containerisation was well under way in Chile; its benefits in the United States and Europe were greater due to the integration of railways, road transport and ships. In South America, such advantages were not then attained due to the inferior terrestrial transport network. To add to PSNC's difficulties, Grace Line announced, in 1966, a new service that threatened the operation of many shipping firms operating in South America. The North American firm, having purchased one of Moore McCormack's routes, planned to inaugurate a new service extending down the Pacific Coast, passing through the Strait of Magellan to Buenos Aires and thence to Brazil to load coffee. Ships would then retrace this voyage to return to the US Pacific Coast. The Argentinean Line ELMA and the Chilean CCNI were the companies most affected by the Grace Line proposals. The two South American shipping firms in conjunction with Brazilian Lines, were prepared to counter the North American threat but Grace Line eventually withdrew its plans.[452]

The old PSNC "S-class" workhorses, the *Sarmiento, Santander, Salaverry*, and *Salamanca* were sold in 1967; the *Salinas* followed in 1968. They were replaced by vessels transferred from Shaw Saville & Albion, sailing under the PSNC flag as *Orita (II), Oropesa (III)* and *Oroya (IV)* [all 6311 gross tons].

The year 1970 saw the *Kenuta, Cotopaxi* and *Pizarro* transferred to Royal Mail, and the three Island class boats *Eleuthera, Somers Isle* and *Cienfuegos* built specifically for the Caribbean routes, were sold after a lengthy lay-up. The disposal of the *Potosí* occurred in 1972. In 1973, three modern vessels were added to what remained of PSNC's fleet. These were the self-loading ships the *Orbita (II), Orduña* and *Ortega (II)*; the capacity of each one of these vessels was almost equivalent to the combined total of four PSNC's S-class ships. In 1980, ironically, the *Orbita* was sold to one of PSNC's oldest competitors, the Compañia Sudamericana de Vapores

mv Santander **(S-Class)**

The impact of containerisation, self unloading ships and larger vessels, led to the development and integration of modern special facility docks such as those at the new UK container ports Tilbury, Felixstowe, Immingham, Plymouth, Southampton and elsewhere. The older ports, following the general trend, have mostly relocated their operations to new deep-water positions at river mouths or estuaries leading to their respective old ports. The historic Ecuadorian port of Guayaquil now has its Terminal Maritimo located about six miles outside the City. In Liverpool, a large sector of the old docks and many of the old port's massive warehouses have been demolished. Some have been converted to luxury apartments and office accommodation; several modern hotels have been constructed along the riverside, close to the world famous floating Pier Head, which once attracted countless passenger vessels from all over the world. This transformation is in keeping with the general trend of many ports throughout the world, often incorporating modern marinas in the re-developed former dock areas.

About two miles from the Canada Dock, which together with its neighbouring Huskisson Dock, provided the former principal cargo berths for PSNC vessels, a new Royal Seaforth container berth has been constructed. This complex, with its massive cargo handling capacity, is about as far up the River Mersey as ships now proceed. It is quite rare to see vessels passing beyond that point, and those that do are usually small coastal craft, ferries and the occasional visiting cruise liner.

Royal Seaforth Docks Container Terminal.
Photo courtesy of Ron Davies Liverpool Photo Library

Valparaíso has also undergone a considerable transformation. It is hard to imagine that the calm image of Valparaíso Bay can be an arena for sudden and vicious northeast winds that have struck with such tragic impact on ships moored there. Valparaíso has embraced the wind of change quite effectively with its modernization process and the move to containerisation handling. An enterprise called TPS (Terminal Pacífico Sur de Valparaiso) acquired a 20 years lease on the Port's No. 1 Terminal. It covers an area of 16 hectares of which 13 are allocated specifically for container stacking. The terminal comprises five berths, intended to increase to six, which can be serviced simultaneously. The Europe-South America Lines (Eurosal) consortium currently enjoys a permanent berth there. This enterprise was formed from five shipping companies: Hapag Lloyd, Hamburg Sud, P&O NedLloyd, Compañia Sudamericana de Vapores and CGM-CMA. The Pacific Steam Navigation was a member of the Eurosal consortium, having committed *Andes III* to the pool. This latter vessel was, in 1985, the only remaining sign of that shipping company.

Valparaíso's Maritimo Terminal.

ss. Andes. Furness Withy owned but assigned to PSNC. She was constructed to operate as one of seven ships on the Eurosal service. The vessel had a self-unloading gantry for use at ports where no container cranes were available. Reproduced from "Liverpool Docks. Four decades of Change", courtesy of Philip B. Parker

Eurosal operates a weekly service between Europe and Valparaíso. Chile, according to TPS,[453] is the principal market for the European Community. So successful has this terminal been that TPS has managed to entice Evergreen, the Taiwanese shipping company, to Chile for the first time. The extra annual tonnage passing through Terminal 1 arising from the Evergreen's contract with TPS is estimated to be 200,000 tons. On the West Coast, as elsewhere in the world, ports large and small have had to modernize to survive.

Wallace G.Carter, a Purser on the Company's passenger liner ss *Orca* in the 1920s, retraced his voyages along the West Coast in the early 1970s, gathering information for his book "*Where the Incas Trod*". When visiting Callao, he recorded the benefits gained from a US 5 million dollars (£2,800,000 approximately) modernization programme for the expansion of port facilities, including the provision of 16 gigantic grain storage silos and extensive docking areas, a five-berths pier, cold storage warehouses, and a transport system fully able to cope with the increasing volume of imports and exports. Carter also noted that considerable progress had been achieved in shipbuilding; yards had been provided, which at the time, were constructing vessels up to 13,000 tons to strengthen the Peruvian merchant fleet. The Port of Callao, in 1973, had one dry-dock and two floating docks capable of accommodating vessels up to 5000 tons. Plans were also in hand, in association with a Japanese shipyard, to provide yards capable of building tankers up to 200,000 tons by 1976.

In July 2002, Lima's El Comercio daily newspaper announced that enormous ships were unloading at Callao. Activity in the port, it wrote, was unceasing and levels of cargo movement amounting to 11.3 million tons in 2001 had made it the most important port in Latin America. Nevertheless, it warned, giant steel freighters were arriving from all over the world, only to find that some of the port's infrastructure was almost obsolescent. It quoted the local Mayor as declaring that it was necessary to re-shape the port's development in view of the worldwide assortment of ships that visited Callao, only to encounter stowage-handling problems in the docks. The Lima newspaper recommended that the port needed to be supported by the installation of new cranes and similar equipment, which were then lacking. Commenting that the Empresa Nacional de Puertos (National Ports Authority) had estimated that restructuring would cost US218 million dollars (£121,000,000 approximately), it still considered that carrying out such redevelopment would make Callao one of the leading ports in the world.

Even the smaller ports on the Peruvian coast have modernized. Salaverry in the early 1970s was an important sugar exporting outlet, which used to load and unload cargo by lighter. Vessels now go alongside purpose-built docks to accept full cargoes of other commodities such as mineral ore. The port's two piers can now accommodate vessels of up to 20,000 tons. Typical of the modernization process and changes in trade was the development, in 1953, of the small port of San Juan, about 250 miles south of Lima. It was specifically developed to ship high-grade blast furnace iron ore from the Marcona mine about 18 miles inland. According to Wallace Carter, production advanced so rapidly that, by 1960, a concentrating plant was installed at San Nicholas Bay where a dock was constructed. Shipments from the new port began in 1962 and, by 1965, San Juan had been phased out as an exporting port. The entire Marcona output amounted to ten million tons of ore concentrates, of which 80% was exported to Japan.

In December 1971, Marcona Mining secured a contract to undertake a US26 million dollars (£14,500,000 approximately) expansion programme aimed at improving docking and loading facilities, and increasing speed and operational capacity. Up to December 1971, the largest visiting ship had a loading capacity of 165,000 tons. Similar restructuring has taken place at other small ports, which, in the 1960s, still employed lighters to ferry cargo to and from vessels anchored in the open sea.

Those ports heavily involved in processing fishmeal, have felt the most telling change. Mention of this commodity will surely bring back painful memories for many cadets and deck officers. A close watch had to be kept when loading bags of this finely ground material; some occasionally fell from the loading slings into the sea. Standing instructions required that damp or wet bags be returned to shore via the lighters. However, once recovered from the water, the lighter men, when the supervising cargo officer was deliberately distracted, would furtively place them back in the next load. Loading wet bags had to be avoided at all costs; often halfway across the Atlantic, wet or damp fishmeal cargo had a habit of smouldering, growing hotter with each passing day; the smell was sickening. The vessel was often met on arrival by fire tenders.

By 1965, according to Wallace Carter, a tremendous amount of money had been invested into the Peruvian fishing industry, 40% of which was foreign-owned, mostly by United States' corporations. Peru then claimed to produce 45% of the world's total fishmeal supplies,[454] earning US230 million dollars (£128,000,000 approximately) in the 1969/70 seasons. The Peruvian Ministry of Fisheries revealed at that time, that there were 123 fishmeal plants along the 1400 miles coastline, served by twenty-three ports.

PSNC used to convey considerable fishmeal cargoes to Britain, but availability of this commodity was subject to the vagaries of the phenomenon known as El Niño. Every year about Christmas time, hence the name, El Niño (the boy child), flows from the north into the Humboldt Current, but usually no further south than northern Peru. However, every seventh year, the current flows much further south, causing the plankton on which the anchovies feed to migrate to cooler and greater sea depths. Apart from problems caused by over-fishing, the El Niño affect can cause further severe shortages, which, in turn, affect exports and shipping. In 1972, the Peruvian Ministry of Fisheries deemed the whole of the 1972/73 fishing season as a write-off. A seven-years loan of US70 million dollars (£39,000,000 approximately) was made available to avoid liquidation of some of the fishing companies, but this did nothing to alleviate lost cargo revenue for PSNC and other shipping companies during a very lean period.

Ploughing The South Sea

Change comes to everyone eventually; even the Panama Canal with its proud motto "*The land divided-the world united*" has been subjected to it. By 1964, there were approximately 100 merchant vessels that were too wide and 600 ships, when fully laden, too deep to negotiate its locks. The canal's significance for the United States Navy has also diminished as a result of her aircraft carriers now being too large to pass through it, and her developing and transferred reliance on military aircraft and missile systems. An alternative Nicaraguan waterway is still officially under United States' consideration; a sea level canal without locks had been reported as a feasible proposition and, in 1964, the estimated costs of excavating a canal through Nicaragua using nuclear explosives were US1093 million dollars (£607,250,000)[455]. The subsequent Nuclear Test ban Treaty, however, thwarted any such plans.

The once invulnerable looking Grace Lines also finally succumbed to the affects of change in the world economies. This company acquired by Prudential Line in 1970 was renamed Prudential-Grace Lines. In 1974, the name changed to plain Prudential Lines. All Grace Lines' former passenger ships were sold to Delta Lines. Some shipping concerns have been more adaptable and responded to the challenge that changing trade patterns brought. Those shipping firms that were most likely to succeed were those able to operate on the Pacific Rim. They are likely to continue to be profitable as Far East economies continue to develop rapidly.

CCNI's *Potrerillos* **leaving Seaforth Container Docks.**
Photo: courtesy Philip B. Parker.

The West Coast of South America is strategically situated to take advantage of these opportunities, as the stoic Chilean shipping companies, the Compañia Sudamericana de Vapores (CSAV) and the Compañia Chilena Naviera Interoceánica (CCNI) have done. Other British and European companies, like the Pacific Steam Navigation and Royal Mail Steam Packet Company, found that circumstances militated against them. There was little, if anything, that could have been done without massive injections of capital, which due to their size, they could not possibly have hoped to raise by themselves. Even the mighty Grace Line could not provide for its continued existence; it was consumed by the massive cost demands of containerisation. Grace Line, like The Pacific Steam Navigation Company and Royal Mail Lines, have been integrated into larger and more capital rich units, their operational identity lost, but their names and memories committed to history.

16. Conclusions

By the end of the 18th Century, the Spanish colonial system had developed sufficiently to generate substantial commercial sailing-ship movements along the West Coast of South America (WCSA); vessels had gradually improved in size and in the use of technology. The North Americans and the English were adding to the number of voyages following the liberalisation of West Coast ports to meet a continuing and growing demand by the region's residents for European manufactured goods. In the first quarter of the 19th Century, many foreign business houses were attracted to and settled on the American sub-continent, bringing with them that valued expertise and capital craved by the newly independent republics. Their presence and business activities promoted an increasing merchant maritime activity that was clearly well organised at the beginning of the 19th Century.

Three factors contributed to a technological jump in the evolution of West Coast merchant shipping. Firstly, land communications on the WCSA were either non-existent or extremely difficult and hazardous; travel and transport of goods mostly depended on shipping. The London Times newspaper, in 1838, reported a population of 4 millions extending from Valparaíso to Panama, over 2500 miles of coastline embracing approximately 35 ports; 9000 travellers a year were conveyed by sailing ship. Secondly, sailing ship voyages were slow and unreliable in a region where calm conditions and unfavourable light winds prevailed. Accordingly, there was a clear, strong and unsatisfied demand for any mode of transport that would significantly reduce the duration of such voyages.

Thirdly, there was the desire of the West Coast Governments to harness new technological developments created by the enlightened Anglo Saxon and European powers for the benefit of their own nations, together with the finance and expertise needed to introduce and implement them. This desire to embrace new technology was also heightened by military considerations. In the first quarter of the 19th Century, West Coast Governments realised that strong and viable national merchant fleets were essential to their national defences. Deep mistrust and animosity between Peru and Chile had steadily intensified as each sought to make their principal and respective ports of Callao and Valparaíso the dominant maritime trading centre. Liberator Bernardo O'Higgins, dreaming of a Chilean alliance with Great Britain, had wanted to encourage the formation of a merchant marine superior to that of the United States. It is clear, therefore, that political, economic and social conditions, in the first quarter of the 19th Century, were very conducive to the introduction of steamships.

In these circumstances, should William Wheelwright have been credited as the steamship pioneer on the West Coast of South America? He had, by 1826, established a prosperous trading concern in Guayaquil. His prestige and influence

Conclusions

were such that he was appointed as the United States Consul in that port, a position that he also later held in Callao. He would, consequently, have been aware of steam-powered riverboat development on the Colombian River Magdalena, sanctioned by Simón Bolívar in 1823, and probably also, of the appearance of steamships in Brazilian waters in 1819. He had also revealed to his biographer, Juan Bautista Albérdi, how Fulton's late 18th Century steamboats had impressed him. He would also have been alerted to the first appearance of a commercial steamship in the South Pacific in 1821, when the sailing bark *Telica,* having been fitted with a steam engine in Guayaquil, was tragically blown-up, whether accidentally or deliberately by her frustrated young captain.

Wheelwright had certainly noted the naval success of Admiral Cochrane's steam war ship the *Rising Star* in 1822. Accordingly, no credit can be bestowed on him for having introduced marine steam technology to South America decades after it had already appeared. Neither was Wheelwright the first to have solicited a Decree from the Chilean Government for the sole concession to launch a steamship enterprise in her waters. That accolade must be reserved for North American Daniel S. Grisnold in 1821. Chilean President Bernardo O'Higgins had backed Grisnold's application for a fifteen years' period of exclusive rights to operate a steamship service in Chilean coastal waters. In support of his petition, Grisnold had even identified the lack of sea links between the Chilean northern and southern provinces, an issue that was still not addressed for the next thirty years.

O'Higgins had envisaged that regular steamship services would pass through the strategic Strait of Magellan, presenting Chile with commercial and military advantages over other West Coast nations. He saw Grisnold's proposals as the catalyst for the fulfilment of his national ambitions, prompting him to grant Grisnold a Decree for an exclusive ten years' privilege to operate 750 tons steamships in Chilean waters. It is not known why Grisnold had not taken-up this concession; possibly negotiations on the terms of subsidies and/or other conditions broke down. Unluckily for Grisnold, O'Higgins' popularity was waning at that time; opposition, therefore, railed against the latter's support for proposals to introduce the steamship service rather than against its feasibility.

Clearly, Wheelwright cannot be truly labelled a steamship pioneer when fourteen years had elapsed before his own scheme was submitted. But why did Wheelwright's plan receive considerable support when Grisnold's failed? The latter, it seemed, not only got his timing wrong, but also backed the losing horse. When Grisnold appeared on the scene, O'Higgins' power and influence were becoming so ineffective, that Chilean politicians generally sidelined any proposals he espoused. Wheelwright, on the other hand, had attracted and cultivated contacts with many very influential people, for example Lord Scarlett, Admiral Cochrane, the extensive business community of Valparaíso, and not least, the

Ploughing The South Sea

politically powerful and influential business figure of Diego Portales, the unofficial ruler of Chile at that time.

Opinions of these prestigious and influential élites, Portales especially, either coincided with, or were shaped by Wheelwright's convictions and proposals to introduce a merchant steam shipping service. Some identified the commercial advantages his scheme would provide, others would have undoubtedly perceived benefits for the military. Portales who, by his own ambitions for the nation's shipping infrastructure, smoothed the way for Wheelwright to obtain the required privileges; Grisnold only had the declining influence of O'Higgins.

Is there anything for which Wheelwright should be applauded? One can only judge his accomplishments and qualities by 19th Century standards. The conduct and moral codes of contemporary historians and business acquaintances, who observed and recorded his activities, were vastly different from today's highly regulated business requirements and ethics. Wheelwright's main successes derived from being able to frequent the most influential of social circles, and an ability to convince business communities and Government executives of the plausibility of his proposed enterprise. His influence even extended to regular meetings with Chilean and Peruvian Presidents. With the assistance of local commercial undertakings, he convinced the Peruvian Executive to follow Chile's action in awarding him its steamship concession. Peru, probably, would have done so in any case, not wishing to fall behind her southern rival. She would also have calculated that his proposed enterprise would not only give Peru greater access to Great Britain, then the world's financier, but perhaps saw his proposed shipping company as a possible source for securing future loans, as was her custom with foreign business houses.

Promoting his ideas was one thing, raising the necessary capital and implementing them was another. Had Chile been able to raise the necessary finance, she probably would have introduced a steamship operation herself; she had, by that time, made longer-term plans for such provision through the Strait of Magellan *"to make Chile the Emporium of European commerce in the Pacific"*.

Despite Wheelwright's efforts to launch his scheme on the West Coast, he encountered opposition in both Peru and Chile. Such resistance was founded on a reasonably held premise that the Great Powers were reluctant to finance his venture because it was too risky, dependent on supplies of coal not readily available. Perhaps to sway doubters, Wheelwright had already convinced many that the United States Government would financially support his scheme. This was a highly relevant factor generating significant support. Wheelwright's claim, however, was untrue, but he may have honestly thought, at the time, that he would receive such financial backing from the United States Government given his previous position as American Consul, and the excellent business reputation he had acquired in Guayaquil. Certainly, confirmation of United States' involvement would have been welcomed by the West Coast nations; they had insisted that his enterprise be formed either in the United States or in Great Britain. On returning to his native land in 1836 to secure such US Government funding, he found that the more extensive influences of William H. Aspinwall and his financier associates had already secured promises for funding towards the Panama Railroad and the proposed connecting shipping lines on the Atlantic and Pacific coasts. More notably, Aspinwall had already submitted plans for a steamship service along the WCSA.

It is clear, therefore, that if Wheelwright had not proceeded with his steamship enterprise, then someone else surely would have done so. The Government of Chile was similarly convinced. In fact, it had concluded a back-up arrangement in case Wheelwright had failed to deliver his part of the contract; the concession would then have transferred to Pedro Allessandri who was then successfully operating a sailing packet service between Callao and Valparaiso. Success and heroic status would, inevitably, have been bestowed on whomever introduced a West Coast steamship service, such were the widespread expectations of the proposed operation throughout Chile and Peru. The élite ruling class needed to promote their heroes, not only to justify to their respective nations and the outside world, that their method of government was the correct and only way to progress, but also to ensure that that their system was sustained, thus preserving their privileged lifestyles.

In promoting his scheme, Wheelwright had emphasised the availability of abundant coal resources on the West Coast, especially in the south of Chile. Admittedly, he was not alone in highlighting this fact; highly placed and respected individuals, such as Lord Scarlett and Admiral Cochrane, had resolutely confirmed its existence in Southern Chile, as had Bernardo O'Higgins and Grisnold in 1821. Wheelwright though, did not appear to have assessed whether it had been practical to extract this resource, and certainly, there is no evidence that he had actually commenced or even planned mining operations until the two pioneering steamships were forced to lay-up because of coal shortages.

The Editor of the Mining Journal had confirmed in 1845 that there existed abundant supplies of coal and iron ore on the West Coast of South America, the only thing it needed, he claimed, was the means to mine it. If coal had been in abundant supply, and this fact was clearly broadcast by Wheelwright's widely circulated prospectus, the question must be raised as to why shipments of coal were sent out to the West Coast; it would have been logical to mine the coal locally or arrange for its extraction by a third party. Wheelwright proved, by his later efforts to acquire a mining lease in Talcahuano, that he knew of the precise location of this coal resource. He had informed the National Institute in Washington in September 1842, that after working the mines in Talcahuano, he had been able to supply his two steamships with coal, *"which had been used very successfully*. It must have amounted, therefore, to a serious failing on his part, a fault possibly shared with the then Board of Directors, not to have organised such essential mining operations before the launch of the two pioneering steamships, and thus avoid their three months' lay-up.

Finance for Wheelwright's steamship venture was eventually forthcoming in the UK, once the British Government had granted the young Pacific Steam Navigation Company its Royal Charter, and offered it mail contracts to make the overland link via the Isthmus of Panama with Royal Mail Steam Packet Company, a viable proposition. The formation of the latter company and the British Government's desire for rapid mail services to and from the WCSA must have provided a more powerful rationale for Wheelwright's proposals. The success of the *Great Western* in crossing the Atlantic must also be accepted as contributing to the contemporary notion that investment in steamships was a risk worth taking.

Wheelwright's influence and efforts in selling the merits of his proposed enterprise were faultless, but his rush to select iron plating for the hulls of the two pioneer vessels suggests an impetuous dash to embrace new technology without considering all the implications of its use on the West Coast. Iron hull construction was then clearly cheaper than its timber equivalent, and had a longer life span, barring accidents. On the negative side, it was relatively untried on the WCSA where related repair facilities were non-existent. These material requirements, which should have been foreseen, were not established until after the steamship *Chile's* accident, indicating initial shortcomings in operational planning.

Wheelwright's greatest assets and major contribution to the PSNC operation were his influence and status within the élite ruling class and business community. His initial organisational ability, on the other hand, in view of the lack of strategic supplies of coal and absence of adequate repair facilities, must be regarded as suspect. PSNC's London Board of Directors certainly had a case against Wheelwright, on this basis, when trying to dismiss him, but his influential connections and his popular personality seemed to have won him through. Added to which, were the Board of Directors' own failings in purchasing the unseaworthy sailing ship *Elizabeth,* contrary to the advice of the Lloyds' Inspector, loading her with coal and then having to sell both without her ever having left the dock. The Board had also dispatched the *Portsea* with coal to the West Coast without ever having tested her cargo for quality. Wheelwright was thus able to use these error prone events to deflect valid criticism from himself.

Wheelwright had probably also taken advantage of internal company politics to protect his position. Many of the shareholders were from Liverpool and Manchester; they had wanted the newly formed PSNC's headquarters to re-locate to Liverpool, but the London Board had refused. It is likely that the northern contingent, aided and abetted by Wheelwright, used the latter's accusations to dismiss the London directors as an effective weapon in this strategy.

So why was Wheelwright given so much acclaim? Recall that he belonged to an élite class at a time when it needed to identify its heroes, possibly to fortify its own position in society, but more probably, to stand as an example of the achievements of European and Anglo Saxon technology and enterprise in the young independent South American countries. To encourage others from the Great Powers to follow their example, it was fashionable for contemporary historians to eulogise at least one individual from amongst their ranks who had brought benefit to the nation, that is, for the élites themselves.

Wheelwright's proposed steamship venture was truly adventurous, certainly firing the imagination of the public and press in particular. The London Times alluded to him as the *"Father of the (PSNC) company"*. The vessels' arrival in Peru and Chile had provoked even more press coverage, resulting in huge celebrations in Valparaiso and Callao. Public expectation of immediate success had been immense, and one that was significantly raised when the two vessels sailed triumphantly into their respective ports.

Chilean honours were heaped on Wheelwright; his portrait was especially commissioned, medals were struck to mark his steamships' success and a statue was erected in his honour, despite some achievements attributed to him being the work of others. He did not undertake, for example, the establishment of a gas distribution network in Valparaiso, only being involved in the project at one stage. Such was Wheelwright's reputation as an entrepreneur that, it seemed he only had to become associated with a successful project for him to be credited with having pioneered it. It is possible that any proposed project was then considered a sound investment if Wheelwright was involved at some stage. Wheelwright was also credited with founding the Caldera to Copiapó railway as if its construction was intended to benefit Chile as a whole. The line was only constructed following discussions between the Chilean President, Wheelwright and a group of businessmen in that region. Its objective was simply to deliver copper and nitrates to PSNC vessels and to convey supplies to the mines.

After his initial setbacks with lack of coal and repair facilities, Wheelwright's organisation did bear fruit, but his subsequent success was established not only on his ability to engage with and influence highly placed contacts, but also as a result of fortunate and timely economic and political circumstances over which, neither he nor PSNC, had any control. The Californian Gold Rush, for example, caused many Chilean merchant ships to be sailed north to San Francisco where they were abandoned, thus leaving a vacuum for PSNC ships to fill. Lack of meaningful competition in the company's early years, particularly on the southern provinces' routes, contributed hugely to the English company's good fortune.

Did Wheelwright bring meaningful benefits to the West Coast of South America? He undoubtedly enabled, but not intentionally, spin-off employment for stevedores and office workers, and as a result of engaging those firms specialising in providing supplies, stores and cleaning services for the vessels. There is, however, no evidence to suggest that PSNC, during Wheelwright's tenure as West Coast Marine Superintendent, directly contributed to the social fabric, welfare or educational structures on the WCSA. On the other hand, it is clear that a substantial number of poorer people were able to travel more efficiently on PSNC steamships, although the majority appeared to have travelled as deck passengers. This class of passengers may have previously voyaged in similar conditions aboard sailing ships; their journeys would have been longer and more arduous. Accordingly, one could argue that PSNC provided the means of improved sea-travel for everyone. It is also acknowledged that PSNC vessels transported foodstuffs and other essential merchandise when trading between Peruvian and Chilean ports. In these terms, Wheelwright's scheme did benefit a wider sector of the WCSA than the élites.

While it is undeniable that Wheelwright and PSNC enabled other business houses to achieve their own commercial successes, their profits like those of PSNC, were mostly repatriated to Great Britain, the United States and Europe, adding pressure on the currencies of the respective West Coast nations. Moreover, whatever benefits Wheelwright and PSNC brought to the West Coast nations, they tended to consolidate the most favourable position of the resident élite ruling class who, for much of the 19th Century, had taken steps to keep the majority population disenfranchised.

The simple answer, therefore, is that the Peruvian and Chilean nations hardly benefited directly from his works, it was the élite minority who believed that they alone comprised these nations who gained. If Wheelwright is to be judged by the ruling classes' own standards, then, of course, his reputation and achievements are beyond reproach, but it is unfortunate that, in terms of historical accuracy, this exaggerated version has been allowed to perpetuate.

Did the West Coast nations, Chile in particular, use the English company for their own ends? It is quite evident, overall, that they did. Wheelwright had warned that those concessions that were due to expire in October 1850 might not be renewed, and that the West Coast nations would eventually demand a greater role in merchant shipping. The Chilean Government had not then intended to automatically renew the concession granted to PSNC, the inference being that if Chile had been sufficiently powerful financially, she would have taken express measures to ensure the development of her own merchant steam fleet. One also needs to take account of the business community's constant fear, one that lasted well into the next century.

Chilean business houses relied upon shipping for exports and imports; maintenance of low freight charges was their utmost concern. If a steamship company was seen to operate as, or perhaps show signs of becoming a monopoly, then pressure would have been applied to provide suitable competition. Many suspected that if PSNC's licences were renewed, a monopoly would be created in the process, and in this eventuality, freight rates would be set as high as the economy could bear. The Chilean Commission formed to enquire into the matter of renewing PSNC's licences, and of providing a specific steamship route to the southern provinces, was the result of intense business community pressure for its introduction; it was still then favourably disposed to PSNC. Many of its members were also business associates of the English company and fully aware of its operational capabilities.

This advisory body, therefore, recommended the renewal of PSNC's licence, but advised the Chilean Government to retain the right to contract with other enterprises to provide a direct steamship service through the Strait of Magellan to carry mails to Europe, United States and the West Indies. One could argue that the Commission only acted out of loyalty to PSNC, but the reality was that the Commission believed that the English company was the only one then capable of undertaking the service to the southern provinces, and not only of providing a European service, but also of meeting the requirements of the then existing concession. The business community, by initially supporting Henry Griffin's proposed Chile-European route, demonstrated that it had not cared who provided those services, as long as they were introduced and continued in operation.

PSNC was awarded the Southern service with generous subsidies, but only by default, due to the failure of smaller companies when trying to launch a Chilean operation, and the disappearance of Griffin's proposed steamship line following the ending of the war with Spain. Chile's merchant fleet then comprised 276 vessels, only seven of which were steamships and the English company was, therefore, able to dictate some of the terms of the concession. For example, the removal of the requirement to call at the port of Constitución, where entry was made difficult by the presence of a submerged sandbank across the river mouth. This had already caused the failure of one small shipping company.

PSNC was at the forefront in using new technology in its steamships. This was probably one of the practical reasons why the Chilean Government had decided to use the English company to cultivate economic links with the outside world. Not only did it see this firm as a bridge between itself and the financially powerful Great Britain, but it also saw it as a means of establishing an alternative shipping route via the Strait of Magellan.

The 1850 Clayton-Bulwer Treaty had been signed because of rivalry between Great Britain and the United States in the Caribbean. The two nations had agreed that there would be joint control over any *"inter oceanic canal"* but this treaty, therefore, did not cover the Panama Railroad completed in 1855. The railroad allowed PSNC and Royal Mail Steam Packet Company to interact more efficiently, and facilitated the conveyance of cargo and passengers across the Isthmus. Chile saw this railroad as militarily benefiting Peru and a threat to her own trade; a direct steamship route through the Strait of Magellan to Europe was, therefore, a better alternative for her.

In 1853, Henry Griffin had been given a ten years' Chilean concession along with a £12,000 annual subsidy to operate a propeller driven steamship service from Caldera via the Strait to Liverpool, operating six 1500 tons steamships. Strangely, PSNC had shown no previous interest whatsoever in this service, at least not officially, possibly because its arrangement with the Panama Railroad Company was likely to be very profitable and, probably, because PSNC was aware that technology had not then advanced sufficiently to sustain an economic steamship service between Chile and Liverpool.

It may well have concluded that the chances of Henry Griffin's scheme failing were quite high, and that in this event, it would step-in with a substitute scheme at the appropriate time and exact better terms from the Chilean Government. PSNC had also not demonstrated any interest in operating monthly steamship voyages to Ancud in the South of Chile when tenders had first been invited. It only submitted a bid when smaller and under-capitalised shipping firms had failed miserably to provide the contracted level of service.

This failure had provoked calls by the Valparaiso press and business community to support the English company with large subsidies, because they believed that it was then the only shipping company capable of maintaining that operation. PSNC, accordingly, might have reasonably believed that if Henry Griffin's scheme did not materialise, it could count on the same kind of support from press, business community and the Government, given the absence of other interested parties.

The War with Spain had provided a large slice of good fortune for PSNC; the Chilean Government had been obliged to put the European service on hold. Two years later, in 1864, Henry Griffin's British South American Steamship Company had vanished without trace. As PSNC had possibly envisaged, the press and public raised new demands, so anxious were they to have a European service. The Government, accordingly, invited new bids but only that of PSNC was received. The period of the contract was extended from 10 years to twelve and a further grant of £3360 pounds was paid annually for carrying the mails to Europe. Other West Coast nations followed Chile's action and awarded their own subsidies. By 1868, PSNC had commenced its European service, thus avoiding the need to transfer passengers and cargo over the Isthmus.

The strong desire and support of the Chilean business community, the press and the Chilean Government for the introduction of the European operation, provides some foundation for the belief that Chile's Executive provided clandestine support, if not outright encouragement, in PSNC's spat with the Panama Railroad Company. Whether the English shipping company was being deliberately used by the Chilean Government or vice versa, the European arrangements were mutually beneficial. March 1869 saw the introduction of a monthly Liverpool to Valparaiso

Conclusions

service; steam engines began to improve, providing important cost savings; the British Government paid out more grants to construct larger steamships, and by 1872, the Strait of Magellan was the route for most European commerce to the Pacific.

If PSNC's dispute with the Panama Railroad had been a major turning point in the development of merchant shipping on the WCSA, then another contributory factor had been PSNC's inability to effectively apply its customary ruthless tactics to a small Chilean steamship company the Sociedad del Vapor Paquete del Maule. This company was named after its only vessel, *Paquete del Maule,* delivered in 1861, a specially designed sea-going steamship drawing a shallow 9 feet draught, thus allowing her to sail over the infamous sand bank at the River Maule's entrance, even when laden with cargo from the flour mills complex further up river.

PSNC had introduced the 290 tons iron-hulled *Inca* as a temporary counter measure. Her first incursion went smoothly; she managed to sail over the sandbank when entering the river and proceeded safely to the loading point, but found that when fully loaded she could not negotiate the sandbank to return to the open sea. One can almost picture the mirth emanating from the small Chilean company's personnel and its shareholders at that farcical situation. It is reasonable to assume the depth of the sandbank would have been chartered and well known, particularly as PSNC had excluded calling at Constitución because of its existence. PSNC should also have been aware of the draught the *Inca* would draw when fully loaded; it was surely a simple procedure to confirm whether the two were compatible.

Having nothing to fear from PSNC, the Paquete de Maule firm purchased another vessel in 1862, re-forming as Compañia Nacional de Vapores (CNV), but sailed into financial difficulties in 1868. PSNC's attempts to buy-out the company were resisted and it decided, surprisingly, to take no further action. A new firm, the Compañia Chilena de Vapores (CCV), formed in 1870 in Concepción, attracted considerable support from the Chilean press, especially after CCV had announced its intention to operate along the Chilean Coast, from Caldera in the north to Puerto Montt in the south. PSNC also tried to acquire this shipping company but was again rebuffed, and even attempted to purchase a controlling share interest but to no avail. There was then a considerable cross-shareholding in both CCV and CNV; their respective shareholders preferred a joint merger, a proposal that received the backing of the Chilean Government. The new company Compañia Sudamericana de Vapores (CSAV) was formed in October 1872.

These events indicated growing national sentiment and grass roots opposition to the English company. Warning signs were clearly spelt-out for PSNC; CSAV was to be protected by the Chilean Government with generous subsidies because the latter wished to encourage nationally registered companies to provide a requisitioning structure in case of military necessity. Although CSAV struggled initially against the ruthless and aggressive policies of both PSNC and the freight-setting Ocean Conferences, it eventually displaced the English company to become Chile's own *Queen of the Pacific*.

Could PSNC have considered creating another subsidiary with Chilean or Peruvian registry, or have offered a meaningful partnership on some West Coast services? The Central American partnership with the Chilean Line seemed to have worked well enough. No evidence has emerged to suggest that a permanent Chilean partnership or Chilean registration was ever considered, but PSNC seemed to have preferred a combative strategy to try and ruin the young Chilean Company.

The English firm might have benefited from the advice of someone of William Wheelwright's stature, whose diplomatic qualities and later foresight, might have paved the way for a more constructive and co-operative stance than PSNC's chronic haughty and challenging attitudes. These had so embittered Chilean feeling, that they caused it to rail against the monopolistic English shipping firm. It had by 1871, become the largest shipping company in the world; its power and position on the high seas seemed unassailable.

PSNC's main competitor on the WCSA between 1873 and 1877 was CSAV or La Sudamericana. The English company's systematic reductions in freight charges to try to ruin it, although causing serious difficulties for the Chilean company, had only benefited South American shippers with lower cargo rates. Government subsidies, while helping CSAV to keep afloat, did little to encourage the growth of Chile's merchant marine, but rather increased the risk of creating a cartel out of the two firms.

In 1877, CSAV being nearly bankrupt and despite Chilean Government financial assistance, was forced as an unwilling bride into an arranged marriage with PSNC, whereby the latter was able to dictate terms to its younger partner. The marriage was annulled when CSAV, profiting from substantial compensation received as a result of the Chilean Government's requisitioning of its ships during the War of the Pacific, was able to able to continue alone on a financially viable footing.

Wishing to steer away from European shipping influences, the Chilean Government, naturally supportive of CSAV's European initiative, promised further large subsidies. In order to encourage investors, the Chilean Government even guaranteed a minimum investment return of 6.7%. La Sudamericana, having announced its intention to start a European service, surprisingly, in view of its previous humiliating experiences, invited PSNC into a partnership. The English company, while not rejecting CSAV's overtures, deliberately provided high start-up costs to ensure that the Chilean company asked its Government for even higher subsidies. PSNC was then receiving subsidies at half the rate granted to CSAV. A new Chilean Executive rejected the whole scheme.

Conclusions

During the 1870s, Chile's longitudinal Railways were extended as far as Talcahuano and, by 1884, had continued-on further south to Renaico. There were clear advantages for shippers turning to railways rather than coastal shipping and, accordingly, volumes in the latter trade declined. In the northern provinces, nitrates production increased, but the Chilean Government failed to take advantage of this situation by providing sufficient incentives for Chilean ship-owners to expand its merchant fleet; this failure allowed foreign vessels to fill the gap.

The affects of the Industrial Revolution caused most European ports to update their facilities in order to avoid bottlenecks in the discharge and loading of cargo, but such improvements did not figure highly on the agendas of West Coast Governments. Consequently, specialist ships for carrying copper and nitrates were prominent; these were foreign owned and built to incorporate their own highly efficient equipment for loading and discharging of cargo.

The telegraph made the deployment of vessels more effective and world freight charges gradually reduced and became standardised. These cheaper rates, however, were not enjoyed by the West Coast nations. Towards the close of the 19th Century, PSNC's arrangement with other foreign shipping companies to impose inflated freight costs only provoked Chilean shippers into demanding a national merchant marine capable of maintaining lower charges. Cheaper cargo shipments were the main issues at the time, generating almost constant opposition to the Chilean Government's policy of continually subsidising CSAV, because of fears that it would create a monopoly leading to even higher shipment expenses. The Government's rationale for continuing to dispense subsidies was based on the fact that Chile was then a predominantly exporting nation; political and economic groups naturally supported low freight charges.

Accordingly, any action to upset the status quo would have been opposed. Protectionist measures for the same reasons were vigorously resisted, but those groups, previously and consistently supporting the continuation of foreign shipping operating on Chile's coastal trade, performed an about-turn and rejected the foreigners' concerns. They called for action to be taken against them and PSNC, in particular, when learning of the discrepancy between world-prevailing freight rates and the artificially high tariffs the foreign shipping companies continued to impose against the interests of the Chilean nation.

Although some years passed before relevant legislation was introduced, PSNC and other foreign shipping companies had been clearly warned, and only had themselves to blame for eventual protectionist measures directed against them. Moreover, PSNC's imposition of higher freight charges when prevailing rates in the rest of the world were generally much lower, only added to that company's already tarnished reputation from the War of the Pacific, and the arrogant attitude that it had long displayed towards CSAV. The English Company had, naturally, sailed under a British neutral flag during this war. However, realistically, it had been impossible for it to maintain strict neutrality between Peru and Chile, particularly after having established control centres in each and, accordingly, employing British personnel in both countries, some of whom had integrated into their respective societies by marrying nationals of the country in which they were based.

The Chilean view, by 1909, was that PSNC had been more sympathetic to the Peruvian cause; there was certainly some evidence to support this. An example of the double standards operated by the then PSNC management is revealed in an episode with the North American firm, W.R.Grace. The latter was very much a *"Peruvian House"*, and had wished to aid the Peruvians in their conflict with Chile by providing the former with six torpedo boats. PSNC at first, flatly refused to transport these craft on their ships, but was finally persuaded to agree only after the Peruvian Government had consented to purchase two of PSNC's surplus vessels. On the other hand, perhaps for Chilean political consumption, the English company sacked the captain of the *Lima II* for towing a ship full of contraband goods to Peru, as well as the captain of the *Islay* for conveying rifles to that country.

In 1893, new trade patterns emerged in South America; cargo volumes increased, overtaking passenger levels; South America overall had become wealthier, but by the end of the 19th Century, foreign shipping trade to and from the WCSA remained mostly in the hands of companies from the Great Powers. Until the 1890s, the American firm of W.R.Grace had not posed any threat to either PSNC or CSAV. Grace had been reluctant to wholly invest in steamships, often only taking a part interest in a vessel's shareholding, but subsequently sought a partner to share its New York to Peru route. Given PSNC's West Coast virtual monopoly, it had approached CSAV who declined the invitation, opting instead to retain links with the English Company. Refusing Grace's offer was a costly mistake for CSAV. Although initially suffering losses on its operation, Grace soon became very profitable but attracted more competitors to this route.

The Chilean Government's continuing inability to resolve the crisis in its merchant shipping fleet prompted Grace, then known as the Merchants Line, to petition for a £25,000 subsidy. Due to counter-petitions from a Chilean registered shipping agency, the Chilean Government decided not to accept either request. The important factor supporting the Merchants Line petition was the fact that it had expressed a willingness, not only to re-register all its vessels under the Chilean flag, but also to employ Chilean personnel, an issue often passionately aired in the Chilean Congress.

Because of growing trade, PSNC joined forces with its main competitor CSAV to operate regular steamships services from Valparaiso to Panama. The operation was heavily subsidised by the Chilean Government; the service was later extended to take-in the five Central American republics who also provided financial assistance to the *"Chilean steamships"* towards maintaining a weekly operation between Panama and Ocós in Guatemala. The operation initially suffered from a major management blunder. Soon after the service commenced, it was discovered that Panama Railroad Company, on whose facility the partnership was to have relied, was contracted exclusively to the US registered Panama Mail Steamship Company (PMSC). That such an obvious fact was not discovered before the introduction of the planned service suggests lack of management planning.

PSNC, consistently preferring confrontation rather than diplomatic negotiation, applied pressure on British shareholders in the Railroad company to secure beneficial arrangements for the partnership resulting in PMSC's contract being annulled and allowing the Chilean partnership to trade profitably for five years. The tables were overturned in 1902 when PRC was sold to an American company who restored the PMSC contract.

The Chilean merchant fleet was further reduced towards the end of the 19th Century; demand for cargo carrying capacity had increased due to the British Government's willingness to pay higher rates for freighters and transports to convey materiel and troops for the Boer War (1899 to 1902). Such had been the need for cargo space, that the British had resorted to chartering and purchasing freighters; Chilean ship owners, availing themselves of this opportunity, disposed of many of their vessels.

For nine years to 1909, debate had continued to rage in the Chilean Congress on the merits, or otherwise, of appropriate measures to reserve Chilean coastal trading to national vessels. That particular legislation never emerged, but a 1908 Decree was introduced requiring a tax on a vessel's tonnage to be paid when entering Chile from a foreign port. While the Chilean Government claimed that it had not discriminated against foreign shipping, it had affected Kosmos, the German shipping line, more than others; its ships were larger than its main competitors PSNC and CSAV, and it eventually withdrew from Chilean coastal trading. The German and English companies had been involved in a bitter rates war, only ending on Kosmos' entry into the freight rate-setting Europe/South Pacific and Magellan Ocean conference.

High freight costs continued to be the main concern of the Chilean Congress. It had not wanted to discriminate against foreign shipping in favour of Chilean registered vessels, because there was then a widespread belief that continuing to subsidise Chilean ship owners, CSAV particularly, would have led to the creation of a monopoly and, consequently, even higher freight charges than would have been the case had coastal trade been open to foreign vessels. This was despite foreign companies such as PSNC, Lamport & Holt, Kosmos, Gulf Line and others establishing higher uniform cargo rates for South America when freight charges prevailing in the rest of the world were still much lower.

It was clear that the completion of the Panama Canal would affect the operations of shipping companies the world over. United States' shipping enterprises benefited mostly; their vessels were thus able to communicate directly between the North

Atlantic and North Pacific coasts avoiding the long and dangerous haul round Cape Horn. More threateningly for PSNC and European shipping companies, the Panama Canal brought the WCSA closer to the North Atlantic ports of North America. It meant the total or partial loss of some of PSNC's lucrative first class passenger and emigrant trade on its direct service vessels to the WCSA via the Strait of Magellan; the Canal favoured the growing and influential Grace Line.

A delegation appointed by the PSNC Board of Directors had been despatched to Panama to assess the Canal's likely affects on the company. Its conclusions must have been ominous and inevitable; proposals for a take-over of PSNC by Royal Mail Lines were accepted shortly afterwards in 1910. It would have been surprising if the PSNC Board had not also taken into account the political warnings regularly broadcast from the Chilean Congress, and detailed in the press, when the debates about protectionist policies continued to rage, as they had done for decades. The PSNC Board must have realised that the Company's privileged position on the Chilean coast was rapidly ending. Political developments and a growing and educated middle class, more resentful of foreign enterprises, gave rise to more intense national feelings and heated debate over whether Chile's coastal trade should or should not remain open to foreign shipping lines. Public pressure was such that political discussion was translated into meaningful policy. National opinion had become increasingly hostile to foreign enterprises, non-Chilean foreign shipping lines, in particular, fuelled by the already tarnished historical reputations of PSNC and Grace Line.

Cabotage, the reservation of coastal shipping to Chilean registered vessels, duly passed into law in February 1922. The fact that it had not been intended to take affect until 1928, but brought forward to Aug 1922, was an indication of that strong national sentiment supporting the measure. Its emergence was a signal for huge celebration on the scale that had welcomed the arrival of the two pioneering steamships to the port of Valparaiso in 1840. The Chilean nation as a whole saw the new law as marking the beginning of what it perceived as a new era of prosperity in the shipping industry.

Neither PSNC nor other foreign shipping companies should have been surprised at the introduction of this new Cabotage statute; Chile did nothing more than implement a law long practised by other leading nations, including the United States and Great Britain. Neither was the Chilean action a new strategy; it had been debated for decades; William Wheelwright had consistently warned his company of this possibility. PSNC and other foreign shipping firms had had, accordingly, sufficient time to make alternative arrangements, possibly including the re-registration of part or all of its coastal fleet as a Chilean subsidiary, just as the Grace Merchants Line had formerly proposed.

It was possible that coastal trade was not really that profitable or would eventually be less so to PSNC. New roads and the subsidised speedy longitudinal railroads, enjoying certain advantages over coastal shipping, had already enticed trade away from coastwise companies, and would continue to do so when it was extended further southwards. Coastal vessels, however, were still preferred for the transport of bulkier low-value cargoes such as coal, salt, and mineral ores. Moreover, the CSAV and CCNI would both eventually conclude that earnings from one ship assigned to foreign-going trade could earn twice as much as one confined to coastal trade.

It was believed that Peru, in bringing about her own cabotage law, had merely copied Chile's action so as not to fall out of step with the public and political situation on the WCSA. Her southern neighbour may have influenced her in this respect, but the conditions surrounding the Peruvian action were entirely different from the Chilean situation. Corrupt officials of the Peruvian Steamship Company (the Peruvian Line) had promoted cabotage merely to preserve the kickbacks from the then remunerative coastal trade; to achieve this, it sought to promote cabotage for political ends by appealing to patriotic sentiment. At the end of the 19th Century, CSAV, due to the absence of any real Peruvian competition on coastwise operations, was meeting the demands of the majority of the Peruvian coastal shippers, despite the presence of PSNC and Grace Line.

The Peruvian Government, in trying to redress this situation, had formed the Peruvian shipping Line in 1906 acquiring 10% of her initial stock. The company was beset with financial and managerial problems from the start, but World War 1 was a boon to the Peruvian Line; it managed to raise sufficient revenue to redeem all its debt and purchased three German freighters interned at the outbreak of hostilities; their high acquisition costs, however, left the Peruvian Line with insufficient finance for replacement vessels. The pre-war freighters had been expensive to operate and unfortunately, one burnt-out at sea; inevitably, substantial losses were incurred and the company's development was curtailed.

The Peruvian Government continued to pour money into the company but its management permitted the continuation of corruption and inefficiency, leading, in 1913, to a suspension of its services. The Peruvian Government had tried unsuccessfully to place the company in the management of other firms. PSNC had been secretly negotiating with the Peruvian Line while still contractually obliged to CSAV and had, perhaps, considered a partnership; its inefficiency and corruption were so widespread that PSNC withdrew from further discussions.

The Peruvian Line introduced a service from Callao to Valparaiso in 1912. This, together with the knowledge of PSNC's secret dealings with the Peruvian company, stunned CSAV and only added to its perception of the already blemished reputation of the English company. Because of poor management and inefficiency, the Peruvian Lines' services began to decline as Peruvian shippers transferred to CSAV's services. The Cabotage law failed to protect the Peruvian Line and its last vessel was withdrawn in 1930. The opportunistic Chilean company immediately conducted secret negotiations with the Peruvian Government to obtain a two years contract to undertake Peruvian coastal trade, and one that was extended to last until the 1940s.

War again saved the Peruvian Line from total oblivion; the 1932-34 conflict with Colombia caused the Peruvian Government to resurrect the shipping company as a military option, but it chose to manage the enterprise as if it was another bureaucratic Government institution. It also tried to place orders with German shipyards for two new vessels in 1939, but the outbreak of WW2 prevented this. Unable to lay replacement orders, the Peruvian Line found itself in a worse position at the start of WW2 than it had suffered at the end of WW1.

PSNC's fleet, comprising just 14 vessels before the onset of WW2, is a measure of its decline. The war generally proved a boon to West Coast national shipping lines. Not only was substantial revenue earned by merchant fleets conveying raw materials and foodstuffs to the United States to supply the Allied war effort, the nations themselves accumulated large surpluses in their balances of payments, thus enabling the clearing of national debt and the creation of strong capital reserves to promote industry. They also benefited from loans and technical expertise provided by the United States to help the latter process. The war had led to a strengthening of their respective shipping enterprises, and to a consolidation of trade between South America and the United States at the expense of Europe.

At the end of WW2, Great Britain and the other war torn nations, being dependent on the US Marshall Aid Plan, had frightening levels of debt and were in no position to promote large scale investment to modernise their respective merchant fleets or replace lost vessels while focussing on the rebuilding of ports and national infrastructures. PSNC, however, had managed to take delivery of five "S" class vessels, completed towards the end of the war and just after. The Chilean Line, on the other hand, had been able to take advantage of a bargain arrangement it had concluded with the US State Department whereby Chile purchased five C-2s Liberty style cargo freighters, then in very short supply, at very favourable prices. These cheaply acquired cargo ships, which were also economical to operate, along with CSAV's careful management, had enabled substantial profits to be made, which were re-invested in mainland projects rather than returned to Chilean shipping. A series of protectionist measures assisted in the development of West Coast shipping except during a convulsive political period in Chile, and at the time of further decline in the mal-administered Peruvian steamship company.

The development of merchant shipping has never stood still; those companies that did not embrace new technology eventually could not compete and were absorbed by more powerful and capital rich units. In the 1960s, maritime passenger traffic was rapidly being lost to long-haul aircraft routes, and at a time when containerisation was emerging to become the model for the future. Political problems, especially, were beyond the control of both national and foreign shipping companies, but a return to free trade policies had enabled steady growth in the West Coast countries.

The following comparison of the *Andes III* with the five listed PSNC S-class vessels clearly demonstrates the economics of containerisation. The gross tonnage of the five break-bulk cargo vessels, the *Salamanca, Santander, Salaverry, Sarmiento* and *Salinas* totalled 32862 tons. The total crew complement for the five vessels was approximately 275 persons. Each ship had an operational speed of 13 knots. The multi-purpose *Andes,* built in 1984, and of the type proposed in the Andes project, grossing 32150 tons, was almost equivalent to the total of the five S-class ships, but only had a minimal crew of 24 and a service speed of 18.5 knots. Her cargo holds 1,3,4 and 6, specially constructed to carry and load bulk copper, were able to support 2145 TEUs over them. Holds 1 and 5 were reserved for hazardous and refrigerated cargo respectively with 254 TEU's over for bananas. All holds were strengthened for forklift trucks operation. The vessel was, importantly, equipped with a railed 40 tons overhead gantry operating over all forward sections for use in ports lacking container handling. This not only constituted considerable savings in staffing costs, but also resulted in reduced waiting days in port for the unloading and loading of a vessel.

The *Andes* was one of seven such ships forming the 1984 revenue-pooled Europe South America Line (EUROSAL). Furness Withy, PSNC's parent company, was one of the steamship companies participating in the fleet, whose combined gross tonnage was equivalent to approximately 35 S-Class ships. The original names of the Eurosal group were: Johnson Lines (Sweden), Armement Dieppe (Belgium), CSAV (Chile), Hapag-Lloyd (Germany), Lineas Navieras Bolivinas (Bolivia), Ned Lloyd (Holland), Furness Withy-PSNC (UK) and Transnave (Ecuador).

The following table was extracted from one of CSAV's typical schedules for its North Europe to WCSA weekly service in conjunction with Eurosal; it highlights the very short stays in port compared with those experienced by the S-class and other PSNC cargo freighters in the 1960s. Dates shown are sample departures:

Rotterdam	Holland	29 May
Felixstowe	UK	30 May
Hamburg	Germany	01 June
Antwerp	Belgium	04 June
Le Havre	France	05 June
Bilbao	Spain	08 June
Kingston	Jamaica	17 June
Manzanillo	Panama	22 June
B'naventura	Colombia	24 June
Guayaquil	Ecuador	27 June
Callao	Peru	30 June

| Arica | Chile | 03 July |
| Valparaiso | Chile | 06 July |

Many famous British shipping firms disappeared by absorption into larger companies because they were unable, by themselves, to provide the necessary capital to modernise and keep abreast of changes in trade patterns and technology. Even the American Grace Line, which pioneered container services, unable to cope with the cost and pace of modernisation, was merged with Prudential Lines before the Grace name was discarded. Shipping companies have been obliged to combine with others to provide the huge capital required for the provision of ever-increasing sizes of vessels, designed to cater for the constantly changing structure of shipping influenced by new and shifting patterns in world trade. The cost of constructing a large container vessel in 2000 was approximately £31,000,000 (US 55,800,000 dollars). What does the future hold?

A study commissioned by Lloyd's Register in 1999 in association with Ocean Shipping Consultants Ltd., concluded that ultra-large containers ships (ULCS) of up to 12,500 TEUs were entirely feasible, and that the first of these vessels could well be in service by 2010. One reservation, however, suggests that at this level, infrastructure limitations may constrain the operational flexibility of these ships. It noted that since the introduction of containerisation over 40 years ago, the size of containers ships had increased dramatically.

Until the mid 1980s, the dimensions of the Panama Canal (the Panamax) limited the size of such vessels, principally 32.2 metres beam. By the end of the millennium, approximately 30% of the world's fleet was post-panamax. The largest container vessels on order, at that time, would accommodate 8000 TEUs. It seems that the even larger capacities will be available. David Tozer, Lloyd's Register's Business Manager remarked:

"Prediction of the basic dimensions of the next generation of ultra-large container ships must commence with an understanding of the current and anticipated future capabilities of the infra-structure with which these ships must interface. It is nonsense to consider ships in isolation; they must be considered as part of a complete intermodal transport process. This is a necessary change of philosophy from previous generations when the ship would be designed to provide optimum performance at sea, knowing that the terminals could provide whatever capacity and capability was required to service the vessels during their brief periods in port"

According to a September 2004 release by the Chilean News Agency La Prensa, the Taiwanese Government is similarly convinced. It is reported as having decided to participate on its own account, or together with international consortia from the United States and Japan, in a scheme to expand the existing Panama Canal. The Taiwanese have already dispatched a team of experts to assess the scheme's viability. However, at the time of this report, a consortium of United States, French and Belgian firms were already conducting studies on the affects on the Panamanian environment, the climate, and the displacement of some of the inhabitants due to proposed deliberate flooding to permit the canal's expansion. Current cost estimates are between 7,000,000,000 and 10,000,000,000 US dollars (between £3,900,000,000 and £5,600,000,000). Before the project can start, the Panamanian Government must hold a referendum on the issue.

Such a scheme is likely to make a significant contribution to world shipping. It will, undoubtedly, affect shipping pools such as Eurosal, which now includes the two Chilean companies, CCNI and CSAV that were once in competition with both each other and PSNC on the West Coast. CSAV, moreover, has a branch office within the container port of Felixstowe. Perhaps the Chilean Government's policy of continued and generous subsidies was the right approach, but even these two Chilean shipping companies have finally had to succumb to financial reality. They are now under the control of larger consortia; CSAV is a subsidiary of the Claro Group while CCNI is part of Urenda, which has extensive shareholdings in Chile's ports and their infrastructure.

Famous British names have disappeared from the scene, and it is likely that in order to meet the ever-increasing capital costs of larger and more complex vessels, the trend will be towards international mergers and partnerships. ULCS vessels will require less crewmembers and therefore, there is likely to be less employment in merchant marines, although the few positions that will remain will need better trained and higher qualified personnel. If one is to identify the source of the decline of the British merchant navy, as witnessed in the 1960s, no person, company or Government is to blame, the finger can only be pointed at technological progress and changing patterns in world trade. These, and often scare capital, were the very conditions existing on the West Coast of South America when William Wheelwright first promoted his steamship plans and will continue to dominate merchant shipping for the foreseeable future.

Bibliography

La Vida y Los Trabajos Industriales de William Wheelwright En La America del Sud. (The Life and Industrial Works of William Wheelwright in South America). Biography of William Wheelwright by Juan Bautista Albérdi. 1876. Librería de Garnier Hermanos. Paris.

William Wheelwright, His Life and Work.
A Memorial Address delivered by Rev. John Webster Dodge at the Corliss Memorial Hall. Newburyport. Mass. December 1898. Cambridge University Press 1899. Relies mainly on Albérdi's biography.

William Wheelwright.
An English version of lecture given in Spanish at the Peruvian-North American Cultural Institute on September 30, 1959 by Edward G.Trueblood. The latter was Resident Representative of the Technical Assistance Office of the United Nations. Copied from the collection of Cecil B.Lyon Papers, courtesy Georgetown University Library. Washington D.C.

El Vapor Conquista El Pacifico. Anales de Las Hazañas Marítimas 1840-1940.
(The Steamship Conquers the Pacific. Annals Of Maritime Prowess 1840-1940). A commemorative publication marking the centenary of Pacific Steam Navigation Company by Arthur C. Wardle. Universo S.A. Valparaíso. Chile. 1940.

Heirs of Great Adventure. History of Balfour Williamson and Company. 1851-1901. Wallis Hunt. An internal production for Balfour Williamson & Company. 1901.Provides useful contemporary economic background.

Historia de la Marina Mercante de Chile.
(History of Chile's Merchant Marine). Refers to period 1824-1922. Claudio Véliz. Universidad de Chile. 1961. Gives detailed explanations of the political struggles involved in establishing Chile's Merchant marine.

W.R.Grace & Co. The Formative Years 1850-1930.
A history of W.R.Grace & Co. Supplies important facts and details of the Guano trade in the Chincha Islands of Perú and the development of the company into shipping. Lawrence A.Clayton. Jameson Books Ottawa. Illinois. USA. 1985.

Bibliography

The Panama Route, 1848-1869.
History of steamship routes on the East and West Coast of North and Central America via the Isthmus but mainly the Panamá Railroad connection. John Haskell Kemble. University South Carolina Press. 1990.

Panama in 1855. An Account of the Panama Railroad, Of the Cities of Panama and Aspinwall with Sketches of Life and Character On the Isthmus.
A light-hearted travelogue with some useful facts on the Railroad and citizens of the area. Robert Tomes. Harper & Bros. New York 1855.

Isthmus of Panama. History of The Panama Railroad and the Pacific Mail Steamship Company. F.N.Otis, M.D. Harper & Brothers New York, 1867

El Pacífico Sudamericano; Punto de Encuentros y Desencuentros.
(The South American Pacific; Scene of Engagements and Withdrawals). A paper by Jorge Ortiz Sotelo of the Escuela Superior de Guerra Naval. Perú. 2000.

The Golden Isthmus.
A History of the Isthmus of Panamá 1502-1966.
David Howarth. Readers Union-Collins. London 1967

Chile Since Independence.
Extracts from The Cambridge History of Latin America. Edited by Leslie Bethell. Professor of Latin American History. University of London. Cambridge University Press 1998.

Oil and Coffee. Latin American Merchant Shipping from the Imperial Era to the 1950s.
René De La Pedraja Tomán. Greenwood Press. 1998.

Diary of Dr. Robert Robertson 1871.
Surgeon aboard ss. Araucania. Glasgow University Archives. Ref HB/98/1/2

Globalización Al Interior de Los Imperios Mercantiles Perú, Chile y España. 1660-1810. (Globalisation within the Trading Bloc of Peru and Chile with Spain 1660-1810). Joint Paper by Carlos Newland (Universidad Argentina de La Empresa) and Andrés Alberot Gallo (University of Illinois).

Importancia de La Marina Mercante En la Historia de Chile.
(Importance of the Chilean Merchant Marine in Chile's History). Archivos de La Armada de Chile. 2001.

La Política Oceánica Durante El Decenio Del Presidente Don Manuel Montt (1851-1861). (Ocean Politics During the 10 years of Don Manuel Montt's Presidency 1851-1861). Paper by Hernán Ferrer Fougá. 19th February 1994. (Archivos de La Armada de Chile 2001).

Latin American Merchant Shipping In The Age Of Global Competition. René De La Pedraja (Greenwood Press 1999).

Boundaries. Possessions And Conflicts in South America
Gordon Ireland. Cambridge, Massachusetts Harvard University Press. 1938. Detailed study of treaties, conflicts and disputed territories

By Reason Or Force: Chile and the Balancing of Power in South America, 1830-1905. A detailed political history of Chile and relations with her neighbours. Robert N.Burr. University of California Press 1965.

La Campaña Del Pacífico (1862-1866). (Campaign in the Pacific 1862-1866). West Coast War with Spain. Paper by José Ramón García Martínez (The Don Castro Méndez Núñez Maritime and Naval Centre. Madrid. Spain.).

Strategy In The Southern Oceans. A South American View.
Detailed South American perceptions of the value of the sea. Contains two case studies of which Case Study One is relevant, Bolivia's outlet to the Pacific Ocean (pages 1-64). The other case study refers to Falklands War and teritorial claims on Antartica. Virgina Gamba-Stonehouse. Pinter Publishers Ltd. 1989.

The House of Gibbs and the Peruvian Guano Monopoly.
Well-sourced work, providing comprehensive accounts of the financial and political situations prevailing in Perú. W.M.Mathew. Published by the Royal Historical Society. 1981. Period covered 1840-1880.

The Nitrate Clippers.
History of the sailing ships and shipping firms involved in the WCSA nitrate trade. Basil Lubbock. Charles E.Lauriat Company 1932. Boston

The Poverty of Progress. Latin America in the Nineteenth Century.
A Social perspective of Latin America E.Bradford Burns. University of California Press. 1980.

Latin America. A Concise Interpretive History.
E.Bradford Burns. University of California Press. (Second Edition) 1977.

Spanish America 1900-1970. Tradition And Social Innovation.
Fredrick B.Pike (Thames and Hudson London 1973).

The Modern History of Peru.
Fredrick B.Pike. Published by Frederick A.Praeger, Inc. New York. 1967.

Bolivia Y Perú. La Fraternidad Escindida. Bolivia and Peru.
(Bolvia and Peru. The Divided Fraternity). A Paper by Nelson Manrique. Pontifica Universidad Católica del Perú. 2002.

Globalization in Latin America Before 1940.
Paper by Luis Bértola (Universidad de La República) and Jeffey G.Williamson (Harvard University). February 2003.

The Path of Empire. A Chronicle of the United States As a World Power.
By Carl Russell Fish. (Volume 46 of the Chronicles of America Series, edited by Allen Johnson was donated to Project Gutenberg by The James J. Kelly Library of St. Gregory's University USA. Courtesy Alev Akman)

Estados Unidos Y El Mar Boliviano.
(The United States and the Bolivian Sea) Paper by Dr. Jorge Gumucio Granier. Pittsburgh University Pa. USA and Universidad Mayor de San Andrés, La Paz. Bolivia. 2001

A Todo Vapor.
(Full Steam Ahead) A history of steamboats on the River Magdalena in Colombia. Antonio Montaña. Editorios Nomos. Santa Fé de Bogotá. Republic of Colombia. December 1996.

The Pacific Steam Navigation Company. Its Maritime Postal History. 1840-1853 with particular reference to Chile.
A.R.Doublet FRPSI. Royal Philatelic Society. London 1983.

The Age of Capital 1848-1875.
E.J.Hobsbawm. Abacus 1992.

The Triumph of the Middle Classes. A Political and Social History of Europe in the 19th Century. Charles Moraze. Doubleday, New York. 1966

South America. Observations And Impressions.
Travelogue by James Bryce (Macmillan 1912)

Railways of The Andes.
Brian Fawcett. George Allen and Unwin. Publication date unknown.

Where The Incas Trod.
Wallace G.Carter. Morriss Printing Company. Canada. 1973. Carter was a Purser with Pacific Steam Navigation Company. In this work he retraces the voyage of the PSNC liner ss *Orca* and addresses issues of historical importance relating to the Inca period.

The Age of Reform England. 1815-1879.
Llewellyn Woodward. Oxford University Press 1992.

Birth of the Modern. World Society 1813-1830.
Paul Johnson. Weidenfeld & Nicolson 1991

Pinochet In Piccadilly. Britain and Chile's Hidden History.
Andy Beckett. Faber & Faber 2002.

History of Latin America. Edwin Williamson. Penguin Press. 1992.

History of the United States of America. Hugh Brogan. Penguin Press 1999.

Historia Marítima del Perú. La República-1850 a 1870.
Fernando Romero Pintado. [Tomo VIII Volumen 2]. Instituto de Estudio Historico-Marítimos del Perú. 1984. A history of Perú's Navy between 1850 and 1870 and details of naval battles with the Spanish Expeditionary Force.

Endnotes

Introduction

[1] There are two publications: "Oil and Coffee" and "Latin American Merchant Shipping in the Age of Global Competition". See Bibliography.
[2] Although this book is out of print, it does appear to form the basis of a PSNC history provided at Red Duster Web sites.
[3] There was a simultaneous publication by Universo in Valparaíso entitled "El Vapor Conquista el Pacífico. Anales de Una Proeza Marítima". This is the copy that I have used in my own research.
[4] A South American either born in the Iberian Peninsular or born in South America of Spanish or of Portuguese descent as opposed to the majority non-élite indigenous population.

Chapter 1. Setting The Scene. 1503-1835

[5] Page 103. "History of Latin America" Edward Williamson (Penguin) 1992
[6] The combined area of modern day Colombia, Panama, Ecuador and Venezuela
[7] Page 105. "History of Latin America" (Edward Williamson)
[8] Recited by E.Bradford Burns (Page 54) in his "Latin America. A Concise and Interpretive History". California Press 1972.
[9] The name given to colonies in Central America and part of what is now the United States.
[10] Now forms part of modern Bolivia.
[11] "Criollos" in Spanish, a word used to describe a native of South America but of Spanish descent.
[12] Source: Armando De Ramon y José Manuel Larrain Page 282 "Orígenes de la Vida Económica Chilena 1659-1808", Centro de Estudios Públicos, Santiago 1982. Recited at page 4 of a paper entitled "Globalización Al Interior de Los Imperios Mercantiles:Peru, Chile Y España 1660-1810". Carlos Newland-Universidad Argentina de La Empresa and Andrés Alberto Gallo, University of Illinois. (2000)
[13] Page 5 ibid
[14] Page 3. "El Pacífico Sudamericano Punto de Encuentros y Desencuentros". Jorge Ortiz Sotelo. Escuala Superior de Guerra Naval. Lima. 2000
[15] Page 126 "History of Latin America". (Williamson)
[16] Page 3. "Pacífico Sudamericano..." Jorge Ortiz Sotelo.
[17] Page 4. Jorge Ortiz Sotelo.

[18] ibid
[19] "Globalización al Interior etc.." (Newland and Gallo). Page 7
[20] "History of Latin America" (Williamson) Page 104.
[21] Pages 318-319. Dorothy Burne Goebel. "British Trade to the Spanish colonies, 1796-1823". Agricultural History Review, 43. No.2. (1938). Recited at page 9 by W.M. Mathew in "The House of Gibbs and the Peruvian Guano Monopoly". London Royal Historical Society 1981.
[22] "By Reason or Force". Robert N. Burr. University California Press. 1965
[23] Page 17 "La Historia de La Marina Mercante de Chile". Claudio Veliz (Universidad Santiago 1961)
[24] "Viajeros en Chile, 1817-1847." Samuel Haigh et al. (Santiago 1955). Recited by Veliz p28.
[25] Claudio Veliz. Page 28.
[26] Veliz describes this operation (P29 footnote Historia de La Marina Mercante de Chile) as involving British ships chartered by shippers in British ports who loaded them with merchandise. The vessels would then set sail for Chile, the cargoes having been consigned to associates there. Having unloaded the cargoes brought from Britain, the vessels would proceed to northern ports where they would load copper, ore and other precious metals. This latter cargo would be transported to Calcutta or other Asian ports where it would be sold and the proceeds used to purchase tea, spices and other Asian products. The vessels would then proceed to the UK via the Cape of Good Hope. .
[27] "El Libro del Cobre y de Carbon de Piedra en Chile" Benjamin Vicuna Mackenna. Santiago 1883. Quoted as source by Veliz as footnote 25. Page 32.
[28] Vicuna Mackenna. Cited as source by Veliz .Page 32.
[29] Diego Barros Arana, " Historia de Chile". Tomo xiv. Page 78. Also "Sesiones de Los Cuerpos Legislativos", Tomo vi, pages 166-170. Both recited in Veliz Page 38.
[30] Veliz. Page 36.
[31] "Leyes Promulgados en Chile. Desde 1810 hasta el 1 de junio de 1912. Santiago. Tomo 1. Pp 84-102. Cited as source by Veliz.
[32] Variations of up to 50% in the annual tonnages arriving at the port are attributed by Veliz partly to the irregular pattern of both Chilean coastal and foreign trade; voyages from Europe to Valparaiso took at least three months and this coupled with the limited consumption of Chile's interior market periodically caused an excess of supply over demand in the shops and stores in Valparaiso which consequently affected exports to that port for a year a two. Veliz states that for example, (British) Consul Rowscroft reported that rolls of high quality cotton fabric exported from Manchester were selling at six [old] pence per yard in Valparaiso and that between Valdivia and San Blas there were enough textiles to satisfy the [West Coast of the] Pacific for a further year. Sources cited by Veliz: Foreign Office 61/3, 8th October 1824 and Board of Trade reference 6/60, 1st November 1824.
[33] Claudio Veliz at page 43 recites the population of Chile during the 1820s as being less than one million, the vast majority of whom were outside the capitalist monetary economy.
[34] Based on data at Veliz. Page 55.

Endnotes

Chapter 2. Visions of Steamships And Political Conflicts 1824-1839.

35   At this time Buenos Aires was an independent nation.
36   The owner was William Bartlett; Wheelwright was later to marry his daughter.
37   Page 113. Published by University of California. 1972.
38   Page 8. "The Poverty of Progress" by E.Bradford Burns. University of California Press 1980.
39   Europe for this purpose would not have included Portugal and Spain at the time.
40   The Chilean Congress had, in 1828, rejected the idea of constructing a railway between Valparaiso and Santiago. Source: Veliz p.68
41   Recited by A.R.Doublet "Pacific Steam Navigation Company-Its Maritime Postal History 1840-1853, with particular reference to Chile (published in 1983 for the Royal Philatelic Society, London).
42   Page 17. "By Reason or Force: Chile and the Balancing of Power in South America, 1830-1905" (Robert N.Burr). University California Press. 1965. "By Reason or Force" is also Chile's national motto.
43   The amount of $100,000 was recited by Alberdí who was living in exile in Chile at the time. It is likely to refer to Chilean pesos and would be valued at around 20000 pounds sterling or US 36,000 dollars, a considerable fortune in 1828.
44   Page 22. Robert Burr (By Reason or Force)
45   Page 23. Robert Burr
46   Page 10. "The Nitrate Clippers". Basil Lubbock.. Charles E.Lauriat Company. Boston 1932.
47   Page 11. Lubbock.
48   Page 16-17. Rev. John Webster Dodge. Memorial Address re Wheelwright
49   ISSN 0250-7161. Pontifica Universidad Católica de Chile 2004.
50   Source cited as "Municipalidad 19:10-11 and 18:287"
51   Page 16. Wardle.
52   Page 18. Rev. John Webster Dodge.. "Wheelwright Memorial"
53   Page 9. Ortiz Sotelo.
54   Ibid
55   Page 36. Burr.
56   Page 9. Ortiz Sotelo
57   Source: Page 3. "Boundaries, Possessions and Conflicts in South America". Gordon Ireland. Published Cambridge. Massachusetts Harvard University Press 1938

Chapter 3. A Problematic Venture. 1835-1840.

58   Page 18. "El Vapor Conquista El Pacífico". Wardle.
59   "Europeanization" in this context excludes Spain and Portugal

Ploughing The South Sea

[60] Source: A paper entitled " La Politica Oceánica Nacional Durante El Decenio del Presidente Don Manuel Montt (1851- 1861), produced by Hernán Ferrer Fougá. Archivos de La Armada de Chile 2001.
[61] Page 13. Mathew. The House of Gibbs…
[62] ibid
[63] Page 15. Mathew.
[64] Page 64. "Modern History of Peru". Pike
[65] Page 17. Mathew.
[66] Page 94 Pike
[67] Ibid
[68] "Memoria del Ministro del Interior al Congreso Nacional de 1,844". Documentos Parlamentarios, II,223. Page 71 Burr.
[69] Page 20. "El Vapor Conquista El Pacífico". Wardle.
[70] Kemble quotes his source as the New York Herald of May 19, 1848.
[71] Page 19. Rev. John Webster Dodge.
[72] Translation of letter extract appearing in Veliz who cites at page 69 the source as "Documentos Historicos Oficiales Relativos a Los Primeros Pasos Y Medidas Tomadas para Introducir La Navegación a Vapor en las Aguas de Chile, "Revista de Marina, Tomo II, 1886, pp 545-560 et al.
[73] Veliz, page 69.
[74] Veliz page 70
[75] Page 383. "The History of the USA". Hugh Brogan (Penguin)
[76] "Square-riggers on Schedule". R.G.Atkinson. Princeton NJ. Recited in "Birth of the Modern"
[77] Recited in "The Birth of the Modern. World Society 1813- 1830. Paul Johnson (Weidenfeld & Nicholson 1991)
[78] "Robert Fulton Engineer and Artist" (London 1913). Quoted in "Birth of the Modern".
[79] This claim was first attributed to Wheelwright by Alberdí Page 92 "La Vida Y Los Trabajos de Wheelwright en La America del Sud"
[80] The proposed voyages to South America from England, and vice-versa, would rely on a link with Royal Mail Steam Packet Company sailing between the Isthmus of Panama and England.
[81] The responsibility for letting Mail contracts fell to the US Navy which had oversight for supervising and vetting the design and construction of vessels to be used.
[82] "The Panama Route, 1848-1869". California University Press". 1943
[83] Source Boletin de Leyes y Decretos. Tomo III (libros VIII, IX, X, XI). Cited by Veliz P74.
[84] The majority of PSNC shareholders at the time resided in or near Liverpool and appeared to be more disposed to Wheelwright..

Endnotes

Chapter 4. First Steamship Line . 1839-184

85 The Bolivian Government later tried to involve the Company in territorial disputes with Chile when it lost its ports within the Atacama coastal strip.
86 Page 22. "Boundaries, Possessions and Conflicts in South America". Professor Gordon Ireland. Harvard University Press, 1938.
87 "Fuerte Bulnes". Armando Braun Menéndez. Emecé Editores S.A. 1943. Buenos Aires. Cited by Burr Page 71.
88 Source: Tratados (Treaties) de Argentina 1911. Cited Page 22. Ireland.
89 Page 22. Ireland
90 Page 25. Ireland...
91 Page 40. "El Vapor Conquista El Pacifico" (Wardle 1940). PSNC actually received significant subsidies for long periods from the Chilean Goverement. There are also significant reference to British Government subsidies. These are detailed in later pages.
92 Page 51. Memorias de Hacienda. Recited in "La Politica Oceánica Nacional" (Fougá)
93 Page 241 "History Latin America". Edwin Williamson. Penguin Press 1992
94 A tax based on $1/10^{th}$ of annual production or income, usually relating to agriculture for the support of the priesthood and/or religious establishments.
95 The name given to a South American resident of European descent.
96 Page 33. "William Wheelwright. His Life and Work". An address by Rev. John W. Webster Dodge. 1899. Cambridge University Press.
97 Pages 29-30. Webster Dodge(supra).
98 "La Vida y Los Trabajos Industriales de Wm.Wheelwright en la America del Sud "(1876).
99 Page 30 .Webster.
100 Most probably Aspinwall and associates.
101 Pages 30-31. Webster.
102 Then a village on the outskirts of Valparaíso

Chapter 5. Growing Pains. 1845-1849

103 The Caldera-Copiapó railroad was the third railway service in South America but the first in Chile.
104 Arica, a port in the pressent day Province of Tarapacá which was then, and prior to 1866, was in the Province of Tacna-Arica under the sovereignty of the Republic of Peru

Ploughing The South Sea

[105] Iquique being part of the Province of Tarapacá was the subject of a subsequent dispute and war between Bolivia, Chile and Peru, but at this time was within Peruvian territory.
[106] Cobija was at this time Bolivia's main port but is now in the Chilean Province of Antofagasta.
[107] Cited at page 132. La Vida Y Los Trabajos de Wheelwright
[108] Wheelwright's surveys of likely coal deposits in the Callao region had already proved fruitless.
[109] "Genesis of the Pacific Mail" (San Francisco 1934). Page 35 of Kemble's "The Panama Route, 1848-1869".
[110] San Francisco Daily Alta California. June 14, 1849. Recited in Kemble's "The Panama Route, 1848-1869". Page 120.
[111] Aspinwall to Robinson New York May 22, 1849. Daulton Mann Letter Book collection. New York. Page 121. " The Panama Route 1848-1869". Kemble.
[112] Lord Abinger was in fact the Hon.P.C.Scarlett, one of Wheelwright's closest supporters in the Company.
[113] Cited by E.Bradford Burns, Page 104, "Latin America History".
[114] From later sympathetic comments made by Peacock, the captain in this instance seems to have been Pinhorn, promoted from Chief Officer.
[115] Page 18." Oil and Coffee. Latin American Merchant Shipping from the Imperial Era to the 1950s" . (Greenwood Press 1998). René de La Pedraja.
[116] Page 61. Wardle.
[117] Veliz. Page 112.
[118] Memorias de Marina 1852, recited by Veliz. Page 113.
[119] Page 64. Wardle.
[120] The talk appears to have been based on a prepared paper entitled "Ejes de lo feminino/masculino y de lo blanco/no blanco, en dos textos literarios". (Masculine / female and white and non-white issues appearing in two literary texts).
[121] Natives of Latin America descended from Europeans.
[122] Edwards-Bello uses "Criollo", the Spanish word for "Creoles".
[123] The Almendral is the old "village" on the outskirts of Valparaíso.
[124] Glasgow University Archives Ref HB98/1/2
[125] Page 209. "Where the Incas Trod". Wallace G.Carter.
[126] Page 15. "Spanish America 1900-1970.Tradition and Social Innovation" F.R.Pike. (1973 Thomas and Hudson London)
[127] Page 18 "Spanish America...".Pike Page
[128] Page 5 "Poverty of Progress: Latin America in the 19th Century" (E.Bradford Burns). University of California Press 1983.
[129] Page 23 Rev John Webster Dodge
[130] ibid
[131] ibid.
[132] Page 14. "Modern History of Peru". Pike.
[133] Recited at page 15. Pike.
[134] Page 16. Pike.
[135] ibid

Endnotes

[136] Page 87. Pike.
[137] The title of "Colonel" was believed to have related to a Youth Army Training Corp unit which he helped to establish and finance. Participating in its activities he assumed the title of "Colonel".
[138] Page 71. .Arthur Wardle. "El Vapor Conquista El Pacifico".

Chapter 6. Political Developments 1845-1848

[139] Page 78. Wardle. "El Vapor Conquista El Pacífico".
[140] Page 80. Wardle.
[141] Wheelwright did not obtain a concession to operate in the waters of the then Colombian province of Panama until 1845.
[142] Page 82. Wardle.
[143] Memoria de Ministro de Guerra y Marina al Congreso Nacional de 1,844. Documentos Parliamentarios. Pp 309-321. Page 72 Burr.
[144] Burr calculated these figures from Chilean Government revenues reported in "Historia de Chile: Historia Económica" (Daniel Martner). Santiago de Chile: Establecimientos Gráficos de Balcells, 1929, Pages 224 and 298.
[145] Wallis Hunt in "Heirs of Great Adventure" quotes at page 37 that 180,000 pesos equalled approximately £45,000. (About 4 pesos to the £)
[146] Burr at pages 75-76 cites source: "Pan-Hispanism: Its Origin and Development to 1866". Mark J.Van Aken.University California Press 1959.
[147] Source: Documents on Inter-American Co-operation, 1810-1948. (Roland D.D.Hussey and Robert N. Burr) University of Pennsylvania Press 1955. Vol 1 pages 102-10, cited in Burr.
[148] Source: "Historia de La República del Peru". Jorge Bennett. Editorial Cultura Antádida. S.A. 1948. Pages 218-220. (Vol 1). Recited in Burr.
[149] Page 87. Wardle.
[150] Letter from W.R.Grace to John W.Grace. Page 83." W.R.Grace". (Lawrence Clayton)

Chapter 7. Panama and The Railroad 1849-1860

[151] Pages 69-70. "Panama in 1855, An Account of The Panama Rail- Road of the Cities of Panama and Aspinwall, with Sketches of Life and character of the Isthmus". Robert Tomes, Harper & Brothers. New York. 1855. (Hereinafter "Tomes Panama Railroad").
[152] Pages 102-103. Tomes. "Panama Railroad."
[153] David Howarth describes other routes, one of which was the Camino Real, an ancient trail used by the Spaniards and which he suggested would have been easier to negotiate than the Chagres route.

Ploughing The South Sea

[154] Véliz. Page 80.
[155] Source: Page 78. Veliz. See footnotes 99 and 100.
[156] Page 80. The Blanco Encalada letter was published in the Valparaiso newspaper, El Mercurio on Aug. 17, 1849..
[157] Véliz. Page 81. (footnote 106)
[158] Véliz. . Pages 85-86
[159] Véliz. Page 83.
[160] See notes 6 and 7, Page 41. Paper by Capitán Hernán Ferrer Fougá entitled "La Politica Oceanica Nacional Durante El Decenio del Presidente Don Manuel Montt (1851-1861)
[161] Veliz Page 117.
[162] El Mercurio September 10, 1849. Cited in Veliz, page 117.
[163] Page 29. "Railways of the Andes" (Brian Fawcett).
[164] Boletín de Leyes 1851 page 4. Quoted in Véliz page 118.
[165] Boletín de Leyes 1851 pp 168-170. Quoted in Véliz page 118.
[166] Boletín de Leyes 1852 pp 148-149. quoted in Véliz page 119
[167] Véliz. Page 120.
[168] Source: "Memorias de Hacienda" recited in "La Política Oceánica Nacional &..." (Fougá)
[169] " El Tratado de Amistad, Comercio y Navegación entre Chile y los EE.UU."
[170] Véliz. Page 88.
[171] Véliz. Page 89.
[172] Page 90 Veliz who cites as source Ramon Guerrero Vergara page xv.
[173] Veliz. Page 96. In footnote Veliz indicates that technological improvements in construction methods also contributed to lower building costs.
[174] "La Historia de La Marina Mercante de Chile". Page 101.
[175] Page 224. Mathew.
[176] Source: Footnote 147. Page 111. Veliz
[177] Page 116. Mathew.
[178] Page 117. Mathew.
[179] The Times 26 November 1853(page 18) and 16th February 1854 (page 7). Recited at page 117. Mathew.
[180] Extracted from Table 1. Appendix IV. Page 252 Mathew.
[181] Page 37. Mathew.
[182] Based on Casa Gibbs' figures that in March 1857, there were 128 ships waiting at the Chinchas which were capable of carrying 160,000 tons of guano.
[183] Page 121. Mathew.
[184] Page 118. Mathew.
[185] Page 180. W.R.Grace (Clayton)
[186] Page 48. Lubbock.
[187] Further details of Wheelwright's activities in South America are described in Albérdi's "La Vida Y Los Trabajos Industriales de Wheelwright en Sudamérica".
[188] "History of the Panama Railroad". PART 2 Chapter XVI. Ira E.Bennett.
[189] Source: Kemble "The Panama Route, 1848-1869" page 194.
[190] Tomes. "Panama Railroad 1855" Pages 116-117

Endnotes

[191] Bennett records that the Company frequently transported 1500 passengers, the US mail and the freight from 3 steamships, all on a daily basis.
[192] "The Panama Route 1848-1869" John Haskell Kemble
[193] Now in the Republic of Colombia.
[194] Source: Kemble, "Panama Route, 1848-1869". Page 96
[195] Highly popular holiday resort on Merseyside, particularly in 19th Century.
[196] A philanthropic shipping and forwarding agency operating from Liverpool in 1851. Its main activities included Shipping merchandise to West Coast of South America. and importing nitrates and minerals.

Chapter 8. War With Spain. 1860-1871

[197] The American Civil War might account for the overall downward trend in tonnage figures in table "Chilean Merchant marine". Page 216. Véliz.
[198] An explanation of this and its affects is more fully explained in Chapter 11
[199] When Williamson became the senior partner, the name of the firm changed from Balfour Williamson to Williamson Balfour.
[200] Page 191. Véliz
[201] Page 179. Véliz.
[202] Page 90. Burr
[203] Page 153 "House of Gibbs".." Mathew.
[204] Paper by Gregory T.Cushman (October 10, 2002) South Western University USA. Cushman claims that the 1856 Guano Act created a legal "precedent" for the subsequent colonization of Hawaii and Puerto Rico.
[205] Page 13. Ortiz Sotelo.
[206] Page 92. Burr.
[207] Page 115. Pike. Modern History of Peru
[208] Page 185 Véliz. Footnote 281. Representations to the British Government are listed as: being made by I.R.Tennet & Co. Glasgow, Shipowners of Aberdeen, Panulcillo Copper Co.Ltd., Chambers of Commerce of Dundee, Lerith, Glasgow, Bradford, Birmingham. "In addition, various important business houses from New York with commercial interests in Chile, signed a petition to the US Secretary of State requesting his intervention as a mediator in the conflict. Those firms signing the petition included Alsop & Co., Fabbri & Coucey. Theodore V. Tizley, Loring & Shute, C.P. Hemnway & Co. Samuel D.Crane & Co., Heywood Haydn & Co. J.E.Manning. Listed in El Mercurio January 23, 1866.
[209] Source Francisco Vidal Gomez. Cited by Véliz Footnote 282. Page 187.
[210] Page 187. Véliz
[211] Reproduced in Véliz opposite Page 208.
[212] Page 117. Pike.
[213] Page 119. Pike.
[214] Page 125 Pike.
[215] ibid

Ploughing The South Sea

[216] Page 126. Pike
[217] Page 194. Véliz
[218] Page 194. Véliz
[219] Page 112. Wardle.
[220] ibid
[221] Panama was at that time still a state under the jurisdiction of the Colombian Republic.
[222] Page 148. Burr.
[223] Page 114. W.R.Grace & Co." (Lawrence A.Clayton)
[224] According to Véliz, the Chileans considered the PSNC to be pro-Peruvian.
[225] Page 125. W.R.Grace & Co., 1850-1930". (Clayton).
[226] 1867. Harper Brothers Publishers. New York
[227] El Mercurio de Valparaíso October 8, 1853. Cited by Véliz page 159.
[228] Source: Boletín de Leyes 1853. pages 564, 633-638. Recited pp 159-160 Véliz.
[229] Véliz. Page 160
[230] ibid
[231] Véliz. Page 162
[232] Page 162. Véliz
[233] Véliz. Page 165.
[234] Page 126. Burr.
[235] In 1840 the fleet comprised only the **Peru** and **Chile** but the writer may have thought to include the later **Ecuador**.
[236] Veliz. Page 75.
[237] Extracted from Wardle.
[238] Punta Arenas
[239] "Inicios de La Marina Mercante de Chile 1800-1870"
[240] Diary of Dr. Robertson. Ref HE98/1/2. Glasgow Health Authority Glasgow University Archives.

Chapter 9. West Coast Competition 1869-1878.

[241] Approximately 1.9 tons per hour
[242] Page 199. Véliz.
[243] El Mercurio January 2, 1860. . Véliz. Page 166.
[244] Véliz.. Page 166.
[245] Véliz at page 167 describes this company as Chilean but the question of its nationality was to play a vital diplomatic role in the later Bolivia-Chile conflict. See Chapter 12.
[246] El Mercurio July 23, 1860. Véliz, page 167.
[247] El Mercurio. October 17, 1860. Crónica Nacional. Concepción.
[248] El Mercurio. October 8, 1861. Page 168. Véliz.
[249] Véliz.. Footnote 254. Page 169.
[250] Véliz.. Page 169.

Endnotes

[251] El Mercurio de Valparaíso. September 11,26 and October 28 1863. Véliz page 174.
[252] El Mercurio, October 26, 1863. Page 173. Véliz.
[253] ibid
[254] Memoria de Marina 1862. March 11 1862. pp 71-75. Cited in Véliz, page 179
[255] Archivos de La Armada Chilena. "La Importance de la Marina Mercante".
[256] That is the Pacific-Panama-Atlantic routes.
[257] Kemble referring to competitors of the Pacific Mail Steamship Company. "The Panama Route, 1848-1869"
[258] Page 199. Véliz
[259] Source: Page 284 "The Economic Development of France and Germany." Cambridge 1955, Recited at page 200 by Véliz.
[260] Pages 78-113. "The Development and Decline of Copper and other Non-Ferrous Metal Industries in South Wales. The Transactions of the Honourable Society of Cymmridorion Session". 1956 London. R.O.Roberts. Recited as footnote 264 page 200 Véliz
[261] Although Caracoles was in Bolivian territory, it was by arrangement with the Bolivian Government being worked and developed with Chilean expertise and capital.
[262] Page 206. Véliz. Footnote 298,
[263] Page 210 Véliz.
[264] Page 212. Véliz
[265] Santa Rosa is the patron saint of Lima
[266] Page 215. Véliz
[267] Page 217. Véliz
[268] Page 219. Véliz.
[269] Dr. Robertson, in one of his diary entries, records visiting a production of "Macbeth" presented by the resident workers.
[270] Dr. Robertson of Hamilton. Ref HB98/1/2. Glasgow Health Authority. Glasgow University Archives.
[271] A terrible outbreak of Yellow Fever occurred in Buenos Aires in 1871. It lasted four months during which time, schools, churches and public buildings remained closed. Despite these measures 14000 persons died and a special cemetery was created .
[272] Similar information was described by F.N.Otis in his "History of the Panama Railroad. The dry dock enterprise was operated independently of PSNC.
[273] "The Panama Route , 1848-1869".
[274] Source: Page 26. "Pinochet in Piccadilly. Britain and Chile's Secret History". Andy Beckett (Faber 2002)
[275] A zealous political agitation in 1850s Chile. Founded politically influential Egalitarian society.

Chapter 10. Preludes To Protectionism. 1873-1889

[276] Page 96. "Heirs of Great Adventure. The History of Balfour Williamson and Company Ltd." by Wallis Hunt.
[277] A suburb of Valparasio
[278] Chile then exported grain on Balfour Williams sailing ships to the United States.
[279] Page 222. Véliz quotes an exchange rate of 44d to the peso making it equivalent to £183,334 (US 33,000 dollars).
[280] Page 223. Véliz..
[281] Pages 219-221. Véliz.
[282] Report of CSAV Directors of April 26, 1881, Recited at page 127. "Oil and Coffee", Réné De La Pedraja.
[283] Page 57. Footnote 54. De La Pedraja..
[284] Letter from John Train(PSNC) to CSAV Directors in Valparaíso. 15th November 1881. Quoted by De La Pedraja, page 27 from Allard CSAV.
[285] Page 22. De La Pedraja. "Oil and Coffee".
[286] Footnote 307 on pages 222/223. Véliz
[287] Page 30. "Oil and Coffee". De La Pedraja.
[288] El Mercurio. August 11, 1874. Véliz. Page 225.
[289] Recited page 120. "Panamá Route, 1848-1869". Kemble.
[290] This floating dock was actually fabricated in Glasgow and transported in sections on the Company's own vessels. The sections were assembled in Callao.
[291] Wardle. Page 155
[292] "Major James Rennell and The Rise of Modern English Geography", Sir Clement R Markham. London 1895. Véliz. Pages 146-156.
[293] Page 37. "W.R.Grace & Co. The Formative Years 1850-1930". Lawrence A.Clayton. Published 1985. Jameson Books. Illinois.
[294] Véliz Page 242. Footnote 334,
[295] "The Last of The Windjammers", Basil Lubbock, Glasgow 1927. Pages 384-389. Recited at Page 242. Véliz.
[296] Page 250 Véliz.
[297] Page 252. Véliz
[298] Page 263. Véliz
[299] Page 266. Véliz
[300] Page 258. Véliz.
[301] "De la Protección a la Marina Mercante Nacional". Pages 281-287. Recited in Véliz page 257.
[302] Footnote 345. Page 258. Véliz,
[303] Page 259. Véliz.
[304] This was not the end of the matter. Another 20 years would pass before such legislation was approved by both Chambers.
[305] The petition was signed b Vorwerk & Cía acting for German Kosmos Lines; J.W.Sharpe for PSNC; Duncan Fox & Co. for Lampert & Holt; Allardyce Brett & C.

Endnotes

for Gulf Line; W.R.Grace y J.F.Fowler for Merchant's Line (owned by W.R.Grace Co Footnote 356. Page 275. Véliz.
[306] Page 275. Véliz.
[307] Footnote 360. Page 277. Véliz.
[308] Recited at Page 279 Véliz
[309] Page 280. Véliz
[310] Recited at page 260 Véliz.

*Chapter 11. War Of The Pacific.
Causes And Affects 1879-1898*

[311] Prior to Bolivia's independence, Potosí was the name given to the Spanish Intendency in the Vice-Royalty of Rio de La Plata.
[312] Recited at page 83." La Vida Y Los Trabajos Industriales de Wheelwright". Wardle.
[313] A General and former lieutenant to Bolívar. He was the first President of Bolivia.
[314] One reason for the Elites' lack of support, it is claimed, was that Santa Cruz was not of European descent like them.
[315] "La Cuestion de limites entre Chile i Bolivia (Santiago 1836)". Page 53. Ireland.
[316] 55. British and Foreign state Papers 860-861. Recited by Ireland Page 53.
[317] Page 90. Burr.
[318] Page 119. Burr.
[319] Page 55. Boundaries, Possessions and Conflicts .Gordon Ireland. Cambridge Massachusetts Harvard University Press. 1938.
[320] Complete mining complexes including plant, offices and auxiliary units.
[321] Page 113. "W.R.Grace" (Clayton)
[322] Page 14. "Strategy in the Southern Oceans" Virgina Gamba-Stonehouse). Source cited: page 32 "Historia del Tratado "Secreto" de Alianza Defensiva entre Peru y Bolivia (Lima 1978), J.Pardo.
[323] Page 57. .Boundaries. Possessions and Conflicts. (Ireland)
[324] Page 142 Pike.
[325] Page 114: "Heirs of Great Adventure" (Wallis Hunt).
[326] Page 142, Pike
[327] From an article entitled "A Very Mischievous Boy". Harper's Weekly. Nov.14.1891.
[328] Page 56. Andy Beckett's "Pinochet in Piccadilly" (Faber and Faber 2002)
[329] Source: "The Alsop case" presented to the US Department of State, Foreign Relations 1910. Pages 139-189. Recited in "United States and the Bolivian Sea Coast" (Chapter 4).
[330] Page 205. "Pinochet in Piccadilly-Britain and Chile's Hidden History" (Andy Beckett)
[331] Page 116. "Heirs of Great Adventure". (Wallis Hunt)
[332] Page 227. Véliz. Footnote 315.
[333] De La Pedraja. Page 21. "Oil and Coffee".
[334] Page 228. Véliz.
[335] Cámara de Senadores. Boletín de las Sesiones Ordinaries 1911 .Page 454 et seq. Véliz Page 227.

[336] Page 229. Véliz.
[337] www.Chile.golatin.com
[338] Page 11. Ortiz Sotelo
[339] Pages 153-155. Pike.
[340] Page 159-161. Pike.
[341] Page 171.Pike.
[342] Page 11. Ortiz Sotelo
[343] Page 172. .Pike

Chapter 12. Sailing Towards Protectionism. 1890-1915.

[344] Page 283 Véliz
[345] Ministerio de Relaciones de Chile. Informe Relativo al Establecimiento de Una Linea Directa de Vapores entre Chile y Centroamérica. Santiago. 1906. Recited as Footnote 368. Page 284. Véliz.
[346] Pages 283-284. Véliz
[347] Page 31, De La Pedraja.
[348] Page 254. Véliz.
[349] Page 200. W.R.Grace & Co. The Formative Years 1850-1930. L.W.Clayton.
[350] W.R.Grace y Cia. (Chile) was founded in Valparaíso in October 1881 with the object of exporting Chilean nitrates to the USA.
[351] Page 286. Véliz
[352] Page 287. Véliz
[353] The first ocean conference on trade to the Pacific Coast of South America was organised in 1893 but comprised mainly British companies because Kosmos line had refused to join until 1904. Source page 104 Royal Commission on Shipping Rings. (Report of HMSO London 1909). Recited at page 43. De La Pedraja.
[354] Pages 301-303, Véliz,
[355] Page 288. Véliz
[356] Page 290. Véliz
[357] El Mercurio. 13 June 1903. Recited at page 290. Véliz.
[358] Page 33, De La Pedraja. Recited from pages 71/73 Castro Mendoza's "la Marina Mercante de La República. Vol.2.
[359] Lamport and Holt's services were mostly provided on the River Plate and the East coast of South America with a Belgian subsidiary effecting West Coast voyages.
[360] Page 34. De La Pedraja.
[361] Page 43. De La Pedraja.
[362] Page 174. "El Vapor Conquista El Pacífico". (Wardle)

Endnotes

*Chapter 13. Affects of protectionism.
Return to a Free Market. 1915-1994*

[363] Page 16. "Report on the Finance, Industry and Trade of Peru 1919." HMSO 1920. Recited at page 86. De La Pedraja.
[364] Page 80. De La Pedraja. "Oil and Coffee".
[365] "Financial Standing of the Peruvian Steamship Company." October 18, 1929. Report of Record Group 59, National Archives 165,006 Washington. Recited as Note 16. Page 86. De La Pedraja ("Oil and Coffee")..
[366] Page 82. De La Pedraja. "Oil and Coffee".
[367] Page 89. Castro de Mendoza. "Historia de La Marina Mercante de la República". Vol..2 .Recited at Page 86. Note 21. De La Pedraja.
[368] Source: "Hog Islanders" by Mark H.Goldberg.
[369] Page 193.. Wardle
[370] Page 76. De La Pedraja. "Oil and Coffee".
[371] Page 195 Wardle.
[372] Page 355. Véliz.
[373] Page 356 Véliz
[374] Extracted by Véliz from Memorándum 84-62-A-89-94. Fusión de Empresas Navieras del archivo de la Subsecretaría de Comercio, 17 junio de 1930. See Page 356 Véliz for respective annual totals.
[375] Page 357. Véliz.
[376] Acta (Minute) No.2983. CSAV. August 14th 1933. Recited in Spanish, note 3 Page 85. De La Pedraja.
[377] Véliz. Pages 342-344 and 348-355.
[378] "Cia. Chilena de Navegación Interoceánica: Un Cuarto de Siglo través Dos Mares. 1929-1950".(Valparaíso-Intercoceánica 1954. Page 7-9). Recited at page 77. De La Pedraja.
[379] CSAV's Board of Directors' minutes No. 2846 (Oct 10, 1930), 2848 (November 19, 1930), 2861. (March 9, 1931). Also New York Times June 25, 1931. Recited at page 85, Note 6. De La Pedraja.
[380] Page 85, Note 8. De La Pedraja..
[381] Note 9. Page 85. De La Pedraja.
[382] Minute (Acta) 2976 June 5, 1933 quoted in "Cien Años de La Compañia Sud American de Vapores". Allard. Notes 10 and 11. Page 85. De La Pedraja.
[383] Pages 11-12 "Interoceánica. Un Cuarto de Siglo a través Dos Mares": Recited at page 85. De La Pedraja.
[384] Note 13. Page 86. De La Pedraja.
[385] Note 13. Page 86. De La Pedraja. "Oil and Coffee".
[386] Archivos de La Armada de Chile: "La Importancia de La Marina Mercante en la Historia de Chile".
[387] Now the Republic of Colombia.

Ploughing The South Sea

[388] Treaties and Conventions concluded between the United States and other powers since July 4 1776. Recited by Kemble page 3 "The Panama Route, 1848-1869"
[389] The Treaty was named after John Hay, the US Secretary of State and Dr. Thomas Herran, the Colombian Chargé d'Affaires in Washington.
[390] Page 212. The Golden Isthmus. David Howarth.
[391] Page 212. Howarth
[392] Page 222. Howarth.
[393] Page 225 Howarth.
[394] Page 226. Howarth
[395] Page 51. "Heirs of Great Adventure" (Wallis Hunt)
[396] Grace Line's early steamers were built in Britain and registered there.
[397] At this time only ships built in the United Sates could be registered there. Grace's earlier vessels had been constructed in Great Britain.
[398] Source: Page 12. "Latin American Merchant Shipping in the Age of Global Competition". René de La Pedraja.(Greenwood 1999)
[399] ibid
[400] PSNC was a member of this Conference.
[401] Ibid
[402] Minute 3626 December 1943 and 3666 October 1944 of CSAV's Archives. Recited by De La Pedraja in "Latin American Merchant Shipping". Page 7.
[403] Note 14. Page 70. "Latin American Shipping".
[404] Page 65. "Latin American Shipping".
[405] Note 2. Page 121. "Latin American Shipping".
[406] Note 3. Page 122. "Latin American Shipping".
[407] Note 4. Page 123. "Latin American Shipping"
[408] Note 6. Page 124. "Latin American Shipping".

Chapter 14. Peruvian Line, Grancolombiana...

[409] Gran Colombia was the name of the country formed from the three participating countries in the early 19th Century.
[410] Page 109. "Oil and Coffee". (OAC). René De La Pedraja. Greenwood Press. 1998.
[411] Pages 36-37. "La Marina Mercante" (Becerra). Recited at Note 4 page 120. De La Pedraja (OAC).
[412] "La Marina Mercante y El Desarollo Nacional de Colombia 1988." Pages 18-20. Carlos Martinez Becerra. Recited by De La Pedraja Note 3. Page 20 OAC.
[413] "La Grancolombiana" should not be confused with the Colombian Steamship Company (Colombian Line) which was established by the US Shipping Board. Between 1918 and 1921 the Board established several routes and services and one of these was the American-Colombian Line managed by the Clyde steamship Co. This led to a trade war with United Fruit Co. and it was agreed that the Caribbean trade of Clyde Steamship Co would be separated from their domestic coastal trade.

Endnotes

The latter shipping company was then formed to operate a route from New York to Puerto Rico, Colombia, Cartagena and later to Haiti. The service was expanded to take in the Leeward and Windward Islands and later Brazil and other US East coast ports. In 1938 the Colombian Line was extinguished on its incorporation with Grace Line. in 1938.

[414] Page 120. Note 6, De La Pedraja. (OAC)
[415] Author of "Oil and Coffee". Greenwood Press 1998 which was supported by the History Department of Canisius College. USA.
[416] Page 112. De La Pedraja. (OAC)
[417] Pages 112-113. "Oil and Coffee". De La Pedraja.
[418] Page 120. Note 11. De La Pedraja.
[419] Page 114. Note 12. De La Pedraja.
[420] Recited at page 114. De La Pedraja.
[421] Page 120. Note 12. De La Pedraja.
[422] Page 115. Note 17. De La Pedraja
[423] Page 121. Note 19. De La Pedraja.
[424] Page 121. Note 21. De La Pedraja
[425] Page 121. Note 22. De La Pedraja.
[426] Page 121. Note 23. De La Pedraja.
[427] Note 17 Page 9. "Latin American Merchant Shipping in the Age of Global Competition". René De La Pedraja. Greenwood Press. 1999.
[428] Page 9, "Latin American Shipping". De La Pedraja.
[429] Page 10. "Latin American Shipping".
[430] Note 22. Page 10. "Latin American Shipping".
[431] Page 11 "Latin American Shipping".
[432] Note 24. Page 14. "Latin American Shipping"
[433] Sourced from New York Times November 20, 1972 and form correspondence from Simón David Zevallos Menéndez to Alvarez Díaz, Guayaquil. October 19 1971. Recited by De La Pedraja Page 66. "Latin American Shipping".
[434] Note 27. Page 71. "Latin American Shipping"
[435] Page 67. "Latin American Shipping".
[436] Page 67. "Latin American Shipping".
[437] PSNC suffered similar experiences with Peruvian fish meal. Not only did it contaminate other cargo but if loaded damp, tt tended to smoulder when the vessel was half-way across the Atlantic.
[438] Note 28. Page 71. "Latin American Shipping".
[439] "La Marina Mercante en La República 1821-1968. Vol 2 pp 103-113. Recited as Note 1. Page 69. "Latin American Shipping ". De La Pedraja.
[440] Note 3. Page 70. "Latin American Shipping " De La Pedraja.
[441] Note 8. Page 70. "Latin American Shipping". De La Pedraja.
[442] Note 18. Page 128. "Latin American Shipping".
[443] Note 20. Page 129. "Latin American Shipping".

Ploughing The South Sea

Chapter 15. Modernise Or Wither. 1946-2000

[444] Page 87. "Latin American Merchant Shipping In The Age of Global Competition". Greenwood Press 1999. René De La Pedraja.
[445] Note 4. Page 98. "Latin America Shipping". De La Pedraja.
[446] Page 94. "Latin American Shipping".
[447] "América Latina". November 2, 1978. Recited at note 25. Page 98. "Latin American Shipping".
[448] Page 95. "Latin American Shipping ".
[449] Note 9. Page 95 " Latin American Shipping".
[450] Note 8. Page 125. "Latin American Shipping ".
[451] Note 10. Page 139. "Latin American Shipping".
[452] Page 75. "Latin American Shipping ".
[453] Information from TPS Press statements
[454] Wallace Carter states that five tons of fish need to be caught to produce one ton of fishmeal.
[455] Source: US Atomic Energy Commission's preliminary report1965, recited at Page 262. in David Howarth's "The Golden Isthmus"

Printed in the United States
44937LVS00004B/79-150